VICTORIAN LONDON

Also by Liza Picard

Elizabeth's London
Restoration London
Dr Johnson's London

VICTORIAN LONDON

The Life of a City 1840–1870

Liza Picard

St. Martin's Press ❧ New York

www.stmartins.com

ISBN 0-312-32567-3
EAN 978-0-312-32567-1

First published in Great Britain by Weidenfeld & Nicolson

First Edition: March 2006

10 9 8 7 6 5 4 3 2 1

Contents

List of Illustrations

Preface

Isabella Beeton began her *Book of Household Management*: 'I must frankly own, that if I had known, beforehand, that this book would have cost me the labour which it has, I should never have been courageous enough to commence it.' Give or take a few commas, I feel much the same. Yet it has been fun, uncovering the 'real' Victorians, or trying to. So much was written about them in their own time, and so much has been written since. Where to draw the line? What kind of line, come to that? Journalists make their living through vivid reportage; just how accurate were the Victorian journalists? Anyway, are we not entitled to adopt their viewpoint, so as to see as their readers saw?

The best evidence would be an unbiased account by someone who was there, and had no axe to grind, but they are few and far between. Friedrich Engels was in London for a few weeks between November 1842 and August 1844, but he had a very definite axe to grind: the appalling condition of the working class in England, which should if properly understood lead to a revolution.[1] It didn't, quite, and most of Engels' work concerned Manchester, where he was looking after his father's cotton industry interests like the good bourgeois son he was; but he did try to understand the working men of his time. As he put it, 'I forsook the company and the dinner-parties, the port wine and champagne of the middle classes and devoted my leisure hours almost exclusively to the intercourse with plain working men.' What the plain working men made of him is not on record.

Flora Tristan was another foreign visitor with a mission, in her case to denigrate the aristocracy.[2] This was understandable when you know her life story. Her father, a wealthy Spanish-Peruvian nobleman, had married her mother, a French émigrée, in Spain. They settled in

Paris, and lived the well-padded life of the aristocracy until he died, his property was confiscated by the French government, and Flora discovered that she was illegitimate, because her father had never got round to marrying her mother in a civil marriage as the law required. She was reduced to earning her own living by writing, at which she was triumphantly successful, becoming known for her feminist and egalitarian views. I have included excerpts from her *Promenades dans Londres*, published in 1842, although the *Promenades* described the London she last visited in 1839; I have assumed that the English aristocracy went on disgracing itself as she described.

Hippolyte Taine was a French savant, scholar, philosopher and teacher, who visited England in 1859, 1862 and 1871.[3] His *Notes on England* are good value. How can one fail to sympathise with his account of a wet Sunday in London: 'the aspect of a vast and well-kept graveyard'. Emerson and Nathaniel Hawthorne contributed sidelights, even Dostoevsky was here and wrote about it.

An incomparable source of objective reporting has recently become available: Heather Creaton's *Unpublished London Diaries*, published in 2003. I regret not having had the time to read all the ones which concern mid-Victorian London. I recommend them to anyone who shares my love of London social history. There are many published first-hand accounts of Victorian life, from Queen Victoria's own letters to Thomas Wright's *Some Habits and Customs of the Working Classes*, published in 1867. He was one of the founders of the Amalgamated Society of Engineers. There are biographies and autobiographies of many famous Victorians, and collections of their letters. It would be otiose to list them here; they are fully referenced in the text.

Henry Mayhew towers above his contemporaries as a source of information on how the poor of London lived. He was one of the seventeen children of a London solicitor. In 1841, with two other men, he founded *Punch*, mocking the lives of the affluent classes. To salve his conscience perhaps, or to tap another readership, he began a series of articles, mostly for *The Morning Chronicle*, about the myriad ways of scraping an honest livelihood in the lower depths of Victorian London. Most of these articles were published in three volumes, in 1851, as *London Labour and the London Poor*. In 1861 a revised edition was published, with a fourth 'additional' volume concentrating on the criminal underworld. This is the edition I used. Not all his articles were included in *London Labour*; they can be found in *The Unknown Mayhew – Selections from the Morning Chronicle 1849–50*, edited by E. P.

Thompson and Eileen Yeo and published in London in 1971. In 1862 Mayhew began another book, *The Criminal Prisons of London and Scenes of Prison Life*, but he was beginning to run out of steam by then and that book was completed by John Binny. Mayhew's technique was to interleave his verbatim reporting of the poor people he interviewed, with paragraphs of statistics. His people are completely convincing, although sometimes one wonders just how typical they were, despite his assurance that 'I seek for no extreme cases.' His figures are not always so convincing, but they are certainly impressive. The ineluctible conclusion from his figures for the earnings of poor needlewomen producing the elaborate gowns of the Victorian rich – that they could not live on their earnings and were driven to prostitution – shocked society.

Gustave Doré's pictures of the poor districts of London are well known, but I had not realised that they were the illustrations to a book – *London* – produced with a journalist, Blanchard Jerrold, in 1872. Jerrold's text deserves more attention. There were also many earlier descriptions, handbooks and guides to London, aimed at the tourists arriving in London in 1851 for the Great Exhibition. There were maps of London, of very varying reliability, except for the magnificent *Library Map of London and its Suburbs* published by Stanford in 1862.[4] Many a happy hour could be spent, with a good magnifying glass, examining the astonishing amount of detail it shows.

Punch and *The Illustrated London News* began their long lives in 1841 and 1842. There were many other illustrated periodicals and newspapers around.

By now, if you are still with me, you must be dreading a quick run through Victorian novelists, foremost in their ranks Charles Dickens, with Anthony Trollope hard on his heels. You are saved. I took an authorial decision at a very early stage: no novels, no poems. Otherwise I would never have finished, and my efforts would have been dwarfed by erudite scholars of Victorian literature.

Another decision I took was that this book would cover only the middle years of Victoria's reign, 1840–70. These are arbitrary dates, chosen in the hope of limiting the book to a manageable compass for reader and writer.

Archivists, librarians and curators are unfailingly helpful and patient: is this a qualification for entry into their profession or an acquired trait? I have acknowledged with gratitude the many occasions when I drew on their knowledge, in the notes to the relevant chapters.

I hope they do not feel undervalued if I do not list them here.

✳

Now I would like to thank everyone who has seen me through *Victorian London*: my friends, who have disguised their feelings when every conversation with me began 'The Victorians ...'. Henrietta Wilson, whose keen and well-stored mind constantly inspired me. My son John, who made time in an exceedingly busy professional life to save me from some remarkable medical howlers. My friend and neighbour Peter Stalker, for his patience with my computer-generated chaos and his skill in disentangling it, which have put me, almost, to shame. (It was Chapter 3 that I lost irretrievably. He was abroad at the time.) My dear editor, Benjamin Buchan, whose gentle, percipient guidance and encouragement have kept me on the straight and narrow path when I was tempted to despair. And Ms Lawik of the London Library, for her unending patience with my abstruse requests, and her skill in discovering in the recesses of that astonishing institution books that I did not know existed, and relished when they arrived.

Thank you.

Liza Picard
Oxford
February 2005

CHAPTER I

Smells

Cesspits · sewers · excrement · burial grounds · coal gas · slums ·
Bermondsey · water closets · the Great Stink · Bazalgette's intercepting sewers
· Abbey Mills pumping station · the royal inauguration · the salmon

A writer can use words to describe a scene. A painter can paint it. A musician, and a sound-effect studio, can reproduce to some extent the sounds of the past. But that most potent of senses, smell, has no vocabulary. Allied with memory, it can evoke an individual's past as no other sense can. But without the help of memory, when it has to act alone, how can it summon the past? There are only words to describe the smells of the past. Which is why this book begins in the way it does.

Think of the worst smell you have ever met. Now imagine what it was like to have that in your nostrils all day and all night, all over London. But it was worse than that. Every stinking breath was dangerous. Miasma, bad air, or as the Italians called it, *mal aria*, brought disease. Florence Nightingale firmly believed so, and designed her new hospital of St Thomas's in separate blocks with airy verandahs, so that hospital stinks could not accumulate in the wards and poison the patients.

The Thames stank. The main ingredient was human waste. In previous centuries the Thames really did 'run sweetly', and salmon and swans flourished in it. Human excrement was sold as useful fertiliser to the nursery gardens and farms outside London, by the night-soil men who emptied the cesspits.[1] Sometimes chamber pots were upended out of windows on to luckless passers-by, or on to the streets, their contents adding to the rich mix of dead dogs, horse and cattle manure, rotting vegetables. The rain washed most of it away into the Thames. There were indeed sewers, but they were restricted to surface water only, and it was an offence to run the excrement of your household into them.

Then London changed. By 1841 the census counted 1,945,000 people in London, and probably more if you include the shadowy ones who always evade officialdom. There were 200,000 cesspits,[2] full and over-flowing. The night-soil men charged a shilling to empty each one, which many people grudged. In the old parts of London the houses teetered above brimming lakes of filth. The sewers could no longer deal with the surface refuse, and they fractured and overflowed. A concerned citizen wrote to the Home Office in 1840 urging action to improve the drainage of Pimlico, where 'there is scarcely any drainage or sewerage and where the gullies are all open, and are filled a foot or more deep with sand, vegetable offal and garbage, from whence there arises a most horrible stench generating malaria and fever, and all this as the crow flies within 100 yards of Buckingham Palace'. The letter was laconically endorsed by the Master of the Royal Household – 'substantially correct'[3] – but he saw no need for action.

In 1843 the Surveyor of the Sewers in Holborn and Finsbury, where there were 98 miles of covered sewers and no access to the Thames, reported that 'in a large proportion of the covered sewers the accumulation of foul deposit has remained for many years in a state of fermentation, being the cause of much disagreeable and unhealthy effluvia ... the remedy ... was by raising the substance in buckets, to be emptied in the street and afterwards carted away', an operation to be avoided by those with delicate noses.[4] Sometimes, but not always, the sewer itself could be enlarged to cope with the increased flow. In 1849 the sewer running under Fleet Street was reconstructed at a deeper level, with greater capacity, blocking almost the whole of this vital thoroughfare while the work was done. There was a sewer in Westminster – then a slum district despite the grand Palace of Westminster – from which, according to a survey in 1849, a 'sickening smell escapes into the houses and yards that drain into it'.[5]

In the aristocratic districts of Belgravia, and Grosvenor Square, Hanover Square and Berkeley Square 'there are many faulty places in the sewers which abound in noxious matter, in many instances stopping up the house drains and smelling horribly',[6] even inside those upper-class houses. But nothing was done. A labourer working under Buckingham Palace itself said he was 'hardly ever in such a set of stinks as I've been in the sewers and underground parts of the palace'.[7] Some sewers were hundreds of years old, and the brickwork was crumbling. They were all cleaned, in theory, by men and by the force of occasional deluges, but a noisome deposit gradually built up which could not be dislodged.

Another ingredient in the street bouquet was animal dung. Cows were kept in cowsheds all over London, in appalling conditions which allowed no space for thorough cleaning. The cattle, sheep, calves and pigs sold in Smithfield Market walked through the London streets, depositing nearly 40,000 tons of dung a year as they went. The thousands of horses that powered London each excreted 45lb of faeces and 3½lb of urine a day, nearly 37,000 tons of dung in a year.[8] Animal and human excrement was not the only problem. Friedrich Engels was in England between November 1842 and August 1844, gathering material for *The Condition of the Working Class in England*.[9] His middle-class susceptibility was appalled by the smells of London street markets and slum housing. 'Piles of refuse and ashes lie all over the place and the slops thrown out into the street collect in pools which emit a foul stench.' But his starkest *coup de théâtre* was this:

> The corpses [of the poor] have no better fate than the carcases of animals. The pauper burial ground at St Bride's [Church] is a piece of open marshland which has been used since Charles II's day and there are heaps of bones all over the place. Every Wednesday the remains of dead paupers are thrown into a hole which is 14 feet deep. A clergyman gabbles through the burial service and then the grave is filled with loose soil. On the following Wednesday the ground is opened again and this goes on until it is completely full. The whole neighbourhood is infected by the dreadful stench from this burial ground.

It is just possible that Engels had not seen this himself, but was treating a horror story as current because it corroborated his theme, when it really referred to the previous century; but there were church 'burying places' not adjacent to their churches, and increasingly overcrowded, scattered through London, so he may have been right.

The coal gas which was coming into use had a sickening smell, not like modern gas. Predictably, the gas mains leaked. If you happen to pass an excavation in a London street even now, you can sometimes catch a whiff of coal gas; the soil is impregnated with it. It was also 'surreptitiously tapped', not always skilfully, by those with no liking for gas bills.[10] The gasworks scattered through London spread their foul smell far and wide.

.Strangely enough the accounts of foreign visitors and English tourists do not often comment on the awful smells. The Queen was seen to notice them when she went to visit the *Great Eastern* in Millwall, down the river on the Isle of Dogs. One of her entourage wrote to her sister that 'the smell [was] beyond description. The Queen ... smelt her nosegay *all the time*' (my italics).[11] The Great Exhibition of 1851 assembled together more people than had ever met before in one place in London, day after day, during a hot summer. None of the many accounts I have read of it mentions whether Mr Jenning's lavatories, used for a penny a time by 827,280 customers, smelt.

Some districts smelt worse than others. Slums exhaled their foul odours down foetid alleys behind the most fashionable shops and houses. But the prize-winner in the stink stakes was Bermondsey, on the south bank of the Thames opposite the Tower of London. This was where skins and hides were turned into leather, by a long and skilful process including the use of dog turds. Not surprisingly, 'the air reeks with evil smells'.[12]

In January 1862 a respected professional journal, *The Builder*, emphasised the need for change:

> On occasions of high tide the low-lying districts were flooded – not with water but with sewage ... the filth which ... is allowed to ferment and fill our houses and streets with gases of ineffable subtilty [i.e. you couldn't keep them out] includes much more than watercloset liquesencies. There are the percolations of crammed churchyards, the rain washings of the streets ... which carry away with them ... filthy objects, horse and cattle dung, ... refuse from hospitals ... fishmongers' and fishmarket washings and offal; slaughterhouse offal; fell-mongers', glue-makers', candle-makers', bone-dealers', tanners', knackers', scum boilers' and tripe dressers' liquid refuse ... refuse from chemical works, gas works, dye works; ... dead rats, dead dogs and cats, and, sad to say, dead babes.

The Victorians must have congratulated themselves, at first, on having made a breakthrough in cleaning up London, when water closets became a normal part of a house. By 1857 there were 200,000 of them,[13] all duly sidetracking the cesspits, and emptying straight into the Thames, via the sewers. The result, long delayed but inevitable, was the Great Stink of 1858. In June the river stank so badly that the rooms in the Palace of Westminster which overlooked it became not only disgusting but – if you believed in the miasma theory – dangerous.

This at last precipitated the action which various committees had been considering for ten years.

Thinking Londoners were beginning to realise that government through medieval parochial boards was not viable in the nineteenth century, and in 1845 London's first Metropolitan Board of Works was set up. For the first time sewerage could be treated as a metropolitan problem. But it was all very difficult. There were no precedents, and precedents are dear to local government officials. One answer was to compel houses built or rebuilt after 1848 to be connected to the sewers, but this was a reversal of policy that did more harm than good. In 1849 Charles Dickens described the Metropolitan Commission of Sewers as 'that preposterous jumble of imbecility and rottenness'.[14] Fortunately Joseph Bazalgette joined the Commission as an assistant engineer that very year, and when his boss died from overwork three years later he was appointed Chief Engineer.

Bazalgette's grandfather had immigrated from France in the late 1770s. Joseph was born in 1819. After an apprenticeship with a respected civil engineer Joseph had set up in practice in 1842, at the age of 23. His combination of sweeping vision, executive drive and engineering genius achieved the impossible. There is a modest bust of him on the Victoria Embankment, inscribed 'Engineer of the London Main Drainage System and of this Embankment'. But he deserves the epitaph earned by Christopher Wren for his final achievement of St Paul's Cathedral – *si monumentum requiris, circumspice* (if you're looking for his monument, look around you). In Bazalgette's case, you could look at the whole of Victorian London.

London lies on a slight north–south incline, from the heights of Hampstead down to the marshes of Lambeth and Greenwich. Add to that the complication that part of it lies in a shallow bowl, centred at approximately Poplar/Deptford. (Imagine a saucer slightly tipped towards you, and higher on the left than the right, with the river wriggling across the middle of it.) The old sewers had run into the Thames or one of its many tributaries. Bazalgette took, figuratively, a marker pen and drew firm lines along the sides of the saucer, roughly parallel to the river, at right angles to the old sewers and the Thames tributaries. These lines reached the river far downstream, well outside the (then) built-up area. There were three lines north of the river, the high level, the mid level and the low level, which joined together near Stratford in east London, and two on the south bank which joined together at Deptford.

The whole scheme was estimated to cost £3 million, raised by a combination of private investment and government funding, and to take five years, not counting the time spent in the meticulous preparation characteristic of Bazalgette. Often the old sewers had to be traced and charted; no-one knew where they were, which just shows how often they had been cleaned.[15] Work on the 'intercepting sewers' was begun in February 1859, and advanced steadily through London, disrupting the traffic but quelling some of the ancient smells. By August 1859 'it is estimated that 200,000 cesspools have of late years been removed from beneath our dwellings'.[16] But still, in 1861, a London resident could write 'we have come to dread hot summers as we would a pestilence ... for with the dog days there always arises from the Thames such an accumulation of villainous smells as makes its banks hideous and force us to fly from them as far as we conveniently can. But a better time is coming ...'.[17]

By November 1861 'about 1,000 men are engaged upon [the north mid level] and it is progressing rapidly'.[18] In most places the tunnels were built under the streets, by 'cut and cover', sometimes 30 feet below the road surface. The 1,000 labourers worked their way from Kensal Green to Notting Hill, then along Oxford Street – imagine the chaos – across Shoreditch and under the Regent's Canal, to Stratford. Their only labour-saving devices were steam-driven cranes, and of course, horses. By 1862 the Metropolitan Board of Works was even arranging conducted tours. One group inspected the sewer at Old Ford in Hackney, and then 'walked through a long tunnel which was illuminated for us for a mile or so'. Then they all got into a train of ballast trucks and were taken through the 'works' for about 7 miles, to Barking, 'where the north outfall is to be. Here refreshments were provided and after lunch we were conveyed in three steamers [it must have been a large group] up the river to Greenwich, and descended the tunnel which is to convey the sewage of the south side of London.'[19]

Another complication which perhaps emerges from my 'saucer' metaphor was that although the 20 square miles drained by the north high level could rely on gravity to maintain an even flow of 3 miles an hour down to the final outflow, the area drained by the mid and low levels – another 28 square miles – would have to use steam-powered pumps if the system were to function properly. On the south side of the river nearly 20 square miles could be drained by gravity but 22 square miles could not. Two pumping stations were built, one at Abbey Mills near Stratford, east London, for the north levels, and the other at Crossness, on the south bank of the river, again well beyond the built-up area, for the south low level.

These pumping stations had to be seen to be believed. Perhaps Bazalgette was bored by all his magnificent work being out of sight, and decided that here at last was his chance to express his artistic soul, and impress his image on the public. Abbey Mills pumping station, where the north high and mid level sewers joined, was an edifice in which Coleridge's Kubla Khan might have felt at home, minarets and all.[20] The whole network of intercepting sewers on the north side of the river had to wait for the completion of the Thames Embankment in 1868 – another Bazalgette achievement – before it could all function, but there was no such hold-up on the south side. The official opening of Crossness pumping station by the Prince of Wales was breathlessly reported in *The Illustrated London News* on 15 April 1865. He travelled by steamer, from the Palace of Westminster, accompanied by both archbishops, two more bishops, two princes, two dukes, two earls, fortunate MPs and other dignitaries; all available forces were invoked. (Both pumping stations have survived and can be visited by appointment.)

The steamer called first at the north bank, where the various luminaries inspected the northern outfall, at Beckton, and no doubt nodded wisely at the explanations of the Chairman of the Metropolitan Board of Works, and Bazalgette. Perhaps they were able to do that without getting off the boat, because there was nothing very exciting to see. (Abbey Mills is about 2½ miles away from the river.) Then the steamer took them across the river and a little downstream, to their destination at Crossness. 'Shrubs and flowers in pots gave a very gay appearance' to this monument of sewage – one hopes that they were scented. The band of the Royal Marines played suitable music, and His Royal Highness and his entourage were shown the engine house and the boiler house, and taken into the culvert connected to the sewers, 'a long lofty wide tunnel of excellent brickwork ... lighted up by rows of lights'. They were given a unique opportunity to walk about in the vast reservoir 'illuminated by myriads of coloured lights', which would very soon be filled with sewage. Then they filed into a lecture hall and listened to an address by – who else? – Bazalgette, while the fairy lights were hastily dismantled. Next, to the engine rooms:

Here after a careful inspection of the immense pumping apparatus and furnaces, the Prince of Wales, under the guidance of the engineers in charge, proceeded to set the prodigious works in motion. As soon as the handle was turned by His Royal Highness a sensible vibration was felt throughout the building, showing that the engine beams, lifting-rods and fly-wheels were in operation, and that the sewage which had been confined in the great receptacles underground was being pumped into the reservoirs thence to be afterwards discharged into the Thames. The four engines were successively set in motion by His Royal Highness, who was greeted by a loud cheer by a body of workmen perched aloft in the galleries.

His Royal Highness must have been overwhelmingly relieved when the next event was 'an excellent déjeuner for 500', with toasts. They all went home at 3 p.m., arriving at Westminster at 4.15, their duty well done.

One of the enigmas of the occasion is – what did the gentlemen do with their top hats? They are shown in *The Illustrated London News* respectfully carrying them while the Prince demonstrated his amazing engineering ability, indeed some of them are so carried away that they are waving their hats in the air. But at the déjeuner they are all pretty tightly packed at long tables. Where had they stowed their hats? The lecture hall and the eating-place were contrived out of space usually devoted to plans etc.; surely there wasn't room, and organisation, for a check-in room for 500 top hats? Nor of course is there any mention of the needs of the distinguished visitors to add their personal contributions to all that sewage.

The Illustrated London News' account of opening a sewage works combines in a typically Victorian way sycophancy, pride in Bazalgette's achievement, and realism, the glamour of the Prince balanced against the raw material which had occasioned his visit. It took the combined forces of the throne, the Church and the politicians, let alone the expertise of the new profession of civil engineers, to move London's sewage, and no doubt the readers of *The Illustrated London News*, and many others, were fascinated.

But the really important visitor arrived almost unnoticed. By May 1864 much of the system was operating. 'No sooner had things come to this satisfactory outcome than a fine salmon, on the lookout for clean fresh water, made its appearance in the Thames.'[21]

The River

When Victoria came to the throne in 1837 the Thames was still the wide, meandering river that had been the thoroughfare and playground of Londoners since time immemorial, but now it was 'soiled and darkened with livid, false tints'.[1] It was tidal up as far as Teddington, and twice a day it ebbed and flowed. The newspapers gave the times of the high tides.

The annals of the Company of Watermen and Lightermen of the River Thames kept by the Company's Clerk, Henry Humpherus, recorded a more detailed picture of tides and weather.[2] Nine times, between 1841 and 1869, there were abnormally high tides, as high as 3 feet 7 inches above the normal high-water mark, which meant that low-lying areas such as Wapping, Lambeth, Bermondsey, Battersea and Westminster were flooded. In the winter of 1850 the water rose so high that it put out the furnaces at the gasworks in Wandsworth and 'the neighbourhood [was] placed in total darkness'. On 17 November 1852, the day of the Duke of Wellington's funeral, it had rained for two months and there were floods everywhere. A particularly high tide that day was called 'the Duke's flood'. A week later there was another abnormally high tide, and many of the inhabitants of Bermondsey, which was particularly flood-prone, had to be rescued from upper floors by wagons. Flood water was a nasty mixture of mud and sewage.

When the Thames went to the other extreme in 1840, and again

ten years later, it shrank 'to a mere brook', so that 'persons could
walk across it'. It would not be an inviting stroll, no matter how much
you could save in boat charges or bridge toll. You would have to
walk through concentrated essence of sewage; and at every low tide
the exposed mudbanks 'swarmed with bright red worms ... the boys
called them blood-worms'.[3] In very low water the wooden wherries
were more viable than the steamboats, which as Humpherus noted –
with little sympathy – 'suffered considerably from the want of water
and many got aground, and for some time could not run'.

Twice in the winter of 1840 there were fogs so opaque that ships
collided. There was a severe snowstorm, with frost, in January 1842,
and a hailstorm in the summer of 1846 so heavy that it broke panes
of glass all over London, including Buckingham Palace, where £4,000
had to be spent on repairs. Hurricanes sometimes blew for two days,
so that ships had to lie to, and risked running aground, and many
laden barges sank with their cargoes of coal and grain. After one
hurricane 'the river in the morning was covered with timber, spars
and portions of rigging, deals, broken wherries, barges and other
craft'. Twice the Thames froze over, in 1846 and 1855: not so solidly
that the great Frost Fairs of the previous centuries could be repeated,
but enough to prevent the watermen from earning their livelihoods.

The ancient custom of swan-upping was still performed every
August, when the swan masters of the Crown and the two privileged
livery companies, the Dyers and the Vintners, counted all the swans
on the river, and marked the young ones. In 1841 the Queen owned
232, the Dyers' Company 105, and the Vintners 100, a marked
decrease from the 500 they owned three centuries earlier, when the
Thames had been famous for its huge flocks of swans. But in view of
the pollution it is surprising that any swans survived at all. In 1842 a
whale was caught off Deptford pier. It was measured – 16 feet long –
and weighed – 2 tons – and exhibited in a nearby pub, 'where 2,000
persons paid for admission in one day'. Another whale was landed
off Grays, Essex, seven years later, but all that Humpherus had to
say about it was that it was 21 feet long.

Since 1197 the river had been under the jurisdiction of the City of
London. When the new Lord Mayor of the City went every year to
Westminster to be sworn in, he went by river, in a gorgeous procession

of decorated barges. 'It had always been considered a grand Field Day for Watermen as – independent of the number of them engaged on the various barges – many poor Watermen managed to get good employment for the day'. Relations between the City and the Government had often been strained. In 1857 some crisis led to the first Thames Conservancy Act, transferring jurisdiction over the river from the City to a statutory body called the Board of Conservancy (later the Thames Conservancy Board). The Watermen's Company, which had got on well with the City, described the Conservators as 'radically vicious'. One of the first results of the transfer was the ending of the Lord Mayor's river procession.[4] His beautiful barge was sold in 1860, for only £105. From 1857 on, the Watermen's Company had to ward off constant attempts by the Board to oust it from its traditional privileges. Henry Humpherus, never one to spread himself in purple prose (and with a regrettable fondness for '&c'), tended to concentrate more on the in-fighting between his Company – for whom he acted vigilantly and effectively – and the hated Conservators. Old London Bridge with the mill-races between its piers had been demolished long ago, and the nine new bridges presented no particular hazard to river craft, if you discount the 'extraordinary accident [which] occurred during the progress of the Lord Mayor and Corporation up the river in the City barge [in September 1844], by a violent collision with the piers of Westminster bridge, the Lord Mayor, Sheriffs and Aldermen, Sheriffs elect, &c, were thrown from their seats, the mace, decanters, glasses &c rolling on to the floor [plus, presumably, the Lord Mayor &c] causing great consternation'.

But a new danger had arrived, in the shape of steamers catering to the commuter trade, as the suburbs expanded. Steam had begun to challenge traditional manpower as early as 1818.[5] Steam-powered boats with a revolving paddle wheel on each side could do a steady 4 m.p.h. against the tide and 7 m.p.h. and more with it, and they were not above harassing the watermen's fragile wooden skiffs and wherries. In 1844 a steamboat ran down a waterman's boat and killed him. The master was found guilty of manslaughter, but the sentence was only four months' imprisonment. In other cases alleging default by the steamship captains or owners it seems to have been difficult to get a jury to convict. There was constant bickering between the steamboats and the watermen, sometimes taking the form of demolishing the piers used by the opposition. In 1844 a tit-for-tat raid by 40 men was 'eventually stopped by a body of police arriving in cabs'.

Steamboats had a nasty habit of pulling away from the embarkation pier at full speed before the passengers were safely ashore or on board. In 1843 thirteen children were thrown into the Thames in this way. Three drowned, and the chances of survival of the others were slim, if they swallowed much of the filthy river water. There were 'almost daily' collisions between rival steamboats. Sometimes a steamboat simply blew up, without any collision. In 1847 the steamboat *Cricket*, 'having taken in between seventy and one hundred passengers, was about leaving the wharf [at London Bridge] when the engines exploded with fearful destruction. Six persons were killed, twelve very seriously injured, and others slightly, most of the passengers being blown into the river but were rescued by watermen's boats. The engineer was afterwards tried and convicted of manslaughter, for tying down the safety valve' – no doubt hoping to increase speed so as to win a race against a rival. 'An action was brought by a person named Redgrave, who was seriously injured, against Mr Octavius Smith, the owner, for damages, and a verdict obtained ... for £200.'

The busiest stretch of the steamers' route was between Chelsea and Woolwich, collecting middle-class commuters from Chelsea and artisans from Woolwich and depositing them at London Bridge pier, all for one penny. There was a landing-stage under one of the arches of the bridge, which was welcome in bad weather as long as the tide was low. But at high tide the steamer had to keep its funnel dipped, to clear the bridge, and the passengers on deck had to put up with getting dirtier and dirtier from the sooty smoke it discharged.

There were regular services further afield. It was a middle-class habit to evacuate wives and children to some 'watering-place' such as Margate, Gravesend and Ramsgate for the summer, to avoid the smells and pressures of London. The husbands led a bachelor existence until Saturday morning, when they caught the 'husbands' boat' to rejoin their nearest and dearest. These boats were comparatively luxurious. Meals were served, and first-class passengers could relax on the poop deck, under a canvas awning, while quite often a band played. The only drawbacks were the tracts and sermons inflicted on these captive audiences by religious enthusiasts, and the slight risk of sea-sickness, for which 'a reclining posture with the eyes shut [should] be secured and maintained ... a little brandy and water and plain biscuit be taken occasionally'.[6] By 1844 'it was computed that there were two hundred steamers constantly navigating the Thames, the competition continuing very great, the Diamond Company carrying passengers from Gravesend to London at one shilling fore cabin and eightpence after cabin'.

Steam tugs for towing barges arrived in 1848. Like present-day black cabs they could turn in their own length, because the paddle wheels could be worked separately.[7] The hay and straw for London's horses came down in barges, with the tide, and barges bringing grain and building stone came up from Kent, dipping their sails and masts as they negotiated London Bridge.[8] The fleets of 200 to 300 sailing ships that had brought ever-increasing loads of coal to London for centuries were gradually replaced by screw-operated steamers, from 1852. (They in their turn were supplanted by the railways from 1864 onwards.)

Three-masted sailing ships were still the main long-haul mercantile carriers. These 'clippers' were a wonderful sight as they came up-river to the Pool of London or the docks. 'Near the top of the tide, tugs passed every few minutes, with sailing vessels, many of considerable size, in tow. In the early 60s wind-jammers were plentiful, and all but the smallest took steam assistance in the upper river reaches.'[9] Sometimes they came under their own power, especially when they were competing to be the first into London from China to offer the new season's tea harvest. New tea could sell at a premium of 10s a ton, and the captain of the winning ship was paid a bonus of £100. In the 1850s clippers from Boston had won the race, but from 1859 the British took over, sailing in Aberdeen-built clippers.[10] On 30 May 1866 sixteen ships sailed from Foochow in China. Ninety-nine days later, having crossed the Indian Ocean and rounded the Cape of Good Hope, three of them arrived in the Thames on the same tide. The sailing ship *Ariel* won, and won again two years later, cutting the record to 97 days. After the opening of the Suez Canal in 1869 the 'Tea Derby' declined.[11] (The tea clipper *Cutty Sark* can still be viewed in Greenwich, splendidly conserved.)

The quay at London Bridge saw some splendid occasions, such as when the Queen and Prince Albert and a selection of royal children took the Admiralty barge to the royal steam yacht *Victoria and Albert* en route for their annual holiday in Scotland. When the Queen was not too pregnant to enjoy travel by water, the royal pair often used

the river for state visits. Prince Albert made a progress in the royal
state barge, from Whitehall to the Brunswick pier at Blackwall, to
inspect the *Victoria and Albert*, launched at Pembroke on 25 April 1844
and brought to the East India Docks. The barge, which had just been
refitted and regilt at Woolwich Dockyard, was 64 feet in length and
about 7 feet in width, the head and stern were elaborately carved and
gilt, and highly varnished. The vessel was rowed by 22 watermen in
scarlet liveries, and the Admiralty barge which accompanied it by
ten watermen in scarlet coats. The state barge in its progress to and
from Blackwall attracted many spectators on the river and its banks,
and with the Admiralty barge formed a splendid piece of water
pageantry.

In 1845 'the Queen and Prince Albert, with their suite of grand
officers ... embarked in the Royal Yacht at Woolwich, on their way
to Germany' to visit Albert's family. Prince Albert, who appreciated
the publicity value of royal appearances, used the royal yacht in 1849
from Whitehall to London Bridge on his way to open the new
Coal Exchange 'in the absence of Her Majesty the Queen from
indisposition'. This was an almost Tudor progress. At Whitehall Stairs
waited

> a large flotilla of boats, some belonging to men of war, and some
> painted blue with gilt mouldings, belonging to the royal yacht ... A
> row of steamers had been moored on the north side of the river,
> between Whitehall and the Custom House, a row of barges being also
> moored on the south side to London Bridge, so that a space of 100 feet
> was kept clear for the procession to pass, 5 miles of mooring chain
> being used for the purpose. [Six steamboats belonging to various livery
> companies were moored next to London Bridge] fitted up with seats,
> platforms &c, for the privileged visitors. On the procession arriving at
> London Bridge, the shipping in the river below were all dressed up
> [the modern phrase is 'dressed overall'], the crowds on board and in
> the rigging, &c, cheering most lustily ... The watermen reaped a good
> harvest in conveying visitors from the shore to the ships, barges &c
> moored in the line ... The ceremony being finished, the royal party
> embarked and returned to Whitehall in the same manner. The pro-
> cession on the water was witnessed by many thousands, every house,
> wharf, &c and the bridges being crowded with spectators.

The bridges and river banks provided ideal vantage points for other
occasions. In 1848 British seamen demonstrated against a proposed

amendment of the Navigation Laws which would enable foreign sailors to work in British ships.

> About 3,000 formed a procession in boats, carrying numerous flags, on the river. The floating of such a number of boats in a stately line with colours flying was stately and imposing. As they passed, guns were fired from the shore and ships, which were all showing their colours and the men cheering lustily. The sailors all landed at Westminster and proceeded in procession to Trafalgar Square ... the river was lined with boats and craft of all descriptions, full of spectators.

Prince Albert was not alone in using the river as a publicity venue. In November 1841, surely an unpropitious time of year, full of rain and fog,

> Samuel Scott the American diver gave a flying leap from the topgallant yard of a coal brig lying off Rotherhithe, in the presence of an immense concourse of spectators, who he amused first for upwards of an hour, by his feats on the topgallant yard. Although it was blowing a gale at the time, he fixed his head on the mast with his feet kicking in the air, where he remained for some time, ran from end to end of the yard without holding on to any rope. He made a slip noose which he placed round his neck, and threw himself off the yard, remained suspended for a few seconds with a rope under his chin, and raised himself with great dexterity on to the yard, when he said 'come tomorrow and you will see me hang myself again'.

He must have thought he was on to a good thing. He 'kept up his performances on the river, jumping from the bridges into the river when full of ice'. But

> on 11 January [1842] about ten thousand spectators had assembled on [Waterloo Bridge] and in boats on the river. He ascended a temporary scaffold ten feet high over the second arch, and placed a rope around his neck, to carry out some of his performances of dancing on air. After swinging by his head, he swung by his feet head downwards. He again placed it in the rope, which became fixed, and strangled him. He was cut down, but too late, as his friends believed it was part of the performance.

And so, for a while, did the 10,000 spectators. Twenty years later, when the tightrope walker Blondin was thrilling crowds at the Crystal Palace,

A lady calling herself the 'Female Blondin' was about to cross the river on a tightrope extending from [Cremorne Gardens, Chelsea] to a wharf at Battersea. Through some deficiency in the guide-ropes ... the feat was not completely accomplished, and when the lady, who had started from Battersea, had performed about four-fifths of her perilous journey, she was compelled to sit down, and ultimately descended into a boat. The courage displayed under these trying circumstances created almost a greater amount of admiration than would have been produced had the artist walked all the way.[12]

The British do love a gallant failure.

In 1843 the First Thames Regatta was held at Putney. The Boat Race between Oxford and Cambridge was going strong. (It may interest aficionados to know that between 1829, when the race began, and 1882, when Henry Humpherus's records end, Oxford won 21 times, Cambridge 17, and there was a dead heat in 1877. From 1856 onwards, it was held annually.)

Shipping on the Thames was often worth a visit. In January 1845 Brunel's vast iron-hulled, screw-propellered ship the *Great Britain* arrived at Blackwall and

caused a considerable sensation, she being three hundred and twenty feet long, one third longer than the largest three decker. The neighbouring banks were covered with people to greet her passage up the river, and a great number of boats accompanied her to her moorings. During her stay, thousands of people were conveyed daily in steamers and watermen's boats, to the vessel, to inspect the same, causing considerable employment. The charge of admission on board was two shillings and six pence each person ... the *Great Britain* remained until 12th June when her departure was attended by similar demonstrations.

In 1848 a Chinese junk arrived in the Thames. 'For a time it lay off Blackwall, where it was visited by thousands,' then it moved up to near Waterloo Bridge. Charles Dickens was scathing. Apparently the exotic craft had managed the journey from China only 'by the skill and coolness of a dozen English sailors ... it would look more at home on the top of a public building ... than afloat on the water ... imagine a ship's crew without a profile among them, in gauze pinafores and plaited hair, wearing stiff clogs a quarter of a foot thick in the sole, and lying at night in little scented boxes, like back-gammon men ...'.[13] But the junk which arrived in the Thames in 1851 was possibly more authentic. Its captain was the mysterious mandarin who materialised before Her Majesty while she was opening the Great Exhibition; no-one knew who he was, so he was hastily incorporated in the royal procession round the Crystal Palace. His 'great unwieldy' craft was moored near London Bridge, and could be visited for a shilling.[14]

✻

People always enjoy watching tragedies from a safe vantage point, and the fires along the banks of the Thames provided plenty to feed their appetites. In 1842

a great conflagration occurred at the Tower of London, which destroyed the Round Tower, Armoury, Clock Tower, &c. The tide being out, water was supplied by the floating engine by seven hundred feet of hose to the land engines; the White House, Chapel and Jewel House were with difficulty saved, the Jewel House and iron railing were broken open with crowbars, and the jewels removed by policemen passing through a detachment of soldiers; the amount of loss was enormous. The fire continued burning for several days. The view from the river was very grand, and the watermen's boats were crowded with spectators.

Punch, just founded, went to town: 'In the first place, by way of ensuring the safety of the property, precautions were taken to shut out everyone from the building, and as military rule knows no exception, the orders given were executed to the letter by preventing the ingress of the firemen with their countermand. This of course took time, leaving the fire to devour at its leisure the enormous meal that fate had prepared for it.' Humpherus may not have realised that the 'difficulty' in saving the Jewel House was caused by the only key being in the custody of the Lord Chamberlain, who was not immediately available.

Warehouses seem to have been desperate fire risks. Not only the building and its contents went up in flames, but so did ships lying alongside, unless the tide was high and they could be towed away. At low tide, when they were stuck in the mud, they shared the same fate as the warehouse. Often sparks from one fire ignited another nearby, especially in the case of distilleries and timber yards. In 1845

a great fire occurred at Nine Elms [Battersea], destroying Mr Bethel's creosote and naptha works, containing several reservoirs of pitch, tar,

&c. All the saw mills, and many thousands of railway sleepers &c,
shared the same fate ... The pitch in the cisterns boiled over, and
poured into the river, and the surface ... presented the appearance of
a lake on fire.

In the same year a warehouse storing oil and turpentine caught fire:

The boiling turpentine and oil ran out of the windows on to the wharf
adjoining the river, burning one of the [fire]engines and a fireman, the
people escaped on to the various barges ashore near the works, and on
to the floating engine, but the burning turps &c set the barges and
floating engine on fire, which caused it to be abandoned, the heat was
so great that the small boats could not get near the burning barges to
take the people off, as they also became enveloped in fire, and they
were thus driven to throw themselves in the river, covered with blazing
turps and oil, and were then picked up and saved with a few exceptions
... Great fears were entertained for the City Gas Works adjoining, and
orders were sent round to the shop-keepers to light their burners to
reduce the gasometers.

In 1851 the Thames Bank Repository burned down. 'An immense
quantity of furniture, pictures and valuable goods were stored there
which were mostly destroyed, the damage being estimated at
£100,000' – an unimaginable sum in those days, and I doubt whether
the owners were insured.

'The most destructive [fire] in London since the memorable one
of 1666' broke out in Tooley Street on the south bank, in June 1861.
'Blazing fat floated far down the stream and imperilled the wooden
vessels moored in the Pool. For days afterwards as far as Erith [15
miles down-river] the river banks and mud flats were coated with
grease which was energetically salvaged by hordes of men, women
and children.'[15] The fire destroyed three wharves and 'enormous
quantities of the most valuable goods, besides injuring several ships
which only escaped by being towed out when on fire. It continued
burning for several days ... Here Mr Braidwood, the Superintendent
of the Fire Brigade, lost his life by the falling of one of the walls.'
Humpherus did not have the prose style of Dickens, who would have
made much more of these tragedies. You have to imagine, with no
help from Humpherus, the shrieks, and the roar of the flames, and
the reflections in the water.

✳

Further down-river lay the shipbuilding yards. Brunel's *Great Eastern*, then known as the *Leviathan*, was built at Millwall, and launched after innumerable difficulties and crises in January 1858. The Thames failed to deliver the usual abnormal winter high tides, which would have made the launch easier. The press had a field day:

> Men and women of all classes were joined together in one amicable pilgrimage to the East, for ... the *Leviathon* was to be launched at Millwall. For two years London ... had been kept in expectation of the advent of this gigantic experiment, and their excitement and determination to be present at any cost are not to be wondered at when we consider what a splendid chance presented itself of a fearful catastrophe ... [In Millwall] every apartment in every house ... if it commanded even a glimpse of the huge vessel stretching along above the tree tops, was 'turned inside out' to accommodate visitors for friendship, relationship or lucre.[16]

The 'fearful catastrophe' did not happen, unless you count the death of a labourer and injuries to some of his mates, during the first efforts to launch the ship. When she finally slid majestically sideways into the river, she was towed down to Deptford for further work, where, predictably, she was visited by 'enormous crowds'.[17]

A country visitor was unimpressed by the *Great Eastern* and saved his enthusiasm for Deptford dockyard, where he 'saw ... three ships building, one an enormous three-decker to be called the *Ariadne*, the other a single-decker to be called the *Cameleon*'.[18] 'The fine vessels for the East India trade have all along been made principally in the Thames'[19] up to the 1840s, but as iron supplanted wood it made commercial sense to move shipbuilding yards north to the Clyde in Scotland and to the north-east coast of England, where labour was cheaper, and already skilled in working iron and steel. In 1852 the *Agamemnon*, a 'magnificent Government vessel, was launched from Woolwich dockyard ... great numbers of people witnessed it in boats and the river presented a very attractive appearance'. The *Hannibal*, 91 guns, was launched two years later from Deptford. The armour-plated screw sloop *Enterprise* also came from Deptford, in 1864, but after the launch of the screw corvette *Druid* in 1869 the yard was sold, 'being unsuited for the construction of the new class of vessels'.[20] The Thames Ironworks Company was building a new warship, the *Mino-*

taur, at Blackwall, as late as 1865; she had 36 guns, armour-plate 5½ inches thick, screw engines, and five iron masts.[21] London shipyards still attracted a certain amount of foreign trade. The Prussian navy commissioned the *Arminicus* from Samuda Bros at Poplar in 1864, and an armour-plated sixteen-gun frigate the *Kron Prinz* from them in 1867.[22] But the shipbuilding trade was leaving London.

Old ships, like old buildings, could still be useful. The *Dreadnought* had fought at Trafalgar. She was moored at Greenwich as a floating seamen's hospital. When she showed signs of collapse she was replaced by another three-decker. In twenty years the two ships cared for over 63,000 patients. No sick sailor, whatever his nationality, was ever refused admission.[23] Further down the river at Woolwich lay the dreaded prison hulks, two old men-of-war, and a smaller ship which relieved the black tragedy of the hulks by drying the prisoners' washing, like bunting strung between her shortened masts.[24]

The Pool of London, the stretch of river from London Bridge down to Limehouse, had been London's main port since Roman days. By the nineteenth century it had become notoriously congested. Ships could lie there for months waiting to discharge their cargo, at the mercy of storms, fire and theft. The River Police had been founded in 1798, as the first organised police force in the country. In 1839 it was incorporated into the new Metropolitan Police Force. In *The Illustrated London News* of 17 April 1869, the picture of the new embankment from the Temple to Somerset House includes a natty little boat labelled 'Thames Police Station'. It has no visible means of propulsion, but perhaps the artist was not nautically minded. Presumably it had a good turn of steam-powered speed.

✳

The real answer to the endemic pilfering from cargo ships was the system of enclosed docks, built mainly – there had been some earlier ones – between 1802 and 1880. By 1850 they covered 90 acres, including 35 acres of water and a wine-cellar extending for seven acres. The London Dock (1805), the East India Dock (1805), the Surrey Dock on the south bank of the river (1807), St Katherine's Dock near the Tower of London (1828) and West India South Dock (1829) had all been built according to the latest technology of their time, but their designers had not foreseen the advent of the railways, and of steam-powered iron-built cargo carriers. They had no room in which to expand, and to deepen them for modern shipping would have been prohibitively expensive. The Victoria Dock, opened in 1855 (extended to the east by an even larger dock, the Royal Albert, in 1880), was built on a low-lying site of 100 acres, east of the River Lea. It was the first dock to provide hydraulic cranes and lifts for raising ships in a pontoon dock, and was well served by rail links with the Great Eastern line. The Millwall Dock on the Isle of Dogs, opened in 1868, offered similar modern facilities.

W.S. Bell, the tourist who turned his nose up at the Chinese junk, duly visited the London docks in 1851 – 'a most astonishing sight ... We visited the wine vaults and tasted the wines which the guide liberally dispensed ... there were hundreds of visitors here ... the guide rinsed the glasses out with wine.' Then he and his party went on to the sherry vaults, where they 'plentifully refreshed themselves', and they meant to pack in a tour of St Katharine's Dock, but his stamina, or his sobriety, gave out.[25]

When Hippolyte Taine came to London in 1859 and 1862, he was bowled over by the docks:

> The number of canals by which the docks open into the body of the river ... are streets of ships ... the innumerable riggings stretch a vast circle of spider-web all round the rim of the sky ... [they are] one of the mighty spectacles of our planet ... [the docks] are prodigious, overwhelming. There are six of them, each a great port inhabited by a population of three-masted ships ... from every corner of the world. A merchant who had come to check the arrival of spices from Java and a trans-shipment of ice from Norway, told me that about 40,000 ships enter these docks every year, and that as a rule there are between five and six thousand in the docks at any given moment.[25]

Bazalgette's embankments were gradually confining the Thames into a tidy channel between 1864 and 1870. The Victoria Embankment ranks as high as his great intercepting sewers for sheer engineering genius, and it is more visible to Londoners than his drains. But since one result of the embankments was to add to the space available for roads, they are considered in the next chapter.

CHAPTER 3

The Streets[1]

~❧~

Maps · the street layout · medieval survivals · cow-houses · traffic jams ·
new roads · Bazalgette's embankments · traffic control · obstructions · the
suburbs · road surfaces · coaches and cabs · omnibuses · velocipedes

The obvious thing to do before you begin to explore an unfamiliar
city is to buy yourself a map, but this was not straighforward for a
visitor to Victorian London.[2] Many maps on the market were severely
out of date, considering the huge growth in the built-up area. Two
were based on surveys made in the 1820s, while another, which
purported to be so detailed that it even showed the pillar boxes, erred
in the opposite direction, and indicated a rail link between Euston
and Charing Cross stations which had been sanctioned in 1864 but
never built. The Great Exhibition of 1851 provided a heaven-sent
sales opportunity to map-sellers, who flooded the market with souvenir
maps and information booklets for foreign tourists. Meanwhile the
Metropolitan Commissioners of Sewers, realising that the first step
towards an efficient drainage system for London must be a proper
survey of its streets and existing drains, had commissioned detailed
maps from the cartographers of the Board of Ordnance (hence our
Ordnance Survey maps). The survey was completed in 1849, and 326
separate maps were published between 1851 and 1871.

But the master of maps, for the average citizen, was Edward
Stanford. (Stanfords still flourishes, and is still London's premier map-
seller, in Long Acre, near where the firm began.) His *Library Map of
London and its Suburbs* came out in 1862. It could be bought in 24 single
sheets, for 1s plain, 1s 6d coloured, or mounted on a roller, or as a
portfolio of sheets for £1 1s plain, £1 11s 6d coloured.[3] It is a
magnificent work, for which a good magnifying glass is essential. The

gasworks scattered through London are easy to spot, as bold circular blobs. Look more closely and you can see another innovation, large square workhouses in every district. Prisons built on the 'Panopticon' design (explained in Chapter 21) stand out. New cemeteries on the outskirts are shown, as well as the old inner-London burial yards marked 'closed'. Even the design of the gardens in front of the 1862 Exhibition building in South Kensington is clearly and accurately shown. So, after a careful study of *Stanford* in your library and a quick look at the latest 'Pocket Map' – to the streets.

Regent Street had been laid out by Nash, beginning in 1813, to connect Piccadilly with the new Regent's Park. The line of the street survives, but Nash's plan to develop residential chambers above the ground-floor shops never really took off. A covered arcade in front of the shops made a continuous balcony along the windows of the chambers, so that residents could have watched the traffic – in those long-distant days this would have been a pleasure – and chat to their friends passing in their carriages. (The arcade and balconies were demolished in 1848.) Where Regent Street met Oxford Street the buildings at the corners were rounded and set back, creating an elegant circus, and the same plan was followed at the junction of Regent Street and Piccadilly. (Eros arrived much later, in 1893.) Confusingly, both circuses were called Regent Circus.

Grosvenor Square still dominated the streets west of Regent Street. The Duke of Westminster surely disliked the workhouse built just a stone's throw away from the square. Narrow culs-de-sac threaded their way behind the mansions, to house the necessary carriages and servants. Still going west, you arrived in Park Lane, running along the eastern edge of Hyde Park. Turning left (south), you would pass Grosvenor House and Dorchester House (hotels on both sites, now). At the end of Park Lane was Apsley House, the home of that towering idol of Victorian London, the Duke of Wellington (it is still there). Turn left again, along Piccadilly, and you would pass Devonshire House (sold and demolished in 1918). It must have had the most delightful views in London, south over Green Park and north through its long gardens and past Lansdowne House to Berkeley Square. The other eighteenth-century survival in Piccadilly, Burlington House, was not in private occupation any longer by the time Stanford compiled his *Library Map* in 1862, but the Palladian building still survives.

The Duke of Westminster owned another huge parcel of prime London building land, south of Knightsbridge. Here, he commissioned

Thomas Cubitt to lay out Belgrave Square, as the centrepiece of his Belgravia estate, built between the 1820s and 1850s. The Grosvenor family has always kept strict control over the development of its London properties; Belgravia, even more than Grosvenor Square, still breathes Victorian high society and wealth. Victoria took a house in the square for her mother the Duchess of Kent, while Kensington Palace was being refurbished, for £2,000 a year. West of Sloane Street, Stanford showed market gardens scattered among the houses and museums of Earl's Court and South Kensington (now completely built over).

Coming back to the circus at the Piccadilly end of Regent Street, make for Leicester Square to the east: a sordid place, redeemed only by an extraordinary building in the middle of it, Wyld's 'Great Globe', and the Alhambra on the east side (see Chapter 16). Pass St Martin's workhouse, opposite the church of St Martin-in-the-Fields, and you have arrived in Trafalgar Square, with the National Gallery on the north side of it and the two fountains in the open space. Stanford's *Library Map* even gives the names of two occupants of plinths – Napier and Havelock – with marks showing the empty plinths, and, of course, Nelson on his column, described by a visiting Frenchman as 'that hideous Nelson, planted on his column like a rat impaled on the end of a stick'.[4] But then one cannot expect a Frenchman to enthuse over Nelson. From there you could either take Whitehall down to the Houses of Parliament, passing various Government offices, or turn left along the Strand towards the City, with its maze of winding illogical streets still preserving its medieval layout, fascinating to historians but incomprehensible to strangers. The Thames makes itself known to your nose. Its banks are lined with wharves and warehouses, leaving only narrow spaces for the piers and jetties used by watermen's wherries and passenger steamers.

Medieval survivals scarred this modern metropolis. A few flocks of live geese and ducks – 500 or so of them at a time – were still being driven through the streets to Leadenhall Market in the City, as they had been since the fourteenth century. There were stables, dairies and cowsheds everywhere, with unregulated abattoirs conveniently close. At the back of a house in Bethnal Green 'a cowkeeper and dairyman kept in large sheds about 40 milk cows ... The cows were turned out every day into a large yard which was only divided from our premises by a low wall. The smell was at times intolerable, and the flies in summer were a perfect plague.'[5] There were three cow-houses, one with its en-suite slaughterhouse, beside St John's Church in Smith Square.[6] One cow-house near the Strand was in a cellar under a dairy. The twelve cows in it 'must have been lowered to their places by ropes'.

The outbreak of rinderpest in 1865 had a marked effect on the number of cows in London. In St Pancras parish there were only 266 left, of the 1,178 cows normally kept in 100 cow-houses. The 1,288 cows in Hackney's 83 cow-houses were reduced to only 450.[7] 'The wheels of the heavy waggons, laded with bales and barrels, creak and moan ... [there were] the sportive bullocks, too, the gigs, knackers' carts, sheep, pigs, Barclay's drays ...'.[8] Although 'sportive bullocks' and other livestock had mostly arrived earlier in the day, there were still enough of them to fill any space between vehicles, and threaten pedestrians. They plodded slowly across London Bridge, along past St Paul's Cathedral and down Ludgate Hill to its junction with Farringdon Street, where amidst much shouting and cursing they turned across the traffic, north towards Smithfield Market.

Between 1852 and 1854 the principal livestock market at Smithfield sold on average, in two days' trading each week, 5,000 cattle, 30,000 sheep and 2,000 pigs. They all had to walk there somehow, and then they all had to trickle back in small numbers through the streets again to their last homes. 'Our streets are disgraced by the sufferings of over-driven bullocks ... the animals, maddened by heat, ... attack those who are passing by [and] gore those who cannot escape.'[9] Those were the days before de-horning was usual.

Despite the obvious need to relocate the livestock market, nothing was done until 1855, when a new cattle market was opened in Islington, and Smithfield became mainly a meat and poultry market. Billingsgate Market, on the river just downstream from London Bridge, had specialised in fish for many years. Until the railways came, fishing boats unloaded at the wharf. But as the river trade declined, and the railways increasingly carried fish to London, every fish still had to come from the rail termini to Billingsgate, which had no rail link; so the whole area round Billingsgate was solid with fish-smelling vehicles.[10]

❋

Traffic jams were appalling. Omnibuses from the residential quarters barged their way to the Bank of England, cutting across the streams of animals, and the cab drivers, and the more sedate private carriages. There was of course no Highway Code.[11] The most notorious place for gridlocks was the area between Temple Bar, the Bank of England and London Bridge, particularly on weekdays between 11 a.m. and 5 p.m. London Bridge contributed over 13,000 vehicles and horse-riders, at an average of over 1,000 an hour, to the maelstrom seething round the Bank.[12] The crowds of clerical workers employed in the City walked in from the suburbs. They walked astonishing distances, come rain or shine. In 1854 it was officially estimated that 200,000 people walked into central London every day.[13] So many crossed London Bridge that the granite slabs of the footways wore smooth, and had to be roughened with a mallet and chisel. 'The footways were solid masses of moving humanity while the roadway for hours together was packed with horses and wheels often without space for a single addition.'[14]

Clearly something had to be done. If it coincided with slum clearance, so much the better. Victoria Street was built in the 1850s, connecting the new railway terminus to Whitehall, and clearing slum property on its way. In the 1860s New Oxford Street was driven through the notorious slum district of St Giles, to connect Oxford Street and Holborn, whence a splendid cast-iron viaduct (it still survives and is worth seeing) was built over the steep valley of Snow Hill, making a new connection between the City and Westminster.[15] The slum-dwellers were supposed to be grateful for the demolition of their hovels. Certainly the planners felt no obligation to rehouse them, so they moved into adjacent slums, making them even more over-crowded. The new thoroughfares across the crowded centre of London demolished 7,403 tenements in the process, and relocated 38,231 people.[16] Church Lane in Westminster accommodated 655 people in 1841, but six years later there were 1,095 people in the same houses.

The most spectacular road improvement was the work of Joseph Bazalgette. By incorporating in his great system of intercepting sewers an embankment along the Thames, he created out of nowhere a new highway a mile long, making a third traffic artery between Westminster and the City. The work began in September 1862. By 1866 'the paved footway next the river from Westminster Bridge to the Temple [was] opened to the public, complete with the Westminster steam-boat pier',[17] and by April 1869 the stretch between the Temple and Somerset House was finished, with trees along the edge, dolphin-wreathed lamp-posts and seats adorned with sphinxes. It took another year to bring the Embankment as far as Blackfriars. Thirty-seven acres were retrieved from the stinking muddy foreshore of the Thames and added to London.

Bazalgette's genius lay in his sweeping vision combined with searching practicality. He designed the Embankment to cover the last of his great intercepting sewers. Not content – as surely most men would have been – with that, he incorporated in his design a duct to house gas, water and (later) electricity mains, and a tunnel for the underground railway. He used some of the reclaimed land for the gardens which still provide a pleasant riverside promenade. In 1870 Gladstone harboured plans to develop this new space with offices which would be so profitable that he could announce the end of the hated income tax, but he was fortunately thwarted.

Work on the Albert Embankment on the other side of the river – a comparatively simple engineering project to Bazalgette, merely designed for flood prevention – began in 1866 and was completed in four years. It extended from Lambeth Palace to Vauxhall Bridge, resulting in a mile of reclaimed river bank on which Florence Nightingale's newly designed St Thomas's Hospital could be built. Now that the river no longer stank, patients could enjoy the fresh breezes, as well as the visual treat of Barry's Palace of Westminster on the opposite bank. The third embankment, along the Chelsea reach, was finished in 1874. In all Bazalgette added 52 acres to London.

There were a very few innovative traffic-controlling measures. In 1864 Colonel Pierpont had difficulty in crossing St James's Street to his club. He found this intolerable so he bought himself a traffic island in the middle of the street.[18] The Members of Parliament risking their lives to cross Bridge Street to get to the House took a different line; the first traffic light was installed there in 1868. At 20 feet high it efficiently replaced 'the arm and gesticulation of a policeman'. It combined both coloured lamps – red to stop the traffic, green for 'go', there was no amber – and a 'semaphore arm' like a railway signal.[19] The beginnings of a one-way system were applied in Albemarle Street when Humphry Davy's lectures at the Royal Institution there became so popular with the educated classes that their carriages caused a traffic jam every time he was to speak; the carriages had to set down their occupants on the left-hand side. From 1867 omnibuses, too, had to set down passengers on the left-hand side of the road. But in general London traffic was a nightmare.

The streets were constantly obstructed. There were 78 principal toll-bars or turnpike gates within 6 miles of Charing Cross, with 100 subsidiary ones to prevent rat-runs. They were not cleared away until 1864. Pedestrians, even pushing prams or wheelbarrows, did not have to pay, but the charge, which could be as much as 6d, must have deterred some small traders with donkey carts, making for the London markets. At least there were no tolls within the City. London Bridge was toll-free – and hideously overcrowded. (The toll on Blackfriars Bridge ended in 1785, but most other bridges charged tolls until 1877.) The pavements were often obstructed by utility works. The electric telegraph, that 'most marvelous application of science',[20] was 'carried in iron pipes under the foot pavements ... Provisions, called testing posts, are made at intervals of a quarter of a mile along the streets, by which any failure ... in the buried wires can be ascertained' – just like the holes dug by modern utilities looking for leaks. A sewer worker might suddenly emerge from a manhole, or a London borough such as Finsbury, with no direct access to the river, might be cleaning its drains on to the road. The gas and water companies were always repairing their mains. Strings of fourteen or fifteen skeletal horses bound for the knackers' yards, tied to carts carrying dead horses, made their way slowly through the traffic. In residential districts a couple of nice clean cows might be standing still while the milkmaid milked them straight into the customers' jugs,[21] and the traffic had to go round, or wait.

Modern advertising stunts had begun. The birth of *The Illustrated London News* in 1842 was announced by a phalanx of 200 'peripatetic placards' (sandwich-board men) walking through the streets. There was 'a colossal hat, mounted on springs like a gig ... dashing down Regent Street at the heels of a spirited horse, with the hat-maker's name in large letters'.[22] In 1859 the New Adelphi Theatre mounted a smash hit, called *The Dead Heart*; the manager of the theatre sent out sandwich-board men in heart-shaped billboards.[23] The pressure of unregulated traffic inevitably brought accidents. In 1868 'there were no fewer than 200 deaths from injuries caused by horses and vehicles'.[24] This may seem trifling to us, but it was not then, and accidents and collisions all meant crowds and delays, whether or not they were fatal.

Meanwhile the suburbs were burgeoning. The commercial reorganisation of the City created a new class, clerks by the hundred. They needed somewhere to live, and they were not prepared to live in the central slums. The new property developers provided houses – mile upon mile of terraced houses, with two or three bedrooms, a kitchen, a living room, and a garden, some jerry-built but many soundly built and still, nowadays, a delight to live in, once a bathroom has been added. Prosperous businessmen and eminent professional men moved into elegant houses in Beckenham and Clapham. All round London the green fields gave way to bricks and mortar. The new suburbs were served by new roads. The London of 1843 shown on a map published by that invaluable institution The Society for the Diffusion of Useful Knowledge indicated Regent's Park at the edge of the built-up area, and Victoria Park beyond the north-east fringe. Just nineteen years later Stanford, in compiling his *Library Map of London and its Suburbs*,[25] found it necessary to include Clapton, well beyond Victoria Park; and Sydenham, Streatham, Wimbledon, Tooting, Wandsworth, Hammersmith, Hampstead, Highgate and Crouch End. Some of these places were not yet heavily built up, but they soon would be.

The main roads were surfaced with squared granite paving blocks or setts, 'driven home by files of men wielding great wooden rammers which they lifted and let fall in unison',[26] making an appalling noise as they did so, or with 'macadam'. This was a layer of large stones, then a layer of smaller ones, and finally a layer of gravel which was beaten into the crevices of the under-layers by the traffic, or a 'huge iron or stone cylinder painfully hauled by ten or a dozen navvies'.[27] That was at least the theory. Unfortunately the 'drift' from the top layer tended to block the gullies at the sides of the roads. The problem was not solved until the whole thing could be stuck together with bitumen or tar – our tarmac. Meanwhile the macadamised streets of the fashionable quarters were 'covered with gravel, and carefully watered ... to keep down the dust and deaden the rumbling of the carriages and the step of the horses',[28] and if someone were gravely ill, straw was laid in the street outside the house, to give the invalid some quiet.

Some side streets were still cobbled. Some streets, for example outside the Central Criminal Court (the Old Bailey), were surfaced with wood blocks in the hope of enabling proceedings to be audible, since wood made less road noise. But wood had its own problems. In Cheapside in the summer 'the dust used to rise, palpable to taste and smell, higher than the first-floor windows, churned up by the perpetual whirl of carriages'.[29] And frost made it slippery. 'The omnibus horses have been obliged to go circuitous routes to avoid wooden pavement'.[30]

The vehicles on the road were colourful. The most impressive, the stretch limos of the day, were the carriages of the rich, with their gleaming paired horses, their uniformed coachman and handsome footmen.[31] A coach could hold four to six persons, with a substantial seat for the driver in front, and a platform at the back for footmen. A landau, such as the present Queen uses at Ascot, was much the same as a coach, but with a roof which could be folded back. If you were really confident in the weather you might trust yourself in a barouche, a two-seated carriage without a roof at all. A chariot was more dashing; it was the back half of a coach with the front cut off – a coupé. 'It is considered the most elegant for a dress or court carriage'.[32] You could buy a clarence for only £60 as Jane Carlyle did in 1864.[33] These vehicles all had four wheels. Two-wheelers included a cabriolet, 'a convenient carriage for a single man to ride about town in'.[34] They all had springs of a sort, but they were still far from comfortable compared with a modern motor car, and they all shared one snag: they were difficult to get in and out of gracefully, if you were wearing a crinoline.[35] There were little folding steps which the footman would lower, and there was his arm to lean on – but given arthritis, embonpoint and a long, full skirt, an elderly passenger needed all her agility.

Any kind of coach presupposed a coach house, and at least one horse, which needed a stable, and they both needed a coachman. It was a frequent pattern for the paterfamilias to be driven into the City in the morning, and send his carriage back for the mistress of the house to use if she wished, while he came home in due course by cab, so for a large part of the day the coachman might have nothing to do. Some employers used him to wait at table, but he tended to bring a stable smell into the dining room. To save the expense of a stable, if there were no convenient mews, you could put your horse in a livery stable and rent storage for the coach – 3s a week at most. Another answer was to dispense with them altogether, and hire a coach, horse and driver for a day, a week or a month. 'Today I acted the gentleman and hired a carriage and drove round to pay visits with my wife' wrote a Chancery clerk in his diary.[36] An 'excellent-class' carriage could be hired for 80 guineas a year; proportionately less, presumably, if you were only in London for the season.[37]

One-horse cabriolets, 'cabs', were like today's black cabs, except that they plied from cab-stands only, not while moving. The chaises 'with a leather hood being raised or lowered at pleasure' had given way to hansoms and clarences by 1861.[38] They were licensed, and the fares they charged were controlled, although the drivers were notorious for demanding more, especially in fog, or snowy weather, when sometimes they had to use an extra horse. Unlicensed cabbies should be avoided, since they had a reputation for robbing sleeping or drunk passengers.

The middle classes habitually travelled by horse-drawn omnibus.[39] By 1850 there were 1,000 licensed vehicles, belonging to several different companies, which were distinguished by differently coloured liveries, and covered with advertising placards. The exclusive right to use profitable routes, sometimes shared by several operators, could be sold for as much as £400–£500.[40] Most companies charged the same fares – 3d for part of the journey, 6d for the whole way, 1s to the outer suburbs. There were no tickets, you paid the conductor when you got off. The conductor stood on a foothold halfway up the back of the bus, holding on to a long strap. He signalled to the driver to halt by banging on the roof of the bus. There were no regular stopping-points, the driver might or might not stop where you wanted to get off or on, and if he saw a pedestrian who even looked like a possible passenger he would veer across the traffic and pull up abruptly for the conductor to persuade the man aboard. This could be irritating; a clerk of the Law Courts was due at the House of Lords on official business, but 'the driver of the omnibus greatly disconcerted me by going at a foot's pace and touting for custom all the way'.[41]

Most buses began at 9 in the morning, when the middle classes went to work, and continued till midnight. When the City offices closed at 4 'some buses had a complement of regular passengers, started to a fixed time-table, and made non-stop runs to their destination'.[42] During the busiest times you rarely had to wait more than five minutes. Buses were usually licensed to take twelve passengers inside, where they had the benefit of straw on the floor, to keep their feet dry and warm, but this got progressively filthier as a wet day wore on. Another disagreeable aspect of inside travel was the other travellers. Omnibuses were a favourite haunt of pickpockets. A respectable-looking female sitting necessarily close to another passenger might appear to have her gloved hands modestly clasped in her lap, but one hand might be false, while her real hand was busy in her neighbour's pockets. Another risk was, of course, fleas. Some omnibuses were built to allow a lady who wanted seclusion to take a separate compartment about the size of an upright coffin, built into the side of the bus. If she was really unlucky her predecessor had been a gentleman who enjoyed a morning cigar . . .

After 1850 the licence allowed another nine or ten outside passengers, sitting back-to-back on a bench called a 'knife-board' along the middle of the roof, with nothing to hold on to and no protection from the weather. There was no staircase, only metal rungs at the back of the bus up which you climbed. Since the driver saw no reason to wait until his passengers were seated, this could be a tricky operation. In 1851 *The Times* published a letter complaining of having to 'scramble up at considerable personal risk by the aid of an iron step . . .'. Obviously most women would not go up those iron rungs in long skirts, certainly not if they were wearing crinolines, but it could be done. Before Jane Carlyle bought her clarence, she sometimes used omnibuses just for pleasure. In 1858 she treated herself to a trip from her home in Chelsea, to Putney. 'It is as pleasant as a barouche and four, the top of an omnibus; but the conductors don't like the trouble of helping one up.'[43]

Even getting into the inside could be tricky. 'One of [the conductors'] duties in the crinoline age was to lean down from his perch and prevent with his hand the oval that hoops had to assume when squeezing through the narrow doorway from rising to an indelicate height.' When a bus was hired for an outing including ladies, 'a ladder would be provided for their decent ascension while all males looked the other way'.[44] Gentlemen were very obliging: 'when the bus conductor enquired, as he frequently did, "Will any gentleman [seated inside] go outside to oblige a lady?" he never asked in vain'.[45]

The design of buses improved markedly during 1855–9, when most London bus companies were owned by a French one.[46] The inside height rose from $4\frac{1}{2}$ feet to 6, and the width increased from $4\frac{1}{2}$ feet to 5. Small brass rods were installed to mark – optimistically? – each person's share of the seat, strips of wood replaced the straw, and handles and rails made it easier to climb to the top. Conductors were even given whistles, to warn the driver that a passenger wanted to get out. The companies reverted to British ownership in 1859, but the French improvements mostly survived.

All these vehicles used horses, and horses used vast quantities of hay and straw, and deposited vast quantities of dung and urine on the London streets. Man-powered, four-wheeled velocipedes did neither. In the early to mid 1860s they 'became quite familiar objects in the streets'. They were on hire at the Crystal Palace, and several other places in London, or for 100 guineas you could buy the model 'fitted with a sketch desk and umbrella' which would beguile any journey as long as you did not need to look where you were going. Ladies could ride them 'with perfect decorum'. You could attain 9 m.p.h. on a long run, and 60 miles in a day was easily possible.[47] Thomas Carlyle rode from Chelsea to Wimbledon on one, in three hours, but preferred a horse.[48] Odd, that velocipedes never took on.

CHAPTER 4

The Railways

⚜

Speed · railway time · lines and stations · accidents · Cook's Tours ·
travelling conditions · W. H. Smith · the electric telegraph · Parliamentary
trains · railway hotels · the underground railway

The speed of a railway train was terrifying. When Queen Victoria
was whisked from Slough (the nearest station to Windsor Castle, then)
to London in 1842, the train averaged 44 m.p.h. over the 17-mile
journey, and she asked Albert to tell the railway company that she
had not enjoyed it, please go more slowly in future. Yet the engines
displayed at the Great Exhibition by the North Western Railway,
with driving wheels of 8 feet in diameter, had 'taken trains at speeds
... from 60 to 70 miles an hour', the Great Western Railway's
locomotive the 'Lord of the Isles' could *average* 60 miles an hour, and
another monster locomotive was capable, so its makers said, 'of
running with safety at 80 miles an hour with a large express
train'.[1]

Could the human body survive the pressure of such velocity? It
had never before been subjected to such a strain; until the railway
age, the fastest anyone had travelled was on a galloping horse, and
the speed of a stagecoach was reckoned to be as fast as anyone would
want to go. *Bradshaw's Railway Timetables*, which had been available
since 1839, reckoned on an average speed of express trains of 36–48
m.p.h. Before the advent of the railway, peaceful country towns had
set their clocks by whatever time-keeping system they chose. Because
of *Bradshaw*, for the first time ever, Englishmen all over the country
could synchronise their watches. A man standing on Newcastle station
watching the noon departure train pull out would know that his
cousin in Truro was watching the arrival of the noon express from

London, at the very same time – always assuming, of course, that both trains were on time.

From 1830 on, the rail transport system had begun to cover the country with a network of lines owned by different companies, which were vociferously promoted in the City. The 'railway mania' reached its peak in 1847, when 6.7 per cent of British national income was being invested in railway shares.[2] By then the Deptford and Croydon Railway Company's station at London Bridge had been opened, in 1836; it was (and is) a confusing place, which was rebuilt in 1849 without eliminating much of the confusion. Euston station, the terminus for the London and Birmingham line, was opened in 1837. In 1838 it acquired a magnificent entry portico with four Doric columns, and an arch which cost £35,000. The next year saw the opening of the Great Hall, a combination of concourse and waiting room as grand as any public building in London. (It was demolished, with the arch, in 1963, by British Rail.)

Isambard Kingdom Brunel designed the Great Western Railway's spectacular Paddington station, built between 1850 and 1854. He was able to use the same combination of wrought iron and glass which had so brilliantly succeeded in Paxton's Crystal Palace (1851), to create a central aisle 102 feet wide, with side aisles 70 and 68 feet wide. (There is a delightful statue of Brunel, with his stovepipe hat beside him, where the taxis put passengers down. The cathedral-like aisles and transepts are a fitting memorial to him and the great Victorian engineers. So far Paddington has not been radically altered by modern progress.) Fenchurch Street station, the first station to be built within the City, served westbound commuters on the Blackwall Railway from 1841. Until 1849 it must have been the quietest station in London, because no steam locomotives came into it; the carriages were pulled from Blackwall to Minories, at the edge of the City, by cable and continued on to Fenchurch Street under their own momentum. On the outward journey they were set in motion by gravity and 'a slight push from the platform staff'.[3]

After 1847 the pace of development slowed slightly. Waterloo station was opened in 1848 by the London and South Western Railway. (This is another confusing station, made more so by the near-impossibility of finding the way in. The Victorian platforms were swept away and the present station opened in 1922.) The line passed Vauxhall Gardens, that eighteenth-century survival 'half-tumbling to decay', and the 'sickening stench of the bone-boilers' nearby, and paused on the viaduct over

Westminster Bridge Road for tickets to be collected – a cunning way of preventing passengers from making a getaway without buying a ticket.[4] On several lines the tickets were collected before the terminus, but it was not unknown for some passengers not to have tickets at all. A little girl was being sent to her aunt in the country to recover her health after a childhood illness in Bethnal Green. 'About half way on the journey I was pushed under my aunt's crinoline when a man came to look at the tickets ... no ticket had been taken for me.' Even if the ticket collector had suspected her presence it would be unlikely that he could ask a female to raise her crinoline, just in case.[5]

When King's Cross station opened in 1852, as the terminus of the Great Northern Railway, it was the biggest station in England. Its design was refreshingly functional. (Its elegant simplicity is hard to discern, now that the frontage is cluttered with modern development.) Victoria station opened in 1860, serving Brighton and the south coast, and expanded two years later to serve the London, Chatham and Dover line, used by boat trains for the Continent. Charing Cross station for the South Eastern line was opened in 1864 and is still a monument to Victorian technology; the six tracks were roofed by a single arch 164 feet wide and nearly 100 feet high at its apex. The line was extended to Cannon Street two years later; the arch over the tracks there was 680 feet long, 106 feet high and almost semi-circular. (It has been demolished and the site redeveloped.)

In 1868 St Pancras station opened as the terminus of the Midland Railway. Yet again, Victorian technology still amazes the observant traveller who has time to stand and stare. The single arch over the tracks spans 240 feet, and rises to 100 feet. The station stands on a plinth, because the tracks had to clear Regent's Canal, which explains that breathless canter from Euston Road up to the station concourse. The space underneath the concourse made an ideal storage area for the beer barrels coming down from Burton by train; indeed the length of a beer barrel was adopted as a module for the construction of the cellars.[6] In the stations the traveller's every need was catered for – refreshment rooms, lavatories, and even 'large chained Bibles for travellers to read while waiting'.[7]

By 1870 the main railway network had spread over England, and most of the familiar London termini were in place.[8] Not everyone liked them. The line from Greenwich to London Bridge was built on raised arches, the passengers looking down into the wretched houses and backyards of the unfortunate residents. Euston, St Pancras and King's

Cross stations swept away shanty towns where poor people had been trying to scratch a decent living. They were evicted with no hope of compensation or rehousing. Victoria station had a different problem. The residents of nearby Belgravia had more than enough clout to insist that the noisy, dirty trains must be covered in by an iron and glass roof for almost half a mile from the terminus, which produced a hideous din for the passengers but maintained the purity of the nearby mansions.[9]

The railway boasted a remarkably low accident rate – fatal accidents 653,637 chances to one, injuries 85,125 to one. And

> many of the railway accidents which are recorded arise from the imprudence and the rashness of the passengers themselves, by far the most frequent causes of such accidents being the getting into or out of the train while in motion [40 per cent], or sitting or standing in an improper place, attitude or position [28 per cent] ... It is a peculiarity of railway locomotion that the speed when not very rapid always appears to an unpractised passenger to be less than it is. A railway train moving at the rate of a fast stage coach seems to go scarcely as fast as a person might walk.[10]

So avoid at all costs sitting or standing improperly, or getting out while the train is in motion. 'Never attempt to jump out, in case of accidents ... by so doing you are *certain* to be greatly injured, and probably killed. In your seat, you have a chance of escape.'[11]

Suddenly the railway enabled people to travel from end to end of the country. In June 1841 Thomas Cook, walking to Leicester from his home 14 miles away, had a brainwave. 'What a glorious thing it would be if the newly-developed powers of railways and locomotion could be made subservient to the promotion of temperance!'[12] So he organised his first 'Cook's Tour': a party of 500 fellow-teetotallers, by special train from Leicester to a gathering in Loughborough, brass bands and all. His venture grew steadily, as he gained experience in negotiating special terms with railway companies. He arranged a tour to Liverpool and North Wales in 1841, and a tour to Scotland in 1846, on the tourist map ever since Victoria and Albert had fallen in love with Balmoral.

When the Great Exhibition opened in 1851 he was ready. Of the six million and more who visited the exhibition, 150,000 had arrived via Thomas Cook. His organising flair produced irresistible bargains. Return tickets from York on the Midland Railway cost 15s, 10s, and 5s for first, second or third class, and you could survey the passing countryside secure in the knowledge that 'in the history of the Midland Lines no accident attended with personal injury has ever happened to an excursion train'. A typical Cook's party was a group of 3,000 Sunday-school children, who arrived in Euston from the Midlands and were safely shepherded across London to the Exhibition, and back to Euston in time for the night train.

A most indefatigable London sightseer – and for the Victorians that is saying something – suddenly realised, after his fourth visit to the Great Exhibition, that he ought to find out about his train back to Newcastle. Surprisingly – he had spent the last sixteen days in a tornado of well-organised activity – he had not bought himself a *Bradshaw* so he walked from his brother's house in Bedford Square to Euston Square station,

> where I found that I must leave this evening. [Surely he was cutting it a bit fine?] At 8 we left Bedford Square in a cab, upon arriving at Euston Square we found the place crowded and such a crushing and confusion took place ere the multitude got seated. We having first class tickets got very comfortably seated, upwards of two hours elapsed ere the train started and our carriage was without a lamp. It happened to turn out a moonlit night so that we did not find this inconvenience so much. The train being so laden having between 1,500 and 1,600 people in it and only one engine moved slowly. It drew up at the Derby Station between 4 and 5 in the morning, when we had some refreshment. At Normanton we were turned out of the train and had to kick our heels for two hours waiting for the ordinary train to take us to York and on our arrival at York we had another two hours to wait. [They went into York and managed to get washed and fed, then back to the station –] where we were packed into a goods van with rough deal boards set across, this scandalous affair called by the porters an Exhibition Coach was crammed full of people.

They arrived home in Newcastle at 6.30 p.m., nearly 24 hours after leaving London, having experienced every level of rail travel. Perhaps he had not booked through Cook's.[13]

Cook was not the only promoter of excursions by train. In 1849 'upwards of 100,000 persons were present' at the public execution of a notorious murderer, 'the railway companies running trains from all parts'.[14] Little did these ghoulish sightseers think that the next time they took an ordinary second-class journey they might sit next to the executioner himself – Calcraft, the Hangman, who frequently travelled from his base in London, where business was decidedly falling off (see Chapter 21, Crimes and Punishments). He operated in at least 45 other venues, from Aberdeen to Devizes, Norwich to Swansea. Once, at Dundee, the event was called off – the prisoner was reprieved – so the best thing the expectant crowds could think of was to see the Hangman himself at the station on his way back to London. He was an obliging man, not wanting to disappoint his public. 'Evidently anxious that all should have the fullest opportunity of inspecting him, after taking his seat in a second-class carriage he rose to the window and kept his head out till the train left the station.'[15]

There were more idyllic treats arranged by the rail companies. You could take a day return ticket on the Croydon line, to Anerley, enjoying the beautiful scenery on the way, and rest in the marquee put up by the railway company in the woods near Anerley station, or settle down for some fishing in the nearby canal. There was no need to worry about the train back to London: a porter rang a large dinner bell in the road five minutes before the train left.[16]

Railway engines made a great commotion and a loud noise, emitting plumes of steam and showers of smuts; it was advisable to keep the windows shut. Of course if your travelling companions were smoking pipes or cigars the attraction of fresh air might overcome the risks. The first-class carriages, seating eighteen people, were as comfortable as any form of mass transport has ever been. If you preferred you could travel in solitary state in your own vehicle, loaded on to a flat car and securely wedged. The 8.20 up train from Scotland provided 'a luxurious moveable drawing room, where well-dressed men lounged around the table and smoked'.[17]

Should your journey be a long one and your intention be to travel by a first class carriage bring with you a travelling cap, and hang your hat [this must be a gentleman's top hat] up to the lines placed in the roof. Should you travel a long journey in a second class carriage it is advisable to take with you an air cushion to sit on. On some of the lines the inferior carriages are made as uncomfortable as possible, in order to drive people to the first class.[18]

The third-class carriages were slightly improved cattle trucks, open above waist height with no protection from the weather or the engine dirt. In 1847 the most money came from the sale of second-class tickets (24 per cent), next the first-class (20 per cent), the third-class contributing only 15 per cent: 'merchandise' produced the highest proportion, at 30 per cent, and 'private carriages' less than one per cent.[19]

In 1848 W. H. Smith and Son had become official bookstall contractor to the London and North Western Railway, paying £1,500 for the monopoly, which was gradually extended to all the other main termini. There the prudent traveller could buy all the morning and evening newspapers, and pick up a weekly if ordered in advance, and some light reading – nothing costing over 1s[20] – and also rugs, candles and maps.[21] Reading a newspaper was not always a simple matter, since they were sold with the pages uncut, and 'railway passengers habitually carried folding paper-knives – kept on sale at the bookstalls – in their vest pockets and it was a common sight to see a compartment full of voyagers each intent on cutting the edges of a paper just purchased from Smith and Sons'.[22] The 'voyager' might decide to pay a small deposit for a book, read it, and return it at the end of the journey. He might have with him one of the 'roulette boxes' sold by street traders, 'much favoured by train travellers and stockbrokers'.[23]

He would need more forethought to provide himself with one of Alexis Soyer's Magic Stoves, and the food to cook on it, but the irrepressible M. Soyer assured his readers that a good meal could easily be produced, in a railway compartment, on one of his stoves. He did not take into account the feelings of any starving fellow-traveller. It might have been wiser to stock up at the shop opened by the Aerated Bread Company in 1860 (it made its bread by carbonated gas, without yeast) at Fenchurch Street station, or go to the station refreshment bar, an 'elegantly decorated Saloon served by neatly-dressed young ladies',[24] although the coffee was notoriously undrinkable. Some travellers provided for every eventuality. Hippolyte Taine had 'seen travelling English people provided with so many kinds of field and perspective glasses, umbrellas and iron-tipped sticks, capes, woollens, waterproofs and greatcoats, with so many necessaries, utensils, books and newspapers, that in their place I should have stayed at home'.[25]

Another change brought about by the railways was the spread of the electric telegraph, at first only on wires beside the railway lines.

It reinforced the system of railway signalling by exchanging batons, and later by the semaphore signals patented by John Saxby in 1856, and was so useful that 'pocket telegraphs' were carried by railway staff. It was later extended to non-railway business. 'Telegraphic messages are despatched by messengers immediately on their arrival at the stations, and are delivered in carefully-closed envelopes, at a charge of 6d for the first half-mile, on foot, or express messengers – fly, cab, horse or rail – 1s. The messenger is invariably sent by cab, in London, when medical men are required.'[26]

Telegraphs achieved the arrest of Müller for the murder of Thomas Briggs on a railway train in 1864. After a struggle in a first-class compartment Müller had killed Briggs, robbed him of his valuables including – of all things – his top hat, and thrown the body out of the train. He took passage to New York on a sailing ship, but meanwhile the evidence against him was accumulating in England, including that of a hatter who deposed that Müller had brought him a top hat which he wanted cut down to suit the new fashion, and altered to fit him. (The newly fashionable low-crowned hats became known as 'Müller cut-downs'.) Detectives, alerted by telegraph, travelled by fast mail-steamer and were waiting for him in New York. The fateful top hat was found in his trunk. After that, some railway carriages were designed with windows between the compartments, so that an attack or struggle in one could be observed from the next.[27]

As well as the flocks of tourists and the 'well-dressed men lounging around the table smoking', there was another category of passengers, who represented a fundamental shift in social habits. Until now, the average upper-working-class artisan had to live near his work. He could and did walk to it, over distances which we would think unacceptable, but his working day began at six in the morning, and there was a limit to the time and energy he could expend on just getting to work in time. He might prefer to live in the slum district round the corner from his job, provided he could find a tolerable roof. Government slowly considered whether something could be done to improve the slums and the condition of the poor – not, heaven forbid, by any kind of state-funded income support, subsidised housing, and so on, but by persuading the upper working class to better their own conditions. For example, if they could live further

out of London and travel in to their work by this new-fangled railway
system, surely several birds could be killed with one stone? In 1844
Gladstone decreed that every line had to run a train charging only
1d a mile, every day, for working people, who needed to get to their
work long before the civil servants and merchants clocked in at ten
or so. His 'Parliamentary trains' brought into central London crowds
of 'poorly clad creatures, men in patched garments, women in pinched
bonnets and coarse shawls carrying a plenitude of baskets and bundles',
and hordes of '3rd class children' with 'poor little wan faces ... what
a contrast to the quietude of the scarcely patronised 1st and 2nd class
wagons are the great hearse-like caravans in which travel the teeming
hundreds who can afford to pay but a penny a mile'.[28] At least, by
then, the rail companies were obliged to put roofs, doors and windows
into their 'hearse-like caravans'.[29] The idea caught on rapidly. By the
end of 1865, 2,000 'bona fide mechanics and daily labourers, both
male and female' were buying weekly tickets to the London termini
at 2d a day return.[30]

Once a well-heeled passenger had arrived at a rail terminus, where
was he to go? London had always been desperately short of decent
hotel accommodation. The few hotels that there were had been
contrived by joining several houses together, which can be thoroughly
inconvenient. The new stations needed new purpose-built modern
hotels, with impressive frontages to attract the travelling public. The
hotel at Paddington station (1854) was 'in the school of' the French
Second Empire – throw everything in that looked as if it had some
connection with the Renaissance. The Grosvenor Hotel at Victoria
(1861) was opulently built, again in a mixture of Renaissance styles,
with a hydraulic lift, then known as a 'rising room'. The rising room
in the Charing Cross Hotel (1865) even had seats; the complex of
station and hotel cost over £3 million, including a pastiche of the
long-vanished medieval cross.[31] When it came to building the hotel at
St Pancras station (1868), Sir George Gilbert Scott had a chance to
use his High Gothic designs for Whitehall offices, which had been
spurned by the Government, and did so with resounding success.[32] In
its time, the hotel was described as the most sumptuous and best-
conducted hotel in the British Empire.

But the trains only worsened the traffic problems afflicting inner London, as passengers and goods were unloaded and taken by road to their destination, sometimes across London, competing with all the other traffic. The answer was simple and novel: put the rail traffic *underground*. Yet of course it was far from simple. £170,000 set aside to finance the plan somehow disappeared. The subsoil was honey-combed with tunnels and drains and streams, and subject to alarming variations. But after years of dithering, a start was made. *The Illustrated London News* reported jubilantly on 7 April 1860 that

> the Metropolitan Railway has now been commenced in earnest ...
> from opposite the Great Western Railway hotel at Paddington, [it]
> crosses Edgware Road ... enters New Road [now Euston Road] which
> it follows to King's Cross ... it occupies throughout the greater part of
> its journey the under surface of the existing roadway ... [From King's
> Cross to Farringdon Street it runs] in open cutting except when passing
> under roadways ... In this manner the whole of the New Road will be
> taken up and relaid in sections.

The accompanying picture shows most of the road surface occupied by steam cranes and diggers, and horse-drawn carts. There was just room for one lane of traffic on each side, which may have been generous; a rival publication shows the New Road in effect blocked. The underground stations were to be 'commodious, airy and well lighted with gas' where they were not in the open air at the bottom of a cutting, as Farringdon Street station still is. Imagine living anywhere near the New Road, a very busy traffic artery particularly used by omnibuses, as the tunnellers approach. 'In all directions the shopkeepers etc. are complaining of the ruin caused to their trade, by the long-continued stoppage.'[33] *The Illustrated London News* kept its readers informed of the progress of the underground railway, running neck and neck with the intercepting sewers. The Fleet river, which by then was a stream of undiluted sewage, had been contained in a huge iron pipe which the railway had to negotiate. In an appalling accident in 1862 the pipe broke and flooded the underground railway works at Farringdon Road with sewage.

At last, in January 1863, 650 invited guests including Mr and Mrs Gladstone boarded a train at Paddington and went all the way to Farringdon, where 'a banquet had been prepared and was partaken of by the guests'. The difficulties of producing a banquet in the middle of a tube station were as nothing compared to achieving the station itself.[34] Then, on 10 January:

the line was opened to the public ... and it was calculated that more than 30,000 persons were carried over the line in the course of the day ... from 9 o'clock in the morning till past midday it was impossible to obtain a place in the up or cityward line at any of the mid-stations ... they are queer little buildings, those offices on the Metropolitan line ... For the most part they resemble ... half an establishment for baths and wash-houses ... I descend the broad staircase which leads some thirty feet below, and as I do so ... become aware of a certain chill ... there is an unmistakable smell, too, of railway steam, which increases as I proceed; and having at length reached the platform of the subterranean station, I am free to confess it is not a very cheerful place ... a dense fog filled the place when I was there ... we plunge into the tunnel. Not into darkness, though – there is a good steady light from the gas-burner above, which enables you to read ... or you may lean back in the well-cushioned, comfortable seat of the most roomy railway carriage in England [he was in a first-class carriage], and, forgetting that you have 20 feet of earth above you, contemplate your opposite neighbours ... At full speed there is a peculiar vibration noticeable on the underground rail. The carriages are too wide and heavy to sway much from side to side, but there is a kind of undulating movement ...

Second- and third-class carriages were not so luxurious. The third-class passengers sat in open wagons, without any protection from the dirt and smoke. Despite the appalling atmospheric conditions, the general public embraced the Underground with enthusiasm. By 1864 there was a train every two minutes during rush hours, 9–10.30 and 4–6.30, slackening to one every ten minutes at quieter times. Almost twelve million passengers used the line that year, rising steadily to twenty-seven million in 1868.[35] The network of lines spread rapidly. The problem of smoke had to wait for electrification, to be solved. At least, accidents were not complicated by 'live' lines. In 1869 'a woman jumped out of one of the carriages on to the metals, and ... was rather severely shaken, and one gentleman complained of being slightly hurt'. Later that year there was a collision between two trains, which caused the line to be blocked for two hours and 'a great deal of inconvenience', but the injured were taken to the Portland Street station, 'where they were waited on by servants of the Company',[36] no doubt with tea or brandy from the station refreshment room.

CHAPTER 5

Buildings

꿏

*The slums · philanthropic housing · George Peabody · Angela Burdett
Coutts · public bathhouses · terraced cottages · middle-class housing ·
steps and letter boxes · baths · lavatories · earth closets · Belgravia ·
Buckingham Palace · the Law Courts · the Foreign Office · 'Albertopolis' ·
the British Museum · the Pall Mall clubs · the Palace of Westminster*

The very poor lived in slums. Sometimes these were old buildings
surviving from even before the Fire of 1666, lurching over crooked
lanes and nearly meeting overhead. They had been decent houses
erected by prosperous Restoration magnates, before fashionable
London moved west. They seem to have been left unoccupied, instead
of sold. Perhaps there was no market for them. Squatters quickly
moved in and removed anything usable or saleable. Wooden banisters,
doors and window frames, even floors and stairs, could be sold or
burned as firewood. Iron hinges could be sold, fireplaces had been
sold long ago, glass windows had short lives. Once the buildings had
been gutted, the very poor inherited the shells, into which they packed
as many as could find a space to lie on the floor – sometimes more
than that.

These dark, derelict houses loom indistinctly in pictures of the
slums of the time. Whatever progress had been made since they had
first been built had passed them by. They had no drains, no street
lighting, no refuse collection and no police. If there was a cesspit at
all, it had long been full, and overflowed into the cellar. It was
probably broken anyway, leaking into the earth round it. Yet money
could be made out of such housing. The man with a little money
could take a whole house in Jacob's Island in Bermondsey, for a rent
of 4s a week, and let it out in rooms at 2s or 3s each.

For the man in a steady job, even on low wages, prospects were slightly brighter, as public-spirited philanthropists interested themselves in housing for the deserving poor. The Metropolitan Association for Improving the Dwellings of the Industrious Classes was founded in 1841 to buy or build 'dwelling houses to be let to the poorer classes of persons ... more especially in densely-populated districts'. It erected a five-storey block of flats – the first in London – at St Pancras, where 110 families could be decently housed for as little as 3s 6d a week, each with its own water supply, wc and scullery, and a communal laundry and drying-ground. It built another block of flats in Bermondsey, for 108 families, and other blocks and houses built or refurbished by it were scattered through London. Where there was space, further from the centre, it built houses divided into four apartments, each with a small garden, let at 5s–6s a week.[1]

The Association set out to demonstrate that such developments could be commercially viable, producing a return of 5 per cent on the initial investment. This became the general principle of financing such associations: a mixture of commercial good sense and charity – '5 per cent philanthropy'. Prince Albert, as President of the Society for Improving the Conditions of the Labouring Classes, inspired a block of four flats on two floors, with separate access by an exterior central stairway, costed to let at only 20d a week. They could be inspected in Kensington Barracks yard during the Great Exhibition, and thereafter on-site in Kennington. Their exterior favoured an eclectic mixture of Tudor and Gothic, with decorative string courses and a 'Tudorbethan' pediment, but they were more practical than they looked. Each had three bedrooms, two small and one reasonably sized; a living room 14 feet by 10 feet, a scullery and a wc. The ingenuity of the design lay in its adaptability. The module could be repeated both upwards and sideways, to form a large tenement block. The Society's architect also contrived a way of avoiding the pernicious Window Tax (abolished in 1851), by giving each flat access from a balcony.[2]

By 1861 these two bodies, plus smaller concerns and miscellaneous parochial and private charities, probably housed more than 6,000 people, which was a start, at least.[3] In addition there were some enlightened employers such as Thomas Cubitt, who saw the commercial advantages of making houses available for their key employees.[4] Bazalgette provided eight cottages for the workmen at Abbey Mills pumping station as part of his great intercepting drainage system, and 21 at Crossness. These each had five rooms 'fitted with every reasonable convenience'. The house for the superintendent was of course 'more commodious and fitted up in better style'. Since the whole point of Crossness was that it was beyond the built-up area of London, where else would his labour force have lived?[5]

But the drive of the two major companies had slowed. Two individuals took on the challenge of rehousing the poor: George Peabody and Angela Burdett Coutts. Peabody had been born in Maryland, in 1795.[6] At 34 he was a prosperous Baltimore merchant, whose business frequently brought him to London. In 1843 he decided to move from Baltimore to London, and set up as a merchant and banker. He took in a partner, Junius S. Morgan – the firm was still trading until recently as merchant bankers Morgan Grenfell. In 1862 Peabody established a trust fund, the Peabody Donation Fund, with an initial capital of £150,000, with the general object of helping Londoners by residence or by birth who were poor and 'of good character'. The fund was vested in trustees, including the American Ambassador, to whom he gave complete discretion, save that no religious or political criteria should influence them. He suggested that they might use the fund for 'such improved buildings for the poor as may combine ... the essentials of healthfulness, comfort, social enjoyment and economy'.

Two years later, when Peabody was 70, he retired from business to give his whole time to the disposal of his huge fortune of over £1,713,00. Most of his benefactions were to educational or scientific bodies in Massachusetts, but the largest single allocation was the Peabody Donation Fund, increased by successive payments to £500,000. In 1865 its trustees published a report explaining their decision to act, in effect, as a housing society:

> ... In the poorer districts of London the dwellings of the lower classes had been suddenly disturbed by the long pent-up invasion of metropolitan railroads, whose incursions were overthrowing whole streets inhabited by humble and industrious labourers and artisans. This dispossessed population, unprovided with adequate accommodation elsewhere, were thus driven into alleys and courts, already inconveniently crowded by their previous inmates; and discomfort and disease were in many instances added to loss of employment and expense.

Peabody never intended to house the unemployed or the destitute. Someone in steady, albeit humble, employment, who could pay his rent regularly, was the ideal tenant. The first Peabody Buildings were opened in Commercial Street, Spitalfields, in 1864. They were five-storey blocks round a central courtyard where the tenants' children could play, safe from the dangers of the street — and the neighbouring slum-dwellers. The exteriors were sparsely decorated, the interiors starkly utilitarian. There were communal laundries, and baths, on the top floor. The size of the flats varied from one room, for which the rent was 2s 6d, to 5s for a set of three rooms, but all lavatories and washing facilities were on the landings outside the flats, and the interior walls were bare brick — the tenants were forbidden to paint or paper them. (Yet was not this a sensible way of avoiding the bedbugs that afflicted even the middle classes, lurking under paper or plaster?) Rubbish was to be disposed of down a chute on each landing. Other rules brought home the importance of community health:

> No applications for rooms will be entertained unless every member of the applicant's family has been vaccinated ... and [the applicant] further agrees to have every case of infectious disease removed to the proper hospital ... the passages, steps, closets and lavatory windows must be washed every Saturday and swept every morning before 10 o'clock. This must be done by the tenants in turn. Washing must only be done in the laundry ... Tenants are required to report to the superintendent any births, deaths or infectious diseases occurring in their rooms. Any tenant not complying with this rule will receive notice to quit ...

By 1870, estates had been opened in Islington (1865), Shadwell (1866) and Chelsea (1870). Between 1871 and 1885 twelve more were built. Blocks of Peabody Buildings are still a familiar sight in central London. Their originally forbidding exteriors have been cleaned and redecorated, and shared lavatories are a thing of the past.

Angela Burdett Coutts, the richest heiress in Europe, was the granddaughter of Thomas Coutts the banker, and the daughter of Sir Francis Burdett, an MP with radical leanings. She never married. Like Peabody, she believed that the poor would be improved if they had somewhere decent to live. During her lifetime she gave £3 million to housing projects and other charities. She spent £43,000 on four forbidding Gothic blocks in Bethnal Green, housing 600 people. A family could live there, in three rooms, for 5s a week.[7]

It was an enormous step forward to have water laid on, but a bathroom with hot water was out of the question for the working classes. At the end of the week 'a favourite plan of cleaning-up on Saturday afternoons is – among those who live within easy reach of public baths – to take their clean suits to the bath, and put them on after they have bathed, bringing away their working suits tied up in a bundle'.[8] The Association for Promoting Cleanliness Among the Poor opened a bathhouse and laundry in Smithfield, in 1844, where you could bath, and do your washing, for a penny, and even do your ironing for a farthing, and if you had the energy you could borrow a pail and some brushes, and paint your house – such as it was – with free whitewash. The idea gradually spread. Endell Street baths were opened in 1846, where the Oasis Health Centre is now, in High Holborn. The first municipally owned ones, in the parish of St Martin-in-the-Fields, began in 1849. In 1853 baths and washhouses opened in Marshall Street, Westminster, where they were badly needed, and Davies Street, a pocket of slum property in the middle of otherwise plutocratic Mayfair.[9]

There are still acres of Victorian terraced cottages in London. They were mostly built by small speculative builders, who built for sale and not to order. A builder, perhaps a bricklayer himself with a carpenter as partner, would put up two or three houses, identical in ground plan, with a front parlour, a back kitchen and a scullery where there was water laid on, and probably a water closet, downstairs, and two or three bedrooms upstairs. After 1848 every house had to be connected to a sewer. The corner end-of-terrace house was usually more substantial, suitable for a foreman, with a stable for a horse and cart or a pony and trap, unless the site was taken for a public house. As each group was sold, the builder used the proceeds to erect the next few. It is still possible to spot where each spurt of activity ended, using as clues slightly different brickwork, different shapes of chimney pots, different decorative motifs, but all from the same pattern book. Some of the capitals of the pillars adorning the more pretentious terraces are splendidly ornate, garlanded with fruit and flowers which nowadays, in Hackney at least when I lived there, have been painted in cheerful tropical colours. The site might run to a minute front garden, and certainly a back yard, where cabbages could be grown and pigs and chickens kept.

The middle classes, too, lived in terraces, of tall, narrow houses, a

kitchen and a room for the servants in the basement, with stone steps
down from the pavement to the 'area' (the part of the site next to the
street which might have been a small front garden, but if left open
gave the basement a modicum of light and air, and separate access
from the street). More handsome steps led up to the front door. The
ground floor was usually a narrow hall or passageway, and two rooms
often divided by folding doors. Two or three rooms on the next floor
were drawing rooms or studies, bedrooms on the next floor, and
nurseries and servants' rooms in the attics. We have a description,
slightly tongue-in-cheek, of the home of a prosperous Bank official in
1859.[10] 'This is the sort of house that is neatly solidly furnished from
top to toe, with every modern convenience and improvement: with
bath rooms, conservatories, ice cellars; with patent grates, patent
door-handles, dish-lifts [between kitchen and dining room], asbestos
stoves [?], gas cooking ranges and excruciatingly complicated ven-
tilatory contrivances' – the kind of house to be found in the Bloomsbury squares and Manchester and Portman squares. It was replicated
everywhere that the middle classes saw to be habitable, including
Pimlico, between Victoria station and the river. This part of the
Grosvenor estate was low-lying and prone to flooding, so it was never
included in the grander designs of Belgravia further north.

In the suburbs such as St John's Wood, the ground landlord might
favour detached or semi-detached villas instead of terraces. If you
were thinking of buying you would be well advised to have the house
carefully surveyed, because builders using 'dishonourable', i.e. non-
union, labour, accepted scamped work. 'Some of these houses fetch
low prices if they have to be sold a second time, the skirtings and
doors and other work being so shrunk ... the men who build them
only look to sell them once'.[11] The sale would be by one landlord to
another, who bought for investment. It was rare for a house to be
bought outright by the occupier. A young couple setting out on
married life would not take on the burden of a mortgage, as they do
nowadays, and they could give up one tenancy and move to another
without difficulty.

Before putting your foot on those freshly scrubbed stairs, would it
be too much to ask you to take the worst of the street dirt off your
shoes, on the scraper incorporated in the iron railings at the side of
the steps? They are a characteristically functional piece of Victoriana
that often survives unnoticed.[12] There is a blunt vertical blade for the
sole, and others to take off any mud on the sides and the upper

surface of the boot. Another point to notice, on the front door. When letters were paid for by the recipient, the postman knocked on the door to summon the resident, with his purse, so a knocker was needed. When the system changed after 1840, and the letters had already been paid for by the sender, the postman could simply deliver them without waiting – hence, a slot was made in, or near, the front door.

Water was laid on to the kitchen, and often to the upper floors, but the idea of a room dedicated to abluting was slow to spread. After all, it was very pleasant to lie in a comfortable bath of hot water in front of your bedroom fire, until you stepped out and wrapped yourself in the towel which had been warming on the towel rail, leaving the water to be carried down the stairs, as it had been carried up them, by the maid. A house that Charles Dickens rented in 1854, in fashionable Devonshire Terrace, had two lavatories, which by their nature were fixed, but no bathroom. The bath was kept in the butler's pantry.[13]

But for those who enjoyed new inventions, there were various fixed arrangements, which necessitated the devotion of a whole room to them. This accounts for the delightfully spacious bathrooms in some Victorian houses, where a bedroom has been changed into a bath-room. When a bathroom came to form part of the original plan, the space devoted to it was usually less. Some baths were made of zinc, a metal which had made its début at the Great Exhibition in the shape, much admired for her curves, of *Amazon* by the German sculptor Kiss, and an 18-foot statue of Queen Victoria, admired for the maker's tact, all in zinc. It is a nasty material, to my mind, redeemed only when galvanised and given a dull sparkle. The bath in a Victorian house in Holloway, where I lived for a while as a student in the 1940s, was an original fitting made of zinc, with a mahogany surround. It was the shape of a sarcophagus, straight-sided and very deep, and the surface of it remained a sinister dull grey no matter what you did in the way of cleaning. Most baths were free-standing. Some had a comfortable raised back, most had flat bottoms, but bath design has not changed all that much. What has changed is the method of heating the bathwater. In 1842 *The Magazine of Science and School of Arts* recorded that 'many copper and tin baths have lately been constructed in London, with a little furnace attached to one end, and surrounded by a case or jacket, into which the water flows backwards and forwards till the whole mass in the bath gets heated to a due degree ... when the proper temperature has been attained, the furnace must of course be extinguished'.[14]

Or you might prefer the more direct application of heat to the bath itself, such as Defries's Magic Heater, which for the expenditure of 2d-worth of gas would produce a hot bath in six minutes – and, one would imagine, a pool of molten metal and a violent explosion fairly soon afterwards. Then there were those terrifying contraptions aptly called geysers since they were as unpredictable and uncontrollable as anything in nature, often resulting in blowing off your eyebrows. They assumed (1) a room free of draughts which would, and usually did, blow out the vital match which you held at the pilot-light nozzle; (2) presence of mind, at that point, to turn off the gas supply; (3) strong nerves; (4) an unquenchable desire for a hot bath, then, there, and not later or elsewhere: all to be co-ordinated, while appropriately dressed for the bath you hoped to take.

Perhaps after all a cold shower would be just as enjoyable. It would certainly benefit your health more, as Carlyle insisted as he emptied bucketful after bucketful of cold water over himself by a contraption of ropes and pulleys. His wife Jane tried it, but 'whether it strengthens me or shatters me I have not yet made up my mind'.[15] The glory days of showers came a little later in the century, but the essential idea was there: a perforated tank balanced above the bath, sometimes with the refinement of a hand pump operated by the happy bather – or someone else – beside the bath, and possibly a water heater which at least took the chill off the shower water.

The word 'lavatory' used to mean somewhere to wash – the same root as laundry. But now it usually means an apparatus in which to urinate and defecate, which is also called a toilet, which used to mean the cloth on your bedroom table which protected it from cosmetics. With this clarification, let us consider lavatories, in our period. The first surprise is that they were not always water closets. The Reverend Henry Moule, apparently inspired by a passage in Deuteronomy,[16] invented an earth closet in 1860, which had a lot to be said for it. There was a hopper behind the seat, containing fine, dry earth. It had to be dry, to ensure it was free-running: suitable earth could be dried in the kitchen oven. A substantial wooden slab like a low table on four legs had a nicely rounded hole in the middle, with a metal pan fixed under it, and a smaller hole convenient to the occupant's right hand, housing a handle which could be raised to release a flow of earth from the hopper into the receptacle under the seat. It was simple to maintain and repair, easy to clean, and the floor under it could be swept and scrubbed.

Although Mrs Beeton specified the manifold duties of every servant in a household, I have not identified who was charged with filling the hopper and emptying the receptacle. By 1865 Messrs White of Bedford Street were advertising their 'earth closets and commodes' as better than water closets, since 'the deodorising material (dry surface earth) is the best for the purpose, and at the same time is the cheapest and within the reach of all classes ... in all large establishments such as hospitals, union houses [workhouses], schools, gaols and asylums a very considerable sum may be saved annually in the production of a valuable manure'.[17] I am not sure where the poorest of 'all classes' were to procure a supply of dry surface earth, but they were not likely to be constant readers of the *Gardening Chronicle* in which the advertisement appeared.

Earth closets were, however, overtaken by water closets.[18] The delighted first-time users of Mr Jennings's installations at the Great Exhibition spread the word. By 1857 200,000 water closets were flowing – and the Thames suffered.[19] In 1861 Thomas Crapper, whose name has delighted generations of schoolboy historians, began to sell his water closets with the slogan 'a certain flush with every pull'. His 'elastic valve closet' cost £3 9s 6d, worth every penny for its com-plicated mechanism. His high-level 2-gallon cistern was sold with a Water Waste Preventer and Tranquil Inlet Valves, Silencing Air Tubes, and Brass Chain and China Pull – I quote from one of his advertisements. All that for a mere £1 1s 6d.

❋

Sumptuous mansions were commissioned by plutocrats such as the Duke of Sutherland, who needed a town house to add to his other three palaces (it is now called Lancaster House). His brother Lord Ellesmere built Bridgewater House in Cleveland Row, nearby. (It was sold in 1948–9.) Dorchester House in Park Lane was meant by its untitled but even richer owner R. S. Holford to outdo all of them, and probably did (it was demolished in 1929 to make way for the Dorchester Hotel). But the most impressive development was the grand design of Belgravia further west, owned by the Duke of Westminster and built by Thomas Cubitt.[20] Where, in any other district, there would be a pub at the corner of the street, here the pubs were hidden away in the mews, where the servants lived. Belgrave Square, the centrepiece, was begun in 1828 and received the royal seal of approval in 1840, when Victoria moved her mother there while Kensington Palace was being refurbished. Here was the final development of terraced housing, in majestic rows and crescents. Soon the whole district glittered with titles and money. It still exudes a peaceful atmosphere of unlimited wealth and space, swathed in thick layers of cream stucco, and the lovely lines of the terraces are unbroken, due to the control exercised by the ground landlord, the Grosvenor Estate.

We have arrived at the top of the pyramid, royalty itself. Surely, when some of her subjects lived in palatial mansions, the Queen and her family could be as, or more, comfortably housed? Poor Victoria. The only good thing about Buckingham Palace was that Cubitt was employed in its refurbishment. It had never been intended as a royal palace, and had been tinkered with by successive monarchs at vast expense without making it any better. Unpleasant smells from the drains pervaded the building. There was not even a decent ballroom. The existing ones were long and narrow, suiting the formal eighteenth-century dances, but ladies valsing in huge crinolines needed much more space. In 1845 the Queen told her Prime Minister that something would have to be done about the 'total lack of accommodation for our little family', and the exterior, which was 'a disgrace to the country'.²¹ So once again the wretched building was pulled apart, between 1847 and 1855, in hopes that it would emerge perfect at last, hopes that once again were disappointed. Meanwhile the royal pair went off to the Isle of Wight and built Osborne, where they were happy.

London was acquiring a collection of public buildings suitable for its status as the capital of the richest country in the world. The Law Courts had functioned in Westminster Hall since the Middle Ages. As the law grew in complexity the awkwardness of this arrangement became more glaringly obvious. In 1865 a site on the north side of the Strand, then a slum district, was acquired for almost £1.5 million, and £700,000 which was lying unclaimed in the Courts of Chancery was earmarked to pay for the building.

The new Law Courts took seventeen years to complete. The chosen design reflected all too well the state of Victorian law − a whimsical mixture of modern innovation and medieval preservation. The Gothic was much to the fore, with pointed arches, elaborate railings and much wrought iron. Yet an observant eye will have noticed the design of the railings in the front, featuring delightful sunflowers, more Gilbert and Sullivan than Gothic. Over the main entrance, and almost impossible to see, are figures of the law-givers, Christ, King Solomon and King Alfred. The Victorians liked King Alfred, who has fallen out of fame since, except for his culinary carelessness. At the back, the Gothic changes into more or less Venetian, presided over by a figure of Moses. Inside, the Great Hall is so vast that it silences all careless talk – a stark contrast to Westminster Hall, where the details of a claimant's case could be heard by any interested listener. By an ingenious contrivance, the winding staircases are double, the inner spiral being for the use of judges only, the outer one for other members of the legal profession, and the public; never the twain do meet.

Whitehall was the display place for Government buildings. Here, Gothic was finally elbowed out by the Italianate or classical style. Stanford's 1862 *Library Map* has a blank space reserved for 'New Foreign Office'.[22] Britain was then the leading world power, and the office dealing with foreigners had to remind them of that. A competition was held to choose the architect for this most prestigious project, which Sir George Gilbert Scott won, with an elaborate Gothic design. Palmerston, then Foreign Secretary, did not care for it and steamrollered through his own choice, a course which he was all too apt to follow in dealing with foreign affairs; so Scott was out of the running. Then Palmerston fell, and Scott's Gothic design was up again – until Palmerston bobbed back again and Scott's design was out again. The only way Scott could keep the commission, as he was determined to do, was to produce a plan which would satisfy Palmerston – and anyone else who might succeed him – so Scott came up with yet another design, jettisoning the Goths and looking back (or forward) to the Italian Renaissance.

Palmerston has long gone, but the grandiloquent Foreign Office still stands, unspoilt by modernisers. It is so huge that it is difficult to take it in, even from the top of a bus, but unless access is barred for security reasons it is usually possible to see through the arched entry courtyards at the side, which begin to convey a sense of the grandeur of the interior. The staircase alone was a fitting reminder of the superiority of the British Empire to lesser races. Scott was able to use most of his Gothic design for the Midland Hotel at St Pancras Station.

The success of the Great Exhibition in 1851 generated a fund which Albert was determined to use for the same object as his Exhibition: the education of the British public, especially in matters of design. The first step was to acquire a site. The 80-acre Kensington Gore estate in South Kensington was bought by the Commissioners of the Exhibition in 1852, and Albert's great plan to build a whole precinct of museums and galleries to educate the public, which became known as Albertopolis, was under way. The fine art collection housed in Lancaster House had become a treasure house of masterpieces, but like many treasure houses it was higgledy-piggledy, and badly needing some kind of rationalisation. This came with the building of the Victoria and Albert Museum, begun in 1859 but not completed in its present form until 1909. To visit it is to experience some of the elation and despair of the visitors to the Great Exhibition. It is superlative, exhausting, and best taken in small and repeated doses (it has seven miles of corridors and the lofty display halls necessarily imply interminable stairs). Round every corner there is a masterpiece of Victoriana.[23]

The Albert Hall was begun in 1863, funded by a contribution by the Great Exhibition Commissioners and by an ingenious idea: the sale, on 999-year leases, of individual seats, entitling the leaseholder to attend any performance in the Hall free, subject to rare exceptions. Over 1,300 seats were sold in this way, at £100 each. In 1867 the Queen laid the foundation stone, and announced that the words 'Royal Albert' were to be added to the existing title of the Hall of Arts and Sciences. Her son declared it open four years later, his mother being too overcome with emotion. Only then, as the Bishop of London's prayers were answered with amens from all over the Hall, several times, did the notorious echo make itself heard.

The British Museum had been built in stages, between 1823 and 1847, the last stage being the construction of the imposing pillared entrance, with a pediment showing the progress of civilisation. The central blocks were grouped round an open square, in which the famous round Reading Room was built in 1852–7. It was a typical combination of Victorian vision and utility: the most comfortable reading room, perhaps, that I have ever used. The wide mahogany desks had plenty of space for your notes and the several books you were consulting, and there were even – but I did not use them – two inkwells, one for quill pens and one for 'steel pens', i.e. metal nibs, in pen-holders. The stacks, where the books were stored, shared a feature with other libraries, in the old Public Record Office in Chancery Lane, the library of the Patent Office nearby, and the private London Library, founded in 1842: stairs and floors made of iron grids. While admirably designed to prevent or contain fires, they did not take into consideration female footwear: the size of the mesh is just wide enough – or so it feels – to trap a stiletto heel. And if you are working on the top storey of the London Library stacks, and drop your pen, you can hear it tinkling its way through the floors down to the basement.

For grandiloquent buildings that were not inhabited by Government servants, you needed only to look at the stately procession of gentlemen's clubs in or near Pall Mall. The Athenaeum (1830), unmistakable with its classical frieze and statue of Pallas Athene, stands at the corner. Facing it across Waterloo Place was the United Services Club (1827, remodelled by Decimus Burton in 1859; it closed in 1976, the building is now occupied by the Institute of Directors). West of the Athenaeum is the Travellers' Club, designed by Barry and completed in 1832. Then comes the Reform Club, again by Barry, opened in 1841. (The Carlton Club, the Conservative Party stronghold, also in Pall Mall, was rebuilt in 1854. It was bombed during the Blitz and the club moved to St James's Street.) They were all monuments of the Victorian way of life.

The apotheosis of Victorian public building was the Palace of Westminster. The old Palace, with its ramshackle accumulation of mismatched buildings, had burned down in 1834 and at last, after 300 years of discomfort, Members could hope for a purpose-designed legislative building. The inevitable competition was won by Barry, with a Gothic design, and work began in 1837. His plan admirably summarised the British constitution. The Commons Chamber is at one end of an axis leading through the Lobby, where constituents can meet their MPs, to the Lords' Chamber, for the Lords Temporal and Spiritual (the Bishops). There is a separate entrance into this Chamber, for the monarch. Thus all three estates are comfortably housed and yet decently separated.

The elegance of the ground plan is somewhat obscured by the magnificence of the surface decoration, by Pugin, the past-master of Gothic. Some practical snags, particularly the heating and air conditioning systems, became apparent as the building progressed. The bell on which the hours are struck in the huge clock in the Victoria Tower, which became known as Big Ben, had a chequered history of cracks and miscalculations which were not resolved until 1859. It weighs over 13 tons, and needed a team of sixteen horses to pull it through the city streets from Whitechapel, where it was cast, to Westminster. But when the Palace was completed, in 1860, it was rightly acclaimed as a masterpiece.

Despite two wars and the ravages of modernisers, many Victorian buildings survive. Once you have your eye in, you can spot them at a hundred paces all over London, from small houses to magnificent commercial and public edifices. But some have gone. The saddest loss, perhaps, is the Coal Exchange, which Albert journeyed down the river in the royal barge to open in 1849. It was a masterpiece of cast iron and glass. Its circular central hall, with four cast-iron galleries, was covered by a glass and iron dome, and its wooden floor was patterned as a mariner's compass, a reminder that coal still came down from the coalfields by sea. Having survived two wars, it was demolished in 1960. A banking hall in High Holborn, with a huge, and apparently continuous, circular mahogany counter (how did the bank clerks get in? Did they hurdle over, or crawl under?) and gorgeous terracotta dragons, went the same way. There was a Museum of Practical Geology in Jermyn Street, the walls of which were lined with sheets of polished stone. It was opened by the Prince Consort in 1851, and survived until 1936, when it was demolished. Tastes change, but with any luck the surviving Victorian buildings may outlast their critics.

CHAPTER 6

Practicalities

London's size and population · its government · contrasting districts ·
the police · the fire service · water supply · gas · refuse collection and
dust heaps · air pollution · the postal service

To the Romans, Londinium was the area of approximately one square
mile on the River Thames, fortified by strong walls. The walls survived
until the eighteenth century, but London had burst out of them long
ago, like a fat lady taking off her stays. After the Great Fire of 1666
many people preferred the new developments outside the walls to the
cramped quarters of the old 'square mile'. Although bankers and
merchants maintained their establishments in the City, fashion moved
west. St James's Square was followed by Belgravia. Green fields
receded further and further from central London.[1]

At least the Romans knew exactly what they meant by Londinium.
Since their day it had grown increasingly complicated to define
England's capital city. In a *Handbook of London* published in 1849
London was said to be 'about 30 miles in circumference'.[2] In September 1850 that indefatigable number-cruncher Henry Mayhew took
the Metropolitan Police district as his guide: a fifteen-mile-wide circle
centred on Charing Cross, plus some outlying parishes which disturbed
the neatly drawn circumference. He computed that there were 315
parishes, 3,686 miles of streets, 365,520 inhabited houses, 13,692
uninhabited houses, and 5,754 houses being built. But even he said
'where the capital begins and ends it is difficult to say'.[3] It certainly
included 20 miles of the Thames, from Hammersmith to Woolwich.
From Holloway in the north to Camberwell in the south was 12 miles.
From Bow in the east to Hammersmith in the west was 14 miles.[4]
Mayhew – again – calculated the density of London housing, parish

by parish, in 1862. The average density for the whole of London was 4.1 houses per acre, but this covered a wide diversity. Kensington had only 2.5 houses per acre on its 7,374 acres, Hampstead (2,252 acres) had a density of only 0.8. But St Luke's parish in central London had the highest density of all, at 30 houses per acre.

In 1851 the population of England was nearly twenty-two million, of whom 54 per cent were urban dwellers – a proportion which steadily rose to over 58 per cent in 1861, 65 per cent in 1871. London accounted for three and a half million of them. The next biggest English city was Liverpool, with a population of 395,000; then Manchester (338,000) and Birmingham (265,000). Over the border, Glasgow competed at 375,000.

Parishes have largely lost their importance in the modern world. An observant pedestrian may sometimes see, set into the walls of old buildings at ground level, a small stone with two sets of initials on it, standing for the parishes on either side of the stone. Until the Victorian era parishes and their boundaries were important to residents, because local government was organised – if it was organised at all – by the parish. Many London parishes could trace their history back to the eleventh century, before the Norman Conquest. Interesting as this might be to a historian, it was increasingly irksome to anyone who hoped to move London into the nineteenth century. In painful spasms, the old parochial machinery was sloughed off like a snake skin and a new, shiny London emerged. The Metropolitan Police Act of 1829 (extended in 1839) replaced the notoriously inefficient parish constables with a paid force of uniformed men who could operate over the whole area – except, of course, the City, which insisted on keeping its own force. Next, the archaic Commissioners of Sewers found themselves swept away – except in the City – and in 1855 the Metropolitan Board of Works was given power to impose a drainage system regardless of parish boundaries, which might have prevented the Great Stink of 1858. Other functions were transferred piecemeal. Even the numbering of houses and the naming of streets became matters for the central London government. The process took time, partly because of the City's reluctance to let the light of day – or even the new gaslighting – into its arcane secrets, but by 1888 the London County Council had taken over the whole administration of London.

The City livery companies which had exercised such power in the sixteenth century had changed, for the most part, into social and financial clubs administering their considerable estates. Only the Stationers' Company was confined to members of that trade. In others, freedom of the company could be bought for £105, with no prior apprenticeship.[5] The Company of Watermen and Lightermen of the River Thames, not strictly speaking a livery company because it had never instituted a livery for its members, still maintained an effective apprenticeship system, necessary in the shifting sands and technological changes of river navigation.

There was an appalling, visible contrast between the way the rich lived, and the dreadful existence of the poor under their noses. Just off Chancery Lane, in the lawyers' quarter, was a passage where 'frightful, one-eyed, pock-pitted creatures ... peer distrustfully through the patched and papered windows. Rickety children paddle in congenial dirt. Here are shops where victuals are offered for sale much less eatable ... than the cat's meat of a reputable tripe shop ...'.[6] In Fulwood's Rents nearby, there was a thieves' kitchen 'up an alley, through an iron gate, down a narrow passage, down a rude old stair, across a rude lobby ... a large long antique cellar [where there were] men and boys, perhaps 15 in all, all thieves'.[7] 'There are criminal districts in the metropolis, hot beds of particular crimes ... a school for coiners, another for burglars, another for shoplifting, another for horse stealing ...'.

> There are terrible highways and passages round about [Westminster] Abbey. At the back of Regent Street and Oxford Street are alleys of houses where some of the most miserable of London's citizens abide. There are purlieus in Kensington, Belgravia, Westbournia and the Regent's Park as heart-sickening as those that skirt the highway in Shoreditch.[8]

Over the river, in Bermondsey near the stinking tanneries, the houses of Jacob's Island had 'wooden galleries and sleeping rooms at the back of the houses, which overhang the dark flood and are built on piles ... Little rickety bridges ... span the ditches ... [which were] the common sewer for drinking and washing water [and excrement]'.[9]

Yet parts of what we now classify as the East End were not too terrible. In Bethnal Green a family of fourteen lived in a three-roomed 'detached villa' built by a man and his father in their spare time. Crowded, certainly, but 'like every house there, nearly everyone kept either pigs or chickens or ducks, sometimes all three' – a country touch that contributed usefully to the family finances.[10] Other districts had their distinctive characters. The silk weavers in Spitalfields hung on to their declining trade by their fingertips. They had always been known for their love of flowers, and still, in 1849, some of the houses had back gardens 'filled with many-coloured dahlias'.[11] Savile Row was the Harley Street of the time, inhabited by eminent medical men. The suburbs varied from the prosperous tree-lined avenues of St John's Wood, Clapham, Ealing and Kensington, to the long two-storey terraces of Hackney and Brixton. And 'there is, in London, a whole quarter which is qualified as "Australian", inhabited by people who made their fortune in Victoria or Melbourne'.[12] Unfortunately the writer did not say where it was.

※

The new Metropolitan Police Force quickly established a reputation for efficiency and probity. They were a smart body of men, minimum height 5 feet 8 inches, physically fit and mostly literate. Their uniform distinguished them in a crowd, and their tall hats of varnished leather, replaced by the familiar helmets in the late 1860s, gave them protection and added height. Each man carried a truncheon, a lamp and a rattle – like the ones heard at football matches – which could alert colleagues on the next beat that there were criminals about. They patrolled their allotted streets at a steady two and a half miles an hour, contacting the bobby on the next beat at regular intervals, trying doors to assure themselves that the owner had locked up properly, and shining their lanterns into dark corners to see that there were no thieves, or stray boys, lurking there. They walked on the outer edge of the pavement, to avoid missiles such as the contents of chamber pots emptied out of upper windows.

They were not allowed to go into a pub for a meal. They carried a small packet of food in their pockets, and they slaked their thirst from a public drinking-fountain. (Possibly this was the ideal, and the actual fell a little short and was not always immune to an invitation from a hospitable cook to join her for a bite of something in her kitchen, where, after all, he was still on his beat.) After the establishment of the force the figures of reported crime markedly decreased. Perhaps this was due to the wise policy of concentrating on crimes apt to endanger people or property, rather than pursuing small boys perpetrating heinous offences such as ringing doorbells and spinning tops in the street. The criminal fraternity, the army of prostitutes and the police maintained a wary balance, with which the average citizen was satisfied, except for the more rabid Sabbatarians who wanted the police to enforce the laws prohibiting Sunday trading and amusements.

The police had to be prepared for violence. A prostitute called Cross-eyed Bet was ordered by an Inspector of Police to stop loitering in Clapham Park one night. 'She had chloroform in her handkerchief and instantly applied it to the Inspector's face, who was immediately rendered incapable of resistance. She then robbed him of his watch and was decamping when two detective officers, who were on the other side of the hedge ... captured her. She was transported.'[13] On one occasion there were only six officers to quell hundreds of rioting Irishmen in Saffron Hill. One of the officers put a charge of red powder in his pistols, which he fired at 'a great chap' advancing towards him. The great chap fell back, red all over his face, and the mob retreated, unnerved at the sight of so much blood. The sufferer was taken to St Bartholomew's Hospital just round the corner, where his face was washed and he went on his way, thoughtful but unscathed.[14] There was a pioneering attempt at traffic control, which impressed Hippolyte Taine: 'At Hyde Park Corner I have watched the policemen on point duty ... they never speak: if there is any mix-up in the traffic, they simply raise an arm to stop the coachman, lower it as a sign for him to move on. The coachman obeys immediately, and in silence.'[15] Traffic control in places like the Bank was noticeable by its absence; perhaps the City authorities could see where they were beaten.

The Fire Brigade was another service that badly needed centralisation. The parochial system was so ineffective that the insurance companies set up their own crews, who would rush to the site of a fire – and pause to check that the premises were indeed insured with their company. If, not, they went home. At one time there were 150 parochially funded fire stations, and seventeen others.[16] The terrible Tooley Street fire in 1861 demonstrated the need for a strong unified system able to respond to any call from anywhere in London, yet it was not until 1865 that the Metropolitan Fire Brigade was set up. Their horses could be harnessed and the men equipped and ready within three to seven minutes of a call-out, and the engine would proceed through the streets at the furious pace of 10 miles an hour.

But with every sinew strained, and given no traffic blocks, it could still take almost half an hour for the gallant firefighters to reach a fire only a mile away.[17]

�֍

When London was younger, and smaller, clean drinking water was within the reach of every citizen.[18] But by the nineteenth century it was a luxury. An 1849 guidebook warned visitors against drinking 'the unwholesome water furnished to the tanks of houses from the Thames. Good drinking water may be obtained from springs and pumps in every quarter of the town, by sending for it,'[19] – just as one drinks only bottled water in some tropical countries. But the springs and pumps which had supplied potable water to everyone in the previous century, drew from sources that had become polluted with sewage from cesspits dug deeper and deeper as the old ones proved inadequate. The problem was worst on the low-lying south bank of the Thames. Local residents abandoned the familiar conduits which had served their fathers and grandfathers; the only users were poor passers-by who did not know the reputation of the water.[20]

In 1847 Edwin Chadwick urged the importance to public health of drainage, refuse collection and improved water supplies, the latter being 'absolutely necessary'. But somehow nothing was done. (Chadwick was a brilliant pioneer of public health reform, who would have been as famous as Brunel and Bazalgette, if only he had not upset everyone with whom he worked, so that few of his ideas came to fruition in his time.) Apart from local springs, eight different commercial companies supplied water of varying quality. They often laid their mains pipes next to the sewers, under the roads. If both leaked, as they often did, the mix could be lethal.[21] Only three companies made some attempt to filter the water. The East London Water Company alleged that it filtered all supplies through its filter beds at Lea Bridge (disused now, but preserved as a magnificent wildlife sanctuary), but nevertheless two customers found eels in their water pipes.[22] The northern suburbs took water from the Chadwell, the Lea and the New River, which ran through perhaps twenty villages before reaching London in a comparatively clean state. South of the Thames, the water companies drew from the sewage-flooded Thames. In Mayhew's words, 'we drink a solution of our own faeces'.[23]

The difference was graphically illustrated in the incidence of cholera, a water-borne disease. In the terrible epidemics of the nine-teenth century, deaths from cholera on the south bank were three or four times as high as on the north bank.[24] For all domestic 'consumers', supply was intermittent, and none was supplied on Sundays. The poor stored water in whatever receptacle they could find, and put it in the yard, next to the privy. When they ran short they resorted to the nearest river or canal, which was already heavily polluted, and they emptied their chamber pots into the same source. In Stepney, a poor parish bordering the Thames, there were 200 deaths from cholera within as many yards from the Regent's Canal.[25]

More than 17,000 houses had no mains supply whatever, relying on polluted wells. In the poorest districts 70,000 houses were supplied by standpipes, one to a group of 20 to 30 houses, giving a feeble flow of water for an hour a day, three times a week. If you missed your turn, or the water stopped, at one tap, you would have to carry your bucket or jar to the nearest, hoping for better luck there. Those familiar horse troughs, now mostly filled with tasteful flower displays, date from 1859, when the Metropolitan Free Drinking Association (later known as the Metropolitan Drinking Fountain and Cattle Trough Association) began to supply clean water to the poorer classes, and to animals on their way to market, in the interests of furthering the temperance movement.[26]

The middle class could afford to build storage tanks, but even those were often uncovered and open to pollution. Many private houses drew water from a well in addition to piped water. The Carlyles' house in Chelsea had a well under the kitchen with a pump, which they continued to use after water was laid on to the house, in 1852.[27] Piped water came in at basement or ground-floor level – the 'low service' – but for 50 per cent more than the standard charge you could buy the 'high service', still intermittent, but pumped up as high as 13 feet which would just reach a bathroom on the first floor. The high service needed special mains, and was little used. Charles Dickens, writing in 1855 from his house in Tavistock Square, was one of the 3 per cent of the New River Company's customers who took it. 'My supply of water is often absurdly insufficient and … although I pay the extra service-rate for a Bath Cistern I am usually left on a Monday morning as dry as if there was no New River Company in existence – which I sometimes devoutly wish were the case.'[28] The urgent need to rationalise and improve London's water supply was recognised by everyone, except the shareholders in the extremely profitable water

companies. The companies survived until 1902, when a new Metropolitan Water Board bought them out, for about £40 million.[29]
Only in 1904 did water run constantly through the water mains.
Earlier legislation requiring companies to provide a constant supply
had proved too easy to evade.

Another area where the new centralised body was beaten by
entrenched private interests was the supply of gas. About twenty
companies, the leading one being the London Gas Light and Coke
Company, divided the market between them and held off any attempt
to control them by Government, except in the City, which in this
instance managed to exert its strength and acquire control over the
price and quality of the gas supplied by the companies. Domestic
consumption was increasing, but the undisputed realm of gas was in
public street lighting. Many streets and bridges had been lit by the
gas supplied by the London Gas Light and Coke Company since
1812. 'As evening is drawing on the lamp-lighter is seen busily
hastening from lamp to lamp, placing his slight ladder against the
street lamp-irons and kindling the flames.'[30] The last oil lamp in
Grosvenor Square was replaced by gas in 1846.[31]

⁂

The refuse of a Victorian home may not have presented the problems
of packaging that we try to dispose of now, but it still mounted up
alarmingly. As well as the ashes and cinders from open fires, there
were vegetable peelings and meat bones, rags and paper, sweepings,
spoilt food and broken furniture. In theory, everything was collected
by parochial employees and disposed of hygienically. In practice, of
course, this simply did not happen at all in the poor, populous East
End districts, and 'the poor man dare not carry away the dustheap
which offends the nose and disgusts the eye, lest he be punished for
breaking the contract with him who is pledged, but slow, to remove
it'.[32] Refuse collection was supposed to be provided free of charge,
but if you wanted your rubbish properly removed you would be well
advised to slip the dustmen a tip, to make sure they remembered
you.[33] Two-men gangs came round the streets with high-sided carts,
shouting 'dust oy-eh'. They took their carts to one of the dust yards
scattered through London and the suburbs.

These yards could be considerable enterprises, employing up to 150
people. 'Some time since', wrote Mayhew in 1862, 'there was an

immense dust-heap in the neighbourhood of Gray's Inn Lane which sold for £20,000, but that was in the days when 15s or £1 per chaldron could easily be procured for the dust.' There was a combined sewage and refuse yard at Spitalfields in 1848, beside the workhouse there. It was 'a heap of dung the size of a tolerably large house, and an artificial pond into which the contents of cesspits are thrown. The contents are allowed to desiccate in the open air, and they are frequently stirred for that purpose' so that the 'patent manure factory' associated with the yard could manufacture patent manure cakes for sale to farmers and gardeners, for 4s–5s the cartload.[34] There was one in Bethnal Green, 'pestiferous with mountains of house refuse, road mud, offal and filth', until Baroness Burdett Coutts had it cleared away to make room for a row of model houses in 1856.[35]

Often a family worked together on a dust heap. The man carted the rubbish in, the boys carried it to their mother and threw it against her huge wire sieve – she was called a 'sifter' – and they sorted it all into rags and bones which could be sold for manure and paper-making, coal and cinders for brick-making, old shoes for the dyeworks,[36] and food scraps for the pig-breeders.[37] Sometimes a gang of women worked together. That extraordinary diarist Munby, who was fascinated by working women, described the 'gangs of dust-women' returning from Paddington, where there must have been a dust heap, in 1860. 'One, a broad-shouldered creature in a thick brown greatcoat [was] carrying a sack of perquisites – odds and ends from the dustheap – on her back.'[38] He noticed them again, five years later, in Kensington Gardens, where 'the languid belles ... lay supine under a cloud of pink and white fluff in the barouches ... and meanwhile the mob of coarse and ragged able-bodied wenches were creeping and darting between the wheels, anxious only to save their limbs and their loads of cinders'.

The trade of dustman could be profitable. It was also respectable. Dodd the Dustman (the origin of Boffin in Charles Dickens's *Our Mutual Friend*) used to give an annual tea party, at which the sifters 'often looked charming' and the dustmen 'with clean smocks, ribbons and flowers were like model ploughmen'.[39] Dustmen could earn good wages: more than 10s a week, and over double that if they also worked as night-soil men clearing cesspits. It was a hereditary job. Practitioners could boast that they were 'born-and-bred dust men'.

✳

'Pea-souper' fogs were notorious. A good pea soup is appetising. A London 'particular' fog was foul-smelling, opaque and yellow. The Clean Air Act of 1956, and the change to gas and electric fires and central heating, abolished the multitude of coal fires belching sulphurous smoke from every chimney, so that now it is difficult to imagine how polluted London air was. In 1855 Nathaniel Hawthorne remarked how St Paul's Cathedral 'has grown black with the smoke of ages, through which there are gleams of white'. The fog he encountered was 'more like a distillation of mud than anything else ... So heavy was the gloom, that gas was lighted in all the shop windows'.[40] Another visitor, Hippolyte Taine, noted how 'a thick yellow fog fills the air ... the palace they call Somerset House ... with every crevice inked in, porticoes foul with soot ... even in the parks, smoke-laden fog has fouled the very greenery ... on the façade of the British Museum the fluting of the columns is full of greasy filth'.[41] A resident of Savile Row observed that 'in the early part of September London was different from what it was at other times. The air was so clean; there was no smoke, for houses [in the fashionable West End] all seemed to be shut up. One could see the Crystal Palace at Sydenham from Piccadilly.'[42]

The Victorian postal service can only strike us with awe, when nowadays we are lucky to get one delivery, on weekdays, at an unpredictable time. There were ten collections a day from local sorting offices and pillar boxes, beginning at 9 a.m. Delivery within the inner London area was promised within one and a half hours, and within a 12-mile radius of Charing Cross within three hours.[43] Mid-Victorian Londoners could expect *twelve* deliveries, one every hour during the day.[44]

The letter-carrier ('postman' came later) wore a splendid scarlet tunic and a tall black hat.[45] Since, after 1840, he no longer needed to hand over the letters and receive payment for them from the addressee, because the charge had to be pre-paid, he put the letters through a slot in the door. Pre-payment was by buying a small piece of stamped paper snipped off a sheet, until perforations were invented in 1853, and sticking it on to the letter or the envelope. Envelopes were gradually replacing the old-fashioned fold-and-tuck technique, and some provident correspondents still saved paper by 'crossing' – writing over, and at right angles to, what they had already written, which tends to make both lots illegible. Pillar boxes in the streets are said to have been invented by Anthony Trollope, then employed by the Post Office, in 1855, when the first one was installed in Fleet Street.

As the latest time for posting to the provinces, 6 p.m., approached, the head office of the postal service in St Martin's le Grand was a popular London sight. One window was for newspapers, which were either thrown through it in small packets, landing in a huge box beyond, or delivered in bundles. Meanwhile 'clerks and apprentices stagger breathlessly past with baskets of letters on their heads, or with letter-bags of all colours ... in their hands', to the other window and the box for letters. With only five seconds before closing time, ' "Gents, go on!" cries the red-coat at the letter box ... everyone strives to get his right hand free to throw and the next minute hundreds of letters fly through the air and fall like autumn leaves into the depths of the box ... The 6th stroke sounds and with a crash the chest closes and the board flies in front of the news-paper window ... the crowd of spectators ... breathes again, and disperses.'[46]

In the 1860s Southwark Town Hall was demolished. In its cellars were found crates of petrified plum puddings, addressed to the troops at Sebastopol, during their year-long siege of 1854–5.[47] No doubt they would have enjoyed them. Was this a late postal delivery?

CHAPTER 7

Destitution and Poverty

*Mayhew · the pauper children · beggars · 'bone-grubbers, rag-gatherers
and pure-collectors' · mudlarks and others · selling goods and services · slum
dwellings · window boxes · Soyer's soup kitchens · low lodging-houses ·
the workhouse · the 'Monster School' · the work test*

Mayhew's *London Labour and the London Poor*[1] is an unparalleled source
of information on the ways that the very poor found to stay alive,
when a modern reader's reaction is that 'I would rather not'. Unless
otherwise noted, the information in this section comes from Mayhew.
The dimension missing from his books is one I noticed only slowly –
the numbers of those who did *not* survive. Behind every survivor there
is a grey shadow.

'The mighty capital comprehended whole townships of the almost
hopeless poor.'[2] In 1820 the Society for Affording Nightly Shelter to
the Homeless had opened a refuge in Whitecross Street near the
Barbican, for up to 600 'destitute wretches', men, women and children.
They were given a sleeping-place – a trough on the floor divided
from the next by a low partition, with a waterproof palliasse stuffed
with hay, but it was at least dry – warmth, a compulsory bath, and
8oz of bread. Londoners could stay only three nights, others had a
week to find their feet. Many were foreigners. A crowd would gather
round the door as darkness fell, waiting to be admitted, 'with their
blue shoeless feet ulcerous with the cold'. A surgeon checked them,
and seriously ill cases were looked after.[3] 'To hear the cries of the
hungry shivering children and the wrangling of the greedy men,
scrambling for a bed and a pound of dry bread, is a thing to haunt
one for life ... [they are] the very poorest of this the richest city in
the world.'

If the refuge was full, or if a destitute person simply did not know about the refuge or could not find it, or preferred his freedom, then what? He could beg, or steal, and sleep rough. If the police saw him, he risked prison, depending on how enthusiastically the local force applied the law. Sleeping in a London park was an offence, but hundreds of people did it. Tothill Fields prison, just east of Victoria station, housed boys most of whom had been committed for up to fourteen days, for stealing goods worth under 6d.

> The place is called a House of Correction; but rightly viewed it is simply a criminal preparatory school ... here we find little creatures of 6 years of age, branded with a felon's badge ... the jail ... is really made an asylum and a home by many of them ... there is but one way to empty our prisons, and that is by paying attention to the outcast children of the land.[4]

A contemporary writer estimated that there were 100,000 pauper children in London.[5] This looks suspiciously like a rounded-up figure; it seems safe to say there were very many of them. In Bethnal Green, in the East End, 'everyone had a lot of children. Some were too poor to let them out to play, because they had not enough clothes to cover them. The children of one mother were left alone and they got out into the street with only a piece of sacking tied round them.'[6] Some parents were in prison, or in the workhouse, or dead. Other children were among the many entrusted to a 'baby-farmer' to be looked after while the mother worked – the parents were usually single, and either did not want to, or could not, check that their child prospered. One mother earned 6s 3d a week, making paper bags. She paid 4s 6d to another woman to look after her baby, but the 'nurse' got drunk, the baby got cold, and died. In the cheaper newspapers 'the baby-farmer fishes wholesale for customers'. For a payment of £12–20 – usually stolen – parents could be free of all responsibility for their offspring:

> Adoption: A person wishing a lasting and comfortable home for a young child of either sex will find this a good opportunity. Advertisers having no children of their own are about to proceed to America. Premium £15 ...

Or perhaps

> Nurse child wanted or to adopt. The Advertiser, a widow with a little family of her own, and a moderate allowance from her late husband's

friends, would be glad to accept the charge of a young child. Age no object. *If sickly* [my italics] a parent's care. Terms, 15s a month, or would adopt entirely if under two months for the small sum of £12.

The parents were free of their burden, the 'adopters' were at least £12 to the good, and the child was disposed of as soon as the coast looked clear – not always by murder, because awkward questions might be asked, but by simply taking it to some unfamiliar part of London and leaving it there.[7] Whoever found it might, or might not, look after it, for a while, but by the time the child was six or so it could earn its own living, and it was cast loose.

There was a vast army of beggars, all with heart-rendering stories, many with real or faked disabilities. Here is where the baby or toddler could be useful to a beggar woman, who made better money if she ostensibly had a child to support – even if the child was returned to its mother, or abandoned, once the day's begging was done. 'Old soldiers' did well out of the Crimean War (1853–6). 'The Crimea's been a good dodge to a many, but it's getting stale' by 1862.[8] Mayhew asked this beggar whether he might not find honest work more profitable, and was answered 'Well, sir, perhaps I might, but going on the square is so dreadfully confining.' A beggar who opted for the ex-sailor life had to be careful to behave like an ex-sailor, and spit in the right direction. 'A real sailor never spits to wind'ard, why, he couldn't.' There was a motley horde of foreign beggars, Frenchmen, Poles, 'Hindoos' and Negroes. But the Mendicity Society was gradually reducing the number of allegedly afflicted beggars. It made an exception for genuine blind men, who were allowed 'to sit on doorsteps or in the recesses of bridges without molestation by the police. It would be heartless cruelty to drive [them] into the workhouse, where no provision is made for their peculiar wants.'

How could you scrape an honest living on the London streets, without any money to buy stock? Mayhew estimated that there were almost 1,000 'bone-grubbers, rag-gatherers and pure collectors' in London. You had to be alert to find any bones or rags lying about in the streets, but not many competitors would beat you to a nice pure (dog turd). The tanners in Bermondsey bought it for 8d–10d a bucket, depending on its condition, but it might take a day or so to fill the bucket; meanwhile you took it back to wherever you were living, to keep it safe. A good harvest was perhaps eight buckets a week. Pigeons' dung too was worth collecting for sale to the tanners. Cigar butts could be reconstituted into something smokable and saleable.

'Mudlarks' waded up to their thighs in the river mud – and remember the sewage, and the bright red worms on the mud banks. If they trod on an unseen piece of glass or metal and cut their feet, septicaemia would surely result. (Here is where I first began to see the shadows behind Mayhew's characters.) Yet grubbing about in the cold, slimy, toxic Thames mud sustained all ages, from six-year-old boys to old women, just for the odd lump of coal, a copper nail, a bit of old iron, an end of rope or a bone. No wonder that one young mudlark preferred prison, where he got food and clothes and a bed without worrying. Crossing-sweepers might make 7s a week in a good district, but trade was seasonal, depending on the London Season for its best takings, and they had to spend 3d on a new broom every month. One 80-year-old woman did well from 'people going to their offices at 6 or 7 in the morning [who] gives me a ha'penny or a penny' – but she got 2s a week from her parish, as well. Children as young as five could earn the odd penny for running an errand, or holding a horse, or carrying a parcel, especially from the piers and railway stations, or turning somersaults and amusing passengers stuck on an omnibus in a traffic jam, or making themselves useful in the criminal world.

The docks operated wholly on casual labour, taken on for the day, and paid at the pitiful rate of 3d an hour, in 'tickets', not cash – and often short-changed even then.[9] General labourers could hope to make about a pound a week when there was work. Their ranks were swelled in the late 1840s by Irishmen leaving their famine-stricken homes. In 1845 Prince Albert foresaw a crisis 'when the innumerable railroads now in progress shall have been terminated ... this will throw an enormous labouring population suddenly out of employment'.[10] Fortunately, however, there were always more engineering projects such as the docks, and the underground railway, and Bazalgette's great sewers, looking for labourers. But £1 was not enough for any kind of decent life. No wonder the Irish, alone among the poor, found the workhouse quite acceptable.

There was an infinite variety of ways to earn a scant living by selling goods or services. German bands and Italian opera singers and organ-grinders with monkeys tootled and screeched their way round London, but there was little money in it. There were street sellers of ballads and accounts of 'barbarious and horrible murders'. One of my favourites is the entrepreneur who thought up the idea of standing near a dirty bookshop shiftily offering sealed envelopes ... but when the panting purchaser opened the envelope it was full of old tracts. To show you just one of the characters Mayhew evoked, here is 'a watercress girl' aged about eight, who 'had entirely lost all childish ways':

> I go about the streets with water-creases [*sic*] crying 'Four bunches a penny, water-creases' ... I've been very near a twelvemonth in the streets ... I used to go to school ... mother took me away because the master whacked me ... The creases is so bad now, that I haven't been out with 'em for three days. They're so cold people won't buy 'em ... besides, in the market they won't sell a ha'penny handful now – they're riz to a penny and twopence. In summer there's lots ... but I have to be down at Farringdon market between four and five, or else I can't get any creases, because everyone – especially the Irish – is selling them, and they're picked up so quick ... No; people never pities me in the street – excepting one gentleman, and he says 'what do you do out so soon in the morning?' But he gave me nothing – he only walked away ... It's very cold before winter comes on reg'lar – specially getting up of a morning. I gets up in the dark by the light of the lamp in the court ... I bears the cold – you must; so I puts my hands under my shawl, though it hurts 'em to take hold of the creases, especially when we takes 'em to the pump to wash 'em. No; I never see children crying – it's no use. Sometimes I make a great deal of money. One day I took 1s 6d, and the creases cost 6d; but it isn't often I get such luck as that.

Overcrowded slum dwellings were disgraceful: the authorities disapproved of them strongly, so new roads were cut through the worst slums, and the tottering, teeming old houses were demolished. This did not help, since the slum-dwellers usually had no choice but to move into their neighbours' patch, making it still more overcrowded. 'The Metropolitan Railway projects of 1861 are estimated to destroy 1,000 houses in low neighbourhoods and displace a population of not less than 20,000.'[11] A room in a slum tenement might cost between 2s and 3s a week. The whole family would crowd in, sleeping where they could find space on the floor, or five or six adults in the bed and the children in a row across the foot.

There was no sanitation. 'Whole courts and alleys are furnished with but one water closet, and that is in a perfectly unapproachable condition.' The London City Mission had been founded in 1835. One of its missionaries, from whose autobiography this is taken, described how 'bugs and fleas and other vermin abound ... whilst visiting at night I have sometimes seen numbers of bugs coursing over my clothes and hat ... the stenches have sometimes been so bad that I have been compelled to retreat'.[12] There were horror stories galore. This came from an official report: 'I found [one room] occupied by one man, two women, and two children, and in it was the dead body of a poor girl who had died in childbirth a few days before. The body was stretched out on the floor, without shroud or coffin.'[13] Yet even there, 'in some of these repulsive courts the inhabitants cling to a rude love of flowers, and many an unsightly window-ledge is fitted to resemble a garden enclosure, with miniature railings and gates'.[14] And in one of the worst districts, Whitechapel, there were public baths and washhouses, where you could have a 'first-class warm bath' for 6d, or a second-class warm bath for 2d – which most people did – or just a second-class cold bath for a penny.[15]

There was no means of cooking in these dreadful rooms, so poor people had to buy from street vendors pre-cooked food such as puddings and pies, or food needing no cooking such as whelks and oysters, shrimps and watercress. A hot baked potato cost a halfpenny. Sometimes crumbs could be harvested from rich men's tables. You had to have a ticket to share the unconsumed food from Buckingham Palace, but the Benchers of Lincoln's Inn, for example, sold the leavings of their Bar dinners to middlemen who retailed them at 4d to 8d a pound. Twopence-worth would make a nice change. Alexis Soyer's soup kitchens probably saved many lives. The one in Spitalfields fed 350 children, another in Leicester Square fed 200–300 people, another in Farringdon Street fed an astonishing 8,000–10,000 people daily. They only got bread and soup, but it was hot, and nourishing, and undoubtedly tasty. In 1852 Soyer gave a Christmas dinner for 22,000 poor people, with 9,000lb of meat, twenty roast geese, 5,000lb of plum pudding, various pies weighing 10–30lb, a 'monster pie' of 60lb, and a whole ox roasted by gas, while a band played waltzes and polkas. What a man.[16]

'Low lodging-houses' were a persistent scandal, even after the Common Lodging Houses Act of 1851 tried to impose minimal standards of hygiene. The exceptional ones were fairly decent, with reading rooms where newspapers were provided, and a washhouse and drying-yard, but most of them were filthy and full of lice and bedbugs. 'A pail in the middle of the room, to which both sexes may resort, is a frequent arrangement ... Some of [them] are of the worst class of low brothels, and some may even be described as brothels for children ... a few new lodging-houses, perhaps half a dozen, have been recently opened, in expectation of a great influx of "travellers" and vagrants at the opening of the Great Exhibition.' A night's lodging cost 2d or 3d. It was usual for each inmate to do his own cooking, at the open fires in the communal kitchen, of whatever scrap he had managed to beg or buy during the day. Fish could be picked up for little or nothing at the end of the day, at Billingsgate and other markets, for it would be unsaleable the next day. Mayhew estimated that more than 10,000 people were domiciled in low lodging-houses. Some of the owners neatly manipulated the system. They got themselves on to the parish Board of Governors, and in that capacity recommended that their tenants be given outdoor relief – which no doubt they nabbed before the unfortunate tenant laid a finger on it – and also on to the District Boards, where they managed to minimise the work statutorily required to bring the lodging-houses up to a proper standard. Some of them owned as many as 30 lodging-houses, and lived in comfort, in the suburbs, on the profits.[17]

But the street people had their freedom, of a sort. To enter the workhouse[18] meant giving up all self-respect, and abandoning family ties. It was dreaded with unimaginable fear. The Poor Law Act of 1601, which in its turn had replaced the old monastic charities, had set up parochial Poorhouses. They were suddenly seen by the Establishment to be too lenient. Things had to change. The poor could not be allowed to go on sponging on their richer neighbours. In 1834 the law was drastically altered. Every parish had to provide a Workhouse. Sometimes parishes pooled their resources and built a 'Union'. No longer should an old or disabled person who just needed a bit of help to stay in his or her own house draw 'outdoor relief' from the parish. Spouses who had lived together for decades were to go into the workhouse and be separated into wards for 'male paupers' and 'female paupers'. Their children were taken from them. Brothers might never see their sisters again. It was the workhouse, or nothing.

And yet ... as so often happens, the law did not coincide with practice. Outdoor relief continued. In 1861 the Marylebone workhouse, for example, relieved 2,039 'in-door poor' and 3,332 'outdoor relief'.[19]

Inside the workhouses conditions were hard. Journalists tended to over-sensationalise them, but there are a very few first-hand, reliable accounts. One boy had lived peacefully in one room in Woolwich with his sister, his parents, his uncles and his grandparents until he was seven. Then his world fell apart: his mother died, his father absconded, and his uncles disappeared. He and his sister found themselves in the Union workhouse, which was at the other end of London from Woolwich. He hated it, and was beaten for his rebelliousness. He was taught tailoring – a frequent option in workhouse circles – by a sadistic master who thrashed him twice a day and once knocked him unconscious. He did not see his sister for a month, and thereafter they met at rare intervals, until she fell ill and died. His grandmother somehow managed to make the journey from Woolwich every month, on visiting day, until she died. Then he was on his own. The food was 'not enough': bits of bread in a basin of water and milk for breakfast, meat occasionally for dinner, with three potatoes, often rotten, and 4oz of bread and butter and half a pint of watered milk for supper. 'The utter impossibility of getting away, and the terrible certainty of the cane for misbehaviour, inspired me with terror.'

And yet this unconquerable spirit managed to become a teacher. 'I had a great deal to be thankful for ... I was now nearly 14, knew how to read, write and calculate pretty fairly ... as a monitor I got 2d a week, as head-monitor 4d.' He was moved to the Central London District School for Pauper Children which had over 1,000 pupils. It was popularly called the 'Monster School', 'monster' being a favourite Victorian word for 'huge'. There 'I was thoroughly depauperised'. The first time he was allowed to go for a walk by himself he was terrified. 'I don't think anyone but he who has undergone the same thing can thoroughly enter into the emotions of a workhouse boy being trusted out for the first time alone.'[20] Although 'in many instances a child descends from generations of paupers', in this way he was given a chance to attain the respectable middle class as a teacher.[21] (The school closed in 1933. Its most famous pupil was Charlie Chaplin.)

Another first-hand account comes from a doctor employed in the Strand workhouse. Stanford's *Library Map* shows it just west of Tottenham Court Road, near Charlotte Street.[22] Dr Rogers's brother describes how he 'had to deal with sordid London vestrymen [the parish officers responsible for raising the poor rate to pay for the workhouse] ... and the officials of the Poor Law Board, who were determined ... to shirk all responsibility'. Dr Rogers was appointed as Medical Officer of the workhouse in 1856, for the princely salary of £50 'and provide all medicines'. I shall describe the medical aspects of his time there in the chapter on health, but here is his account of the building itself. It was

> a square 4-storeyed building fronting the street, with two wings ... projecting from each corner. Across the irregularly-paved yard in the rear was a two-storeyed leanto building ... used as a day and night ward for infirm women ... sheds on either side for the reception of male and female able-bodied people, ... in the yard, a two-storey building ... for the reception of male and female casual paupers ...

Somewhere in this considerable complex were a carpenter's shop, a mortuary and a tinker's shop with a forge. The male insane ward 'for epileptics and imbeciles' was above the male casual ward, and the female insane ward was sandwiched between the Board room and the lying-in (labour) ward. The nursery ward was 'damp, miserable and overcrowded – death relieved these young women of their illegitimate offspring'. There were never less than 500 inmates. When Dr Rogers was first appointed, the Master was 'so ignorant that he could only write his name with difficulty'. After the Master was sacked things began to improve.

Hippolyte Taine found much the same variety of buildings serving the same variety of purposes, but a less depressing environment, when he visited St Luke's workhouse in the City Road, in 1859 or 1862.[23] Stanford's *Library Map* shows it was a considerable building.

> There were 500–600 inmates, old people, abandoned or otherwise helpless children, and men and women out of work. The workhouse also gives outdoor and domiciliary relief; that week it had assisted 1,011 people. The cost per inmate is 3–4s a week ... the whole place was adequately clean and wholesome, but I gather that other workhouses are a great deal less pleasant. The children sang – out of tune, but they looked healthy enough ... the food and cooking looked very adequate ... the public rooms are airy and there is a fire in all of them. The old people get tea, sugar and newspapers. There are a few books to be

seen ... one touching detail; there was a vase of fresh flowers on the table.

The parish of St Martin-in-the-Fields had its workhouse, just behind the National Gallery. Gladstone's niece Lady Frederick Cavendish visited it regularly, when in London. 'The look of the sick-ward certainly takes away all romantic notions of ministration; everything most uncomely and meagre, and some of the poor old folk repulsive enough.' Her idea of visiting undoubtedly cheered up 'the poor old folk': one day she brought 'a good load of [country] daisies and clover for my poor old workhouse bodies', but they may have preferred the pinks and roses contributed by a friend, because country daisies do not last in water. Her diary records 'Old folk charmed'. A year later she added St George's parish workhouse, in the East End, to her good works. It was 'a paradise of freshness, good order and comfort compared with St Martin's. I am to have a ward of decrepit old men, who enjoyed some peppermints', and, without doubt, her pretty, cheerful company. But the grimness of the surroundings almost daunted her at times. 'It is very wrong and shocking, how they allow poor people to die in the midst of a crowded ward, without even a curtain to draw round the bed.'[24]

To claim relief, you had to show some connection with the parish, before it would even consider you.[25] Then your fitness to work was assessed. Those who could work, in the view of officialdom, were sent away to do so. A 70-year-old seamstress with deteriorating sight was refused entry to the poorhouse because she was 'young enough to work'.[26] Alternatively they were given work in the casual wards of the workhouse itself. Stone-breaking was a favourite with the authorities, both for male paupers and for convicts sentenced to hard labour. St Mary's workhouse in Islington put its able-bodied male paupers to work in an open shed with no protection from summer heat or winter frost, hammering lumps of granite into setts for road-making, next to the convicts sentenced to hard labour. Some of the experienced convicts could earn 9d a day, but paupers weakened by starvation, and convicts in for only a short stretch, who had perhaps never used their hands except for holding a pen, never attained this expertise and hammered away helplessly, still 'tenaciously assert[ing] their right to wear ... those badges of respectability, the tall hat and the black coat', no matter how tattered.[27] At St Luke's, about 100 paupers were employed in oakum-picking – unravelling old rope into heaps of tow, for caulking ships. St Marylebone workhouse went in for both stone-breaking and oakum-picking. For this the pauper got no pay, only an allowance of bread: 4lb a week if he was married, plus a 2lb loaf for each child. With any luck he could sell enough of it to buy necessities. And yet in the Westminster Union a vagrant applying to the casual ward was admitted at any time of the day or night, and given 6oz bread and 1oz cheese, and a space to sleep on a board strewn with straw, with two or three rugs, which were fumigated daily. When the inmates left, at eight in the winter, seven in summer, they got more bread and cheese. There was no requirement to work. Which all goes to show how parishes and Unions could still, despite the legislation, run things their own way, generously or grudgingly.

Workhouses may have been hated, but they were an effort to solve the perennial problem of poverty in London, and were reluctantly recognised as such by those who needed them. In the bitter winter of 1860–61, when outside work on building sites and in the docks and shipyards stopped, 'the distress and suffering ... particularly among the labouring classes at the East End, are truly horrible. Throughout the day, thousands congregate round the approaches of the different workhouses and unions, seeking relief.'[28] This blind faith that something could be done for them by the authorities is touching. It was the same impulse that led crowds to gather outside the police courts, where a magistrate had always been able to find some money for a deserving case from the poor-box. 'So far as possible each case was examined to eliminate undeserving cases', but sometimes the 'examination' was confined to inspecting their hands; those with work-worn hands passed. On 17 January 1861 there were 2,000 poor people waiting for hours in the bitter cold outside Thames Police Court. Two days later the crowd had doubled. As the weather improved, and labouring work could be found again, they gradually melted away, without a fuss.[29]

More than £2 million was spent annually by charities trying to relieve metropolitan poverty, yet 'pauperism, want and suffering are rapidly growing ... the administration of the Poor Law is as unsuccessful as that of private benevolence ... in London alone the cost of relief has doubled [in 1862] since 1851, from £695,000 to £1,317,000'. The weekly cost of feeding a workhouse inmate had risen from 2s 9d in 1853, to 4s 11d in 1868.[30] It would take many decades before the relief of poverty was seen as a national duty to be funded by national taxes.

In April 1865 the Prince of Wales started the engines at Crossness, the pumping station designed by Bazalgette as part of his great metropolitan sewerage scheme: see pages 7–8. Right at the top of the picture four workmen look down. All the other men are carrying or waving their top hats, except for the Prince and his equerries, who are wearing theirs.

Southwark Bridge and St Paul's, 1841. Paddle steamers took over the passenger trade from the old-established Watermen, until they in turn were ousted by the overland and underground railways.

(Detail of paddle steamers) Services to the City ran from Chelsea and as far out as Woolwich. The two ladies in the right foreground had perhaps spent the day shopping, and were waiting for the Chelsea boat.

The morning rush-hour at London Bridge. The man on the right has opted out of the scrum and bought a newspaper to read, instead.

Riverside warehouses caught fire frequently and spectacularly. Shipping anchored nearby was at risk. In this picture of a fire in Bermondsey in 1843, one ship is shown ablaze and two more downstream have been set alight by flying sparks. For those not directly involved, it was a thrilling sight. The curious tower beside the burning church was part of a commercial telegraph system signalling shipping news from the south coast to the City.

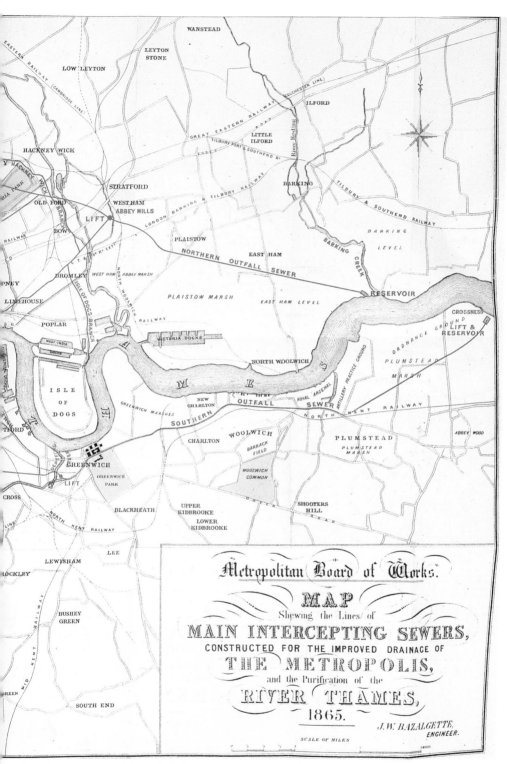

Two passengers have paid extra for first-class travel in separate compartments in this omnibus. Another woman has an inside seat. Male passengers have clambered on to the roof by the steps and rungs at the back. The conductor, standing on his outside step, is holding the door open for a dilatory customer.

Hansom cabs waiting for fares, 1860. Two horses are enjoying their nosebags. The drivers are probably enjoying theirs in a nearby pub.

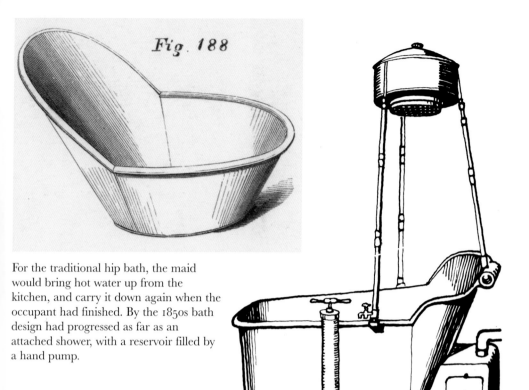

Fig. 188

For the traditional hip bath, the maid would bring hot water up from the kitchen, and carry it down again when the occupant had finished. By the 1850s bath design had progressed as far as an attached shower, with a reservoir filled by a hand pump.

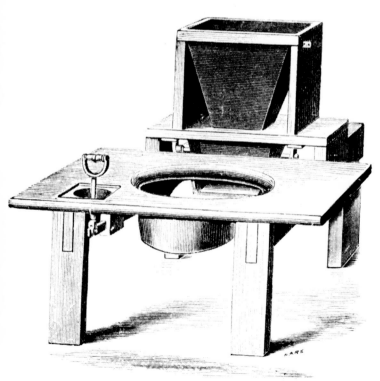

The earth closet invented by the Revd Henry Moule in 1860 (see page 52) rivalled the water closet for a brief period. The imminent world shortage of water might justify a re-assessment?

This map published by John Tallis is a typical souvenir designed for the Great Exhibition tourist trade in 1851. The thick coloured lines are the boundaries of the six London boroughs, including the City, which is coloured pink. The thin red circle is marked '3 miles around Post Office', the Post

Office headquarters in the City. The green patches show London well supplied with parks and open spaces, including the new Victoria Park to the north-east, and Kensal Green cemetery to the west, near the edge of the map.

This 1850s terrace in Hackney is typical of thousands throughout London, built for the Victorian working class. Most had two bedrooms, two rooms on the ground floor, and a scullery at the back.

LEFT: These elegant 1840s semi-detached houses in St John's Wood have steps up to the front door, front gardens, and kitchens in the basement.

OPPOSITE: These 1860s houses in Kensington have all the hallmarks of middle-class prosperity – an area basement, steps up to the front door, and two substantial bay-windowed storeys, with two more floors for bedrooms and staff. Note the Wardian cases (see page 138) on the ground-floor window and the window above the front door of the house in the middle.

There had been a livestock market at Smithfield since 1200. This picture shows it just before it closed, in 1855.

Ten years later the new Smithfield market opened as a meat market. Its Victorian buildings are still functional. Note the variety of vehicles parked outside, in this 1870 photograph.

CHAPTER 8

The Working Class

৵৯

A labourer's expenditure · costermongers · street sellers · fast food · milk women · the knackers' yard · brewing · sugar refining · road transport · Cubitt · the leather industry · Christy's hat factory · shipbuilding · holidays · trade unions · Friendly Societies · Samuel Smiles

The Victorians liked to have social classes clearly defined. The working class was divided into three layers, the lowest being 'working men' or labourers, then the 'intelligent artisan', and above him the 'educated working man'.[1] But London life was not so tidily demarcated. In 42 houses in a stretch of Broad Street in Soho, in 1855, there were two grocers, a baker, an ironmonger and a second-hand clothes dealer, a surgeon and a 'veterinarian', two tailors and a furrier, an undertaker, an umbrella-maker, a jeweller and a 'lapidary', a firm making per-cussion caps employing 150 workers, another making 'mineral teeth' employing 42 workers, a straw bonnet-maker and a trimming-seller and a lodging-house. In several of the houses there were between 20 and 30 residents, in one case 50. The surgeon shared a corner house with the furrier, and their two households comprised only five people. There were two pubs, and a brewery employing 80 workers.[2]

A 'mechanic', or labourer, with a wife and four children wrote to a popular newspaper, *The Penny Newsman*, to say that he earned an average wage, £1 10s a week. His rent, for two rooms, took 4s, 5s went on food and fuel, 3d on tobacco, 'a halfpenny for each child as a treat', and 9d sick club due; with other items, the total expenditure came to £1 8s 1d. Not much was left for contingencies and clothes.[3] Another labourer, married but with no children, earned 19s 6d a week, and he could 'bank on Christmas boxes, £2–£3'. His expenses for a typical week in 1856 were:

Rent (2 rooms)	5s
¾ cwt coals (less in summer)	1s 1d
coffee, tea, sugar	2s 6d
bread, 6 4-lb loaves, at 9d (could eat more)	4s 6d
vegetables	1s 1d
soap, soda salt and pepper	5½d
meat (or fish, when cheap)	2s 6d
beer (frequently have none)	4d
milk (often go without)	3d
wear and tear of utensils – should think, about	2d
wood	2d
total	18s ½d

'Clothing we buy as we can spare the money – generally after Christmas.' He was castigated by the writer who published these unfortunate figures: 'rent and luxuries [coffee, tea, sugar] absorb more than one-third of the entire earnings ... it cannot be a matter of surprise that bread and other necessaries are often wanting, and that there are no savings'.[4] But he seems to have got a bargain in the way of rent, although we are not told where the man lived. The once-grand houses near Golden Square, behind Regent Street, were inhabited by 'the most respectable of the labouring classes – porters, policemen and the like', who might pay 1s 6d for a cellar, up to 5s for one large upper room.[5]

Costermongers, definitely 'working men', with no skills other than their trade experience, made a reasonable living, selling food and a wide range of goods from their carts and barrows. They tended to live south of the river or in the East End. You would find at least one of them in any traffic jam, sometimes pushing his barrow but more often with a donkey and cart. A donkey cost anything from 5s to £3 at the weekly Smithfield Market. Its working life must have depended on how it was treated, but as a vital part of the enterprise it was probably well looked after. Feed cost 4d or 5d a day. Mayhew estimated the number of costermongers in London, in 1861, at 30,000, and rising. (He scorned the 1841 census, which set them down at only 2,045, because, as he said, costermongers did not fill in forms.)

One third of all the fish landed at Billingsgate Market was bought for resale, by costermongers, three or four thousand of them in the winter, slightly fewer in the summer; which, considering the size of the place, must have made it extremely crowded – and noisy: the auctions were conducted by shouting. Trading was confined to regular fishmongers until 7 a.m. when the costers could move in. Eels, a favourite fish with Londoners, were sold live, from the Dutch eelboats moored midstream.[6] Oysters were sold from boats moored at the wharf. There could be up to 1,500 men breakfasting in the course of the morning, at Rodway's Coffee House, on watery 'coffee' and two slices of bread and butter, for a penny,[7] or a favourite beverage – gin and hot milk. Mayhew reckoned that a coster with a fish round could clear 8s a week during the lean months of January and February, but by May he could add plants to his stock, and by July he was clearing 5s or 6s a day.

At Covent Garden Market in the strawberry season there could be as many as 4,000 costermongers, totally blocking the streets round about, waiting to buy from the 'great carts ... sternly stalking in elephantine dignity of progression ... [and] great vans, long, heavily-built, hoisted on high springs and with immense wheels' coming in from the market gardens round London.[8] 'Sometimes a huge column of baskets is seen in the air, and walks away in a marvellously steady manner'[9] – the market porters carrying fruit and vegetables in round baskets stacked on top of each other, perhaps twenty at a time, on their heads. Despite the throngs of people and vehicles, there was little shouting, except by the porters understandably demanding right of way.

Mayhew lists a bewildering assortment of objects offered by itinerant vendors: Britannia metal teapots and china ornaments, rat poison and fly papers, plants and flowers, penny slices of pineapple or a whole pineapple to take home to the suburbs, 'sparrow-grass' (asparagus), ropes of onions at 6d for three or four dozen, live poultry, dead game including grouse – 'they are legal eating on 12 August, but as there's hundreds of braces sold in London that day, and as they're shot in Scotland ... they're killed before it's legal. I've hawked venison but did no good, though I cried it at 4d the pound.' Mayhew estimated that 5,000 grouse, 12,000 partridges and 12,000 pheasants were sold in London streets annually.

A boy who sold birds and snakes in the streets must have made a fair living, in the summer, without expending anything but energy. He told Mayhew he walked 30 miles a day, twice a week:

Birds' nesties I get from 1d to 3d apiece for ... the 3d ones has 6 eggs ... snakes is 5s a pound ... adders is wanted dead ... I kills [them] with a stick, or, when I has shoes, I jumps on 'em ... hedgehogs is 1s each [they were useful for killing black beetles]. The frogs I sell to Frenchmen ... I've had an order for 6 dozen from the French hotel in Leicester Square. The snails I sell by the pailful at 2s 6d the pail ... the French people eats 'em. I reckon I sell about 20 nesties a week ... for 4 months in the year ... some people buys snails for birds [tame thrushes, which eat snails, were popular indoor pets], and some to strengthen a sick child's back, they rub the back all over with the snails.

He sold all kinds of wild birds, and green stuff for their feed, as well as small pieces of turf for caged larks, which would not roost on sticks but retained this pathetic instinct to nest in grass. According to Mayhew 'the whole extent of turf cut for London birds yearly, if placed side by side, would extend ... from London to Canterbury'. Possibly his grasp of figures has let him down slightly here. Small squares of turf for sale were piled up between the spikes of St Paul's churchyard railings, in Covent Garden Market. Much of it was cut in the suburbs of Shepherd's Bush and Notting Hill, 'in which may be seen a half illegible board inviting the attention of the class of speculative builders to "an eligible site" for villas'. A well-trained thrush could fetch as much as £2, twice the price of a 'caged and singing nightingale'. Sparrows were sold for 1d each, tied by the leg for children to play with.

Sellers of fast food proliferated. Many working men breakfasted on 'coffee' (coffee, which was dutiable, was mixed with chicory and baked carrots, which were not) and a slice of bread and butter, at a coffee stall on their way to work. The average earnings of the coffee-stallkeepers, who were often women, were about £1 a week. There were stalls selling eels and pea soup, sheep's trotters and fried fish, meat puddings and eel pies, cakes and crumpets and, in summer, 'the more novel and aristocratic luxury of street-ices'. Mayhew estimated the number of food and drink street sellers at over 6,000, but many were seasonal or temporary.

Milk was delivered by milk women – there were only a few milkmen. A milk woman carried her stock in pails hanging from a harness, on a wooden yoke made to fit her shoulders and displaying the name of her 'master', the dairyman. As well as her pails she carried many individual metal cans, from a quart size downwards, one for each customer on her round. At 6 in the morning, when

no maid servant was up yet ... [she] left her pails by the lamp post, took with her one of the smaller cans, and with her yoke still on her shoulders and the harness hooked together across her chest she tramped down the street, her iron-shod boots ringing loudly ... she carries with her a coil of stout string with a hook at the end. Taking this out of her pocket she hooked it on to one of the little cans and rapidly unwound it through the railings, let down the can into the area, jerked the hook off and drew up the string.

The cans had to be collected again at the end of the day and returned to the dairy before the girl could go home. For a day beginning at 5.30 a.m. and ending at 7 p.m., she was paid 9s a week, and her meals.[10]

The weekly budget of a journeyman carpenter with a wife and three children, whose weekly wages, including overtime, averaged £1 12s, was meticulously set out in the book already quoted, Tegetmeier's *Manual of Domestic Economy*. He spent 5s 6d on rent for two rooms, 2s 6d on clothing, 4s 3d on meat at 6d per lb (a 'large' quantity), 1s 9d on 1½ lb of butter (strongly criticised) and 2s 4d on beer ('unnecessarily large'); but he did allow 4d for 'schooling', 1s 6d for tools and 2d for periodicals. Tegetmeier laments, 'If the people of this country could be prevailed upon to use oatmeal for breakfast, as the Scotch and north country folks do, there would be no such items in a working man's expenditure as Butter, 1s 9d.' But surely there would be an item for sugar, or even treacle; only native-born Scots can face unsweetened porridge for breakfast.

There was a 'fair living' – about £2 a week – to be made in the sewers. 'Shore-men' or 'toshers' usually went down in gangs of three or four, to avoid getting lost, which was very easy, and to fend off the rats. They found coins, sometimes jewellery, but it was a dangerous calling. The bite of a sewer rat was poisonous. They had to operate unseen by the public. 'Whenever the shore-men come near a street grating they close their lanterns and watch their opportunity of gliding past unobserved.'

There was work for a thousand men at the twenty knackers' yards in London, rendering horse carcasses into dogs' and cats' meat. Three carcasses at a time were boiled in huge vats 9 feet in diameter, 4 feet deep, for six hours beginning at midnight. 'One woman – a black –

used to have as much as 16 pennyworth every day. This person used to get out on the roof of the house and throw it to the cats on the tiles ... between 10 and 11 in the morning the noise and cries of the hundreds of stray cats attracted to the spot was terrible to hear.'[11]

The silk-weaving industry of Spitalfields, which had flourished a century earlier, was just surviving. A weaver would buy in the warp (the strong threads that run lengthways through the piece, and bear its weight) and the weft (the decorative threads that show on the face of the textile), and 'work it up in his own poverty-stricken apartment, which often contains his loom, his bed, his kitchen, his family and his birds and flowers'.[12] When Victoria and Albert gave a fancy-dress ball, it was not just for fun, but to encourage the London silk weavers, because everyone had to wear English silk. And there was a steady demand for silk woven especially for the interior of coaches.

To buy a coach you would go to Long Acre, where more than a third of the houses were coach factories. The best coaches had their roof, upper front, back and sides all covered with one hide of leather, which was given many coats of paint and six or eight coats of varnish. As well as silk, embossed leather and fine Spanish cloth were used for linings. A skilled coach-maker could earn 3 to 5 guineas a week, high up in the pecking order of skilled tradesmen.[13]

London was the centre of piano manufacture. Every middle-class home had to have a piano, so the demand was huge. Broadwoods had a factory in Horseferry Road, using imported mahogany from Honduras and Spain. Three mahogany logs 15 feet long and 38 inches wide cost two or three thousand pounds. 'Those workmen who possess this skill are not likely to be supplanted by any automatic machinery.'[14]

Brewing was a major London industry. In 1781 Samuel Johnson had promoted the sale of his friend Henry Thrale's brewery in Southwark (on the south bank, where the New Globe Theatre now stands) by promising that it would earn its buyer 'riches beyond the dreams of avarice'. It was bought by Barclay and Perkins. By 1850 it was reckoned to be 'the largest of its kind in the world';[15] it certainly covered 10 acres. At 4 a.m. every morning up to 200 drays (the hgvs of the time), each pulled by two huge horses which had their own retinue of minders, left the brewery to deliver butts of Barclay's famous 'Entire' and other beers to public houses all over London. The brewery was one of the sights of London. When Flora Tristan, the French social reformer, visited it in 1839 she was impressed by its size, but 'what strikes one most about this brewery is how few workers are employed in such a vast enterprise'.[16] There were 30 or 40 clerks, whom she may have missed,[17] and she did not mention – perhaps was not shown – the malt being mixed in a huge vat by ten men standing in it waist-deep, naked except for loincloths.[18] There were thriving competitors whose names are famous in the history of beer, such as the Albion brewery in Whitechapel (Mann, Crossman and Paulin), the Anchor in the Mile End Road (Charrington), the Horse-shoe brewery in Tottenham Court Road (Meux) and many others. The Black Eagle in Brick Lane produced a famous porter (black stout) and by 1873 had taken over the title to be 'the largest company in the world'. The City of London brewery in Cannon Street had been brewing since the days of John Stow, who died in 1605. The Stag brewery in Westminster was even older; it began in about 1420. Fuller's (since 1845, Fuller, Smith & Turner) had been brewing at its Griffin brewery in Chiswick since the 1500s. Whitbread's brewery in Chiswell Street can still be visited.[19] Small family breweries were scattered throughout London.[20]

Sugar refiners or 'sugar bakers' were mostly within half a mile of Aldgate. If you ever considered how sugar cane ended up in your teacup, you would find that it was an exceedingly complicated process, confused by the fact that 'loaf sugar' in 1843 did not mean our sugar lumps.[21] It began with hogsheads of 'moist', mostly from the West Indies. This was purified by steam, filtered, 'de-coloured' by filtering through charcoal made from burned bones, boiled, the molasses removed, and the hot sugar poured by hand into cone-shaped moulds. (A burn from molten sugar is extremely painful, as many a jam-maker knows. This process was mostly done by Irishmen, so one can infer that despite its danger it was badly paid.) After twenty-four hours any liquid remaining was drained off and made into treacle, and it was washed again, still in its moulds. After some days the 'loaves' – the finest quality – and 'lumps' – the next quality – were knocked out of the moulds and dried in a hot oven, then wrapped in blue paper ready for sale. Blue was thought to deter flies. There is no record of the labour force needed, but it seems reasonable to suppose that it was considerable, involving a range of skills.

London transport was a major employer. At the mainline termini there were porters and cabbies, and men to look after and drive the horses needed to transport goods from the station to the London addressee, or across London to another station. In 1851 the 3,000 London buses employed 6,000 drivers and conductors, 3,000 'horse-keepers' and 2,000 odd-job men.[22] By 1861 a thousand more drivers and conductors worked on the buses, as well as horse-keepers and odd-job men. Eleven or twelve horses were needed by each bus. Although the norm was two horses for each bus, in bad weather three might be needed, and there had to be enough to provide for the animals to rest, even if the men were expected to go on working for a fourteen-hour day. Conductors could keep 4s a day out of the fares they collected. Drivers were paid 34s a week on most lines, for a working day beginning at 7.45 and sometimes ending past midnight.

The construction of the Underground Railway, begun in 1861, was a huge engineering undertaking, building a network of tunnels and cuttings with nothing but manpower and a little steampower. Two thousand men, 200 horses and 58 'engines' built the District Line between Sloane Square and Westminster, alone, with two massive kilns at Earl's Court making the necessary bricks.[23]

From 1859, Bazalgette's great intercepting sewers required a huge labour force. Two thousand men worked on the north high level sewer, and another 1,000 on the mid level one, let alone the third drain on the north side, and the drains on the south bank.[24] Another major single employer was Thomas Cubitt, who built Belgravia and Pimlico and many other developments. He was unusual in keeping his men on during slack times instead of following the normal practice of laying them off until work picked up. In 1828 he employed 1,000 men in Belgravia alone. With growing demand his premises off the Gray's Inn Road were not big enough, so he bought 50 acres along the Thames (where Dolphin Square stands now) for a storage area and workshops. He was an enlightened employer, providing cooking and clothes-drying facilities on site, and water closets, and a reading room and a lending library. 'The best workmen are anxious to be employed there.'[25] Skilled trades such as masons, bricklayers, plumbers, and carpenters earned 30s a week in 1849, 32s–33s in 1859. Labourers were paid an average of 18s a week, rising over ten years to 20s. Apart from Cubitt, there were countless small building firms constructing those endless working-class terraces in the suburbs, employing perhaps two or three men while trade was good and laying them off until capital came in for the next few houses.

The leather industry in Bermondsey, down-river opposite the Tower of London, was the fourth manufacture in England, after cotton, wool and iron. It reached its zenith in the nineteenth century.[26] It was a major employer of every level of skill, from the multilingual clerks who dealt with overseas suppliers and customers, and the skilled workers, to the labourers heaving the raw hides about. The skins from nearly all the sheep slaughtered in London were dealt with there. Exotic imports included buffalo and seal; goat skins came from Switzerland, Germany, the Baltic, North Africa, the East Indies, the Cape (South Africa) and Asia Minor (Turkey). One of the many and complicated processes – all stinking – depended on a shrub, sumach, which was brought in from Sicily, Italy and Hungary. Fine kid skins from Italy were treated with the yolks of 70,000 eggs imported from France annually. (How did they survive the Channel crossing unbroken?) At an early stage the hides were de-haired by soaking them in lime pits for four or five weeks, and the hair was sold to carpet-manufacturers and plasterers. Then the 'pure' – dogs' turds – which had been so laboriously collected by the very poor removed the lime. This was admittedly 'the most disagreeable in the whole range of the manufacture'.

An irrelevant but irresistible detail. 'Chamois' was the name of a process applied to the skins of sheep, goats and deer. Breeches made of it were worn by most of the cavalry of Europe, and very smart they looked too. But 'in the campaigns in Spain in the last war [Wellington's Peninsular campaign, 1808–14] it was discovered by the British commander that the health of the horse-soldiers was seriously affected in wet weather by the leather that they wore, which, fitting close to the skin and being long in drying, chilled the men and rendered them liable to rheumatism and other diseases. Woollen cloth was accordingly substituted, not only in England but in Austria and Prussia. Therefore this branch of the leather trade declined' – which was regretted by the workers of Bermondsey but not by our gallant horse-soldiers, nor, presumably, the Austrians or the Prussians.[27]

Associated trades and skills gathered in Bermondsey, such as fellmongers, the smelliest of all the trades, dealing in the untreated hides still bloody as they had left the animals; curriers, who produced fine coloured leather; parchment-makers, and leather merchants. Most of the tanneries were family concerns, varying from a one-man business to 'one of the largest and most complete private establishments in the world' with five tanneries spread over two and a half acres. In 1850 a smaller tannery specialising in thin, soft skins employed 85 men and a six-horsepower steam engine, processing 470,000 skins a year, using 150 tons of sumach, 18 tons of alum, 30 tons of salt, 60 loads of lime and those 70,000 imported eggs.

Yet another 'largest in the world': Christy's hat factory, conveniently close to the tanneries in Bermondsey which supplied wool to it. There were 200 jobs for women there, earning all of 8–10s a week, and they must have been only a small part of the labour force.[28] A surprising variety of furs was used – beaver, bear, marten, nutria from coypus, musquash, mink and rabbit. The ubiquitous silk-covered top hat began as a 'body' of coarse felted wool or stiffened cambric, which was covered with silk plush (a pile fabric like velvet, woven for Christy's in Lancashire). The tall black hats worn by 'persons much exposed to the weather' such as police constables and railway employees were covered with heavily varnished canvas.

Further down the river on the Isle of Dogs, Millwall Iron Works Company employed 4,000 men and boys in 1867, building the *Great Eastern* for Brunel, and armour-plated vessels for the Navy, as well as turning out armour plate for export to Russia. In all, 15,000 skilled men ('journey-men' who had served their time) and apprentices were employed in the shipyards there. The journey-men were paid 30s or more a week, the apprentices working out their seven-year term, 8–10s. The plutocrats were the fitters in engineering works, at 35–37s a week. Thomas Wright, using the *nom de plume* 'An Engineer', wrote a vivid account of life in those shipyards:

> There are traditions, customs and usages ... in a great measure constituting the inner and social life of workshops, a knowledge of which is as essential to the comfort of those whose lot is cast in them ... as technical proficiency is necessary to obtaining or retaining employment ... When an apprentice enters a shop, he will in all probability be taught to 'keep nix' before he is told the names of the tools ... Keeping nix is a really important job [which] consists in keeping a bright look-out for the approach of managers or foremen, so as to be able to give prompt and timely notice to men who may be skulking, or having a sly read or smoke, or who are engaged on 'corporation work' – that is, work of their own.[29]

Many men had come from the Clyde, and still spoke their Scottish dialect, which was incomprehensible to southerners. They retained their Scottish traditions too. There was a Scottish kirk on the island, which had a small following, and several pubs such as 'The Burns' and 'Highland Mary', which did rather better. Working hours were the usual twelve, from 6 a.m. with forty minutes for breakfast at 8, and an hour for dinner at 1. To be at work by 6 meant a struggle on

a cold, dark morning. Some men arranged to be called by a professional caller, who had a long stick with which he tapped on the
bedroom window. Or the local policeman might oblige; 'the policeman
on night duty often makes a considerable addition to his income by
calling workmen'. During occasional depressions the community held
on as best it could, with discreet help between neighbours.[30]

Thomas Cubitt was unusual, in the early 1840s, in letting his men
off on Saturdays two hours early, at 4 p.m. instead of after the normal
twelve-hour day, starting at 6. But by 1867

the Saturday half-holiday is already enjoyed by hundreds of thousands
of working men. On each of the three great occasions, Christmas,
Easter and Whitsuntide, the bulk of the working classes secure from
three days to a week's holiday, holding revel in parks and other places
during the day, and filling the theatres and other public places of
amusement at night ... In most establishments in which any considerable number of workmen are employed, the annual 'Shop Excursion' – the benefits of which are frequently extended to the wives and
families of the men – is now an established institution, and two or three
days a year may be safely put down for holidays arising out of special
occurrences. [Can this be the 'burying my grandmother' day off?]

But the most noticeable holiday, the most thoroughly self-made and
characteristic of them all, is that greatest of small holidays – Saint
Monday ... The general introduction of steam as a motive power, and
the rapid invention of machinery applicable to all kinds of manufacturing work, gave rise to a numerous body of highly skilled and
highly paid workmen [who] ... would at the end of the week put off
their working clothes with a sense of relief. [When Monday came these
could not be found, or needed washing ...] By running, the half-
dressed and breathless martyr to Monday morning circumstances would
just manage to rush through the workshop gates as they were closing
... Driven by their sufferings ... a large number of the operative
engineers adopted the practice of regularly losing the morning quarter
on Mondays, a proceeding which no other body of workmen would
have dared ... to have carried out! [The practice spread to other trades
...] Did a man feel more than usually inclined for a 'lie-in' after his
Sunday-evening ramble, he would remember him that it was Monday
morning, and indulge himself in 'a little more sleep and a little more
slumber.' Or did a 'Lushington' get a drop too much at the suburban
inn to which *his* Sunday-evening ramble had taken him, he would

remember, when he came to 'think of his head in the morning', that it
was Monday, and have another turn round in the sheets ... On Monday
everything is in favour of the great unwashed holding holiday. They
are refreshed by the rest of the previous day; the money received on
the Saturday is not all spent ... besides, the remains of the Sunday
dinner being on hand ... our wives and families are afforded an
opportunity of sharing the forms of holiday ...[31]

And what had begun as a slight tardiness, for which a quarter or a
half day's pay was docked, turned into a whole day off. So if you
reckon up, say, 49 Mondays, and three weeks at Christmas, Easter
and Whitsun, and odd days, it comes to more than eleven weeks a
year during which you could be absent from your work without
risking the sack. But – it was unpaid.

Trade unions were gradually emerging from the dark ages when any
'combination' of workers to enforce a pay claim might be treated as
a criminal conspiracy. According to Mayhew writing in 1849, there
were 21,000 'operative tailors' of whom 3,000 belonged to a union
and so were 'honourable', the rest, mainly in the slop-making workrooms, were 'dishonourable' and would work for whatever they could
get.[32] In 1850 2,000 workers in the building and allied trades belonged
to a union which enforced wage agreements – 'the society men' – but
18,000 – 'the dishonourable men' – still took whatever work they
could find, at whatever rate was offered.[33] The Amalgamated Society
of Engineers, Machinists, Millwrights, Smiths and Patternmakers was
formed in 1851. In its first year its membership was nearly 12,000,
and by 1865 it had grown to over 30,000, with 295 branches, mostly
in England and Wales, with a scattering in France, Malta, America,
Australia, Canada and New Zealand. Members had to be between
20 and 40, and to have worked in their trade for five years. They
paid an age-related entrance fee of between 15s and £3 10s, and 1s a
week fixed contribution. One of them was Thomas Wright, whose
description of 'keeping nix' is quoted above. Here he is, on 'A
Prosperous Trade-Union':

> The object of this society is to raise from time to time, by contributions
> among the members thereof, funds for mutual support in case of sickness,
> accident, superannuation, emigration, for the burial of members and

their wives, and also for members out of work ... Each candidate for admission must be proposed, seconded and recommended by two members of the branch which he wishes to join: the proposer and seconder must be prepared to state (and if necessary prove by evidence) that [the candidate] is possessed of good abilities as a workman, is of steady habits, and good moral character; and everyone who is elected must be a member twelve months before he is entitled to the benefits of the society.

Unemployment benefit was 10s a week for 14 weeks, thereafter 7s for 30 weeks and 6s a week 'so long as he remains out of employment' ('out of collar' was the colloquial term for it), with a maximum in any year of £19 18s. Sickness benefit was 10s a week for 26 weeks, thereafter 5s a week until recovery. A member disabled by an accident, or supervening blindness, epilepsy etc. could draw £100. A 'retiring allowance' of 7s was payable for life to members over 50, with a membership record of eighteen years, 'if they chose to apply for it'. The retiring workman would not, probably, burden the Society's funds for long. The death benefit for a member's funeral was a handsome £12, and for a member's wife's funeral £5, with the remaining £7 payable on the member's own death. 'Any particular or unusual case of distress' could apply to a benevolent fund; grants varied between £2 and £8. If an unemployed member wanted to try his luck elsewhere he was given a 'travelling card' which enabled him to draw his allowance from any other branch, where the secretary would help him to find work. No wonder that this union was copied by other groups of skilled workers.

In addition to a trade union, a skilled workman might decide to join a Friendly Society, which provided much the same benefits. Thomas Wright was scathing about some of them, describing a (presumably hypothetical) Ancient Order of Goodfellows wasting its funds on drink, and organising its members into degrading 'march[es] through the streets bedizened with gaudy scarves and ribbons, in a style that would be considered *outré* in an African chief'. But 'so far as their primary and ostensible functions are concerned [they are] among the best institutions to which a working man can belong'.[34]

No chapter on the working class would be complete without a reference to Samuel Smiles's book *Self-Help*, published in 1859.[35] Perhaps he was inspiring at the time, and certainly his advice was, and is, excellent; but a little turgid? Some quotes:

There is usually no want of desire on the part of most persons to arrive at the results of self-culture, but there is a great aversion to pay the inevitable price for it, of hard work.

One of the most valuable, and one of the most infectious, examples which can be set before the young is that of cheerful working.

The battle of life is, in most cases, fought uphill.

In other words, pull yourself up by your own bootstraps. The most interesting thing about his book is what he *did not* say. There is only one mention of God, and that was in a quotation from someone else. Self-reliance, not religion, was his gospel. His other book, *Workmen's Earnings, Strikes and Savings*, published in 1861, deplored resorting to strikes for more pay. The building workers had gone on strike in 1859–60, ostensibly for a reduction of the working day from ten to nine hours, but in fact for more pay. 'Many public works stood still. The masters sustained great losses. The men stood out as long as they could' – but in the end they went back to work on the same terms they had rejected.

Another much-quoted book was Thomas Malthus's *Essay on the Principle of Population*, published in 1798. He saw clearly that the problem for the working class was the over-supply of labour by their persistent breeding. 'The working classes have their fate in their own hands': if they stopped procreating it would only take twelve years to achieve higher wages by creating a labour shortage. About as easy to follow as anything in Smiles.

CHAPTER 9

The Middle Class

*Who were they? · clerks · the Post Office · the Bank of England ·
private banks · cashing a cheque · the professions · moving out of central
London · how to be a lady · gentlemen's clubs · marriage · good causes
· the Income Tax · Jane Carlyle's tax appeal*

Since it was so easy to define the upper layer of the lower class, it should be fairly easy to find the interface between it and the lowest layer of the middle class. In 1867 Dudley Baxter took a long, hard look at the figures of the Census Tables of 1861, and produced a class analysis of the population of England and Wales:

	income per annum (£s)	number
UPPER CLASS	over 5,000	7,500
	1,000–5,000	42,000
MIDDLE CLASS	300–1,000	150,000
	100–300	850,500
	under 100	1,003,000
WORKING-CLASS:	all under £100	
skilled labour		1,123,000
less skilled labour		3,891,000
agricultural and less skilled labour		2,843,000[1]

If income were to be the sole criterion of class, the boundaries between working class and middle class merged, below £100. But there were other differences which distinguished a low-paid middle-class man from a working man, and neither of them would have had any difficulty in categorising themselves.

Clerks, for example, were middle-class, because they used their brains and not their hands. There was an explosion in the number of white-collar workers – as we would describe them – although they probably saw themselves as top-hat-and-black-coated workers. There were over 20,000 'commercial clerks' in the 1841 census. Charles Booth estimated the number of 'commercial clerks, accountants and bankers' at 44,000 in 1851, 67,000 in 1861, and 119,000 in 1871.[2] Both government service and the private sector had grown immensely more complicated in the last 100 years, and they needed a corresponding increase in staff. As any civil servant can tell you, a job comfortably done by one man will need two to do it if it increases by the slightest amount, and two need a third to supervise them, and those three each need another to fetch and carry, which necessitates a pool of assistants ... The Post Office had functioned happily with 26 clerks in 1839. By 1862 there were 60 of them; by 1866 there was a staff of more than 200.[3] In 1850 there were 700–800 clerks in the Bank of England, 60 in the Paymaster General's department, and 900 assorted Government servants in Somerset House. The London and North Western Railway alone employed 775 clerks. Barclay's huge brewery in Borough required 30 or 40 clerks.

As postal communications improved, more clerks were needed everywhere. Every letter had to be painstakingly written, copied, filed, and posted, by hand.[4] Every entry in a ledger had to be written legibly by hand. It would be beyond the abilities of the present computer age. These clerks were considered to be in a class above the workmen in the last chapter, even though their intelligence and training may have fallen far short of those of a skilled shipbuilder. One difference was the way they dressed. Another was their working hours. The little girl who lived in Bethnal Green and went out to work at the age of ten remembered her father as 'a well-educated man, [who] was employed in a government situation working from 10 a.m. to 4 ... my father's position compelled him to keep up an appearance which an ordinary workman, earning the same wages, would not have had to do. He always went to business in nice black clothes and a silk hat', and when he came home he had time and energy for a bit of DIY, or to do odd jobs for his neighbours which supplemented his income.[5] The 'ordinary workman earning the same wages' had worked exactly twice the number of hours.

In 1839 – and there was no significant change in later years – an assistant secretary in the Post Office had a salary of £700–£800, but the clerical staff under him were paid on a scale starting with a lowly junior clerk 2nd class, who might have to manage on £90[6] – not very much on which to sustain his top hat and respectability.[7] Anthony Trollope became a clerk in the Post Office, on £90, which he found impossible to live on without going into debt. He was supposed to be at the office in St Martin's le Grand at 10 every morning, which he found equally impossible. In 1841, after seven miserable years during which he was constantly threatened with dismissal for being late, he was earning £140. The clerks who dealt with the foreign mails were paid slightly more, and they had to live in the building. Trollope recalled how the foreign mail clerks had 'a comfortable sitting-room upstairs ... Hither one or two of us would adjourn after lunch, and play écarté for an hour or two. I do not know whether such ways are possible now in our public offices.'[8] (He was writing in 1876.)

The Governor of the Bank of England was paid £400 a year, not, one would think, a vast amount for the responsibility he carried, especially compared with the Post Office.[9] Each of the Directors got £300. There were 700–800 clerks, who were 'elected' annually, not appointed for a specific period, but since there was no compulsory retirement age they might still be there sixty years later. The entrance examination was simple: if a man could add a few figures, and count a bag of silver coin, and had a good character, he was in. Re-election, every year, needed more care. Even if a clerk behaved soberly at work he could be dismissed for being 'a smoking, singing, public-house man' outside working hours. Until 1844, clerks who were under 21 were paid on a scale designed to reach £50 at 21 by £10 increments, so a 17-year-old – the minimum age – must have started at £10, needing family support as much as if he were apprenticed to a trade. At this level he was surely one of the many who lunched off sandwiches made at home, until he could afford to patronise one of the countless City eating-houses 'crammed almost to suffocation', and put back meat and vegetables, cheese and even a pudding. How did he stay awake after that?[10] Further increments brought him up to a maximum of £250, on which a middle-class lifestyle was possible, with some prospect of promotion to a Principal, on £300. In 1844 the scale was revised so that at 21 a clerk would earn £100.

A bank clerk's life was not unduly onerous. Working hours were from 9 to 3.30, or until 5 with one and a half hours off for dinner. In 1834 the eighteen 'holy-days' previously enjoyed by clerks had been cut to the statutory Good Friday and Christmas, with 1 May and 1 November off, when the Bank was closed for the annual election of clerks, and balancing the ledgers. This deprivation left clerks so stressed that they quarrelled and fought and swore on the least provocation, such as who should sit on a particular stool or use a particular ink-stand. In 1845 the perturbed Directors decided to give the clerks an annual leave allowance of six to eighteen days, depending on length of service, and allowed some of them to come to work as late as 9.30 or 10. Banking business was to cease at 4.

Gradually the conduct of the Bank's business, and of its clerks, came under stricter control. In 1846 they were forbidden to smoke cigars in the Bank. In 1850 new rules forbade them to receive 'any gratuities from customers of the Bank or from the Public', which had formed a nicely profitable sideline. From 1852 a daunting entrance examination required a hopeful candidate to 'write from dictation; enter and add a column of figures, and work out a simple sum in division and interest'. Three years later clerks were warned not to wear moustaches. 'If this hint be not attended to, measures will be resorted to which may prove of a painful nature.' To soothe ruffled feelings the Directors funded a clerks' library. The clerks even had the temerity to ask the Bank to pay the new-fangled income tax for them. This was not granted, but annual 'gratuities' were paid in most of the years 1855–65, and an improved salary scale was introduced, paid monthly instead of quarterly.

A new policy of lenience seems to have wafted over the Directors, as long as they were spared the sight of a moustachioed, cigar-smoking clerk. One young man was foolish enough to be spotted 'witnessing the Boat Race from a steamer' when he should have been at work. He was reprimanded but not sacked. On the other hand a man who took 190 days' 'sick leave' in two years, 'to attend most of the principal races', was called upon to resign. One young clerk, William Burgess, diverged spectacularly from the general standard of honesty in 1844 by manipulating a customer's account to the tune of £8,000 in gold – a vast sum in those days. He and his accomplice escaped to Boston on the steamship *Britannia*, but they were traced and arrested. The accomplice hanged himself in prison, Burgess was transported for life.

There were many private banks, all in or near Lombard Street in the City, and all employing clerks. The collapse of one, Overend, Gurney and Company, in 1866 caused a panic in the City known as Black Friday. But in general the City of London was respected worldwide for its probity and efficiency. In 1851 Herr Fischer, visiting from the Continent, went to a City bank to cash a cheque. He arrived shortly before the official opening hour at 9, so he was asked to wait. At 8.55 'an official arrived behind the counter'. Herr Fischer showed him the cheque but there was no reply. The official silently emptied some bags of gold coins into a drawer, and got out his 'little cash shovel that is used for coins in the banks. And then he just waited. At the stroke of 9 he asked me if I wanted gold or bank notes' – and Herr Fischer left the bank very impressed.[11]

A clergyman of course had no need to prove that he was a gentleman, 'often by birth and fortune, almost invariably by education. The average stipend [a parson's salary] is £140 a year. An ordinary living [the post held by the parson] is £200 to £300 a year. The least are £80.'[12] Army officers were indubitably gentlemen, but they were not likely to be middle-class, since they tended to be scions of the aristocracy. Barristers were gentlemen, even when they were hard-up. It was all too easy to starve at the Bar, but at least it could lead to an obscure post in the interstices of the Civil Service which provided a genteel livelihood. Teaching was progressing from a little-respected, ill-educated drudgery to a well-trained profession (see the chapter on Education). One boy who had got his education through the workhouse system did so well that he emerged from a teacher training college as a fully fledged teacher, and therefore a member of the middle class, although he would have been surprised to hear it.[13] Karl Marx would surely have qualified as a member of the middle class, even when he was so broke that when he tried to pawn his wife's family silver he was turned away by the pawnbroker, who suspected him of having stolen it, he looked so disreputable. With the help of his patient friend Friedrich Engels, and miscellaneous legacies – not, at any time, by the normal expedient of working for a living – he made good eventually, in north London, and sent his daughters to a Young Ladies' Seminary.[14]

Most of the middle class moved out of central London. There were clear demarcations between the suburbs. The rich withdrew to Sydenham, Barnes and Richmond. The upper middle class went not quite so far out, to Hampstead. Penge and Ealing, with no direct railway, were middle-class. Camberwell, Hammersmith, Leyton and Balham, all accessible by train, were for the lower middle class. 'City men' gravitated to Bayswater, Brixton and Clapham, well served by omnibuses.[15] A clerk might choose a suburb such as Hackney, within walking distance of the City. 'Persons of moderate income [may] prefer residing within 2 or 3 miles of the Bank, within a 6d ride in fact. If the distance is not more than 3 miles, a walk one way ... and if the occupation be sedentary, such as a clerk's, the walk both ways, when the weather is dry, is not more than sufficient exercise for one in health'.[16] The Victorians walked astounding distances.

Ladies who were not exactly married, but enjoyed the protection of only one gentleman, mostly, favoured St John's Wood, where many of the *cottages ornées* had a convenient covered way from the pavement to the front door, so that an inquisitive onlooker hardly had time to identify the top-hatted figure emerging from the cab before he disappeared.[17] Writers and artists in search of peace chose Chelsea, where Thomas Carlyle optimistically expected total silence to allow his genius to operate. He probably never realised the lengths to which his wife Jane was driven, to quieten all the cocks and hens and dogs of his neighbours – she even gave English lessons to the son of the owner of a particularly obstreperous dog, as a bribe to keep it quiet.[18] The resident population of the City declined from 129,000 in 1851 to 76,000 twenty years later.[19]

❋

For a woman hoping to be taken for a member of this fortunate class, there were many sources of good advice. Indeed, so many that I compiled an amalgam of them.[20]

> Firstly we must consider the possibility that you may occasionally be apt to omit an h. This tendency must be eradicated before even thinking of aspiring to be taken to be a lady. There are several books of advice on the matter, which I will leave to your ingenuity to identify. Nothing would so ruin your prospects as a missing aspirate.
>
> This difficulty having been overcome, I proceed to more general matters. Firstly of course your background cannot contain any trace of trade. How this is to be managed is hard to see, if the leisure that will stamp you as a lady is funded by your father's shop, but such is the requirement. Then, you must be sufficiently well-read to be able to share in the conversation when necessary, gently introducing subjects of which you have read in the latest informative magazine, and on which the stupidest gentleman can shine. But you must at all costs avoid any hint of being intelligent. If a dubious joke is made in your hearing you have a choice. Either you may show your disapproval, by a frigid glare – but this shows that you have understood the double-entendre; or you may take the easier course and ignore it, so demonstrating your pure innocence.

Then, you must never be seen in an inelegant posture. Blowing out a candle is decidedly inelegant. If there is no handy extinguisher, let someone else distend their cheeks. When smiling or laughing, bear in mind that dental deficiencies are more evident than you think. A careful examination in a mirror in a good light should determine the width of your smile. As to laughing, it is usually inadvisable. Music gives opportunity for frequent elegancies, especially playing the harp if your arms are well-rounded and marmoreal, but pause a moment before embarking on lessons. Your audience, while dwelling on the grace of your figure, may expect you to please their ears as well as their eyes, and this is not easy if you have no musical gift. Most wind instruments are decidedly inelegant, they should be left to the gentlemen. Playing the violin-cello is of course out of the question, while the violin, although not so openly obscene, necessitates an awkward position of the head and neck which is not recommended. The piano-forte is an elegant woman's best friend. There is room on a properly designed piano stool for two, in delightful proximity, when attempting pieces for four hands. Remember that if your companion stands up you may be deposited on the floor unless you stand at the same time. Pages need turning, by someone standing close behind you. This will be present to your mind when adjusting the neckline of your dress before a musical evening. Do not spare the application of perfume.

Never be in the company of an unmarried man alone, unless considerations such as the imminence of an acceptable proposal of marriage outweigh the normal rules. If about to faint with emotion, make sure there is a convenient sopha on which to subside. Not all gentlemen can be relied upon to catch a falling female in time.

At assemblies and dinner parties, do not eat more than a bird-like morsel. Never, I need hardly say, drink more than to touch the glass to your lips when called upon to partake in a toast. Alcohol combined with tight stays unfailingly results in unbecoming floridity. A well-trained lady's maid will see that there is a cheering glass awaiting your return, along with a cold fowl.

When at the opera, assume an expression of transported delight, and ignore any tendency of the gentlemen in your party to spend their time surveying the other ladies in the house through their opera glasses.

Mounting into, and descending from, any form of transport is an art in itself. Omnibuses pose constant problems, but, surely, few real ladies will patronise them. Carriages can be as bad, since the effort needed to get in and out of them, no matter how stalwart the footman's arm or how solid the folding steps, can still involve an unbecoming expenditure of energy, accompanied in the worst cases by an exhalation of breath which in one's enemy would be called puffing and blowing. Practise in the privacy of your room. Many emporia will bring out for you the items you require, for inspection, when you have specified their general nature. Thus it will not be necessary to leave the carriage.

When other peoples' children are presented to you, express delight and admiration, no matter how unprepossessing the infants. Resist any temptation to call attention to their running noses, wet pantaloons, or digital nasal explorations. One can only hope that all these matters will be taken care of by some third party such as the nursemaid. Mothers are often blind to any imperfection in their offspring. Meanwhile try your utmost to avoid physical contact with them, combining an adroit management of your skirts with uninterrupted paeans of praise. Much the same applies to other peoples' pets, with obvious amendments.

If invited to view your host's garden, and walking in it is unavoidable despite the dampness underfoot, the advisable method is to admire anything in flower, extravagantly, not omitting a tribute to your host's sagacity in employing such a knowledgeable gardener. References to Mr Paxton rarely come amiss. If bitten by the insects which abound in gardens, try to ignore the irritation. Do not swipe at wasps, it looks inelegant and only enrages them the more. If you step in something undesirable, wait until you have a chance to wipe your shoe, discreetly. This is the only advantage of wet weather in a garden, you should be able to find some wet grass without ruining the hem of your garment. Try not to carry the offending matter into your host's house, no matter how deeply you feel that the original blame lies with him for putting you in this unfortunate predicament. Never ask for a cutting or root of anything in your host's garden. The worst crime you can commit is to take a slip of some precious plant without – you think – his knowledge. An enthusiastic gardener never fails to notice. There is nothing you can do to acquire what you want, save to express pointed praise of this particular specimen and refer to the ease of propagating it. Assume grateful surprise if called for.

A lady never outstays her welcome. For short calls this is easy to observe, but for the prolonged visit care must be given to divining your host's wishes. If he shows a tendency to prefer his own company, at certain times of the day, treat this as an amiable idiosyncracy. But if he positively avoids you when he sees you approaching, it may well be that you should begin to consider leaving in the near future.

With all these hints as to advisable demeanour for every day, the reader may think that nothing remains to suggest for the delicate business of husband-hunting. Alas, in these days when any gentleman belongs to a club where he can find *almost* every advantage of matrimony, potential husbands are like shy animals, vanishing when most hotly pursued. Do not be tempted to offer, in your own person, those advantages of matrimony which are not available in his club. He is all too likely to obtain these, too, elsewhere than at the domestic hearth. Subtlety is needed, and evasion on your part, never fleeing so swiftly, of course, as to be beyond the reach of the most ponderously slow suitor if he is potentially acceptable. As to your own appearance, I suggest, as with the management of carriage steps and the width of your smile, some consideration in the privacy of your own room. Which is your most advantageous profile? Or is an umbrageous candlelight advisable? An expression of admiring pleasure should be possible to sustain for most of the evening without becoming a rictus. Practise daily, for increasing periods. A conviction that your intended is the most desirable gentleman in every possible way already resides in his breast. Show him, shyly but unmistakably, that you share this conviction.

I have touched on the matter of dress above, but would add one or two more hints. No matter how desirable a tiny waist, it must be achieved without the noise of creaking stays. If you rely on those slight aids to beauty widely available nowadays, make sure, by prior experiment, that they are not likely to fail you. I have known several courtships brought to untimely halts by eye-black running, rouge rubbing off on to pale waistcoats, false hair becoming detached, bust improvers deflating, and teeth falling out at quite the wrong moment. In that context may I earnestly advise you *never* to attempt a sticky pudding.

I have said enough to show that the pursuit of a husband is a weighty matter. When discouraged – and what hunter does not suffer occasional setbacks? – remember the alternative: at best, a position in a relative's establishment, filling the offices of governess and confidante, sometimes with honour but never with salary. One investigation I must advise, however, before any notable expenditure of time and effort takes place: what is his financial position? You may not be able to ascertain this in person, but bend every effort to persuade a male member of your family, or a friend, to help you. If – as I would expect, since my advice would be wasted on the pursuit of a poor man – the gentleman in question appears to have money, in what form? Is it in the funds, or dependent on some relative's whim? If he has landed property, is it entailed? Has he any embarrassing debts? Has he expectations? When, and if, the happy day comes when he asks your parent for your hand in marriage, that parent should satisfy himself that your suitor has the means to keep you in the condition to which you aspire. But not all relationships will produce this happy outcome. You should take energetic measures to ensure that you do not waste your charms on an unworthy object. As we all find, time marches on, and destroys that beauty which may be your most potent weapon. Fine whiskers are delightful, but a good income is infinitely more attractive.

It was no wonder that every woman's magazine lamented gentlemen's clubs. They were comfortable male hideouts, affording all the amenities of a well-organised home without any responsibility other than the annual subscription. The normal entrance fee for most clubs was 20 guineas, the annual subscription perhaps 10 guineas. They were much used by professional men and impecunious younger sons of the aristocracy. 'The dinners are good and cheap, compared to the extortionate prices of the London hotels ... five shillings is charged for a dinner which in a hotel would be charged at least four times that sum.'[21] If you felt like talking, you could find kindred spirits there; if not, you could read in the usually excellent library without having to listen to the domestic tittle-tattle that might assail you at home. You could even live there. In the Reform Club, founded for Radicals in 1836 and occupying its magnificent new clubhouse since 1841, 'every bedroom has a recess fitted with a white marble basin into which, through two taps, hot and cold water can be poured at any time' – no need to worry about the idiosyncracies of domestic water-heating systems – and there were 'highly trained valets always in readiness to dress or shave one'.[22] The kitchens were, of course, designed and run by Alexis Soyer, who pioneered the use of gas for cooking. There was even a captive gas flame in a little alcove by the main doors, at which gentlemen could light their cigars. (The club, and the cigar-lighter, are still there.)

Next to the Reform Club, in Pall Mall, is the Travellers', founded in 1819 and since 1832 occupying a clubhouse designed, like the Reform, by Barry. Further along Pall Mall comes the Athenaeum, founded in 1824, where bishops and scholars hobnobbed. Its clubhouse was designed by Decimus Burton. The beautiful frieze above the main windows, periodically repainted in blue and white, is a reconstruction of the frieze on the Parthenon (whence Lord Elgin removed parts, which have ended in the British Museum as the Elgin Marbles. Easier to see the whole thing in reproduction, from the top of a bus.)[23] The Carlton Club in Carlton House Terrace (it was bombed in 1940 and moved to St James's) was for Conservatives or Tories, just as the Reform was for the more liberally minded. (The National Liberal Club, where a large statue of Gladstone broods over the cash desk in the dining room, was not built until 1871.)

The Garrick, named after the famous actor David Garrick, was founded in 1831 for actors, writers, painters and other artists. 'A lover of the English drama may spend two hours very profitably in viewing the large collection of theatrical portraits' if he had the personal introduction of a member.[24] Boodle's, in St James's Street, had been founded in 1762 and survives still. You can identify it by the beautiful fan window on the first floor. White's, also in St James's Street, is the oldest of them all, tracing its history to 1693. It was at one time notorious for gambling, but by the nineteenth century was principally a social club for the rich, including the Prince of Wales.[25]

A few of the eighteenth-century coffee houses survived in the City. Merchants trading to the East Indies, China and Australia congregated in the Jerusalem Coffee House in Cornhill. The Jamaica Coffee House nearby could be relied on for the latest information on the West Indies. The merchants, underwriters and insurance brokers who comprised Lloyd's were functioning in a room above the Royal Exchange, where in 1859 the Lutine bell was installed which still signals good news, with two strokes, or bad news with one. Next in importance to Lloyd's was the North and South America Coffee House round the corner in Threadneedle Street.[26]

So, one way or another, there were plenty of places where a middle-class young man could feel at home, without assuming the bonds of matrimony. Yet, by the time his thirtieth birthday approached,[27] and his friends were enjoying delightful suburban villas with wives, children and gardens, the club began to be uncongenial. Worse: members only fifteen years older had developed a habit of dying.[28] So steps must be taken towards a happy married life, before too long. If he frequented London society during the Season, there should be no shortage of candidates. For those who did not move in those circles, there were many ways of meeting respectable eligible brides. The congregation in the church which he attended might include a desirable young female to whom introduction could be achieved through the officiating parson. The Victorian passion for amateur choral singing should yield some sopranos. The wide ramifications of the Victorian family surely contained among his cousins and second cousins and their friends a girl whom his mother could inspect, and approve for his consideration. Ladies spent an inordinate time doing Good Works. For a short period he might take up some such charitable endeavour, since he had plenty of time and energy left after his six-hour working day. He might even find some voluntary work that rewarded him, without necessarily ending in matrimony.

There was a dizzying proliferation of good causes. Parliament set up Royal Commissions and Select Committees to examine every unsatisfactory aspect of Victorian life. Sometimes legislation resulted, always witnesses were called and a thick report was produced, bound in blue – hence, the 'Blue Books'. In case these were not enough to address every social problem, well-meaning men and women formed societies and sat on committees, often duplicating their efforts but all filled with goodwill. There were societies to improve the housing of the 'industrious classes' and societies to improve their morals and give them baths. There were societies urging men to give up drink and Take the Pledge, and others urging women to give up prostitution and take up sewing. There were benevolent societies looking after governesses and general domestic servants and young girls who only needed a training in laundry work to keep them on the straight and narrow path of virtue.

There were countless educational schemes, such as the Ladies' Sanitary Association which organised miscellaneous medicos to tell the working class how important, for example, fresh air is – when they could get it. The Female Aid Society helped unemployed female servants, and prostitutes 'weary of sin'. The Workhouse Visiting Society energetically visited workhouses. The Society for the Suppression of Mendicity was not popular with mendicants, because instead of yielding to the Victorian version of 'can you spare any small change?' in cash, its members gave out tickets, to be exchanged by 'deserving' cases, for welfare payments. The Society for the Suppression of Vice has not yet succeeded in its object, but perhaps the Society for the Rescue of Boys Not Yet Convicted of Any Criminal Offence caught them in time.

All these bodies needed people – mostly gentlemen but with some ladies – to sit on their committees and run, in an honorary capacity, their offices. Occasionally a middle-class man actually involved himself with the poor, in person, for instance by giving free medical advice or teaching in a Ragged School. Charles Pugh, a clerk in the Chancery Court, 'went to see the poor boys at the dormitory for ragged boys' in 1861, and must have been persuaded to take an active part, since his diary shows him two years later teaching a small class there. He hated doing it, but gradually 'their smiling faces ... and the stories they have to tell me, attach me to them' – a two-way traffic.[29] 'Almost every want or ill that can distress human nature has some palatial institution for the mitigation of it.'[30] In 1862 there were 530 of them, by far the most prosperous being the fourteen Foreign Mission Societies, with an income of £460,000. The next were 92 medical charities, with a joint income of £267,000.[31]

There were civic duties which a middle-class man was expected to perform, such as membership of his local Parochial Church Council or 'Vestry' – so called because that was where they met – to see to the poor rates, and the multiple functions not yet taken over by a general London authority. Even Karl Marx, that scourge of the middle class, found himself elected to the municipal sinecure of 'Constable of the Vestry of St Pancras'.[32] At least he was not enrolled as a Special Constable, as many men of the middle class were when the Chartist agitators threatened London and hundreds of Special Constables were enlisted to support the Army if needed.

And, of course, there was the Income Tax. In 1798 this had been a good way of financing the war against the French, and was duly abolished in 1816 when that emergency was over. Peel reinstated it in 1842 at the rate of 7d in the pound on incomes over £150,[33] and Gladstone doubled it in 1853, to pay for the Crimean War. It has been with us ever since, although in theory it is only a temporary measure which has to be agreed by Parliament every year, after it has considered the Budget. As you complete your Return of Income you may wonder why it has to be so complicated. The reason is a presumption that a taxpayer would deeply dislike his neighbours knowing how much money he had. He had a right to appeal against an assessment, to General Commissioners, unpaid male members of the middle class whose principal qualification was that they knew local conditions, and local men. If the assessment were to show the whole of a taxpayer's income, he would resent those local worthies –

neighbours, perhaps, or members of the same club – getting to know his total wealth. To avoid this, the ingenious machinery of Schedules was adopted, keeping each category of income separate, so that appeals to General Commissioners dealt only with an assessment under one particular schedule and there was no danger of an appeal Commissioner meeting a friend and saying 'I had no idea old George was worth so much.'

This was vividly illustrated when Jane Carlyle, a redoubtable Scottish lady, appeared before the Kensington General Commissioners in 1855, to appeal against an assessment on her husband Thomas's literary income. She described the proceedings in one of her inimitable letters. The startled Commissioners first told her she had no right of audience, but she seems to have dismissed that out of hand. Then she produced her husband's account with his publisher, which showed that he had not published anything for several years. The Commissioners, feeling somewhat browbeaten, rallied with a question as to what he had been living on, in that case. 'I am not here', countered Jane magnificently, 'to explain what Mr Carlyle has to live on, only to declare his income from literature for the last three years.' She added somewhat grudgingly that she believed he had landed income, ' "of which" – said I haughtily, for my spirit was up – "I have fortunately no account to render in this kingdom and to this board".'[34] (If he did have 'landed income', it would be assessed under a different schedule, and appeals against that assessment would be heard by different commissioners.) While this is not the way I would advise any taxpayer to conduct an appeal against assessment, she did succeed in making the unnerved Commissioners tell their clerk to 'take off £100', which seems to have meant total victory. As an ex-Revenue lawyer I find the matter not wholly clear, but as a feminist I cheer from the sidelines.

CHAPTER 10

The Upper Class and Royalty

ॐ

Florence Nightingale · Lady Frederick Cavendish · the Army · the 'purchase system' · the Guards · the Season · a royal ball · Albert's unpopularity · his relations with Victoria · money · Victoria · effect of Albert's death

Why have women passion, intellect, moral activity ... and a place in society where none of the three can be exercised? ... women often long to enter some man's profession, where they would find direction, competition (or rather the opportunity of measuring the intellect with others) and, above all, time ... [but the family system] dooms some minds to incurable infancy, others to silent misery ... marriage is the only chance (and it is but a chance) offered to women to escape this death; and how eagerly and how ignorantly it is embraced! ... a man gains everything by marriage: he gains a 'helpmate' but a woman does not ... the woman who has sold herself for an establishment, in what is she superior to those we may not name? ... The ideal life is passed in noble schemes, of good consecutively followed up. The actual life is passed in sympathy given and received for a dinner, a party, a piece of furniture, a house built or a garden laid out well, in devotion to your guests ... in schemes of schooling for the poor which you follow up perhaps in an idle half hour, between luncheon and driving out in the carriage − broth and dripping are included in the plan − and the rest of your time goes in ordering the dinner, hunting for a governess for the children, and sending pheasants and apples to your poorer relations ...[1]

This was Florence Nightingale, anguished by the trammels of her upper-class existence, entangled in the claims of her unreasonable mother and her hysterical sister. It was very slightly better, perhaps, to be a middle-class woman, who at least could take an active part in the housework from time to time, and possibly even look after her own children. Fortunately for Miss Nightingale's sanity, she was able to escape, very soon after writing *Cassandra*, and begin her career.

And yet some women found it possible to lead busy social lives and still engage in rewarding good works. They did not have Florence Nightingale's appalling family. A 'very busy day' in 1867, in the London life of Lady Frederick Cavendish:

> At 10½ I paid a flying visit to the workhouse. Soon after 11 went ...
> shopping for the [Cholera Orphans'] Convalescent Home ... Luncheon,
> and at 2½ I drove off to Westbourne Terrace to call on Mrs Martineau
> ... looked in at St Paul's, Knightsbridge, but the service was just ending;
> visited [an aunt] who was out, and Lady Albemarle ... [went] to
> Paddington to meet [a relation] but, being a few minutes late, missed
> her. And finally we dined at Lady Estcourt's ...[2]

Some women managed to circumvent the system altogether. Lady Florence Paget was engaged to marry Henry Chaplin. They went to do a little pre-marital shopping, in Marshall and Snelgrove, the new department store in Oxford Street, opened in 1848. They separated while she went into the lingerie department to look at trousseau undies, he – of course – waiting outside. But he waited in vain. She had gone straight through the shop, out by the door to Henrietta Street, into a cab where the Marquis of Hastings was waiting, and she married the Marquis that very morning.[3] Another girl, 'grand-daughter to an Earl, and well known in society, has gone astray and become a mother ... they say that when she was asked who was the father of her illegitimate child she replied "How should *I* know?" '[4]

For men it was different. Emerson, from the egalitarian United States, thought England 'the paradise of the first class: it is essentially aristocratic, and the humbler classes have made up their minds to this and contentedly enter into the system'.[5] If he was right, it was just as well for the British Army, where 'the humbler classes' were prepared to obey orders that sometimes made no kind of sense, out of the long habit of deference to their social superiors.

The gentlemen who commanded the troops in the Crimean War had impeccable pedigrees.[6] After all, as Wellington said, 'the description of gentlemen of whom the army were composed, made, from their education, manners and habits, the best officers in the world, and to compose the officers of a lower class would cause the Army to deteriorate'. They might be stone deaf, one-eyed, lacking an arm or a leg, and approaching senility – all but one of the Generals commanding the British forces in the Crimea were over 60, which was old, for those days – but as long as they were socially 'the right sort' they were welcomed.[7] Their hunting expertise ensured that they could at least stay on a horse, even if they were unable to read a map and sometimes had little idea of where they were going; and riding gave them a pleasant recreation, when they could take time off from the rigours of the Crimean War to organise a steeplechase. Apart from idiosyncracies such as missing limbs, they were curiously similar, for it was obligatory in cavalry regiments to cultivate a heavy moustache, and fashionable to pronounce 'r' as 'w'.

Officers had little education, since the public schools most of them had attended had inculcated Latin and Greek and not much else, except how to endure privation and poor food, and 'wear the wight clothes at the wight time'. In 1849 Wellington imposed an entry examination on prospective officers, but it was directed only to establishing that they had 'good abilities and had received the edu-cation of a gentleman', so attendance at Eton was enough for a pass, no matter how little the candidate had learned there. Very few aristocrats failed at their second attempt, but the exam had its uses, since it could be manipulated to exclude the newly rich middle classes.

There were exceptions to the aristocratic monopoly. General Ches-ney's Army career began in 1798 when he walked 20 miles, barefoot, at the age of nine, to join his regiment of Irish Volunteers, in which he rose to the rank of Sub-Lieutenant. He won a coveted cadetship at the Royal Military Academy at Woolwich, but only just; the minimum height required was 4 feet 9 inches, which he passed with a quarter of an inch to spare – with cork inner soles in his shoes. He never grew taller than 5 feet 1 inch. His outstanding abilities made him a Major-General in 1855.[8]

The most astonishing aspect of the Victorian Army was the purchase of commissions. Wellington again – 'it is promotion by purchase which brings into the service ... men who have some connection with the interests and fortunes of the country'. Putting it another way, the land-owning aristocracy could be trusted to defend their land, but the middle class had no such stake in the country, therefore they would not make good officers. The system had the advantage, to the Treasury, that the officer class maintained themselves by their own efforts, instead of the state having to pay them a proper salary. This had been attractive to Charles II, who came back to his throne in 1660 to find the coffers empty; and the system remained in place until 1871, despite occasional half-hearted efforts to change it. It had never applied in the Navy, nor, after 1755, to the Royal Marines. If they could manage without it, why could not the Army? But it was very difficult to eradicate, because every officer who had paid for his commission wanted to see a return on his investment.

The 1844 edition of *The Queen's Regulations and Orders for the Army* provided a table of the 'Established Prices of Commissions', from the Foot Guards down to the 'Regular Regiments of Infantry', and from Cornet/Ensign/2nd Lieutenant (all the same thing) up to Lieutenant-Colonel. The scale for the Foot Guards ran from £1,200 for a cornetcy, to £9,000 – an enormous sum in those days – to be a Lieutenant-Colonel. (The scale stopped there, because promotion to full Colonel was automatic after seven years.) Quarterly returns had to be made, of 'all Officers prepared to purchase Promotions ... It is to be most strictly observed, that no person shall be employed in the Purchase, Sale or Exchange of any Commission in Her Majesty's Forces, except such as are [duly authorised] Agents of Regiments ...' and anyone who paid any more than the Regulation price would be cashiered. But it did not work that way: another splendid example of Victorian double-thinking.[9] From 1720 to 1871 every commission had a dual value, the official cost and the 'over-regulation' or 'regimental' value. The Foot Guards headed the league, but prices varied, depending, as ever, on supply and demand. Lord Brudenell, later the 7th Earl of Cardigan, who, as commanding officer, led the charge of the Light Brigade at Balaclava, is said to have bought the colonelcy of the 11th Hussars, part of the Brigade, for £40,000, implying a hugely inflated over-regulation price.[10] The Duke of Cambridge, the Commander-in-Chief, told the Select Committee appointed to examine military organisation,

A military authority can only take cognisance of what comes to him officially, and as such I state positively that we are not aware of any more money being paid than in the usual way, because if an officer sells out he sends in his request to retire by the sale of his commission; they do not say what is given ... we can only take it for granted that the regulation is complied with ... if a case of that kind were to be brought before a court, no court would be able to decide that the officer had paid more than regulation ...

He must, surely, have known, 'unofficially', of the auctioneers in Charles Street who handled the buying, selling and exchanging of commissions, and negotiated the 'over-regulation' rates; but the 'unofficial' part of his mind did not talk to the 'official' part.

It was a complex system. The general outline worked as follows. Suppose that Lord A, whose father is an Earl, holds the rank of Major in a regiment of Dragoon Guards. His commission is officially 'worth' £8,300, plus that unknown 'over-regulation' amount, £X. He meets an attractive heiress whose father is prepared to make a handsome settlement on her and the man she marries. She is swept off her feet by Lord A's beautiful moustache. They marry, and depart for the Continent for a short wedding journey, using his annual leave entitlement of eight months. While they are away, Lord A's father dies. Lord A decides to sell out of the Army and set up home in the family seat. He tells his Colonel, and the regimental agent, who will deal officially with the sale of his commission. He also tells the Charles Street agency, which will fix the all-important £X factor.

There are several men interested, of whom one is Albert Bloggs, only son of 'Enery, a Birmingham manufacturer who is rolling in money but occasionally drops his aitches. Albert has a consuming ambition to be an Army officer. He is an intelligent young man, prepared to work hard, and he has studied military history and tactics. 'Enery, who is no fool, recognises the difficulties, and sets himself to gather as much 'interest' as judicious donations to charities, energetic canvassing and hospitality to county magnates can generate. Despite his missing aitches, he manages to compile an impressive dossier of testimonials to Albert's character, and he can provide whatever cash may be needed.

Meanwhile young Captain B, in an Infantry regiment, sees a possibility of 'exchanging' into the Dragoon Guards to fill the vacancy created by Lord A's departure. His pedigree begins with the Plantagenets, but cash may be a slight problem. He can sell his own commission for £1,800, plus the unknown 'over-regulation' amount, but there is still a wide gap to fill. He tells his Colonel and the official agent of his regiment that he is, so to speak, in the market, and goes round to Charles Street to see how much the 'over-regulation' price of his own commission is likely to be, and how much Lord A is expecting for his commission. After a family whip-round, and a loan from the Charles Street agency which is prepared to invest in him at a reasonable rate of interest, the cash is raised, and he applies to the Colonel of the Dragoon Guards, who has known his family for years. Captain B is stupid, lazy and uninterested in military matters, but languidly keen on the added social éclat of the Guards, and their generous leave allowance – he has to toil at being an Infantry officer for all of six months every year. The Dragoon Guards Colonel has, of course, no hesitation in choosing him.

Another advantage of service in the Guards regiment was that the Guards were usually stationed in London, since their prime duty was to protect the person of the monarch, and the monarch did not lead his or her Army in the field by then. Some regiments saw no active service for decades. The 2nd Life Guards saw no action for nearly 70 years after Waterloo. If a regiment was sent to perform garrison duty somewhere like Canada, the West Indies or Australia, it was perfectly acceptable for an officer to avoid such a dire fate by selling out, or exchanging into a home-based unit. But if the foreign posting was on active service, such as in the Crimea, he would be ostracised if he tried to avoid it.

The Crimean War, vividly reported by journalists such as W. H. Russell of *The Times*, aroused public indignation at the 'incompetency, lethargy, aristocratic hauteur, official indifference, favour, routine and stupidity' rampant in the Army command.[11] There were many opponents to reform of the system of commissions by purchase, including the Queen, but finally in 1871 Lord Cardwell as Secretary of State for War achieved its abolition, at a cost of £6,150,000.[12]

An alternative to soldiering was Government service, in the House of Commons or the Lords, or in the diplomatic corps. The Civil Service was beginning to inch towards a more meritocratic organisation, but meanwhile there were plenty of safe family seats, and nepotistic appointments, for any tolerably able young nobleman who was attracted to the life.

'The Season' lasted from Easter until August, when Parliament rose and everyone could go back to their country houses and think of shooting, hunting, and 'Friday-to-Monday' (*never* 'the weekend')

entertaining. Devonshire House, in Piccadilly, had a magnificent ballroom fit for many 'a magnificent ball ... to which "all the world" went'[13] – all the world, that is, who mattered. At one 'big party' there, Lady Cavendish saw 'one foreigner who actually had white powder in her hair! She looked lovely'.[14] Further along was Bath House. In 1850 the Carlyles went to a ball there, with 'from five to seven hundred select aristocracy', including, of course – he went everywhere – the Duke of Wellington. Thirteen years later they went to another ball there. Jane was glad, in retrospect, to have seen 'all the Duchesses one ever heard of blazing in diamonds, all the young beauties of the season, all the distinguished statesmen ... and all the rooms hung with artificial roses looked like an Arabian nights entertainment'.[15] Further west along Piccadilly was Cambridge House, the home of Lord and Lady Palmerston.[16] She was one of the great political hostesses of the day. Stafford House, near St James's Palace (now Lancaster House, used for Government entertaining), was the London home of the Duke and Duchess of Sutherland; she was Mistress of the Robes, a considerable Court appointment, until her husband died in 1861. Norfolk House in St James's Square was big enough for a banquet and a grand ball attended by the Queen and Prince Albert in 1849. Grosvenor House in Park Lane, the home of the 2nd Marquess of Westminster (father of the 1st Duke), had a magnificent picture gallery, and more gold plate than the royal couple could have raised.

Queen Victoria's courts were not as grand as some of her subjects' entertainments. She gave childrens' balls, which sound as if they were fun, all her children and other young guests romping and galloping and enjoying themselves. Four times a year, until Albert's death, she held 'drawing rooms' at which the young daughters of the nobility were presented to their Queen. Young Lucy Lyttleton (later Lady Frederick Cavendish) was presented in 1859, when she was eighteen. Thereafter she was invited to royal balls.

What a beautiful sight it is [her first royal ball]! the glittering uniforms, the regal rooms and the Royal presence. We made our curtseys rather ill I'm afraid, such a slippery floor, and difficult to take the Queen's hand, from her eminence of two steps. However, we did better than most, for at all events we went low down [in their curtsey] and the rest of the world made nothing but nasty little bows and inclinations ... the Prince of Wales ... and Princess Alice [his sister] valsed together with marvellous grace and dignity ... slowly, so unlike the fierce fluttering whirls in a tight embrace that one sees elsewhere.[17]

Poor Lucy Lyttleton: she had been strictly brought up, and was not allowed to 'valse'.

Albert was not regarded with favour by the old English aristocracy. He was, after all, only a foreigner, whose family tree was not nearly as impressive as their own, for all its galaxy of double- and triple-barrelled titles. 'The Prince was misunderstood and disliked by the Englishmen of his generation almost without exception. Being extremely German, Albert was unpopular from the start ... he was rendered ridiculous in public by the Queen's adoration ... though she was often petulant and excessively exacting.'[18] The gentlemen he had brought with him in his suite from Germany did not meet with her approval. They had to go, despite his gentle protest –

> Think of my position, dear Victoria; I am leaving my home with all its old associations, all my bosom friends, and going to a country in which everything is new and strange to me – men, language, customs, modes of life, position. Except yourself I have no one to confide in. And is it not even to be conceded to me that the two or three persons who are to have the charge of my private affairs should be persons who already command my confidence?[19]

No, it was not, and what must have felt even worse, he was given as private secretary a young man in Melbourne's household, George Anson, thus running the risk – which Albert saw so clearly – of identifying him with Melbourne's Whig Party. He grew very fond of Anson, as the years went by; but Anson died suddenly in 1849. The only sentient being remaining to remind him of his beloved Rosenau, where he had been brought up, was his beautiful greyhound Eon. He had a silver collar made for it in Paris, inscribed 'Le Prince Albert de Saxe Coburg et Gotha', and Landseer painted Eon wearing it, in 1842; but Eon died.[20]

The undeniable success of the Great Exhibition, 'the fulfilment of a much-derided idea of Prince Albert', did make him more popular in some circles, yet three years later 'Prince Albert's appearance in a dissolving view [a kind of static news film, shown in a theatre] was hissed and hooted at'. There was a feeling that he should not presume to advise the Queen about state affairs, although the populace at large were never to know how much they owed to his quiet guiding hand as Victoria grew to lean more and more on him. 'Being decidedly German in all his ways and thoughts, he is offensive to English people, even to some who ought to know better.'[21] Fortunately he could shoot stags, in Scotland, and hunt, in England. In 1843 Victoria was able to tell her Uncle Leopold, 'Albert's riding so boldly and hard has made such a sensation that it has been written all over the country, and they make more of it than if he had done some great act!'[22] Possibly his position would have been easier if he had become a Freemason, as most of the royal males were. He might then have been made more welcome in patrician circles; but he expressed no interest in joining.[23]

Perhaps it would have helped if he had managed to lose his German accent, in speaking English. This may not have worried the people to whom he spoke. The courtiers were accustomed to Victoria's slight accent – after all, her mother was German, so was her governess Lezhen, who was very close to her until after her marriage. There was, then, no 'received English pronunciation' and of course no broadcasting, so not many people got a chance to hear him. When they did, they may have regretted it; his speech on the opening of his triumph, the Great Exhibition, was long, ending with the unmemorable words:

> It is our heartfelt prayer that this undertaking, which has for its end the promotion of all branches of human industry and the strengthening of the bonds of peace and friendship among all nations of the earth, may, by the blessing of Divine Providence, conduce to the welfare of your Majesty's people, and be long remembered among the brightest circumstances of your Majesty's peaceful and happy reign.[24]

And that was only the last bit. Poor Albert, he could never do anything right, for the xenophobic Britons, nor anything wrong for his wife. Parliament refused to do as Victoria wanted, and confer on him the title of Prince Consort, so in the end she did it herself, by royal Letters Patent, in 1857; which meant that he got some priority on state occasions over miscellaneous foreign archdukes, but it made clear the attitude of Parliament.

One can only feel sorry for him. He had known all his life that he was expected to marry Victoria, provided, of course, that she finally decided that she wanted to marry him. When, after some other flirtations, she did choose him, and fell passionately in love with him, he had no get-out. The life he had lived until then was that of a cultured young Continental noble, widely travelled, and interested in current thought on literary and scientific subjects. But he had no function in the British constitution. He followed the Queen on ceremonial occasions, wearing uniforms that showed off his manly figure, and at home he functioned impeccably as her stud. The encyclopedic educational regime he advised for his eldest son ought to have produced a princely paragon. Inexplicably, Edward grew up ungovernable as a boy, and dissolute as a young man. His first-born child, Princess Victoria, was much more his intellectual companion than Edward, or even his wife. He was devoted to Vicky, and missed her desperately when she was married off to the heir to the German Empire in 1858, at the age of seventeen.[25]

It was not even as if Albert as the Queen's consort could compete in wealth with some of her aristocratic subjects. A dozen of them had annual incomes of over £100,000.[26] The Duke of Bedford was said to 'lay by' £100,000 a year,[27] and had his sights set on doubling it. Lord George Cavendish had bought Burlington House, in Piccadilly, for £70,000 in 1815, but decided it was surplus to his requirements so he sold it to the Government 40 years later, for double the price he had paid. In 1865 Lord Derby's annual income was £150,000.[28] The 1st Duke of Westminster's income from the Grosvenor estate in London, alone, was more than £250,000.[29] Parliament had granted Albert, grudgingly, just £30,000 a year. When he lay dying, it was said that he lacked the will to live. Perhaps he was tired out. More probably, his death was inevitable, from the cancer of bowel or stomach which modern diagnosis suggests.[30]

Victoria disliked being trumped in conversation by anyone more intelligent than she was. That would not have been too difficult, but courtiers were trained to hold their tongues and reply to her boring remarks equally vapidly. Her many portraits tended to do her more than justice – she was not really very pretty, despite Herr Winterhalter's best efforts. Her photographs were less tactful, depicting a dumpy little woman, increasingly podgy, with rather popping blue eyes, teeth that sometimes protruded over her lower lip, and a receding chin. As she grew older her mouth drooped sourly, and her jowls sagged. But the public bought her photographs avidly.

Apart from the very few privileged families who met her socially, and the populace watching her pass in her carriage, no-one had ever before been able to see what a real-life monarch looked like, so it was not important that she was not as glamorous as, say, Lily Langtry.

She had a terrible taste in clothes, and saw nothing wrong in loading her small person with as many diamonds as there was room for. She had some ability in, and love of, music and drawing, but books held little attraction for her. She was overwhelmed by Albert's death in 1861. She developed an unreasoning aversion to her eldest son, whom she blamed, quite irrationally, for his death. 'The Queen's conduct in this matter is hardly sane ... the eccentricity cannot be attributed to her misfortune but if it goes on and she lives long it will produce a most painful state of things.'[31] As it was, her entourage was afraid to thwart her in any way, after 1861, in case it should precipitate her into the insanity which – as was then thought – had afflicted George III. She felt entitled to retire from public life almost completely, for many years, which led to popular rumbles of discontent. Why should the British public pay for her upkeep when they got so little to show for it? For the disappointed débutantes, it was not at all the same to be welcomed into London society by a mere stand-in, the Prince of Wales and his beautiful, but tragically deaf and chronically late, consort whom he married in 1863.

More seriously, Victoria found the ceremonial of opening Parliament – symbolically a cornerstone of the British constitution – far too trying, and opted out. In 1864 'the *Saturday Review* ... had a disagreeable sort of threatening article about the Queen's maintaining her retirement; and this (as is supposed) has led to her putting into the *Times* a statement of her determination to continue to delegate to others the matters of mere ceremonial, at the same time that she will never shrink from anything that may be beneficial to the people, of whose loyal affection she speaks warmly'.[32] But it took all Disraeli's persuasive flattery – and the fact that she wanted Parliament to grant a dowry to her daughter, Helena – to persuade her to open Parliament for the first time since her husband's death, in 1866.

She gradually returned to public life, when she felt like it, but Londoners saw little of her. Her unvarying routine swung between Osborne, Windsor and Balmoral, spending only a few days in Buckingham Palace from time to time. When she drove to St Paul's Cathedral in 1872, to give thanks for her son's recovery from typhoid fever, she was surprised by the warmth of the London crowds.

Domestic Service

The Victorian middle and upper classes could not have lived as they did without their servants. The 1841 census gave their number at over 168,000. In 1862 *The Edinburgh Review* put the figure at 'a million and more', 400,000 being the lowest grade, maids-of-all-work. They formed by far the biggest category of employed persons.

The steps up to the front door were a status symbol. Even in the poorest of homes, they had to be clean. If you could not afford even a 'slavey', you might hire a 'Saturday girl' to come in on Saturdays just to scrub them.[1] Poor households which could only just afford a slavey paid her very little, but at least she had a roof over her head, some basic vocational training, and the prospect of the next meal. If the girl had come from a workhouse, which was very likely, she was completely untrained. 'Girls brought up in workhouses ... can never, so long as they remain inmates of those huge establishments, have means of learning any domestic duties ... tradespeople complain that workhouse girls are of no use to them, and are perfectly helpless.'[2] Mrs Beeton wrote in 1861 that 'the general servant, or maid-of-all-work, is perhaps the only one of her class deserving of commiseration: her life is a solitary one, and, in some places, her work is never done'.[3] A little girl who lived in Bethnal Green, in the East End of London, began to earn her living at the age of ten, looking after a shopkeeper's baby for twelve hours a day, for 1s 6d a week. At thirteen she went into service in Hampstead. 'I was fairly happy, but had to sleep in a basement kitchen which swarmed with blackbeetles and this made me very wretched at nights.' In her next job she was paid 3s a week, for looking after four children and a newborn baby and doing all the housework. 'I was often so tired ... that I fell asleep on the stairs on my way to bed.'[4]

Hannah Culwick's employment record was skewed by her devotion to her middle-class lover, Arthur Munby, who dictated what jobs she should take, to suit his convenience. Fortunately for us she was willing, and able, to do as Munby wanted and keep a diary. She was paid £6 a year (a little over 2s a week) in 1847, when she was fourteen, for looking after eight children, 'all their boots to clean and the large nurseries on my hands and knees and a long passage and stairs, all their meals to get and our own [the other servants] ... the water to carry up and down for their baths, and coal for the fire, put all the children to bed, and wash and dress of a morning by 8 oclock'.[5] By 1856 she was a 23-year-old 'general servant' in London. 'I cleaned the knives and boots, the doorstep and all that, and I was content at £16 a year.'

After a spell in Margate, that seaside watering-place convenient for Munby by steamer from London, she came back to London and stayed in the Servants' Home near the Strand, where she heard of her next job. 'I had 5 fireplaces to do every morning, the dining room and study and the halls and steps, the lady's maid's room and all the places on the lower ground floor to keep clean ...'. Doing a fireplace meant clearing the ashes and cinders from the night before, cleaning the fireplace surround, and polishing the cast-iron grate with oily black lead (very difficult to do without getting the stuff all over you and there were no rubber gloves then) before laying the fire with paper, wood and coal ready to be lit. Mrs Beeton described the proper brushes for black-leading, but Hannah Culwick preferred to use her bare hands to rub the black lead in. Was she being over-conscientious, or was this another of Munby's fetishes?

Hannah next took a job in an eating-house near the Temple, where Munby lived. 'I could go out every Sunday evening but must have no one to come and see me ... I felt I was lowering myself to the very bottom of service ... I was to get £16 a year and beer money, as well as tea found ... I cleaned the boots and knives ... I slept well in the old turn-up straw bed in the kitchen' which she shared with the other maid. Sharing beds was normal for servants. The inventory of furniture in a house Charles Dickens rented, in fashionable Devonshire Place, included in the 'women's bedroom' one 'large painted French bedstead' for both his maids.[6] The 'beer money and tea found' meant that Hannah got a cash allowance instead of the beer which most people still drank in preference to the often unreliable water, but she was given a ration of tea.

Cleaning the knives was a daily task, in those days before stainless steel. The blades discoloured every time they were used, and had to be rubbed bright with emery powder: a tedious, dirty job. Some households had 'knife-cleaning machines': boxes in which the knife blades were mechanically burnished by a rotary brush; but they were not common. Hannah did not mention cleaning the silver, another unending job, as the Victorian middle-class family acquired more and more silver and silver-plated objects, all of which had to gleam despite the dulling effect of the polluted air.

Furniture, marble, fire grates, chimneys, carpets, curtains, feather beds, windows, brass, silver: the list could go on longer, and everything in it needed regular cleaning in its own particular way. The only common ingredient was elbow grease. There were a few proprietary cleaners and polishes, but from the advice in magazines it looks as if a woman was expected at least to know how to make her own. 'As modern furniture is now nearly always French-polished, it should be often rubbed with an old silk rubber [duster].' But what about old-fashioned furniture that was not French-polished? That would need beeswax polish and a very energetic rub. Marble round the fireplace tended to discolour with smoke. Make up a paste of soap, pipe-clay, and bullock's gall (which seems to have been the Victorians' secret ingredient for cleaning; ox gall came to the same thing) and leave it on for a day or two, then 'rub it off with a soft rag'.

Chimney-sweeping was difficult now that it was illegal, by an Act of 1842, to compel or even allow anyone under 21 – after that they were too big anyway – to climb up a chimney to clean it. Hannah Culwick dealt with chimneys by stripping naked and doing them herself, but there were other ways, such as firing a shotgun loaded with pellets up the chimney, or using one of the new-fangled 'engines' which we would recognise as a sweep's set of jointed long-handled brushes. Windows got filthy in the sooty London air. 'In large towns, it is usual to employ glaziers to clean the windows.'[7] To sweep a floor, whether carpeted or uncarpeted, 'with prodigal hand [it] must be sprinkled over with moist tea leaves'[8] somehow prised away from the cook, whose perquisite they were. One last cleaning method may still be useful if you have any linoleum, the modern version of 'floorcloth', in the house. 'After having washed the floorcloth in the usual manner with a damp flannel, wet it all over with milk and rub it well with a dry cloth, when a most beautiful shine will be brought out' and, one would think, a smell of sour milk.

Here is Hannah on 23 December 1863:

> I got up early & lighted the kitchen fire to get it up soon for the roasting – a turkey & eight fowls for tomorrow being Christmas Eve and forty people's expected & they're going to have a sort of play, and so they are coming tonight to do it over & the Missis has order'd a hot supper for 15 people – very busy indeed all day and worried too with the breakfast & the bells ringing so & such a deal to think about as well as work to do – I cleaned 2 pairs of boots & the knives – wash'd the breakfast things up – clean'd the passage & shook the door mat – got the dinner & clear'd away after – keeping the fire well up & minding the things what was roasting & basting them until I was nearly sick with the heat and smell – the waiter came at 5 o'clock – I made the coffee & that & give the waiter it as he come for it up to 7 o'clock – Fred Crook came in and help'd me & I was glad of him as well as for company – we got the supper by a ¼ to ten, and we run up & down stairs to see some of the acting – ... we laid the kitchen cloth & had our supper & clear'd away after – I took the ham & pudding up at twelve o'clock – made the fire up & put another on & then to bed – came down again at 4 for the waits [carol singers] woke me just in time – the fire wanted stirring ...

Jane Carlyle chronically suffered from servant trouble, perhaps because few would satisfy her high, Scottish standards.[9] She had to battle against bedbugs, first in the servant's bed, then – horror – in her own, when she came back from a visit to Scotland in 1849, and then once more in the servant's bed. The bedstead had to be completely taken to bits:

> I flung some 20 pailfuls of water on the kitchen floor to drown any that might attempt to save themselves; then we killed all that were discoverable, and flung the pieces of the bed one after another into a tub of water, carried them up into the garden, and let them steep there for two days, and then I painted all the joints [with mercury ointment to

kill the bugs], had the curtains washed ... what disgusting work to have
to do!

Surely most mistresses would have left this disgusting work to the
servant. The mattress on the maid's bed, stuffed with wool flock, was
being eaten by moths, so 'all the wool [was] washed and boiled and
teased; and I have a woman here this day making it up into a mattress
again'. Better mattresses were stuffed with feathers, which needed to
be cleaned every three years. Jane took advantage of a hot summer's
day; 'one bedroom has all the feathers of its bed and pillows airing
themselves on the floor' before being stuffed back into a newly washed
and waxed ticking cover.

Mrs Beeton and an earlier writer, Thomas Webster, from whom I
suspect she took much of her material,[10] both specify in detail what
each servant could be expected to do, and how. If you did not have
a copy of their books, your monthly magazine would tell you. Going
through some of the multitude of Victorian advice books, I was mainly
struck by the infinity of ways to get things clean, using brushes
specially designed for each job, and ingredients I have hardly heard
of (ox gall) and would not know where to buy or how to use. A
selling-point of such books which is not immediately apparent was
that when a prospective employer had risen to more money, more
silver, more clothes and more servants than she was used to, she
could direct them with confidence, having just mugged up 'how to
clean black silk' (you've guessed it: ox gall) as if she had always had
a lady's maid.[11]

The starkest contrast between those days and our own was the
household laundry.[12] 'A family wash should be performed as seldom
as possible', for instance a family of husband and wife and one child,
living in 'a genteel 8-roomed house with a small garden in the
suburbs', could wash every five or seven weeks, although once a
fortnight would be better.[13] The cycle began on Friday, with the
coloureds and 'body linen and other fine things' put ready for boiling.
This was done on Saturday, when the servant got up at 3 a.m. to
light the fire under the boiler. She had a nice rest on Sunday, subject
of course to church-going, so by Monday she was able to put the
washing lines up in the garden – for this quantity of wet laundry, a
skilled operation in itself – and finish the washing. Tuesday was for
starching the shirts and petticoats, and carefully smoothing and folding
the table linen and sheets to be mangled. They were sent round to

the mangler on Wednesday morning and returned by her later that day, while the servant began on the ironing. Thursday would see the end of the ironing, and everything checked and put away.

An average wash would be 24 day shirts and six night shirts, with 'trousers, waistcoats etc' in the summer. (Was the writer too modest to mention the starched petticoats and drawers and knickers of the household? What about babies' nappies? Let alone those substantial sanitary towels?) It was 'not usual to wash silk dresses', but if you decided that washing would be better than sending them to the 'scourer' to be cleaned, it was best to take the dress to pieces and rub each piece with a soapy damp flannel, and rinse it with a sponge. 'Some finish it by sponging it with gin, but whiskey or spirits of wine are preferable.'[14] The old lady beside you in the omnibus, who reeked of gin, had been trying to save money by washing her old silk dress in gin, without herself tasting a drop, perhaps.

Meanwhile of course the daily routine of housework and cooking was expected to pursue its normal rhythm. Some of the labour could be saved by investing in a dolly tub, the ancestor of washing machines. It was an ingenious contrivance of a long-handled wooden 'dolly', with four or six short, slanting spokes at the end, like a deformed three-legged stool. You put the spoke end in the water, and rolled the long handle round the rim of the dolly tub so that the spokes twisted the clothes in the washing water, and rubbed them against the inner wall of the tub, which was gently corrugated. If all the washing was 'put out' to a laundress it would cost £25–£30 a year. So it might be cheaper to keep two servants, to spread the load and release the mistress from the anxiety of wondering whether dinner would arrive on the table as usual, on a wet Monday. What happened in wet weather?

There was another worry about washing:

In the suburbs, houses rented from £40 to £50 a year are for the most part inhabited by people who keep only one servant, and in many cases the washing is performed at home ... in such cases the drying is effected in the garden, and, as this is the practice in the neighbourhood, there is nothing particular in it: but to hang out clothes in the garden of a house of £70 to £80 rent would be a profanation ... the family would be set down as low and vulgar and shunned accordingly.[15]

And the only remedy would be emigration. So take a careful look

round before you hang the washing out, if you are not sure how
much rent your employer – or husband – pays.

Female servants were not given work clothes, nor expected to wear
uniforms. A good cotton dress cost only 8d, a common working gown
6d. Scrubbing the outside steps leading up to the front door, which
was a constant chore for Victorian servants, was made no easier by
their long skirts, and no less demeaning if – as many did – they
insisted on wearing crinolines. In 1865 Lady Frederick Cavendish was
'triumphant at starting the underservants minus crinoline during their
work!'.[16] They were expected to dress neatly, although as Webster
observed in 1844, 'of late years the low price of most of the articles
of clothing has introduced ... a more showy style of dress [especially]
among maidservants ... a servant of correct taste in dress would
never appear in curl papers'.[17]

Another domestic diarist was William Tayler, a footman who worked
for a rich widow in Great Cumberland Street.[18] He decided to improve
his education by keeping a diary for a year, 1837. It began as so many
diaries do –

> This being Sunday, nothing has transpired of consequence. I got up at
> 7.30, cleaned the boys' clothes [his employer's grandsons were staying
> with her for their school holidays] and knives and lamps, got the parlour
> breakfast, lit my pantry fire, cleared breakfast and washed it away,
> dressed myself, went to church, came back, got parlour lunch, had my
> own dinner, sit [sic] by the fire and red [sic, dear me, William, this will
> never do] the Penny Magazine [an improving periodical] and opened
> the door when any visitors came. At 4 o'clock had my tea, took the
> lamps and candles up into the drawing room, shut the shutters, took
> glass, knives, plates etc into the dining room, laid the cloth for dinner,
> took the dinner up at 6 o'clock, waited at dinner, brought the things
> down again at 7, washed them up, brought down the dessert, got ready
> the tea, took it up at 8.30, washed up, had my supper at 9, took down
> the lamps and candles at 10.30, and went to bed at 11. All these things
> I have to do every day.

Unlike Hannah Culwick he was able, in the intervals of this exhausting
day, to entertain his friends. One day he 'found my tailor waiting for
me, and paid his bill, drank a few glasses of wine with him' –

presumably out of his employer's cellar. Whether he realised that he was in a cushy job was never clear. 'Almost all servants are obliged to find their own tea and sugar', but he does not say whether this applied to him. He fed like a fighting cock. 'This day we had for dinner a piece of sirloin of beef, roasted broccoli and potatoes, and preserved damson pie ...'. His employer's family lunched at one, 'the same time we dine in the kitchen. They generally have some cut from ours' – note the precedence. One evening some of his employer's family went to Drury Lane Theatre and 'the old lady treated me to see it' – possibly, it is fair to say, so that he was at hand when the gentry came out of the theatre, to help them to get home.

His life was not always idyllic. 'In London men servants has to sleep downstairs underground, which is generally damp.' He does not mention black beetles. There were three women servants – probably a cook, a housemaid and a lady's maid – but in a severe 'flu epidemic which laid low everyone else in the household, he was prepared to 'help with the sick'. He got a sovereign at Christmas from his employer's son-in-law, 'but it is no more than he ought to do as they very frequently dine here'. On Christmas Day the servants had roast beef, plum pudding, turkey and a bottle of brandy to make punch. By the end of the year, perhaps still bilious from the brandy, he sadly noted that 'the life of a gentleman's servant is something like that of a bird shut up in a cage'. But at least he was secure in his cage. 'It's surprising to see the number of servants that are walking about the streets out of place ... servants are so plentiful that gentlefolk will only have those that are tall, upright, respectable-looking, young people and must bear the very best character.'

Hippolyte Taine was impressed by

the footmen in great houses. White cravats impeccably tied, scarlet or canary yellow breeches, magnificent dimensions and proportions; their calves, especially, are enormous ... in great houses they are carefully matched: the footmen, like the pair of carriage horses, must be exactly the same size ... fullness of calves, ankles, nobility of bearing, decorative appearance, all may be worth an extra £20 per annum.[19]

Maybe William Tayler's dimensions came up to that level of pulchritude. But as Mrs Beeton warned,

when the lady of fashion chooses her footman without any consideration than his height, shape, and *tournure* of his calf, it is not surprising that

she should find a domestic who has no attachment for the family, who
considers the figure he cuts behind her carriage, and the late hours he
is compelled to keep, a full compensation for the wages he exacts, for
the food he wastes, and for the perquisites he can lay his hands on.

William Tayler, helping with the sick, was not such a bad bargain.

✳

Hannah found most of her jobs through newspapers, or local shop-
keepers or register offices such as the one in the Soho Bazaar, which
charged a fee of 2s 6d, or 5s for cooks and upper servants. 'They
have prayers there together at a certain hour in the morning and the
man over it all ... speaks to us about religion and gives us tracts
before [we go] upstairs to sit in the room where the ladies come and
look at us.' She waited there with other women, 'then the ladies
began to come in ... one lady spoke to me and she asked me to
follow her ... to another room where the ladies sat and hired you or
asked you questions. I stood before her answering her questions.'
    The registry run by the London Society for the Encouragement of
Faithful Servants, in Hatton Garden – not particularly convenient for
potential employers who lived in the West End – charged no fee, but
required evidence that the servant had been in her last place for two
years, or was looking for her first job.[20] *The Times* always carried
advertisements for servants in middle- and upper-class households;
the *Christian World* was the medium for the lower classes. The hiring
was for a year but could be terminated by either side at one month's
notice, which explains why the wages are often expressed in annual
amounts instead of the weekly rates one would expect.[21]
    Magazines such as *The Magazine of Domestic Economy* constantly ran
articles advising on servants. In the ideal world as seen by the editor,
there should be a written contract signed by employer and servant,
who would give a written receipt for each payment of wages. The
magazine suggested that the constant complaints of employers could
be their own fault. The contract of service rarely specified how the
servant was to dress, and if the mistress disliked her maid rustling
about in silk, she should have said so when she engaged her. As to
'followers', 'relations ought not to be denied the gratification of visiting
her occasionally'. One can imagine the hordes of 'cousins' who were
thus gratified.

Mrs Beeton sternly reprimanded prospective employers. 'They do not, when engaging a servant, expressly tell her all the duties which she will be expected to perform ... Every portion of work which the maid will have to do, should be plainly stated by the mistress, and understood by the servant.' (In those days, when the market was over-supplied, this was no doubt more feasible than today.)[22] Mrs Beeton gave a useful summary of the normal number of servants in households of various income levels, such as

About £1,000 a year – a cook, upper housemaid, nursemaid, under housemaid, and a man servant

About £750 a year – a cook, housemaid, nursemaid and footboy

About £500 a year – a cook, housemaid and nursemaid

About £300 a year – a maid-of-all-work and a nursemaid

About £200 or £150 a year – a maid-of-all-work (and girl occasionally)

Men servants' pay depended on whether they were 'found in livery' – their uniform provided for them. If not, a footman would be paid £20–£40. It looks as if William Tayler had to provide his own livery – hence the tailor's bill – so at 40 guineas (£42) a year he was not much overpaid. His employer will also have had to pay an annual tax of one guinea, men servants being regarded by the Treasury as a luxury. Mrs Beeton does not mention the tips William got, which could total £10–£15 a year. A coachman, who was always 'found in livery', was paid £20–£35.

Women, who worked in their own clothes, were not 'found in livery', but again there were two scales, depending on whether or not they were given a cash allowance for tea, sugar and beer. Mrs Beeton assessed a general maidservant's pay at between £9 and £14 finding her own tea etc., or £7 10s to £11 plus an allowance, so Hannah was perhaps not too underpaid, even for the mammoth amount of work she did. A cook finding her own tea etc. would be paid between £14 and £30 a year, otherwise £12 to £26 a year plus the allowance. This is puzzling: surely a normal cook would contrive the odd cup of tea for herself from the mistress's tea tray? Cooks had their own 'perquisites', such as once-used tea leaves, the dripping from the joints, which they sold to street traders who called at the back door, and tips from local tradesmen. One of Prince Albert's earliest reforms of the royal household economy was to fix the servants' wages;

housemaids, for instance, were to receive £12–£18 a year.

Victorian novels often mention 'characters', without emphasising how vital they were to an employed person. When changing jobs, a servant needed to be able to show her next employer the written reference or 'character' from her last. If there was an interval, why? What had she been doing? Had she perhaps spent the time in prison? Obviously the employer was wise not to depend wholly on a written reference, which could easily be forged. It was better to see or write to the last employer, so as to judge both servant and employer; but this was a counsel of perfection. By an Act of 1794 'persons giving characters that are false are liable to a penalty of £20'; but that would not help the unfortunate servant if a mistress threatened to dismiss her without this vital document, or to give her less than she deserved as a character.

An oddity, from Mayhew.[23] A maker of false eyes told him that

> false eyes are a great charity to servants. If they lose an eye, no one will engage them. We always supplies eyes to such persons at half price. My usual price is two guineas for one of my best eyes. The eyes we make move so freely – consentaneously as it is termed – with the natural eye, people don't notice.

Servants were encouraged to save part of their earnings in the newly established Post Office Savings Bank. But how efficient a bulwark against penury even the most carefully hoarded savings would be, when a servant was too old to work, was doubtful. Prince Albert addressed the Servants' Provident Society in 1849. 'How can the position of the domestic servant ever be elevated if the career ends in the workhouse?'[24]

CHAPTER 12

Houses and Gardens

A poor couple might decorate their house with a precious and rare
possession – their marriage certificate, 'displayed on the wall of the
living room as a choice print might be'.[1] There would be a pair of
china or pottery ornaments from a street seller on the mantelpiece.
This was the heyday of cheap pottery figures from Staffordshire,
quickly produced by new machinery to catch public interest, and
easily transported to London by the new railways. Victoria and Albert
were obvious subjects, but the range included criminals and politicians,
generals such as Wellington, sportsmen such as the cricketer Lillywhite,
and even Jumbo, the African elephant which arrived from Paris in
1865.[2] China dogs were never out of fashion, especially the spotted
spaniels that have survived in many antique shops. There might be a
plant in a pot, and a pet singing-bird in a cage, a linnet or a skylark.
As long as the lark had a little bit of turf to rest in, it 'adapted himself
to the poor confines of his prison ... more rapidly than other wild
birds', and was prized 'for his stoutness of song'.[3]

Middle-class visitors to poor overcrowded rooms often remarked
on the awful smell in them. Whitewash, which has a slight antiseptic
effect, might help, and it was cheap and effective. It was made by
pouring water on to cakes of whiting, and adding size or glue as a

fixing agent. A pound of 'green vitriol' (iron sulphate) to every two gallons of whitewash 'gives a very pleasing drab' (the first appearance of 'magnolia'?).[4] A handful of local clay, if it was a pleasant colour, would do instead of this dangerous-sounding mixer, but I have not seen it suggested. The lack of damp-proof courses meant that plaster tended to fall off the downstairs walls as the damp rose, to a height of about a yard, so Victorian cottage walls were often lined with tongued-and-grooved pine or deal, up to that height or higher.

A schoolteacher would need to watch the pennies, although she would not be classed as poor. Her bedroom, sitting room and kitchen could be furnished and equipped for £17 16s 4d, according to an 1867 manual much used by teacher training colleges. Her bedroom contained a 3-foot French bedstead (14s) and bedding (together, £2 7s 3d, with a 'good quilt' for her at 6s 3d), a chest of drawers (£1 1s) and a washstand (5s), with a 'toilet glass', a roller blind, and 2 yards of carpet (1s 6d). Her sitting room was comparatively luxurious – a felt carpet 3 yards square, and a hearth rug, six cane-seated chairs (£1 1s) and a deal table (17s 6d); 'damask window curtains complete with pole and fixings' (£1 7s 6d) *and* a roller blind (6s 9d); bookshelves (5s), a fender and fire-irons (6s) and a table cover (3s 9d). It evokes a cosy scene, with the damask curtains drawn and the firelight gleaming on the fender as she sat at her table reading. But she had no lamp to see by, only two candles, and she had no easy chair. In her kitchen she had two more chairs, 'polished Windsor', and a table and fire-irons. The cooking range was assumed to be built-in. She had a large collection of 'earthenware' including four teacups and saucers (1s 2d) and four breakfast cups and saucers (2s 8d) – who were the other three for? – and four tumblers (1s 10d), but only two wine glasses (11d). Her 'sundries' included a foot bath (5s) but no other bath, a pair of brass candlesticks (3s 11d) and a pair of snuffers with tray (2s 2d), and a coal scuttle (2s 6d).[5]

For the better-off, there was an exuberant flood of objects which could add to the impressiveness of their surroundings. This thirst for ostentation seems to have gathered momentum as Victoria's reign unrolled. In the late 1830s Flora Tristan visited London and did not think much of it. Things were ordered better in France.

If I enter an English home in search of domestic comfort, I shall be very disappointed. In England, if a house is fitted out with carpets from hall to attic, if a handsome tea-tray and [tea] service adorn the drawing-room table, if the fireplaces all have their sets of shovels and tongs in polished steel, then it is generally agreed that it is fit to show its face to the world and possesses every comfort a well-to-do gentleman could demand. The drawing-room chairs are awkward, heavy and lumpy, they are uncomfortable to sit upon, as are the chairs in the dining-room ... let us go up to the bedroom ... An enormous bed occupies the centre of the chamber; a large commode stands in one corner, the table in another, while the dressing-table is set in front of the window, which overlooks a tiny yard (for in London all the bedrooms are at the back of the house ...) Five or six chairs piled high with boxes, parcels, shoes etc stand around the room; gowns, mantles, shawls and hats hang from nails on all four walls in the absence of a clothes-press [wardrobe] ... it is difficult to imagine the disorder; a French woman could not set foot in it without a shudder of disgust ... The English bed sums up to perfection the nature and reality of most things in England. In appearance nothing could be finer! But just lie down on it for a moment and you will think you are lying on a sack of potatoes ...[6]

Oh dear. Perhaps she caught her hostess on a bad day. And to think that French hotels used to promise 'le confort anglais'.

In fact capacious wardrobes had been steadily advancing towards English bedrooms ever since someone realised that they are 'far more convenient for keeping apparel than the chests of drawers formerly in general use'.[7] They could be vast – a dream for a maker of 'antiques' nowadays. They usually had full-length hanging space in one division, space to hang jackets or perhaps skirts in another, with a deep drawer under it for hats and bonnets, shelves or drawers in a third, and a full-length mirror on the outside or inside of at least one of the doors, and wooden knobs on each of the inner walls on which to hang the substantial wooden hangers of the time. An arrangement which we lack now, even if we have a wardrobe, was a 'brushing tray', a pull-out shelf on which to spread a skirt for the day's mud or dust to be brushed off and the cleaning techniques of the lady's maid applied. One charming thing about Victorian wardrobes was the sprigged and flowered paper with which they were usually lined.

As to beds, 'four-poster bedsteads ... are the sort generally used in England for the best beds',[8] but there were less elaborate beds, even the kind that fold up into the wall, and iron bedsteads that had the huge merit of not harbouring bugs, as wood did. A brass bedstead was exhibited in the Great Exhibition. What marvels they were, the frame made of sturdy iron but the head- and footboard a riot of brass balls and tubes which could usually be induced, by a bored, mischievous child sent to bed for some wrongdoing, to unscrew enough to produce a comforting, or sometimes embarrassing, rattle when the occupant(s) moved.

'Feather beds [what we would call mattresses: what you lie on] are now in universal use', but wire-sprung mattresses were a 'recent' innovation in 1844, and a great improvement, I would think, since a feather bed needs very thorough shaking every day, to retrieve the feathers that have migrated to the unused edges of the bed.[9] The 1854 inventory of Charles Dickens's house in Devonshire Terrace lists the items in the best bedroom: a stuffed bird in a case, a four-poster bedstead with chintz hangings, a palliasse, a mattress, a feather bed (that makes three layers of varying softness, to lie on), four blankets and two pillows, a bolster and a counterpane, with a 'French polished mahogany double washing stand with marble top and crockery complete, and a bidet'. But, I have to admit, no wardrobe.

His drawing room was crowded with miscellaneous tables and chairs, and a rosewood cottage piano by Cramer & Co. 'The middle classes are fast becoming real lovers and able performers, vocal and instrumental',[10] as Carlyle found when his neighbour's daughters persisted in practising their piano-playing when he wanted peace and quiet.[11] There is a fiction that Victorians were so prudish that they clothed the legs of their pianos, for the sake of decency. I never saw a clothed piano in any illustration of a domestic interior, but such is the power of myth that I distrusted my own eyes, until I discovered that the notion was only a tall story invented by an American and swallowed whole by the English.[12] Dickens's drawing room also contained two 'couches'. Sofas, or couches, were 'not merely luxuries; they conduce much to comfort, and in our artificial society are sometimes essential to health'[13] – possibly a veiled reference to the Victorian lady's frequent state of pregnancy. Certainly poor Mrs Dickens was almost constantly pregnant, for which her husband seems to have held her entirely to blame.

The Great Exhibition had included a class for 'furniture, upholstery, paper hangings, papier maché and Japanned goods'. English manufacturers did not do well in it, the French scooped the board with four of the five medals awarded and the Austrians won the fifth. The jury explained that 'it is important, both for the strength and good effect of furniture, that the principles of sound construction be carried out, that the construction be evident, and that if carving or other ornament be introduced, it should be by decorating that construction itself, not by ... disguising it', but this did not appeal much to English furniture-makers, busy applying bits of 'antique' carving where it showed most.[14] The Victorians were adept at 'recomposing' Elizabethan and later furniture, to make up marketable pieces, known to cynics nowadays as Jacobethan. This was particularly rife in sideboards. A splendidly blatant example sits in the Great Hall of Charlecote Park, near Stratford-on-Avon. I quote from the National Trust guidebook: 'the "antique" sideboard was purchased for the Dining Room in 1837, after the date on the back had been carved to read "1558" '.[15]

Tables of all shapes and sizes could be had, for any function you cared to think of, from workbox to banquet. If Jacobethan was not to your taste you might prefer Mr Pugin's Gothic designs. There was a complicated religious sentiment here. Gothic cathedrals had soared up to heaven by pointed arches and heavily crocketed towers. (A 'crocket' is that nobbly bit which often appears in ascending rows, on towers, but when incorporated into furniture can be decidedly uncomfortable.) So a reflection of a Gothic cathedral in your drawing room, or in the nation's Houses of Parliament where Pugin was commissioned to design the interior décor, was a testimony to decent religiosity. In 1851 Victoria gratefully received from the Austrian Emperor an appallingly hideous bookcase in the acme of Gothic sentiment, which had been much admired at the Great Exhibition.

In really affluent circles French rococo or 'Louis Quatorze' was the thing: the style that the new French Emperor Napoleon III went in for, in Paris. Portly crinolined ladies and well-upholstered gentlemen had to lower their weight carefully on to those spindly chairs and impossibly elegant settees. To set them off, the walls had to be panelled and gilded, and the ceilings broken up by rococo garlands and elaborate, dust-catching friezes.[16] If the antique was what you were aiming at, especially in your library, and you had not picked up a supply of marble antiques in Italy on your Continental wedding journey, the best place to go would be the London Marble Working Company in Millbank, up-river from Chelsea, where you could find newly made antique urns and pillars and busts, as well as fireplaces, in white marble from Carrara or black marble from Ireland.[17]

❈

Whitewash may have been healthier, in a poor man's house, but when cylinder printing began to compete with the old, labour-intensive, wood-block printing, wallpaper could be made for less than a farthing a yard, and not many yards would be needed for a small room in a working man's house. 'During the second half of the nineteenth century it would have been difficult to find a house with unpapered walls, for mass production, begun in the 1840s, had resulted in the marketing of goods so inexpensive that practically everyone could afford them.'[18] A contemporary, looking back to the 1840s and 1850s, remarked on 'the use of wall paper and floor carpets by the better-paid classes of working men'.[19] The cheapest were often striped, with small bunches of flowers or geometric motifs, in two or three colours; badly painted and crude, but cheerful. After all, a cylinder printer producing 200 12-yard-long pieces an hour might be expected to slip a little. Block printing was catching up, however. By 1850 a block-printed paper using 20 to 30 colours could be sold for 3½d a yard.

Washable papers, infelicitously named 'sanitary papers', had been shown at the Great Exhibition in 1851, but were not commercially available until 1853. 'Nursery papers' filled a perceived gap in the market from 1850 – the collection of mid-Victorian papers in the V&A includes an insipid one of 'eighteenth-century' children – but most children would surely have preferred the 1853 design of scenes at a busy railway station, or a splendidly martial one showing the Duke of Wellington surrounded by all his victories. For more sophisticated tastes, a print of 'Beggar Boys' after (a long way after) Murillo had been shown in the Great Exhibition, and there were impressive 'architectural' and *faux-marbre* papers for the hall and staircase. Scenes of duck-shooting and angling, or salmon-fishing in the Highlands, might suit a gentleman's study.

For the drawing room and her boudoir, a lady could choose from a riot of flowers, printed in brilliant colours after the introduction of aniline dyes. Never, except in a nurseryman's catalogue, were roses so pink or foliage so green. Colours were intensified by applying flock to the background, usually in dark shades of red, purple or brown. Affluence could be satisfyingly demonstrated by the lavish use of gold, reflecting the sunlight and glittering in the candlelight and lamplight. A startling pattern of gold motifs on a red flock ground, or shiny viridian circles on a purple flock ground, should impress the neighbours. Of course, the gold discoloured quite soon, in the polluted air, to a dull green or brown, depending on whether bronze powder or gold leaf had been used; but you could always have it done again.[20]

One of the few people (Dickens was another) who was not delighted with the Great Exhibition was William Morris. He so deeply, viscerally, deplored the examples of modern taste on view there that he had to leave, and be sick outside. Ten years later he set up the firm of Morris, Marshall, Faulkner & Company, to improve – he hoped – the design of furniture, interior design, stained glass, textiles and wallpapers, using naturalistic shapes and plain constructions not derived from any accepted school. Two wallpapers in several colour-ways, 'Trellis' and 'Daisy', which date from 1862–4, were followed by a steadily increasing stream of designs. 'Trellis' could have coral pink briar roses climbing through a soft green trellis on which perch birds in several shades of blue – a lovely effect, and beautifully produced. It demonstrates the qualities that made William Morris so eminent in English design of the time: his insistence on careful draftsmanship and the best and purest colours. (The degree of Morris's success may be judged by the survival of so many of his patterns, especially in textiles and wall coverings. Go into any National Trust shop and you will find a William Morris teatowel. Better still, find your way to the 'green dining room' in the V&A, and enjoy the walls with your coffee.) But Morris could not single-handedly alter Victorian taste, which remained what is politely called 'eclectic': happily lifting bits from any style it fancied, without being true to any of them.

Curtains could be ingeniously complicated. Webster's *Encyclopaedia of Domestic Economy* (1844) suggested, for a bedroom in a small house or cottage, that the main curtain could be nailed on to the architrave and simply looped back in the daytime. Perhaps the nails might be covered with a textile border. But from there on, curtains grew more and more impressive. The curtain pole of wood or brass retired behind a valance of fabric, or carved and gilt wood, and lengths of the curtain material or a contrasting fabric could be swathed over the curtain pole and arranged to fall down each side of the window in elegant swags. The noise of brass curtain rings on brass rods still evokes a Victorian interior. Next to the window glass in the best rooms, muslin curtains, 'richly flowered in large patterns', diffused the sunlight and moved gently in the breeze, when the heavy curtains had been put away for the summer. Venetian blinds presented dust-traps to the weary housemaid, and 'were apt to be out of order' according to Webster. Holland or linen roller blinds with spring mechanisms shot up without notice, which could be maddening when the housemaid was trying to adjust all the blinds visible from the street to an exactly measured uniform height.

In affluent homes some of the windows were converted into mini-greenhouses by 'Wardian cases', airtight glass boxes made to fit the lower part of the window aperture, in which flowering plants or those ferns so beloved by Victorians flourished, unperturbed by outdoor or indoor pollution, and regardless of the resultant diminution of light inside the room.[21] Samuel Beeton recalled in 1872 visiting 'many years ago' a house 'in the very centre of the densest part of London ... Here we found every window occupied by a glass case, in which plants were growing in a manner which astonished us; ferns of the greenest and freshest hue; orchids such as we have rarely seen surpassed ... and we were told ... that the cases were hermetically sealed, and that no water had been administered for many months.'[22] The logical extension of glassed-in window boxes was a glassed-in room, or conservatory. These could, as now, be bought ready-made, or constructed on-site. Here, those ferns were joined by palms and other exotics, to create a lush ambience notorious for amatory encounters.

Floors were usually covered with carpet squares or rectangles, leaving a space between the edge and the wall which was painted or covered with 'oil cloth', the predecessor of linoleum. Synthetic dyes (i.e. man-made, not naturally occurring like old-fashioned vegetable dyes) were discovered in 1856, and their brilliant colours gradually crept into living rooms from then onwards, making possible a ca-cophony of flowers and patterns underfoot. Bedroom and nursery floors were often left uncarpeted so that they could be scrubbed, with perhaps a rug or two to comfort bare feet. The encaustic tiles laid in patterns of black and white, browns and creams on the hall floor and on the path leading to the front door of a middle-class Victorian house are so carefully preserved by proud houseowners now, that they misleadingly give the impression that they were universally used for such houses.[23] Oil cloth, which cost only 2s 6d to 5s a yard, one yard wide, plain or patterned, was often used over bare boards in the hall, covered sometimes by a width of carpet.[24]

Once the drawing room had received its full complement of whatnots, chiffonières, console tables, pier tables, sofa tables, occasional tables and work tables, it could be scattered with yet another layer, of objets d'art, bibelots and knick-knacks. One wonders how, or whether, Victorian ladies managed to traverse a properly equipped drawing room in a full crinoline without sweeping several small tables clear, and over, on their way. Some of the objects at risk would undoubtedly have been daguerreotypes. For the first time it was possible to have likenesses of your family made without paying a portrait-painter or miniaturist. In 1844 Thomas Rogers, a well-to-do partner in a firm of hosiery manufacturers, was courting Emma Ashwell. Her 'miniature was taken at Beard's Daguerrotype Rooms' for 28s 6d. Beard had opened a studio on the roof of the Royal Polytechnic Institution in Upper Regent Street in 1841.[25] Four years later Rogers's mother's 'portrait in Daguerrotype' cost him 6d less.[26] They were no doubt framed in silver or carved frames, and displayed on one of those many tables.

There was a craze for stereoscopic viewers (rather like binoculars, often elaborately decorated) for which sets of exotic images such as the Alps or the Pyramids could be bought by the avid collector.[27] They in turn were supplanted by 'cartes-de-visite', which were not, as you would think, visiting cards, although they were about the same size. They were black and white photographic images of people or scenes, often in sets that could be arranged in 'window' albums. These were the pictures of Victorian working women that Munby collected to illustrate his records of the working girls he met, such as maid servants, who came into the studio 'as smart as ever they can, often, I'm sure, in their mistress's clothes'. The only give-away detail was their pathetic red hands.[28] Where a daguerreotype might cost up to £2, a carte-de-visite cost only a shilling or sixpence, and they could be bought by collectors from shops all over London. Victoria had cartes-de-visite made of herself and Albert with the children, which sold by the million. For the first time her loyal subjects could see what their Queen looked like – a dumpy little woman gazing admiringly up at her husband, and no less worthy of respect for that.

A lady who loved flowers would have several jardinières about the room: stands with metal containers fitted to the tops, filled with wet silver sand in which arrangements of fresh flowers, with trailing ferns cascading down the stand, lasted several days. She might also have displays of wax flowers, or stuffed exotic birds, under glass domes which needed careful dusting. Or she might be strong enough to endure a live bird such as a cockatoo on a perch, or a parrot, bought by a dealer from a sailor in the East End for 50s or so, on her behalf, and warranted to speak. Only when it was brought home did its vocabulary disclose its previous owner's command of swear words. Perhaps a canary would be better, or a linnet or a bullfinch. 'In rooms it is common to let [a skylark] hop about, giving it a retired place in which to sleep.'[29] Poor skylarks; they are tiny, vulnerable creatures, and their hopping about the room, let alone sleeping in retired places, cannot have endeared them to housemaids. A glass globe of gold and silver fishes would be more soothing.[30]

In the Victorian lady's endless leisure hours, once she had interviewed the cook and met her children, she undoubtedly embroidered; her output of cushions in bright colours, and fire screens, had to find a place. Perhaps she painted in watercolour. Middle-class ladies were surprisingly talented, having little else to worry them. Charming watercolours elegantly framed in gold adorned her boudoir and the drawing room. Family portraits in oil were suitable for the library or the master's study, or the dining room, where their heavy gilt frames were sometimes more handsome than the sitters.

Lighting in a London house was dim. Many houses still used tallow candles, which had to be snuffed – the burnt wick cut off – carefully and often: hence the supply of candle-snuffers, like scissors with a box on one blade to catch the burnt wick. In living rooms some light was given by sperm oil (from whales) in poorly designed lamps, again smelling and needing constant attention,[31] but they were being replaced, by the late 1860s, by the 'Argand' paraffin lamp.[32]

'Coal gas is unquestionably the cheapest source of light [but] its economy is not so great as it is generally imagined to be, because, as the flame cannot always be brought near the ... part of the room to be illuminated, a much greater amount of light is necessary than when moveable lamps are employed.'[33] Which, when you think of it, must have cheered the place up enormously, instead of having isolated pools of light from oil lamps, and darkness in between. Until the invention of the incandescent mantle in the 1880s, gas was not really a practical domestic lighting medium. In any case, 'gas lighting should not be used in private houses, because it makes the room hot, it smells, and it smokes'. So declared the editor of *The Magazine of Domestic Economy* in 1842, only to be smartly told by a reader that gas was mainly used in the winter when a little extra heat was welcome;

if it smoked it had not been properly adjusted, if it smelt there was a leak somewhere, and – the final shot – 'nearly all the medical men of my acquaintance use it in their homes'. Two years later Michael Faraday, experimenting with the gas lights in the Athenaeum, improved their design by incorporating a ventilating tube.[34] (Did the eminent scientist, then 53, climb about the ceiling of the Athenaeum library, to the edification of his fellow-members?)

But Mrs Beeton was still dubious. The last paragraph of her section on 'The Doctor' warns of 'the necessity of good ventilation in rooms lighted with gas'. Let Tegetmeier's *Manual* have the last word:

> Dangerous explosions sometimes occur after the escape of gas from a leaky pipe, or a burner that has been carelessly left open. These accidents are almost invariably caused by the folly of some person taking a lighted candle to discover the source of the leakage, when the escaped gas, having mingled with the air so as to constitute an explosive mixture, takes fire immediately and burns with a violent explosion. Whenever a strong smell shows that there has been a large escape of gas, the maincock at the meter should be immediately turned, and the doors and windows opened to allow the gas to escape. No attempt should be made to search for the situation of the leakage with a light, but notice should immediately be given to a gas-fitter.[35]

We are so accustomed to the uniform black of railings and iron balconies on Victorian houses that the green railings outside Apsley House in Piccadilly, the home of the Duke of Wellington, come as a shock; but they are completely 'right'. The Victorians' reasoning was that *if* the Greeks and Romans had had railings they would have been made of bronze, which patinates to a light blue-green, so the classical designs of railings and balconies ought at least to look as if they were made of bronze. Pugin's design for the decoration of the Houses of Parliament revived the Goths, but they too must have looked back to the Greeks and Romans, so it was reasonable to specify bronze for the window frames. The thinking may be convoluted but the practice is admirably utilitarian; bronze is a perfect material for window frames, since it does not corrode or warp.[36]

From those heavily curtained windows one could enjoy the garden. Again there was no shortage of advice. Before planting anything it is

always essential to see to the fertility of the soil. 'The principal vegetable manures which are formed in suburban gardens is the mould
of collected leaves swept up in autumn.'[37] Too late? Then consider
animal manure.

> The most valuable animal manure is that of man, the next that of
> horses, as abounding with ammonia and nitrogen ... in every suburban
> villa, arrangement should be made for collecting all the liquid manure
> into two adjoining tanks, and mixing it there with water. Where urine
> cannot be got, excrement and water form the best substitute ... in
> many suburban villas almost as much manure is lost as would suffice
> for enriching the vegetable garden and producing vegetables for the
> whole family ... next to nightsoil, bones are the most valuable of all
> manures.

So much for Victorian prudery. These were not the ravings of a 'fringe'
recycler, but the sober advice of a much-respected horticulturalist,
J. C. Loudon.[38] When gardeners ceased to collect urine for the garden
is unclear, but a quick trip to the compost heap to increase its nitrogen
content, in the decency of twilight, is still practised by some. It makes
one think again about the advantages of earth closets over water
closets.

   Loudon had a robust attitude to garden pests. 'No mode of subduing
snails but hand-picking is to be relied upon ... slugs can be destroyed
by watering with lime-water or tobacco-waste', or that useful liquid
manure. A later (1877) book on kitchen gardens warns that if slugs
and snails are 'allowed to *riot* on the ground, winter sowings will
have little chance'.[39] Hedgehogs will devour beetles and cockroaches,
indoors and outdoors. 'The most effective mode of destroying ants in
frames or hothouses is by placing toads in them' but first, catch your
toad. As to cats – and I apologise in advance – 'a small quantity of
arsenic rubbed into a piece of meat, either cooked or raw, will do
their business effectually'.

   Most small gardens, then as now (provided that no radical television-
inspired replanning has taken place), are laid out with a piece of
grass, called a lawn, in the middle, surrounded by flower beds. More
formal layouts were giving way to child-friendly grass. Any lawn needs
constant attention. But the bad old days of scything were gone. A
machine for mowing lawns had been invented as long ago as 1830
but had room for improvement. Shanks's 'new improved patent lawn
mowing, rolling, collecting and delivering machine for 1865 was

patronised on five separate occasions by Her Majesty the Queen':[40] surely not in person, she was a lady of considerable embonpoint and 46 years by then. Yet the 10-inch-cutter model was 'easily worked by a lady', so perhaps she did. It cost £3 10s. Successively wider models culminated in the 48-inch model drawn by a horse, £28, with boots for the horse at 24s a pair. As an extra, a 'silent movement' could be fitted to all models, which no doubt would please those neighbours already displeased by your habit of saving urine. Immediately below Shanks's advertisement in the magazine came one by a competitor, Green and Son. Since their machine was already 'noiseless' they 'consider[ed] their machines now as near perfection as possible, and in consequence have continued making them as usual' – so much for Mr Shanks and his copy-writer.

If you wanted to cut down on lawn maintenance you might favour a rockery. This was not just a heap of stones with plants stuffed into holes; it had to be carefully constructed on scientific, botanic and aesthetic principles, and took as much care to keep it weed-free as any flower bed. Alpine travel was becoming fashionable. Surely the passion for rockeries was connected with the discovery of the wealth of tiny plants that flower on the scree between the snow line and the trees, in the Alps? And yet, a gardening magazine directed at the middle-class gardener advised planting a rockery with cannas and Pampas grass, which must have looked incongruous.[41] Messrs Dick Radclyffe and Co. of High Holborn, who sold 'choice collections of flower seeds', from 5s to 42s, offered 'picturesque rockeries, ferneries, caves and grottoes designed and erected with taste'.[42]

Any enthusiastic gardener wants a greenhouse, or at least a cold frame, especially after Mr Paxton's triumph in Hyde Park. 'Hot-houses for the Million' could be supplied by Samuel Hereman of Pall Mall, at prices ranging from £24 for a model 21 feet by 13 feet, £161 for one up to 64 feet by 25 feet, or 'to cover any extent, as also for suburban villas and cottage gardens'. Frames could be bought or home-made, covered with glass or 'transparent calico'.[43] Some garden-owners liked to edge their beds with whelk shells, surely a curious taste.[44] Good dry paths could be constructed from a mixture of road sand, cinders and *boiling tar*.[45]

The choice of supplier depended on whether you patronised one of the numerous nursery gardens on the edges of London, the suppliers in Covent Garden and other City markets, or the travel-ling costermongers, who brought pots of daffodils, wallflowers and polyanthus 'all a-growing, all a-blowing', and rooted plants, as well as trees and shrubs such as privet (so good for hedges), lilac, laurustinus (another Victorian favourite, smelling of cat), and syringa (now called philadelphus: beautifully fragrant). 'The customers for trees and shrubs are generally those who inhabit the larger sort of houses ... three quarters of the trees are sold in a [costermonger's] round.'[46] According to Mayhew, 'there is as much bartering trees for old clothes, as for roots [plants]', which seems a curious way to stock your garden. One costermonger told Mayhew he 'liked it best where there are detached villas, and best of all where there are kept mistresses ... one way by which we know the kept ladies is, they never sell cast-off clothing as some ladies do, for new potatoes or early peas'.[47]

A cottager's flower garden cultivated by a 'mechanic or artisan' would be full of roses, honeysuckle, sweet briars and summer jasmine, grown from cuttings from neighbours; perennials such as monkshood and some irises and phloxes, and snapdragons; and hollyhocks, polyanthus, wallflowers and other annuals grown from seed. 'The great consideration is to have such as will thrive in a smoky atmosphere', the mechanic or artisan not having followed the middle class out to the suburbs. The cottager could keep his family in vegetables, as well as flowers, on the eighth of an acre – 20 yards by 61 yards – postulated by the editor of *The Cottage Gardener*, but these would be fortunate and unusual cottagers, in the middle of London.[48]

Of the many nursery gardens ringing London, perhaps the most famous was Loddiges Nursery in Hackney. It had begun in 1756. The vast palm house had been designed by Joseph Paxton in the early 1830s, before he built the hothouse at Chatsworth. Loddige pioneered steam heating so effectively that by 1845 the nursery could offer for sale nearly 2,000 species and varieties of orchid, and nearly 300 varieties of palms, as well as supplying Wardian cases filled with ferns. By 1849 there were spectacular hothouses, a 'tropical rain forest', and an arboretum that attracted visitors from all over Europe.[49]

Loudon, writing in 1843 *On the Laying Out of Cemeteries*, gave the prices of 300 trees and shrubs, with – what gardeners so often forget – 'the height which it generally attains in the climate of London'. Looking through it for trees which would be suitable for smaller gardens, I noticed Judas trees for 1s 6d, halesia, 'the common snowdrop tree', for 2s 6d, mulberry trees for 3s 6d, an oriental plane for 1s 6d, robinia pseudo-acacia (that tree with bright yellow leaves) for 1s, cotoneasters for 1s 6d (here Loudon's indication of the correct pronunciation of botanical names is particularly helpful; why is a cotohn-ee-aster not a cotton-easter?) and 'the common lilac' for 1s. He did not suggest a monkey-puzzle for the cemetery, even for the well-heeled. It is a little surprising to find asparagus, garlic and rhubarb among perennial herbaceous plants suitable for a cemetery, but they would certainly do in your garden.

Plants have fashions, and never more so than with the Victorians. Monkey-puzzle trees (araucaria aurucana) had been known since 1795, but they were not commercially available until the early 1840s. You could astonish the neighbours with a 5-foot specimen for only £5 (slightly less than the annual pay of a maid). Plant-hunters were scouring the world for new plants. Robert Fortune travelled in China from 1843 to 1846, in discomfort and danger, and sent home the Japanese anemone, a fragrant honeysuckle (lonicera fragrantissima), winter jasmine (jasminum nudiflorum) and its spring companion forsythia (f. viridissima), as well as 40 varieties of tree peonies.[50] Orchids were always fashionable. Loddiges and the Royal Horticultural Society's garden at Chiswick were famous for them. Dahlias were for a time 'the most fashionable flower in this country', according to Loudon, and much advertised, but it paid to be careful. An article in the 1842 volume of *The Magazine of Domestic Economy* listed pages of them, with the glowing descriptions of each by the nurserymen advertisers, but they were nearly all, according to the writer of the article, 'worthless'.

Loddiges' 1836 catalogue advertised over 1,500 different roses for sale. Roses were still fragrant, but not yet repeat-flowering. A rose garden could include standard roses, introduced in 1820. The National Rose Society began its annual shows in 1854, in the Crystal Palace at Sydenham. There was a craze for ferns, both native and exotic. Summer bedding plants such as the low-growing scarlet pelargonium (you may still be calling it a geranium, which is not botanically correct) 'General Tom Thumb', petunias, verbenas, and those exotic-looking calceolarias gave full reign to the Victorians' liking for strident clashes of colour. The brilliant foliage of coleus produced a colourful contrast with the already brilliant bedding flowers.[51] There were 24 varieties of hollyhock to exhibit at shows, and 25 for mere 'garden decoration'.[52] The grand carpet-bedding designs of some large Victorian gardens depended on plentiful cheap labour as well as a supply of plants. A smaller version was the 'parterre', a carefully formal layout of low-growing plants.

❉

The Royal Horticultural Society, which had been founded by a group of gentlemen who met in Hatchards Bookshop in Piccadilly, ran flower shows in its Chiswick gardens from 1827 to 1857, where 'the principal part of the English aristocracy are present, and mix indiscriminately with the tradesman, the mechanic and the gardener'. Admission cost 3s 6d. 'There are omnibuses in abundance by which persons may be conveyed from the metropolis for 1s' – 'persons' being presumably the tradesmen, mechanics and gardeners, the aristocracy getting there in their own carriages. But by 1857 Chiswick had declined, so the chance to begin a new garden in Kensington was all the more opportune.[53] The triumph of the Great Exhibition encouraged Prince Albert to plan a garden (now the site of the Science Museum and Imperial College) in part of the 87 acres acquired by the Exhibition Commissioners, with the profits from the Exhibition. It was to be developed jointly by the Royal Horticultural Society and the Department of Science and Art.

Prince Albert took a personal interest in the details of the landscaping, even choosing the colour of the bricks, and donated several sculptures to it. It was opened by the Queen in 1861 and immediately became the height of fashion, especially during the two Great Shows every year, in May and July. There were parterres and bandstands, refreshment 'carts' (presumably mobile stalls) and a conservatory, and 4,000 feet of arcades.[54] The design was based on coloured gravels and clipped box, which would be as attractive winter and summer, as long as the box survived the weather and the gravel was not too dirty, with annual plantings in the summer.

It sounds to the modern taste fairly hideous – white spar from Derbyshire, purple fluorspar, grey Welsh slate, coloured glass and red brick, laid out in curlicues bordered with clipped box reminiscent of seventeenth-century knot gardens, with only a little space reserved for bedding plants. But the Victorian gardeners enjoyed violent colour contrasts. 'Orange and violet look well side by side in ... a lady's bonnet or dress ... and in a scheme of bedding.'[55] A review of the 1863 Spring Show remarked that 'in some classes the amateurs beat the nurserymen', but a quick look at the prize-winners dismisses the idea of a struggling backyard enthusiast: one winner was Miss (later Baroness) Burdett Coutts' gardener.[56] (The lease ran out in 1888. The RHS then moved to its present site at Wisley in Surrey. The first show to be held at Chelsea was in 1913.)

The opening show included a novelty which is still with us: a competition for floral table decoration. The Victorian dinner table included a space for a vase of flowers in the middle of its crowded surface, but as fashions changed and service 'à la Russe' became more general, the floral decoration was given more prominence. The outright winner in 1861 was a Mr March, with *three* épergnes (table-stands with display space at table level and higher up) the length of the table, decorated with ferns, forget-me-nots, rosebuds and 'small bunches of grapes introduced here and there'. A silver épergne was a standard piece of Victorian middle-class silverware, but Mr March's were made of glass, and the top bowl was balanced on a glass tube 2 feet high, creating a leafy canopy over the diners' heads. It caught the middle-class imagination, and replicas of Mr March's glass épergnes were on sale in St James's Street within a month.[57]

CHAPTER 13

Food

'Valuable suggestions respecting the cheapest and best kinds of food for those persons who are very poor' were included in W. B. Tegetmeier's *Manual of Domestic Economy*, first published in 1858.¹ He was a practical man, writing for 'female students in Training Institutions, and ... the elder classes in girls' schools'. His first suggestion recommends bread; 'a labourer should eat daily nearly 2lb, the wife and growing boys above ten years of age, 1¼ to 1½lb, and every child as much as it likes. If you are very poor, spend nearly all your money on bread.' According to Mayhew a piece of bread and an onion were a popular dinner for a labourer.² Then milk; 'every member of the family should, if possible, have 2 pints of new milk, skim milk or butter milk daily. With plenty of bread and milk, there will probably be health and strength, and no doctors' bills.'

Split peas and maize meal are healthy. 'Keep a pig if it be at all possible to get food for it' – which many very poor people did, in the basements and cellars and backyards of their crowded quarters. 'The cheapest butcher's meat is cow's cheek, sheep's head, liver, ox heart, and sometimes pig's head ... Eat a little meat every day, and do not eat nearly all of it on Saturday night and Sunday ... Buy bits of meat at 6d per lb, and fry them. [These must surely have been oddments of decent steak. To fry a cheap 'bit' would make it as tough as an old boot.] ... the cheapest cuts of meat are from the thick flank and round, at 7d and 7½d per lb. [These would need long, slow cooking.] Buy or beg uncooked bones for broth ... obtain as much dripping as possible from your richer neighbours [here he was perhaps unrealistic, since dripping, the 'kitchen stuff' that cooks sold to the dealers who called at the back door, had a commercial value] or buy it from the shop when its price does not exceed 7d per lb ... Tea is a very dear food ... if you are very poor, do not buy any tea, but spend your money in bread and skim milk. If you are less poor, drink tea only rarely, as on Sundays and special occasions.'

Tegetmeier gives basic instructions on cookery, such as 'there is less waste in boiling than in roasting food, and less in gently stewing than in boiling or roasting it'. Most poignantly – 'if you are very poor, and have not enough to eat, do not drink cold fluids'. The snag with his otherwise admirable suggestions is that they assume that you could resist having a family blow-out, within your limits, on Saturday night, and that the fire was always burning on which to stew meat and boil bones for broth. But at least he put his mind to the problems faced by the poor. His 'tables' were sold on single sheets at 8s per 100, presumably for distribution by those middle-class ladies who visited the poor. He was not alone in the field. In 1847 Alexis Soyer, the famous chef of the Reform Club, published a booklet called *Charitable Cookery or the Poor Man's Regulator*. He deplored waste – the peelings of vegetables, and the gizzards, heads and feet of fowls could all be used for soup. There was a lot of meat on a sheep's head, and the remains made good soup.

The wives of working men did their shopping at one of the hundreds of street markets, or stalls. If they had been domestic servants they would have some idea how to cook, but for others, 'something easily prepared, and carried off to the oven, is preferred'.[3] 'No-one had a cooking stove so the meat and some potatoes and a pudding were all put into one dish and taken to the bakehouse to be baked' in the baker's oven, still warm after he had finished baking his bread.[4] A small open fire could be used for frying or boiling, or the heat could be used by putting a piece of meat to dangle in front of it on a piece of string, turning it gently with an occasional push or, for the better-equipped, using a bottle jack or some form of Dutch oven (explained below). But cooking must often have been an anxious juggling of the cost of coal against the advantages of home cookery. It was no wonder that poor and working people often decided to buy food ready-cooked, from the street vendors and 'penny pie-shops', or food that did not need cooking, such as oysters at three for a penny, shrimps at a penny for a half-pint, and winkles.[5]

Watercress, very popular as a 'relish' with bread, is full of vitamins when hygienically grown, but as grown for the Victorians in sewage-enriched streams was full of germs. Until the discovery that cholera was a water-borne disease, any link between cress and cholera was unsuspected. Tegetmeier does not mention fish, which is odd, because it was the cheapest source of protein available, especially when Billingsgate Market was closing for the day. Middle-class visitors often commented on the pervasive smell of fish in poor people's rooms.

⁂

How did a middle-class housewife manage without a refrigerator? Staples such as rice and flour could, up to a point, be bought in bulk – always mindful of the vermin swarming in the kitchen. But – meat? fish? fresh vegetables? For special occasions she might buy some ice; there was a lane near Bishopsgate, in the City, where 'Ice [was] always for sale'.[6] She might make her own ice at home, mixing nitre and sal ammoniac bought from 'Mr Fuller of Jermyn Street, who likewise manufactures a useful freezing apparatus for making ice creams'.[7] But her normal routine would rely on the perishables she wanted being brought to her door when she wanted them.

Butchers' boys called for orders after breakfast, when the day's menus had been decided, and brought the meat round during the morning, in baskets, or trays on their heads – uncovered, and open to polluted air and bird droppings.[8] The idea of the family was sacrosanct, and a good selling-point for retailers; hence the shop signs that so puzzled me as a child – 'family butcher'. (Surely it was not a good idea to butcher your family?) Jane Carlyle reminisced how 'last Christmas another of our Chelsea Butchers ... regaled the public with the spectacle of a *living* prize-calf, on the breast of which (poor wretch) was branded ... "6d per lb" '.[9] Most meat was locally killed, but by 1860 Scottish beef and mutton was being sent from Inverness by rail.[10] In 1856 Eliza Acton recommended Jewish butchers; 'all meat supplied by [them] is sure to be of first-rate quality'[11] because of the hygiene laws enforced by the Sanhedrin.

For fish, Jane Carlyle relied on her local fishmonger, who was not a 'family fishmonger' but, even more confusingly, a 'wet and dry fish-monger'. The 'dry' fish were smoked. Mrs Beeton was unenthusiastic about Finnan haddock – 'esteemed by the Scotch a great delicacy. In London, an imitation of them is made by washing the fish over with pyroligneous acid and hanging it up in a dry place for a few days'.[12] One man told Mayhew he smoked almost any kind of fish, in his backyard, over ivy, wet firewood and sawdust, and sold them as Aberdeen 'finnan haddies'. Some fish were still alive when they arrived; the cook had to kill them. But at least 'skinning eels while alive is as unnecessary as [it is] cruel'.[13]

A cod's head was a good buy; 'almost every part is considered good eating except the eyes'.[14] A very grand household might sometimes need a turtle; the landlord of the London Tavern in Bishopsgate Street in the City 'always has on hand the largest and healthiest stock of living turtles in London. They will live in cellars for 3 months in excellent condition'[15] (which was why they had been so popular with sailors, who caught them and put them in the hold until needed). Salmon came down from Aberdeen by rail, packed in ice.

Fresh fruit and vegetables were the province of the costermongers, who would have their set rounds in the suburbs. 'Cowcumbers' (cucumbers) sold well until a rumour went round that they carried cholera. Fruit and vegetables were sold when they were at their best. The seasons for 'sparrow-grass' (asparagus) and fresh peas, strawberries and cherries were short, buy them while you could. It might be worth going into Covent Garden Market to choose vegetables and fruit, or Leadenhall Market for meat or poultry.

Jane Carlyle bought her groceries, meat, butter and eggs from local shops in Chelsea, but her tea and coffee from Fortnum and Mason in Piccadilly, that long-established firm which had displayed groceries at the Great Exhibition in 1851.[16] Charles Harrod had taken over a grocery shop in Knightsbridge in 1849, and did very well out of the Great Exhibition just along the road in Hyde Park. William Whiteley had been so impressed by the Great Exhibition that in 1863 he opened a shop in Bayswater, the newly fashionable 'Tyburnia' district. It gradually grew into a huge department store which he boasted was the 'Universal Provider'. The Post Office Supply Association, renamed the Civil Service Stores, was founded in 1864, by a group of Post Office clerks sharing half a chest of tea. It flourished, and opened its membership to all civil servants, selling mostly groceries in its shop in Victoria Street. (It moved to the Strand in 1877, expanding into a general department store, but closed after a fire in 1982.)[17]

Tinned food had been supplied to the Army since 1820, and to

Parry's Arctic expedition in 1824. Its usefulness in preserving food indefinitely was somewhat offset by the impossibility of opening the tin, until an American invented a tin-opener in 1858. You no longer had to use a hammer and chisel, or a bullet from a gun, to get at the miraculously preserved contents. The inventor of the tin-opener wrote that 'a child may use it without difficulty or risk', which, if true, probably meant that no-one else could make sense of it at all.[18] After a British patent of 1857 had developed the technique of ice-making in bulk, frozen meat was imported from Australia – good news for Australian exporters, who were no longer limited to wool and gold, which were not affected by climate, but bad news for English farmers.[19] After 1865, when the American Civil War ended, there was a huge increase in food imports, which brought 'a rapidly improving condition of the labouring classes'.[20]

One of the earliest brand names still familiar to us is Price's candles. In 1830 the company began to make candles from coconut oil imported from its plantation on Sri Lanka, as a much cheaper alternative to beeswax or spermaceti, but not smelling as bad as tallow. By 1840 every loyal subject of the Queen could celebrate the royal wedding by illuminating their front windows with Price's refined tallow and coconut oil candles. In 1847 Price's Patent Candle Company began buying palm oil for candles, from the African countries which had formerly sold slaves, and in the same year it diversified into nightlights. Jeremiah Coleman had been selling his mustard since 1814. In the 1840s Isaac Reckitt marketed his Imperial Wheaten Starch, which after energetic sales promotion he was able to advertise as 'supplied to the Emperor of all the Russias', as well as to the Emperor Louis Napoleon III. The firm of Reckitt & Coleman also marketed washing blue to put in the white laundry to get a good colour, black lead for polishing grates, and Silvo and Brasso for polishing metals.[21] Lea & Perrins' Worcester Sauce has been around since the 1830s (the world-famous HP Sauce came after 1870). Goddard's 'non-mercurial' polish for silver and silver plate had been available since 1839, which was reassuring to those whose household silver was all plated; the thin layer of silver had a disconcerting way of disappearing under some polishes.

In 1847 the first chocolate bar arrived, made by Fry's. Cadbury's was given a royal warrant for supplying chocolates to her Majesty in 1854, and twelve years later perfected a liquid Cocoa Essence. Huntley & Palmer's biscuits, sold in 10lb tins, were in every grocer's shop from the 1860s. McDougall's flour saved the cook the chore of sieving the flour she used, from 1864 onwards. Campbell's tinned soups were available from 1869. Cross & Blackwell marketed the great Alexis Soyer's sauces for him, and he was not above recommending bottled mushroom ketchup and Harvey's sauce. If you are exhausted by this lightning trip round a Victorian kitchen, how about a pink gin? – the 'pink' being Angostura bitters, first made in 1824 and 'extremely popular', according to the label 'for use in soft drinks, cocktails and other alcoholic beverages. It also imparts an exquisite flavour to soup ... stewed prunes ... [and] plum pudding.'

The adulteration of food was becoming a scandal. Pickles were a prolific source of food poisoning; 'in numerous instances those which are sold to the public have been found to be of so deadly a nature as to be eminently dangerous'.[22] Bread, so recommended as a labourer's staple diet, often contained chalk to whiten it, potato flour if it was cheaper than wheat flour, and alum to enable inferior grain to be used. I have never come across a case of alum poisoning; it probably did not do much harm in small quantities, but it just was not wheat flour.[23] Perhaps more relevant was the fact that bakers often kneaded bread with their feet ...[24] In 1860 the Aerated Bread Company began marketing bread made without yeast; quite why is not clear to me unless it was to avoid the bakers' feet. The ABC teashops quickly became a familiar feature of London. Also in 1860, an Act for Preventing the Adulteration of Articles of Food and Drink was passed, but it was permissive, not mandatory – local authorities could adopt it or not, as they pleased. The City did adopt it, but by 1869 'nothing has come of it'.[25]

Every picture of a Victorian kitchen includes a gleaming set of graduated copper pans, a *batterie de cuisine*. But they could be as dangerous as any adulterated food, if they were not cared for. As Mrs Beeton observed, 'people are often taken ill after eating food that has been cooked in copper saucepans'.[26] The outside layer of a copper pan conducts heat well, but copper should not be in contact with food, which is why copper pans are lined with tin. This wears off, with long use or over-enthusiastic cleaning, so it has to be renewed regularly. One of the first things Alexis Soyer did when he arrived in the Crimea in 1854 was to inspect the huge copper vessels used for cooking, in Florence Nightingale's hospital at Scutari. As he feared, there was 'not an atom of tin' on them; they were all, promptly, re-tinned.[27] Iron saucepans did not look so pretty but were much safer.

The famous kitchens that M. Soyer, that irrepressible chef, writer and inventor, designed for the Reform Club in 1841 used coal and steam, meticulously planned for the greatest economy of fuel and the smallest waste of heat. They were one of the sights of London for members and their wives.[28] Most middle-class kitchens were going over to cooking on enclosed cookers or 'ranges' instead of an open fire. Old habits die hard: many designs incorporated a provision of spit-roasting in front of the fire bars, which is a different process from the 'roasting' we do in our ovens, where the meat is enclosed and baked. (No wonder barbecues are so popular.) In 1851 M. Soyer designed a 'Modern Housewife's Kitchen Apparatus, containing an open roasting fire, a hot water boiler, a baking oven, a broiling [grilling] stove, a hot plate, all heated by one fire, height 2ft 4ins, width 2 ft, length 3 ft'. The 'hot plate' or hob looked exactly like the top of an Aga, with adjustable rings for pans. The smoke went under the floor into the existing chimney. There was a removable (I think; the illustration is not clear, but otherwise it would have been appallingly in the way when not being used, and M. Soyer was eminently practical) bottle jack on the hob, an ingenious arrangement whereby a clockwork cylinder on an adjustable arm fixed to the hob turned a hook regularly to and fro, from which the joint hung as near, or as far away from, the fire as you wanted.

Bottle jacks were used on open fires as well as on ranges like Soyer's, and they could be combined with a Dutch oven: a shell-shaped metal hood which stood in front of the open fire, with a hook from which the joint hung, and a dripping-pan on its floor. The heat was reflected from the curved inner sides, which had to be kept clean and shining. An elaboration of the design enabled plates to be warmed at the back. Soyer's literary output included a book of domestic advice for the middle-class woman with a 'rather small' kitchen 'only 12 ft by 18 ft'. A typical touch – the two kitchen dressers (arrangements of shelves against the wall, with one deep drawer at waist height) did not have the usual cupboards under the drawers, where anything could be stowed out of sight. The dripping-pan, frying-pan and gridiron (for grilling) were on open view; 'nothing is hid from the sight, therefore they cannot but be clean'.[29] In the Carlyles' kitchen, the pots and pans were stowed there – and that compartment was painted black. M. Soyer would not have approved.[30]

The 'usual offices' of the ideal kitchen would include a scullery with a cold tap, for messy work such as cleaning vegetables and washing pots; a pantry where china and glass was kept; and a larder, preferably built on an outside wall facing north, with slate shelves, for storing perishable food. There might even be one of 'Ling's Patent ice-safes' there.[31] But kitchens were not always ideal, and all these functions might well be crammed into one inconvenient, poorly lit, badly planned, unventilated basement room, where the servant often had to find a space for her bed at night.[32]

Coal was the usual fuel, delivered through a hole in the pavement covered with a movable iron plate, direct into the coal cellar. (The pavements of Chelsea are still punctuated by these round plates, no longer movable.) Opinion was divided about cooking by gas. 'Some persons have been so sanguine as to suppose that this employment of gas may soon do away altogether with the necessity of open fires in our kitchens ... It cannot be expected to succeed except in the hands of persons whose scientific knowledge enables them to employ it with safety.'[33] But by 1851 M. Soyer thought that 'from the cheapness and cleanliness of the process [it] is likely to become a great favourite'.[34]

At least lighting the stove was less troublesome since Bryant & May began to market their machine-made matches, in 1861. 'Safety Matches' had to be struck on a special strip on the matchbox, whereas 'Strike Anywhere' matches could be ignited by friction on any rough surface. In damp conditions they kept better than safety matches, but they had one drawback: the vapour emitted during manufacture could cause 'phossy-jaw' (necrosis of the jaw) if the worker, usually a girl, had decayed teeth, allowing the phosphorous fumes to penetrate to her jaw-bone.

So, the range is drawing well and the daily orders have arrived. What next? Most cooks probably knew their repertoire without needing to check it in a printed book. But where the mistress wanted to try something new, to impress her friends, she would reach for one of the many cookery books and monthly magazines on the market – or tell the cook to do so. Mrs Beeton's *Book of Household Management* (1861) became the most famous, but she had many competitors. Eliza Acton's *Modern Cookery for Private Families* came out in 1856. She begins with the comforting suggestion that 'the fashionable dishes of the day may at all times be procured from an able confectioner'. She confines herself to explaining 'the first rudiments of the art ... plain English dishes'. She would have done better to stick to her own advice, when it came to a recipe for that delicious Swiss speciality, fondue, which she describes as a 'cheese soufflé', which would horrify any decent Swiss.[35] After her promise to keep to plain English recipes, she branches into curries ('curried oysters: let a hundred of large sea-oysters be opened ...'); and she gives a West Indian recipe for roast 'tomatas'. Many soldiers had by then served in India, Afghanistan and Burma, as well as the Jamaica garrison, and they would relish a reminder of the old days.

Eliza Acton has a curious recipe for 'The Lord Mayor's soup': stew, for five hours, 'two sets of moderately sized pigs' ears and feet, from which the hair has been carefully removed ...'. Another recipe for the same soup uses 'half a fine calf's head with the skin on'. If the fish has got a bit high, 'chloride of soda will restore [it] to a tolerable eatable state if it be not very much overkept'.[36] In her recipe for whitebait I noticed for the first time that odd usage still favoured by cookery writers: *throw* the fish into a cloth, and then *throw* it into deep fat. I cannot be the only cook with remarkably poor aim. Why do we have to keep throwing things about? One of her more outlandish recipes was for calf's ears, which are 'usually filled with forcemeat, or a preparation of the brains, and placed upright when dished, and the upper part is cut into narrow fringe-like strips'.

Some ingenuity was needed for spit-roasting a suckling pig: to avoid the middle bit being burnt before the end bits are done, hang a large flat-iron in the centre of the grate. Disciples of a modern cookery writer would be delighted to find that 'the very simple process [of boiling an egg] demands a certain degree of care'. Neither Acton nor Mrs Beeton used a recipe I noticed in one number of *The Magazine of Domestic Economy* for 1843: sparrows, 'which make an excellent pudding with a beefsteak ... or a delicious pastry'. Larks, too, were 'among our greatest delicacies', so were lapwings; and plover's eggs, which were usually boiled but sometimes eaten raw. Caviar cost 15s a cask of 3lb, from Mr Ball's Italian Warehouse in New Bond Street.[37]

Mrs Beeton had

always thought that there is no more fruitful source of family disc
than a housewife's badly-cooked dinners and untidy ways. Men
now so well served out of doors – at their clubs, well-ordered tavei
and dining-houses, that in order to compete with the attractions
these places, a mistress must be thoroughly acquainted with the theory
and practice of cookery . . .[38]

One feels, reading the finished work, that she might have spared
herself the trouble of tracing the history of cooking – 'Man, in his
primitive state, lives upon roots and the fruits of the earth . . .' – and
describing Lord Hastings's herd of Canadian wapiti. Certainly one's
cook should be able to astonish the neighbours, once she has read
past the educational small print and identified a suitable recipe, but
there was no need for her to be erudite. Both the cooking time and
the cost are included in each recipe, which must have annoyed many
a cook hoping to inflate the cost and keep the difference.

Mrs Beeton sets out 'Bills of Fare' for each month, from 'dinner
for 18 persons' to 'plain family dinners'. Her table settings are arranged
in what was becoming the old-fashioned way, with several dishes on
the table at one time. If you wanted something out of your reach you
had to ask a fellow-diner to give you some, or do without. These
meals assumed a vast selection of food. When Mrs Beeton gets to
'dinners à la Russe' she describes them as differing from 'normal'
dinners. 'In a dinner à la Russe the dishes are cut up on a sideboard,
and handed round to the guests . . .'. But her menus still called for a
huge number of dishes. A dinner for November suggests two soups,
six kinds of fish, *fourteen* miscellaneous fish and meat dishes, then three
kinds of game, and seven puddings. As each appeared over your
shoulder, you gracefully waved it away until you arrived, with luck,
at what you really wanted, if there was still time; these meals must
have lasted for hours. 'Dinners à la Russe are scarcely suitable for
small establishments; a large number of servants being required to
carve, and help the guests . . . Where, however, [it] is practicable,
there is perhaps no mode of serving a dinner so enjoyable as this.'

The evening meal was the cook's apotheosis. Sir William Hardman
gave a dinner for eight, in 1863. The menu – all in French except for
the Cabinet Pudding and the anchovy toast – began with turtle soup
and went on through turbot, six assorted meat dishes, a lobster vol-
au-vent, and several vegetables, through puddings and a savoury,
coming to a full stop with raspberry cream and orange water ices. A

little later he threw a more modest party, with only six courses, Cabinet Pudding (again; it must have been an easy one for the cook) and cheese. The cost of private entertaining could be surprisingly low. Charles Pugh, an official in the Law Courts, gave two consecutive dinner parties, each for eighteen guests, for a total cost of £22, including fourteen bottles of wine for £3 10s, and 'plants' for 6s.[39]

There were no pre-dinner drinks. You stood, or sat, for 30 minutes until you processed in a stately way, according to precedence, in pairs like Noah's animals, into the dining room. 'In genteel society the half hour before dinner is generally accepted as a time of unlimited boredom and social frigidity.'[40] Eliza Acton did give a recipe for mint julep –

strip the tender leaves of mint into a tumbler and add as much wine, brandy or other spirit as you wish. Put some pounded ice into a second tumbler, pour it on to the brandy and mint [and go on pouring, from glass to glass] then place the glass in a larger one containing pounded ice: on taking it out it will be covered with frost-work. Observation: we apprehend that this preparation is, like most other iced American beverages, to be imbibed through a reed [straw, to us]. The receipt, which was contributed by an American gentleman, is somewhat vague.

– but she did not say when the American gentleman partook of it. It sounds just the thing to have got a party going.

When dinner was to all intents and purposes over, the hostess collected the eyes of the female guests, who were on the lookout for this, and they all rustled out, leaving the men to tell dirty stories, talk politics, smoke cigars, and enjoy some of their host's fine wine and liqueurs. The bad old eighteenth-century habits of prolonged male post-prandial drunkenness had gone, with the cupboard full of chamber pots which were a necessary part of it. Quite soon the gentlemen came to join the ladies, for coffee.

In Eliza Acton's words, 'there is no beverage which is held in more universal esteem than good coffee, and none in this country which is obtained with greater difficulty'. She suggests leaving it to settle for ten minutes, and if it is not clear by then, add a clean egg shell, but 'never use mustard to fine coffee with'. Alexis Soyer agreed that 'it is a very remarkable fact that but few persons in England know how to make good coffee'. His method was to heat the ground coffee in a saucepan, pour boiling water over it, strain it after five minutes, and reheat.[41] Simple, surely. In 1844 Thomas Webster referred to 'Platow's Patent Filterer', which seems to have been constructed on the same principles as a Cona coffee machine.[42] (My grandfather used one, at table: a terrifying process, involving a small spirit lamp, a hollow glass tube up which boiling water rushed, into a receptacle containing ground coffee at the top which it filled but never over-filled, although we used to wait with bated breath.) Webster also mentioned 'an essence of coffee [which] may be purchased ... the taste is somewhat peculiar'. Can this have been the unlamented Camp Coffee, a dark brown liquid in a tall bottle with a label showing an Army officer being served by a turbaned servant, presumably in camp? The taste was indeed peculiar.

Sir William's diary for 1863 notes 'fish knives for the first time'.[43] This, like so many events in Victorian life, was redolent of class. If your family had owned its table silver since Georgian days, when fishes were dealt with by two forks, or one fork and a piece of bread, your canteen of silver would not include fish knives. On the other hand, they were handy for eating fish, and they were fashionable, but only among the *nouveaux riches.* So solve the quandary as best you could. In general the Victorian dinner table was loaded with a plethora of eating-implements, all of which could terrify a shy entrant on the social scene: dessert knives and forks, asparagus holders, lobster picks, oyster knives ... as well as the silver épergne and countless silver dishes and bonbonnières, tea sets and coffee sets, enough to keep any housemaid busy. There was even a feeling that finger bowls scented with rosewater were more civilised than linen table napkins, which implied that you were a messy eater.

The normal household routine was likely to be much as Alexis Soyer described in his *The Modern Housewife* of 1851. 'Mrs B' had two maids, a cook, a housemaid and a coachman. 'We are what is called early risers, that is, Mr B is obliged to leave home every work day at 20 past 9. Our breakfast is on the table at 8.30.' Mrs B makes the coffee, and they have eggs or cold meat 'and Mr B sometimes has a cutlet ... which I cook myself at the table with my newly-invented [by Soyer, of course] magic lamp-stove'. Then Mr B leaves for work, in the brougham, which comes back for Mrs B to use. Mrs B writes the menus for the nursery meals, luncheon and dinner and sends them down to the cook. At 10 Mrs B goes down to the kitchen herself and sorts out with the cook what is needed for that day. 'I always get my toilet finished by 12. I then have an hour to write notes or see tradesmen or my dressmaker, and on Monday mornings check and pay my tradesmen's accounts.' She sometimes 'assists the cook' on some new dish. The afternoon is a similar whirl of activity. Mr B comes home by cab or bus, by twenty to five, and at half past five they dine, waited on by the maids. 'If there is no company, the children and the governess come down after dinner. If we have company we do not see them.' The children go to bed at a quarter to eight. 'We have tea and coffee at eight. If there is no company the governess comes and passes the rest of the evening with us. Eleven is our usual hour of retiring, before which Mr B likes his glass of negus and a biscuit or a sandwich.' Soyer sets the B's dinner rather early. The middle class was more likely to dine at six, or soon after.[44]

Mr B was probably not all that hungry for dinner at 5.30, having enjoyed a good midday meal at a coffee house or chop house in the City[45] or Bertolini's famous restaurant in Leicester Square.[46] Jane Carlyle sometimes treated herself to lunch out when the painters were making her home uninhabitable. She went to Verey's, in the Strand, 'a clean-looking shop ... where I had half a roast chicken (which was very small indeed) a large slice of warm ham, and three new potatoes, for a shilling ... I see single women besides myself at Vereys' – not improper [i.e. they were not prostitutes] – governesses and the like'.[47] This was a significant step for women, to trespass on premises which had so far been exclusively male.

Nathaniel Hawthorne enjoyed a chop – 'very good' – with bread and two potatoes, and a glass of brandy-and-water, in a tavern, for 11d, with 1d to the waiter.[48] W. S. Bell, in London to see the Great Exhibition, lunched with his brother, an official in the Law Courts, at a chop house off the Strand. The menu included 'a dish of fish with sauce' for 1s, half a dish for 6d, rump steak with oyster sauce for 1s, 'greens, potatoes or carrots' for 1d, bread and butter for 1d and Stilton cheese for 2d. The prices, again carefully noted, out at Knightsbridge but within easy walking distance of the Exhibition, were, surprisingly, much the same, although what you got for a 'sandwich' for 3d was not detailed. In neither place did the Bell brothers tip the waiter; perhaps it was not expected.[49]

But dining out in a restaurant, in the evening, was a very different thing. You could expect to pay 5 guineas at a top-price restaurant, or just 2s at one of the many taverns that cooked joints to be ready every quarter or half hour, from 5 o'clock until 7, and charged 2s a head.[50] The most famous catering establishment was Soyer's 'Gastronomic Symposium of all Nations' in Lady Blessington's former house in

Kensington Gore, opposite the Great Exhibition.[51] Lady Blessington had been a famous – or notorious – society hostess, rarely out of the newspapers, until her creditors caught up with her and she had to sell up and leave for France with her lover, Count d'Orsay. In 1850 Soyer, who had by then resigned from his post in the Reform Club, leased her house, thinking he could make his fortune in it.[52] He always had big ideas, from fixing a peacock's tail on the dish in which 'the fowl' is cooked, in large families 'where peacocks are plentiful', to cooking soup for 22,000 poor people at a time. This time Soyer bit off more than he could chew, which was a shame because it sounds such fun. Lady Blessington's idea of interior decoration, which had been sumptuous in the extreme, gave him a start, and he bought still more land for a 'Monster Pavilion of All Nations' ('monster' in those days just meant 'mammoth', to us) modelled on the medieval castles of the Rhine; a vast tent where 1,500 could eat at the same time, for only a shilling. Dignitaries such as the Duke of Wellington and Disraeli dined inside the house. The gardens, which Lady Blessington had made magnificent, were used for entertainments, concerts and the ever-popular balloon ascents. There was a Hall of Architectural Wonders, a Transatlantic Chamber supplying every kind of American beverage (mint juleps?), la Salle des Noces de Danäe, and a wonderful staircase decorated with portraits of famous people such as Pitt, Disraeli, Napoleon and Dickens, wreathed in hippogriffs, giraffes, elephants and dragons.[53]

About 1,000 visitors came every day, sometimes in pre-booked parties of 200 bemused country people who had gone round the Great Exhibition, shepherded by their parson, and were only too glad to sit down, which they had not been able to do in the Crystal Palace.[54] From a handbill preserved by that indefatigable tourist W. S. Bell:

> French/English dinner at 2s each ... in the baronial hall, dinner, Anglo-Français, 3s 6d ... joints (hot) every quarter of an hour from 2 until 8. In the mansion, tables d'hôte à la Français, 5, 6, 7 and 8 pm for 6s 6d. Admission 1s which is allowed upon dinners and other refreshments.

But – 'I was however disappointed with the place. It did not come up to my expectations.'[55] It was a wild success at first, but somehow the glittering gilt faded. The last straw was a disapproving visit by the licensing authority, on a particularly crowded night. It closed down at the same time as the Great Exhibition, in October 1851. Soyer had lost £7,000.

CHAPTER 14

Clothes and So On

❧

The very poor · working men · smock frocks · second-hand clothes · Moses and Son · top hats · men's coats · trousers · shirts · smoking-jackets · rainwear and umbrellas · underwear · facial hair · baths · women's wear · the bodice · the skirt · footwear · the crinoline · petticoats · tight lacing · drawers · shawls · dress-makers · sewing machines · ready-made clothes · paper patterns · cosmetics · hair · children

The shivering waifs standing outside refuges and workhouses hoping for admission wore what they could. Even there, they clung to the worn-out symbols of respectability: a woman wore a bonnet, no matter how dilapidated, and a man wore the remains of a hat on his head. Where the parish workhouse insisted on work such as stone-breaking being done before relief could be paid, there were often 'infatuated individuals who so tenaciously assert their right to wear, even in a stone-yard, those badges of respectability, the tall hat and the black coat,' despite their hopelessly tattered condition.[1] The black coat of a middle-class man spiralled down through many hands before it finally disintegrated. 'The English carpenter wears a black tail-coat – like the waiters, the undertakers and the Duke ... [a lemonade-vendor's] dress is that of a prosperous middle-class man – gone to shreds and patches'.[2]

A discharged convict leaving prison must have looked misleadingly honest, as long as he wore the clothes he was discharged in – corduroy trousers and waistcoat and a black 'billycock' hat, a kind of low-crowned bowler. No wonder most men exchanged these glaringly clean garments for cash, and comfortably worn, anonymous clothes, as soon as they were out of sight of the prison.[3] But the prison authorities had correctly gauged the dress of a working man. The hundreds leaving the workmen's train at Victoria station wore heavy boots, thick trousers and jackets, waistcoats, and caps or billycock hats. Even there, some tall hats could be seen in the crowd, but they were likely to be either well past their best, if they had begun as silk hats, or the same shape but covered with tough varnished canvas. Working men in uniform, such as scarlet-jacketed postmen and blue-uniformed policemen, wore these tall hats. At work, skilled artisans wore square paper caps, such as the carpenter wore in Tenniel's illustration to the song of the Walrus and the Carpenter in *Alice through the Looking Glass*. A mere labourer would be bare-headed.

Ancient 'smock frocks' could still be seen on the streets of London. They were a practical form of dress for country working men, made of heavy linen, very long-wearing and almost waterproof. Dustmen wore them as 'best', when they came to the Dustman's Tea Party (see page 67 above),[4] and the rare milkmen wore them on their rounds, looking like model ploughmen, or like the real rustics who so intrigued the Londoners when they came to the Great Exhibition in shepherded groups, the men wearing clean smock frocks. Costermongers selling game and dairy products wore smock frocks on their rounds,[5] but other street sellers went in for flashier ensembles: a cloth cap, a waistcoat with big pockets, trousers tight at the knees and flaring over the boots, and a neckerchief, called a 'Kingsman'.[6]

Costerwomen wore a black velveteen or straw bonnet trimmed with ribbons or flowers, a silk Kingsman, and a printed cotton gown short enough to show their much-prized boots. On Sundays and holidays the costers made an elegant show, the men in brown cloth trousers trimmed with braid, and tall beaver hats, and the women in brightly patterned gowns and new shawls.[7] Every woman wore a shawl, even poor women, even in the summer, though perhaps not many of them were as ingenious as Hannah Culwick, who cut one shawl in half diagonally for the summer, and sewed the halves together again for the winter.

'Every newspaper carries the advertisements of dealers who will come to your house and buy your part-worn clothes'.[8] These advertisements were aimed at the middle-class readers. The dealers would probably unload their stock in the second-hand markets or 'clothes exchanges'.[9] If the previous wearers had been poor themselves, their clothes had been worn for years, rarely washed and never cleaned. 'The stench of the old clothes is positively overpowering'.[10] There were two main 'exchanges'. The one in the Petticoat Lane district, near Liverpool Street station, sold wholesale and retail, 'to anyone, shopkeeper, artisan, clerk, costermonger or gentleman'. Most of the wholesale purchases ended up in Ireland. The other one, in Seven Dials near Leicester Square, specialised in boots and shoes, laid out in sorry rows on the pavement, wrinkled and down-at-heel. Two thousand men and boys found employment in 'translating' them, making them almost as good as new, if there were not too many holes in them.[11]

'Inner wear' (a logical contrast to 'outer wear': to us, underwear) especially flannel waistcoats and drawers, sold well, even if they were patched – the patches would not show. Women's wear was usually sold 'as is', the wearer counting on altering it to fit where needed. There was not much demand for second-hand stays, but a market woman might invest as much as 4s 6d in a fur tippet, as a practical way of keeping her shoulders warm. Fur boas, more glamorous but not so warm, went only slowly.[12] Old silk hats always sold well. They could be refurbished and reblocked, with care and skill. A Jewish 'old clo' man' was always shown in cartoons – he was a stock figure for Disraeli – wearing a pile of hats on top of his own; as he bought them on his rounds, he put them on his head, both as a badge of his trade, and to keep them safe.

E. Moses and Son had opened in the East End in 1832, selling ready-made cheap clothing for the working class.[13] By 1851 the shop in Aldgate was a vast emporium, still selling clothes for 'mechanics', such as a coat for 4s and corduroy trousers for 3s, but also catering for a higher level of trade.[14] 'Dress coats' (the top of a three-piece suit) cost from £1 to £2 6s, tartan waistcoats 'in every clan' only 4s 9d, and there was 'an elegant assortment of summer trousers' from 4s 6d, buckskin or doeskin costing 7s 6d or 10s 6d. 'Mourning... may be had at 5 minutes' notice', a man's mourning suit for £1 12s 6d, or a 'superior ditto' for £3. Silk hats varied from 2s 6d up to 5s 6d for a 'very fine' one.

Men's shoes and boots (called Wellingtons, but made of leather, not rubber; their point was that they could be pulled on in a hurry, not laced) cost from 4s to 9s 6d, ladies' boots only 3s, with the more fashionable satin and kid at 4s 6d or 4s 9d. Ladies could buy their shawls and parasols there, but not dresses. 'Those who prefer being measured will find the bespoke department conspicuous for its advantages'. Many upper-class customers patronised these 'advantages', but 'when the trowser [sic] buttons were stamped with the name of the firm we used to have the garments returned to have other buttons put on them'.[15]

Since the Moses family was Jewish, 'this establishment is closed every Friday evening at sunset until Saturday evening sunset, when business is resumed until 12 oclock [midnight]'. During the short winter days this meant a considerable loss of trade. The late Saturday opening was made possible by a galaxy of lamps, even 'one of the first installations of electric light for shop purposes'.[16] That well-patronised institution Moss Bros can trace its history back to 1860, when Moses Moses began selling second-hand clothes from a barrow. Two of his grandsons opened a business in King Street, Covent Garden trading as Moss Brothers, hiring out men's clothes. The firm still flourishes, on the same site and in many branches.

The Victorian middle-class urban male wore a tall hat, a coat, waistcoat and trousers, with an overcoat in cold weather. Any picture of a crowd is punctuated by these black cylinders. Dickens deplored the 'hermetically sealed, black, stiff chimney-pot, a foot and a half high [he exaggerated slightly], which we call a hat'.[17] They were hot, uncomfortable and unpractical. Although Moses and Son's top price was 5s 6d, they could cost more than twice that amount.[18] But 'every person of any respectability takes care to appear in public in a good hat'.[19] From about 1840 the tall hat was almost universal.[20]

A silk 'topper' is made of silk plush sewn on to a stiff blocked base made of canvas. It needs as much care as a small pet, stroking it the right way to restore the nap if it has been treated roughly, and dried gently with a silk cloth if an umbrella has failed to protect it from rain. 'An economical gentleman never puts his hat down on the crown', always on the brim.[21] To an observant eye its shape changed, season by season – higher (8 inches) or slightly lower (6 inches), a curly brim or a flat one, a straight cylinder or a waisted shape; but as long as the magic object was on your head, you passed as respectable. The captains of steamboats on the river wore them, and sometimes even the deckhands.[22] The conductors of omnibuses wore them. The crowds of clerks coming into the City by steamer and omnibus wore them. In pictures of men at work, the gentlemen and supervisors can immediately be distinguished from the workers by their headgear. Brunel, who was a sartorial mess on-site, wore a top hat, no matter how unpractical; it was simply taken for granted.

There were occasional variations. In the early 1840s versions in straw, felt or beaver, which could be 'sometimes as rough as a Scotch terrier' were still available, in fawn or white.[23] But in the 1850s black silk plush swamped its competitors.[24] The story of Müller the murderer has been told in the chapter on railways, but I will repeat it here because it concerns the victim's top hat. The murderer had taken it to a hatter to be altered and shortened to fit him, and although it had the victim's name in it, the murderer, astonishingly, kept it, and it was found in his luggage when he was arrested in New York. The lower hats that were just coming into fashion became known as 'Müller cut-downs'.

Top hats could be a risk, in the wrong surroundings. There was a fire at Her Majesty's Theatre in the Haymarket, which drew a huge crowd of onlookers. Four middle-class men wearing, naturally, top hats, were set on by some toughs in the crowd, who 'knocked my friends' tall hats over their eyes and tried to pull open their overcoats [to get at their pockets]'. But the thieves got more than they bargained for, when the four top-hatted swells took them on with their fists, in 'the circular space that, in spite of the tremendous crush, was immediately cleared and which the blazing theatre rendered as light as day' – a much more exciting spectacle than a mere fire.[25]

Some improvements in top hats were patented, from time to time, but never took on. In 1855 a patent was registered for a movable crown which could be opened or closed 'at pleasure', by rods which lifted the top of the hat to reveal a perforated strip. A Frenchman addressed the same problem in 1870, by lifting the brim instead, to 'protect the wearer from solar heat'.[26] Bowlers became acceptable for informal occasions, in the 1860s.[27] But most middle-class men persisted in their martyrdom to the tall silk hat, come rain or shine.

There was only one place where top hats, no matter how respectable, were agreed to be impossible: the opera. Here, men wore a gibus, a hat the same shape as a top hat, but made of unblocked black cloth, with springs inside it, collapsible into a flat cowpat-shaped circle, which could be tucked under one arm. When the right moment came, a smart blow of the brim against the back of the stall activated the springs with a loud bang and hey presto! A top hat, almost.

Coats were either 'frock' coats, with a marked waist and a skirt with straight edges to about knee level, in dark blue or black; or, from the 1850s, 'tail' coats in which the front of the body was uncovered from waist level and the coat tails curved to meet at the back. From 1860 tail coats in black became the normal evening wear for middle-class men, and can still occasionally be seen – a long reign.[28] An evening coat, trousers and waistcoat cost nearly £7 from a fashionable tailor.[29] Young men might shock the older generation by wearing jackets, which had gradually become respectable by 1870.

Pockets could be in the coat tails, which were vulnerable to pickpockets, or in the side seams of trousers. Pickpocketing was rife. A tool with a three-way grip that could be inserted into pockets, especially in crowded places such as omnibuses or railway stations, cost only 10s, and was less noticeable than a slash with a knife. To foil the thieves, various 'pocket protectors' were patented, usually involving reinforcing the pocket with steel sheet, with a spring holding it shut, which must surely have disturbed the smooth hang of the trousers. Perhaps that was why they did not take on. A gentleman's watch was carried in another pocket, usually in the waistcoat – wrist watches had not yet been invented. As it was pulled out to see the time, the thief could mark where it was, and try for it – perhaps by creating a disturbance, as was done to the four boxing swells above. There were many patents designed to keep watches safe.[30]

Trousers were white, fawn or pale grey, until the 1860s when the three-piece suit in one cloth became normal. Until the mid-1850s they were held 'in tension' by straps under the instep. There was a brief, and to our eyes ludicrous, fashion, in the late 1850s for 'peg top' trousers, the legs widening at hip level into fullness which was pleated into the waistband. Buttoned fly fronts were usual.[31] Trousers were held up by braces, which, surprisingly, offered prim Victorian ladies too shy to refer to trousers except as 'inexpressibles' a chance to exercise their embroidery skills. They 'form a necessary adjunct to a gentleman's wardrobe and they are generally pleased to have them prettily worked' – or at least so they said.[32]

Colours for men were increasingly subdued. Jane Carlyle described the famous dandy, Count d'Orsay, when he called on her in 1840, 'as gay in his colours as a humming bird'. Five years later 'he was all in black and brown – a black satin cravat, a brown velvet waiscoat, a brown coat ... lined with velvet of its own shade, and almost black trousers, one breast-pin, a large pear-shaped pearl set into a little cup of diamonds, and only one fold of gold chain round his neck ... with one magnificent turquoise'.[33] The fronts of waistcoats could be embroidered, or made of rich stuff, until the dark three-piece suit became *de rigueur* in the 1860s. A white waistcoat could relieve this all-over black, in the evening, or for weddings. A slight relaxation could be indulged in, for the uniforms of the Volunteer force raised during the emergency of 1859 when a French invasion looked possible. Even then, a deep grey or green suit modelled on a gentleman's country wear was as far as they went, but their headgear could be more exotic, such as a tall helmet or 'shako' adorned with cocks' plumes.[34] The regular Army enlivened the scene in scarlet tunics.

Shirts were often made at home. It gave those unemployed Victorian ladies something to do, unless they preferred to 'put out' the making, for 3s or 4s. A shirt should be long enough to come to mid-thigh. Simple-to-follow diagrams and directions were given in a series run by a popular magazine.[35] For evening, the front was frilled. Separate collars, standing up stiffly with a wide gap between the square-cut points, were attached to the back of the shirt neckband by a stud. Some men liked to wear them as high as mid-cheek, giving them an unavoidably disdainful look, others could turn their necks over the jaw-high collar. The necktie varied between a mere band of black or coloured silk tied in a bow, and a cravat of stiff silk fixed in place by a gold – often jewelled – pin.[36]

The new fashion for smoking necessitated a smoking-jacket and a smoking-cap, to keep the smell of tobacco away from other clothes. They could be highly decorative, as could the 'dressing-gowns' worn about the house. Thomas Carlyle, devoted to fresh air and draughts but not to elegance, wore a magnificent draught-excluding one in the picture of the Carlyles painted in 1857.[37] Men's boots were Wellingtons, with a straight plain top, or Hessians with a curved top, both to below the knee. Elastic-sided boots had been on the market since 1837, and buttoned boots from the 1860s. Lace-up shoes came in during the 1840s.[38]

Rain was a constant risk to clothes. The equivalent of a plastic raincoat was shown at the Great Exhibition – a 'water-proof paletot [overcoat] so slight that they may be put in a small case and carried in the pocket'.[39] The trouble with these marvellous inventions is that we have no way of knowing how many of them were sold. I have not met any other reference to what sounds a most useful garment. Another exhibitor was Bax & Co., with their 'Aquascutum' shower-proof wool fabric, which could be made into a cloak or cape. Mr Mackintosh of Glasgow had developed a completely waterproof fabric using 'India-rubber' as long ago as 1823, but it had the disadvantage of any impermeable fabric: it certainly kept out the rain, but it kept in the sweat and became horridly uncomfortable and smelly.

For the city-dweller, an umbrella was essential. The steel-ribbed umbrella frame had been patented by Samuel Fox in 1850. According to Mayhew, writing in 1861, 'not so many years ago the use of an umbrella by a man was regarded as partaking of effeminacy, but now they are sold in thousands in the streets'.[40] James Smith & Co. was founded in 1830, and moved to its present premises in New Oxford Street in 1867, selling walking-sticks, canes, umbrellas and parasols. (It has a superlative Victorian shop frontage.) If you did not wish to buy yet another umbrella, having a collection of them at home, you could hire one from the London Umbrella Company, 4s deposit, 4d for three hours – surely the rain would have stopped by then? – or 9d for 24 hours, returnable at any of the company's 'stations' throughout London.[41] Galoshes or 'India-rubber overalls' – overshoes – were gradually arriving from America. No matter how careful you were, your trousers would be quickly dirty in those filthy streets, despite the best efforts of the crossing-sweepers. 'Scouring' or dry-cleaning them cost only 1s 6d, and running repairs – to a pocket, perhaps, damaged by a pickpocket – cost the same.[42]

Underwear consisted of vest (sometimes called a waistcoat, not to be confused with a waistcoat, called by Americans a vest) and underpants, of linen or flannel, or silk for 'those who are apt to become low-spirited and listless in damp weather'.[43] Perhaps this was solely for low-spirited ladies – do gentlemen ever become low-spirited and listless in damp weather? – the article does not make it clear; but there is a pair of long silk men's drawers, dyed a tasteful pink, in Hereford Museum.[44] A trade catalogue of 1866 offered 'men's drawers and pants of merino [a fine wool], lambs' wool, brown and white cotton, and *chamois* [my italics]'.[45] Night shirts (calf length) or night gowns (floor-length) were worn in bed, with tasselled, sock-shaped night caps.

Now to a gentleman's crowning glory – his facial hair. Cut-throat razors needed a steady hand and patience. King Camp Gillette's invention of a safety razor did not arrive from America until 1905. Most men relied on their barber to trim their hair and beards. The profusion of Victorian facial hair was amazing, even repellent, unless it was kept scrupulously clean. Whiskers, covering the space between the ear, the cheekbone and the beard, allowed some topiary according to individual taste, except for police constables, whose 'conspicuously marked' identification numbers were not to be obscured by overlong whiskers.[46] The ideal was 'black, bright and bushy ... of all things avoid a vulgar whisker,' for instance an 'indomitable red' or 'weak moth-eaten' ones.[47] Should a red-whiskered gentleman purchase some black dye from a reputable chemist, or remain vulgarly whiskered? To keep his whiskers and his hair 'bright', Rowland's macassar oil was invaluable. It was a viscous, reddish-brown liquid alleged to come from Macassar in the Far East. It did impart a glossy sheen, but it also stained any textile it touched – hence those linen mats, usually edged with lace, on the backs of chairs, called anti-macassars.

Bear's grease was an alternative to macassar oil. Barbers used to put out a sign saying 'We kill a bear this week' – order your fresh bear's grease immediately. But instead of the lusty bear promised, the one on view in the cellar below the shop was only 'a poor lean greyish bear' which the writer saw, the next week, displayed under another shop.[48] Hair and beards, whiskers and moustaches all could be greased and pomaded, and moustaches could be waxed and twirled between the fingers into elegant spikes.[49]

Baths seem to have been regarded principally as therapy. People suffering from irritability and general debility would benefit from a cold bath; ten to twenty minutes would be 'sufficient even for the strongest constitution' and it would prevent colds. A tepid bath 'was serviceable occasionally to persons of sedentary habits', but 'when mere cleaning is required' you might use soap. 'A vapour bath is common in this country. The patient is seated naked in a chair and a vessel full of boiling water is placed at his side. A large blanket is thrown over his body and head, together with the vessel of hot water'. Such were the instructions, but they seem to me dangerously inadequate.[50] Thomas Carlyle contrived a cold shower for himself, in the kitchen, greatly inconveniencing the maid, whose bed space it was.[51] He may have been unusual – he often was – in his desire to be clean. In 1842 *The Magazine of Domestic Economy* deplored that in this water-dreading country ... washing the hands and face, cleaning the teeth, taking excessive care of the finger-nails, and washing the feet not oftener than twice a month, constitute the generally received notion of cleanliness'.[52]

An indefatigable tourist came down from Manchester to see the sights of London. After two weeks of walking around, sometimes covering twenty miles in a day, it was worth entering as an event in his diary, 'I washed my feet and put on clean socks'.[53]

Toothbrushes were available, although the old method of chewing a wooden skewer until the end frayed was still used by some. The metal squeezable tube for toothpaste had not yet been invented. Toothpowder could be bought, or made at home, from a mixture of chalk, camphor, myrrh and quinine, which must have tasted impossibly bitter, or honey and charcoal, for the sweet tooth. Either way, 'once a fortnight or oftener, dip your brush into a few grains of gunpowder, breaking them first' – with circumspection.[54]

Ladies' dresses were designed to stress the helpless femininity of the wearers. The narrow shoulders and the cut of the sleeve tops ensured that a Victorian lady could not lift her arms, even to brush her own hair, and an unbelievably slender waist was the ambition of any young girl. The neckline for day dresses was usually high, but evening necklines sank lower and lower – 'far too much so for strict delicacy to approve'.[55] A footman wrote a trenchant description of genteel evening dress: 'The young ladies are nearly naked to the waist, only just a little bit of dress hanging on the shoulder, the breasts are quite exposed except a little bit coming up to hide the nipples'.[56]

It is extraordinary that this display above the waist was linked with such a prurient reticence below the waist. It must have complicated any attempt to remedy a flat chest. 'Bust improvers' padding the front of the bodice could be inserted in day dresses, and were usually included in wedding dresses, but they would be spotted immediately in evening wear. The bodice was elaborately darted and boned, and fastened at the back with hooks and eyes. Usually it was joined to the skirt, but sometimes a skirt would have two bodices, one low-necked for evening and the other high-necked for day wear.[57] Alternatively, 'persons who have not a large store of evening dresses may make the sleeves in two separate parts, the under to come off at the elbow ... when the dress is worn in the evening, a ruffle of lace will make a short sleeve of very pretty appearance'.[58]

Brocaded silk, very like eighteenth century patterns, was fashionable. Often a grandmother's wardrobe yielded enviable silks that could be used again. Shot or 'changeable' silk was popular for day dresses as well as evening wear, and there was a craze for tartan, and the Indian 'cone' pattern, which we know as Paisley from the Scottish town where imitations of it were made. Lace was often used over a coloured base. The lace worn over a wedding gown could be used over many other dresses. The gentle, fugitive colours of vegetable dyes were giving way to the strident colours of the aniline dyes invented and patented by William Perkin in 1856[59] and exhibited at the International Exhibition in South Kensington in 1862. They revolutionised patterned dress fabrics and prompted the Victorian passion for purple, one of the earliest aniline dyes. Hippolyte Taine thought 'the colours [of ladies' clothes] are outrageously crude'.[60]

The skirt of a dress was pleated into a waistband, to dispose of the vast yardage cascading to the floor. To increase the bulk of fabric even further, frills and flounces were often woven into it. The hem was lined and edged with stiff braid, to preserve the dress fabric. The braid was brushed when the garment was taken off, and could be replaced when it was irretrievably grimy; meanwhile it usefully served the purpose of sweeping the floor, for instance in the Crystal Palace. Pockets could be in the side seams of the skirt, or under a flounce. Watches could be stowed in a small pocket at the waist. English ladies looked their best on horseback in fashionable Rotten Row in Hyde Park, wearing skirted, man-tailored riding-habits in dark cloth, with boots and sometimes showing a tantalising glimpse of 'Amazonian riding trouser'.[61] Trousers for women as outer wear were still unthinkable. Mrs Amelia Jenks Bloomer of New York pioneered full Turkish-style trousers (we might call them harem pants) in 1851, and her friends had tried to introduce them to London, but they caused an uproar.[62] When a London brewery dressed all its barmaids in bloomers the fashion died.[63]

Shoes and ankle-length boots for indoors were made of satin or kid. The 'execrable wallow of mud' outdoors forced the Victorian lady into more suitable wear, derided by Hippolyte Taine: 'bottines which are veritable boots, the large feet of a wading species, and a stride and carriage to match'.[64] There is an intriguing description of an 1860s fashion for day dresses: 'some of the skirts ... have inside them an arrangement of rings and cords along the hem. These were for lifting up the skirt of the dress. The cord was manipulated at the waist and the skirt rose in gathered-up drapery several inches from the ground, revealing the ankles or a brightly-coloured petticoat specially worn for the purpose'.[65] Unfortunately the eminent costume historian who wrote this did not suggest when these skirts were worn. To raise the skirt above the ankles was for many years the sign of a prostitute; this must surely have been forgotten by, or unknown to, the wearer of such a skirt. It would perhaps have been useful for the new sport of croquet, or perhaps the brightly coloured petticoat could be seen while the wearer was crossing the street, but veiled again when she reached a clean pavement.

By 1865 the wide skirts supported by crinolines were being super-seded by 'tunic' or 'princess' dresses. By 1870 the fashion was over, and the silhouette changed from a floating bell to a svelte-waisted cylinder, with a growing bustle at the back.

The most famous under-garment worn by Victorian women was the crinoline. It had been preceded by very stiff petticoats of 'crinoline' fabric, made of horsehair and wool, with rows of piping at the hem.[66] Someone must have been looking at pictures of Elizabethan dress, when skirt-wearers had the same problem – how to spread the skirt?[67] The Elizabethans had developed the farthingale, a wire or whalebone frame. The Victorian version, first of whalebone then of covered steel wire, was enthusiastically adopted, yet even at its zenith, in about 1859, it was not universally worn, although it attracted so much publicity that the casual reader of fashion magazines might think everyone wore one. Queen Victoria never did. She even went into print on them, in a letter addressed to the Ladies of England; they were 'indelicate, expensive, dangerous and hideous'.[68]

Indelicate they certainly could be, especially in high winds or crowded trains, but Victoria never had to walk far carrying as much as a stone's weight of the multiple petticoats needed to expand a skirt to a fashionable width by sheer bulk.[69] Expensive? – 6s 6d for a perfectly good one, in 1861. Dangerous they often were when the wearer misjudged her distance from a fire. Hideous, especially on a short, plump woman like Victoria, they could be; but the Empress Eugénie looked superb in her huge-skirted ball dresses when she and her husband Napoleon III visited Victoria and Albert. There were various shapes and structures. The best were made of watch-spring steel, the 'Sansflectum' had its hoops covered with gutta-percha and was washable, some were flounced, some were lined with flannel. The 'American cage' of 1862 weighed only 8oz.[70] They did present problems, especially in carriages, whether public or private, and on stairs. No wonder grand ladies sat in their carriages outside fashionable shops so that the shop men could bring the goods out for them to inspect. There were alternatives. In 1842 'Lady Aylesbury wears 48 yards of material in each of her gowns, and instead of crinoline she wears a petticoat made of down or feathers which swells out this enormous expanse and floats like a vast cloud when she sits down or rises up'.[71] Like wearing a goose-feather duvet; delightful in the winter, but in the summer ... 'Arctic down petticoats' were advertised for 17s 6d.[72]

Even with a crinoline, one or two petticoats were needed. In December 1860 Jane Carlyle, who felt the cold, was wearing 'all my petticoats at once, and am having two new ones made out of a pair of Scottish blankets'.[73] They were to keep her warm, and were probably a decent cream colour, but about that time red, bright blue or purple petticoats, plain or striped, became fashionable, signalling a change in attitude. Until then, underwear was strictly a matter for the wearer, her maid and the laundress, and was white. Now, since it could be seen as the crinolined skirt dipped and swayed, it might as well be worth seeing.

One result of crinolines was the demise of tight-laced corsets. The slanting seams of the bodice, converging towards the waist, and the spread of the skirt, created a visual illusion of a small waist, so stays dropped out of fashion. This greatly relieved medical men and even the Church. 'Tight lacing, from a moral point of view, is opposed to all the laws of religion'.[74] In their day they had been formidable. In 1841,

> the modern stay extends not only over the bosom but also all over the abdomen and back down to the hips; besides being garnished with whalebone to say nothing of an immense wooden, metal or whalebone busk passing in front from the top of the stays to the bottom ... the gait of an Englishwoman is generally stiff and awkward, there being no bend or elasticity of the body on account of her stays.[75]

Laces that had to be pulled and tied at the back, by someone other than the wearer, gave place to front-fastening models by 1851, when Madame Roxy Caplin won a medal for her 'hygienic corset', comfortable but still producing a 19-inch waist.[76] *The Englishwoman's Domestic Magazine* of May 1867, when the crinoline was beginning to decline and stays were coming back, printed a letter reminiscing about the torture inflicted by stays, in the writer's youth:

> I was placed at the age of fifteen at a fashionable school in London, and there it was the custom for the waists of the pupils to be reduced one inch per month until they were what the lady principal considered small enough. When I left school at seventeen, my waist measured only thirteen inches, it having formerly been twenty-three inches in circumference.

This unnatural constriction surely helps to explain the habits of Victorian ladies, of fainting, and preferring to lie on the sofa, to taking exercise[77]. By the 1860s stays were often coloured, for instance in a cheerful scarlet, and they were shorter and lighter than before.

'Drawers are of incalculable advantage to women, preventing many of the disorders and indispositions to which British females are subject', quite how is unclear.[78] *The Magazine of Domestic Economy* of 1840 gave instructions on how to make them. The legs were attached to the waistband, overlapping a few inches at the waist but not sewn together. 'About a yard is a good length'.[79] The hems could be embellished with as much embroidery and lace as the wearer thought fit. The trade catalogue quoted above, from J. & R. Morley, offered 'women's vests and drawers in merino, lambs' wool, white cotton and chamois'. One longs to know how many women actually wore Morleys's leather knickers. They would be useful for bicycling, but that was still in the future.

The other typical Victorian garment was the shawl – 5 yards square, or vestigial, cashmere or wool for winter or filmy lace for summer. The Indian 'cone' or Paisley pattern was everywhere, printed or woven, plain or fringed. As anyone knows who has tried one, there is an art in wearing a shawl. For one thing it cannot be combined with carrying a handbag, a baby, shopping or anything else. *Sylvia's Home Journal* gave useful advice on 'this difficult art'. The shawl should be 'as much as possible draped ... and sustained by the arms being pressed upon the bust', which took all one's concentration.[80] There were several fashionable shops in Regent Street specialising in shawls, including one which would buy or exchange them and dry-clean them.[81]

It was just possible to hold another Victorian accessory, a parasol, while clamping one's arms to one's bust to anchor one's shawl. Parasols could be made to match the dress, or to contrast with it. In 1840 they were small, frequently frilled and embroidered, with jointed ivory or wood sticks to swivel and tilt so as to keep the sun from the complexion, as you sat in your carriage. They grew in size, and altered in shape, from the even curve to the ogee-shaped 'pagoda' shape. They were, of course, no use in rain. In 1857 Barbara Bodichon (née Leigh Smith), an early feminist, fumed at the 'inconvenient modern dress' of women, 'which is only suited in carpeted rooms, where it appears graceful and proper; in the streets it is disreputable, dirty and inconvenient'.[82] 'No woman ought to be without a waterproof cloak with a hood ... Winter boots should always be made with a layer of cork between the two soles; this keeps the feet perfectly dry, and, by adding thickness to the soles, lifts the boots from the mud without adding to the weight' – the new version of pattens, but much safer and more comfortable.[83]

Mayhew described a fashionable West End salon, as related to him by one of its employees:

> [It is] more like a mansion for a nobleman than a milliner's establishment ... these large houses are not only milliners and dress-makers, but they supply every kind of ladies' wearing apparel with the exception of shoes. A lady goes to order perhaps her wedding trousseau, or a train for the Queen's Drawing-room, or her morning and evening dresses. She alights from her carriage. The hall-door is opened by the footman ... who bows her into what is called the 'premier magazin' or 'first show-room'. Then comes a French lady, dressed in a silk dress, with short sleeves, and a very small lace cap, with long streamers of ribbon that fall over her shoulders down to her feet ... These French ladies are styled 'magazinières' or 'show-room women'. There are generally five or six of these showroom women ... The first show room is about 130 feet long and 60 feet wide. In every other panel there is a looking glass from the floor to the ceiling, set in a handsome carved gilt frame. The floor is covered with a very expensive carpet, sometimes of a violet and amber colour. In different parts of the room there are counters of polished ebony, elegantly ornamented with gilding. The lady is then shown an assortment of magnificent silks and velvets ... she asks the Frenchwoman which is most becoming by daylight, and which by candlelight ... she selects one or two dresses [i.e. dress lengths] ... as soon as convenient to the lady, the 'first hand' goes to take her measure ... a one-horse Brougham, with a servant in livery, is brought to the door, and the first hand goes in it ...[84]

The dress will be finished by the next day, if the customer wants it.

When Thomas Carlyle had become celebrated, by 1862, his wife Jane decided to go to a fashionable dress-maker, though not as grand as the one just described. Her charges could be as much as £300, although she charged Jane Carlyle very much less.[85] Ladies of more moderate means employed 'daily' dress-makers who came to the customer's house, charging between 2s and 3s a day. Often the customer did much of the plain work herself, such as the skirt seams and the trimmings, leaving the tricky bits for the dress-maker.[86] At least, the sewing did not all have to be done by hand. The first machine had been invented by a Frenchman, M. Thimmonier, as long ago as 1829; this was the model that had been exhibited at the Great Exhibition in 1851, but it raised little interest, perhaps because it produced a stitch like chain-stitch on the top surface, which could be unwieldy. The next entrant was Elias Howe, who invented and patented his machine in 1846, but it was not a commercial success until Isaac Singer improved it and patented it in 1851, in America. Then others entered the field, until in 1868 there were six different makers, some of them selling from their own shops, and providing machines that could embroider, as well as sew the lock-stitch which modern machines use.[87]

Dresses could be bought ready-made. *The Magazine of Domestic Economy* always ran a feature on 'London and Paris Fashions', often mentioning that they could be seen in Swan and Edgar's in the Quadrant, Regent Street (closed in 1982, but dear to many suburban housewives, who would arrange to meet each other there, innocent of the fact that it was also a profitable pitch for prostitutes). No other shop was mentioned; one suspects that Swan and Edgar's had some commercial tie-up with the magazine. Or the bodice alone could be bought, with enough of the fabric to make up a matching skirt; or vice versa. 'In cases of sudden bereavement ... where a readymade and stylish dress is required at a moment's notice,' recourse could be had to 'Jay's Patent Euthemia, a self-expanding bodice'; quite how it expanded for the grieving widow did not appear in the advertisement.[88]

Paper patterns had been supplied to professional dress-makers as early as the 1830s, but in August 1850 the monthly magazine *The World of Fashion* sold them with every copy, and by 1859 there were fourteen competitors in the field, including Samuel Beeton. The patterns were fiendishly difficult to deal with, since the pieces for several garments were printed on the same sheet of soft tissue paper. 'The models may be traced with ease by the peculiar style of line devoted to each', which sounds very like those assurances about 'simple self-assembly' of flat-packed furniture. But the Victorian ladies persevered, and a rising tide of paper patterns rustled through sewing rooms until recently, when few people would dream of making their own clothes.

The clothes in museum collections often seem impossibly small. There are two reasons: a garment handed down from a previous wearer, or bought second-hand, can usually be induced to fit a smaller wearer, and often was, so garments belonging to larger people have rarely survived unaltered. And Victorian women *were* small, as were the men, by our standards. Saxon men and women had been a stalwart 5 feet 8 inches and 5 feet 4 inches tall, but the Victorians were 3 and 2 inches shorter.[89] Victoria was probably just under 5 feet tall, and was often spoken of as 'our little Queen', but she was not all that much short of the average height of women for her time.

Cosmetics were 'almost out of fashion'. Lip salve could be coloured with a vegetable dye from alkanet, but 'this colouring has frequently the inconvenience of reddening a cambric handkerchief if accidentally touched to the lips'.[90] A weak solution of arsenic could be used to remove facial hair. This was one of the many excuses for arsenic being in the home, available to a poisoner.[91] A fair, unblemished complexion was desirable; freckles could be 'decomposed' by silver litharge or muriatic acid, neither of which sounds safe.

Indoors a frilled and beribboned cap was worn, covering the top of the head and the sides of the face, with 'streamers' or lappets from each side down as far as the chest, loose or tied under the chin. These caps could be delicious confections adorned with lace and flowers: a most useful way of disguising the thinning hair of middle and old age. Emerson was surprised to see that 'English women wear their grey hair', i.e. untinted.[92] Widows wore caps with a peak coming down over the centre forehead, like a smaller version of the widow's cap made famous by Mary Queen of Scots. Victoria wore one for the rest of her life, after Albert's death. Outdoors, the head was always covered, with bonnet or hat. The coiffure could be elaborate, and sometimes needed false hair. Poor women sold their hair, and sometimes women were robbed of their hair by violent muggers.

Little girls and boys wore the same clothes until the boys were 'breeched' at six or more. Little girls wore copies of their mothers' clothes, but shorter, and little boys were often forced into sailor suits, or Highland dress, such as the heir to the throne wore when his mother opened the Great Exhibition, poor child. (To wear tartan, no Scottish blood was called for. Prince Edward's father was German, his mother at least half German. Both parents took to Sir Walter Scott's Scotland with enthusiasm).

One significant invention must be recorded here: the safety pin, patented in America by Walter Hunt in 1849.[93]

Health[1]

Dentistry was emerging into a profession, from the dark days of market-place charlatans. The first drill worked by clockwork was invented in 1863. A dental plate of pink vulcanised rubber could be moulded to the gum, and held in place by a suction pad. False teeth were best made of porcelain, which did not rot or stain, as the teeth of cadavers tended to do.[2] The Duke of Wellington's teeth were human in the front, otherwise made of gold and walrus ivory, which discoloured less than elephant ivory.[3] The dentists in May's Buildings off St Martin's Lane offered 'every variety of artificial tooth ... in every variety of artificial gum, wax, composition or gold'.[4] A full set of artificial teeth could cost from 4 to 20 guineas [£4 4s to £21], as advertised in *The Penny Illustrated Paper* in 1868.

For toothache, laudanum applied to the cheek and also taken internally might help,[5] and it is 'often useful to apply one or two leeches to the gum'.[6] Isabella Beeton recommended a remarkable cure: 'take a piece of sheet zinc, about the size of a sixpence, and a piece of silver, say [the size of] a shilling; place them together, and hold the defective tooth between them or contiguous to them; in a few minutes the pain will be gone, as if by magic. The zinc and the silver, acting as a galvanic battery, will produce on the nerves of the tooth sufficient electricity to establish a current, and consequently to relieve the pain'.

A dentist in Hanover Square charged Hannah Culwick 10s 6d for filling two teeth, even though he must have known she could ill afford it, because she was dressed in her working clothes, as a maid servant. 'He let his pupil see him stop my teeth, I suppose he wouldn't do so for a lady'.[7] For extractions, ether or chloroform could anaesthetize the patient.[8] A society man called Samuel Boddington, a great diner-out, went to his dentist in Brook Street 'who took out my twelve decayed teeth in a minute and a half', which must have been an immense relief to his neighbours at his next dinner party.[9]

❀

In 1842 an official enquiry into the average ages of mortality showed startling differences between the middle class ('gentlemen, professionals and their families'), the skilled working class ('tradesmen and their families'), and the lower class ('mechanics, servants and labourers and their families'). In Bethnal Green, an east London parish, the average age at death of gentlemen etc. was 45; of tradesmen etc., 26; and of labourers etc., *16*. In Whitechapel, another east London parish, the respective ages were 45, 27 and 22. In Kensington in the West End, gentlemen died at the age of 44, tradesmen at 29, and labourers at 26. In all three parishes, children under 5 made up 62 per cent of the deaths of labourers and their families.[10] Statistics can be used to prove almost anything, but these figures do reveal the glaring discrepancy between the general life expectancies of gentlemen and labourers.

The 1834 Poor Law had been designed to reduce the number of feckless claimants by offering them only the repellent workhouse as an alternative to supporting themselves. After 1834 typical applicants changed, from those whom the Elizabethans had called 'lusty vaga-bonds', who refused to work although they could, to the chronic sick and the disabled, who could not. The workhouses could not look after them without medical facilities. Workhouse infirmaries were built at public expense, and workhouse medical officers were appointed.[11]

One of these medical officers was Dr Rogers, who took the job at the Strand workhouse in 1856 when his own practice had been ruined by a cholera epidemic.[12] His starting salary was £50 a year, out of which he had to pay for any medicine he prescribed. 'There were no paid nurses ... such nursing as we had ... for the first nine years I was there, was performed by more or less infirm paupers,' who got slightly better food than the patients they were supposed to be looking after. They also managed to get more gin. They were usually drunk by 7 in the morning, and if there was a corpse to be laid out – a frequent event – they got an extra glass for doing so. One of them 'systematically stole the wine and brandy from the sick'. (Brandy was used as a stimulant in cholera cases).

Dr Rogers ordered the nurses to isolate cases of measles, then often fatal, but they were 'too stupid or too careless to do so'. Things gradually improved. The Master in post when Dr Rogers arrived, an illiterate brute, was finally sacked and replaced by a Master and a Matron who 'treated the inmates with kindness and consideration', and in 1865 a superintendent nurse was appointed. The infirmary was so overcrowded during the bitter winters of 1863–5 that the beds were pushed together and patients could get out of them only by scrambling out of the ends. Dr Rogers fought to get some patients admitted to the large 'voluntary' hospitals, and eventually succeeded. His salary was doubled, and supplemented by the premiums paid to him by several 'pupils', i.e. medical students, so in the end he had a tolerable middle-class income; but the professional press constantly complained that the salaries of workhouse doctors, and of other parochial appointees such as the parish doctor, were scandalously low.

Hospitals were 'voluntary' in that they relied on voluntary contributions, with no state support. In the eighteenth century there had been a wave of philanthropic energy, which had produced Guy's, the London, the Middlesex, the Westminster and St George's, all on the fringe of the then built-up area, to enjoy the fresher air and the cheaper site values.[13] (They have survived into the twenty-first century, as have the medieval foundations of St Bartholomew's and St Thomas's.) They were run by governors, who donated a certain amount to the hospital funds, and had the right to nominate cases for admission. At Bart's, for example, one ward was open day and night to receive emergencies, but for non-urgent cases a petition signed by one or more governors had to be delivered, on the correct form, available from the steward's office. This was where help from a middle-class contact could be invaluable, such as the 'missionaries' employed by the London City Mission, one of whom befriended an ex-soldier who had been discharged on health grounds – he had TB – with twelve months' pay and no prospects. 'I offered my endeavour to procure his admission to the excellent hospital at Brompton for consumption and diseases of the chest'.[14]

Munby, that middle-class man with a passion for working-class women, endorsed an application for admission to the Royal Hospital for Incurables by a girl whose face was eaten away by TB. 'The patients are not elected on their merits, but according to the amount of money and votes that A or B can beg or buy for them'.[15] Hospitals were supposed to be for the sick *poor*, but some governors used 'their' hospitals as free nursing-homes for their own servants; no enquiry was ever made as to the patient's means. The Royal Free Hospital, originally in Hatton Gardens, had been founded in 1828 as a protest against the power of 'governors' letters'.[16] The London, out at Mile End, had never used them. For a hopeful patient, the trick was to know which was which.

Armed with the right paperwork, the sufferer came to the weekly General Admission Day, to be examined and considered for admission. If successful, 'inpatients are visited daily by the Physicians and Surgeons, outpatients attended daily [i.e. in clinics] by Assistant Physicians and Assistant Surgeons'.[17] Hippolyte Taine was taken round Bart's by a young medical student.[18] There were 600 patients when he was there. 'The building is enormous ... the beds 5 or 6 paces apart ... [there is] perfect cleanliness. The place seems to me to be well equipped and run ... [there is an] enormous kitchen, where all the cooking is done by gas'. Bart's was fortunate enough to have an annual income of £40,000, some of it still derived from the City properties with which it had been endowed when Henry VIII refounded it. Most hospitals were chronically short of funds. The Westminster had to close three wards in 1850; it was a common phenomenon.[19]

St Thomas's had been founded in the twelfth century, at the south end of London Bridge, in Southwark. Seven centuries later, in 1859, it had an astonishing windfall when the London and Chatham Railway compulsorily acquired its site to build London Bridge station. After a period in temporary premises it was able to move into a state-of-the-art building on a man-made site on Bazalgette's south embankment, opposite the Houses of Parliament, taking advantage of the most modern planning, approved by Florence Nightingale. Separate, connected pavilions were built, to give every patient the maximum amount of air and light. Queen Victoria laid its foundation stone in 1868, and it was opened three years later.

As well as the general hospitals, there was a growing number specialising in specific diseases. By 1860 there were at least 66 specialist hospitals in London alone. There were four hospitals for diseases of the chest. The Brompton Hospital was founded in 1842, with a nominal capacity of 300 beds; but at least half of them were usually empty because there were no nurses, or no funds. The City of London Hospital for Chest Diseases, founded by the Quakers in 1848, had a nominal capacity of 160 beds – but the same problems as the Brompton. The grand-sounding Royal National Hospital for Chest Diseases had some 20 beds. The North London Hospital for Consumption, established in the 1860s, was financially crippled because someone had run away with a large part of its funds; it was described as 'a doctor's racket'.[20] But some of the specialist hospitals functioned well. One of them was the Hospital for Sick Children, founded in 1852 with 10 beds, in Great Ormond Street (and still there). Children were admitted between the ages of two and thirteen. The under-twos could be brought to out-patient clinics. By the 1880s the little girls' ward held 75 small patients. There were 'pretty iron cots of a cheerful colour, surrounded at the top by a rail on which slides a broad board at a convenient height for the patient to reach when it sits up, and on which is arranged its toys and picture-books. Every thing is bright and light and pleasant-looking, even to the nurses', and a cheerful fire burned in every ward.[21]

The conjunction of medical school and hospital was part of nineteenth century thinking. Bart's had had a residential college for medical students since 1842, to 'afford the pupils [students] the moral advantages, together with the comfort and convenience, of a residence within the walls of the hospital', medical students usually being in need of moral advantages.[22] St Mary's, in Paddington, was a general hospital with 150 beds, opened in 1851. Its medical school for 300 medical students opened three years later. University College had been founded in 1826, with an associated hospital and medical school. Charing Cross Hospital, which could trace its origin back to 1815, had had a medical school since 1822. Its new building was opened in 1834 with 60 beds.

King's College also had its associated hospital and medical school in Portugal Street, nearby. When the University of London was founded in 1836, medical students could work in London schools and hospitals for degrees which until then had been conferred only by Oxford and Cambridge. Tuition fees of £100, and the cost of books, with £50 or so living expenses over four or five years, brought the total cost of qualifying up to perhaps £400, but this could be cut if the student landed one of the miscellaneous jobs available to medical students, such as ward clerks and dressers, as well as writing, tutoring or assisting a qualified general practitioner.[23] Professions often run in families, especially the medical profession. A student might choose to revert to the old system of apprenticeship which had ruled medical education before the rise of medical schools, and live at home for a year or two, apprenticed to his father or another member of the family, saving on tuition fees and living expenses, and probably enjoying the luxury of his mother's care; £50 a year would allow only the barest existence.

Once qualified, at about the age of 21, a young doctor would set his sights on one of the prestigious bodies, the Royal College of Surgeons or the Royal College of Physicians, who together had a tight grip on the hierarchy of the profession. At about 30 he might land a job as assistant surgeon or physician in a hospital, as long as his medical school had given him a good testimonial and the governors had no other more favoured applicant – appointments to staff jobs were notoriously corrupt and needed energetic canvassing. By 40 or so he might hope to be a full surgeon or physician on the hospital staff. These appointments led to useful and remunerative contacts in the world outside the hospitals for the sick poor. If he decided to go into general practice, he could qualify as a surgeon-apothecary, put up his plate and wait for patients. It was to her local apothecary that Jane Carlyle sent her unfortunate servant when a black beetle crawled into her ear. The apothecary flooded it out with soap suds. 'There might be a leg or two left' he said, offering to syringe the ear again in the morning, but the maid had had enough.[24]

John Snow, who rose to be Queen Victoria's anaesthetist, began as a surgeon in 1854, in one-room lodgings in Frith Street, Soho, a crowded street where there were already four other surgeons' practices.[25] There were various part-time appointments to be picked up, such as medical officer to the sick clubs and trade unions that were proliferating, or as public vaccinator, police surgeon or prison medical officer. Snow never married, but most young doctors found that a wife gave them the added gravitas and respectability prized by patients. Practices could be bought and sold through the professional journals. As the practitioner became more eminent there were possibilities of being called to give forensic evidence in criminal trials, particularly in the rash of poisonings that kept the Victorian press focused on the Old Bailey.

Nurses may not always have been 'bright and light and pleasant-looking', but they were becoming better-trained and more self-respecting, less ignorant, less likely to take refuge in gin. In 1850 and 1851 Florence Nightingale had visited a Lutheran training school for nurses, at Kaiserswerth in Germany. She followed it up by training in hospitals run by the Sisters of Charity in Paris.[26] She passionately regretted the lack of any English institution like Kaiserswerth or the Sisters of Charity, where English girls could train to be nurses. In the teeth of family opposition she was at last able, in 1853, to put a genteel toe into the murky water of the nursing profession, by taking on the Institution for the Care of Gentlewomen in Distressed Circumstances at No.1, Harley Street. There she let loose her characteristic maelstrom of organising, so that the Committee ladies and gentlemen scarcely knew what had hit them – a pattern to be repeated throughout her life.

Hardly had Florence Nightingale settled there, when there was an epidemic of cholera, and she volunteered to superintend the nursing of cholera patients in the Middlesex Hospital. Next, a much greater challenge: the Crimean War. The initial euphoria that seems to come over the British public whenever a war begins soon turned to horror as William Russell of *The Times* described the inhuman conditions in the general hospital at Scutari. Miss Nightingale was invited to take a party of 40 nurses out to Scutari and do her best. They were a very mixed bag: ladies, servants and experienced nurses. The seeds were sown, there, of questions which bedevilled the nursing profession for years. What was a nurse supposed to do? Should she look to the religious orders, and offer the patients spiritual consolation, ignoring their need for a bed-pan? Or was she there to look after their verminous, stinking, diseased bodies and follow the doctor's (and Miss Nightingale's) instructions? Was she to be a lady or a ward maid?

By 1856 Miss Nightingale was back in London, haunted by her memories of the British soldier's wretched lot. It took her a year of strain and behind-the-scenes pressure, but in 1857 the Government set up a commission to examine the health of the British Army. In 1860 Miss Nightingale dedicated the £45,000 subscribed by a grateful public for her work in the Crimea, to setting up a School of Nursing, to be based in St Thomas's. It revolutionised the profession. Nurses were to be sober, honest, truthful, trustworthy, punctual, quiet and orderly, clean and neat, and conscientious record-keepers. Although by now she had become a recluse – the most energetic recluse in history – she read and marked her nurses' notebooks every week.

✳

Medical knowledge was expanding rapidly. The old mantra 'Bleed, cup and blister, Purge, physic and clyster' was giving way to more scientific treatments.[27] The word 'consumption', which had for centuries described the patient's wasting away, was replaced by 'tuberculosis', after the discovery of the characteristic tubercles in the lungs. The time-honoured technique of careful observation of the patient was still the physician's first and best approach, but new tools could make diagnosis more specific. The new clinical thermometer was 6 inches long, and took five minutes to register, but it gave an accurate reading of the patient's temperature. In 1816 a French doctor, Laennec, was faced with a female patient with chest problems. Etiquette forbade him to listen to her thoracic noises by simply putting his ear to her chest, so he invented the stethoscope, a wooden tube which could conveniently be carried in a top hat. Blood pressure could be measured by an early version of the sphygmomanometer. Microscopy was becoming more and more sophisticated.

The 1862 *Year Book of Medicine, Surgery and Other Allied Sciences* recommended that 'the bandages and instruments which have been used for gangrenous wounds *ought not, if possible* [my italics], to be employed for a second time';[28] but post-operative deaths from 'hospital gangrene' were gradually coming down, as Lister promoted the idea of antisepsis, lessening the risk of infection by getting the surgeon to wash his hands in carbolic, and spraying the operating room with carbolic vapour. A few old-fashioned surgeons clung to their conviction that some post-operative infection was simply a normal part of wound recovery, and to their comfortable old operating coats, stiff with the blood and pus of earlier operations, sometimes even inherited from an honoured predecessor; but professional opinion gradually turned in favour of Lister, as the statistics of post-amputation fatality fell from 46 per cent in 1864–6 to 15 per cent in 1867–70.[29]

The other huge advance was in anaesthesia. A surgeon's success rate in the previous century had largely depended on his dexterity in completing an operation so fast that the patient hardly had time to feel the pain, until post-operative shock hit him later. The only ways of blocking the pain had been alcohol or opium, in unmeasured doses of unknown strength, taking no account of any idiosyncrasy of the patient. In 1831 James Simpson, Professor of Surgery in Edinburgh, had discovered the miraculous properties of chloroform, by serendipity. The legend has it that he inhaled it, with several of his students, when one of them upset a bottle of it. When Mrs Simpson came to see why they had not come to dinner, she found them all on the floor, fast asleep.[30] In December 1847 Charles Greville, a layman with an interest in current events, went along to St George's Hospital 'to see the chloroform tried':

A boy two and a half years old was cut for a stone. He was put to sleep in a minute ... the operation lasted above twenty minutes, with repeated probings ... the chloroform was applied from time to time ... this invention is the greatest blessing ever bestowed on mankind ... it is a great privilege to have lived in the times which saw the production of steam, of electricity, and now of ether [which is not quite the same thing as chloroform, but lay people do sometimes get their medical terms wrong] ... wonderful as are the powers and the feats of the steam-engine and the electric telegraph, the chloroform far transcends them.[31]

Mrs Charles Dickens would have agreed with him. She was expecting her eighth child in 1849. Her husband first 'made himself thoroughly acquainted in Edinburgh with the facts of chloroform', and then (as described in a letter to a friend) he

insisted on the attendance of a gentleman from Bart's Hospital who administers it in the operations there and has given it four or five thousand times ... It saved her all pain (she had no sensation, but of a great display of sky-rockets) and saved the child from all mutilation [by forceps delivery?]. It enabled the doctors to do ... in ten minutes what might otherwise have taken them one and a half hours; the shock to her nervous system was reduced to nothing, and she was to all intents and purposes well, next day. Administered by some one who has nothing else to do, who knows its symptoms thoroughly, who keeps his hand upon the pulse and his eyes on the face, and uses nothing but a handkerchief, and that lightly, I am convinced that it is as safe in its administration as it is miraculous and merciful in its effects.[32]

It is not often that one can witness the birth of a medical speciality so clearly. The key lay in the fact that the 'gentleman from Bart's hospital' had 'nothing else to do' except concentrate on his patient.[33] In 1853 Queen Victoria, surely prompted by her scientifically minded husband, produced her fourth son, Leopold, under chloroform, administered by Dr John Snow. It all went so well that when Dr Snow was summoned to the Palace for Victoria's next child, he found her already in labour, and Albert methodically administering chloroform to her, dripping it on to a handkerchief. 'I commenced to give a little chloroform with each pain ... the effect of the chloroform was not at any time carried to the extent of quite removing consciousness [which might have raised constitutional questions] ... the Queen appeared very cheerful and well, expressing herself much gratified by the effect of the chloroform,' but she made no mention of sky-rockets.[34]

The royal seal of approval put paid to the mutterings of the medical establishment, including Mrs Dickens's doctors, that women were *meant* to suffer pain in childbirth – they being quite safe from it themselves – because the Bible said so: God had told Eve, after the Fall, that 'in sorrow thou shalt bring forth children'.[35] After Dr Snow had been summoned to Lambeth Palace for the lying-in of the daughter of the Archbishop of Canterbury, the opponents of anaesthesia in childbirth on religious grounds had to admit defeat.[36]

But modern marvels did not make hospitals any less frightening to the poor. They were afraid that their bodies would be taken for dissection, 'clandestinely by the physician and students'.[37] This could happen. In 1840 a mother and her baby died, in Queen Adelaide's Lying-in Hospital. According to the grieving husband, 'my wife was removed from the hospital [for burial] and another application was made for the infant', but no baby's corpse was produced. When he persisted, he was referred to a nearby anatomical school, where he 'received the body wrapt in a sheet of brown paper with an incision in the throat' – he had been just in time.[38] The bodies of people who had died in workhouses were available for dissection in the medical schools if no relative claimed them, but there was a chronic shortage. By 1868 the deathbeds of the pauper sick were more closely watched, their relatives more generally informed, and their bodies more regularly claimed, which made the supply of 'subjects' to the anatomy schools even more difficult.[39]

❈

Rather than go to hospital, many people put their faith in the 'miracle cures' sold in the streets and advertised in the popular press. Various herbal 'remedies' were sold by street vendors, on a 'no cure, no pay' basis, asthma excluded.[40] In 1842 a magazine aimed at the middle class deplored the number of quack medicines available.[41] 'No country in the world is so entirely quack-ridden as Great Britain'. Dr James's Fever powder, containing antimony and ammonia, certainly produced heavy sweating, but also vomiting and diarrhoea. Anderson's Scots pills for indigestion, containing aloes and hellebore root, which is toxic, caused piles and chronic constipation. Morison's pills, containing aloes and a coloured gum, gamboge, resulted in piles and chronic inflammation, and even 'numerous deaths' – and a fortune of £12,000 to £15,000 for the maker. Steel's Aromatic Lozenges, containing cantharides, an irritant long thought to be an aphrodisiac, were 'one of the most mischievous quack medicines ever offered to the public. Its professed use is to repair the evils brought on by debauchery [a veiled reference to venereal disease? or to penile disfunction?] ... it holds out delusions to the young and the old which may lure them to destruction ... the action anticipated from these lozenges does not take place, but only a painful and dangerous inflammation instead.'

In 1863 a new medicine hit the fashionable market: Dr J. Collis Browne's Chlorodine, for stomach problems and anything else you decided to try it for. Jane Carlyle's aunt 'fell into a refreshing sleep' after 50 drops of it, and her pain was much better. It was regularly advertised in the *British Medical Journal*.[42] In 1868 *The Penny Illustrated Paper* advertised Kaye's Worsdell's Pills, 'confidently recommended as the best medicine which can be taken under all circumstances, as they require no restraint of diet or confinement during their use, and their timely assistance inevitably cures all complaints': 1s 1½d a box, family size 4s 6d. At least they would be worth trying. Godfrey's Cordial and Dalby's Carminative (for wind), both containing opium, certainly soothed fretful babies, especially when mixed with a little gin, but their silence might be permanent.

The middle class seems to have resorted to drugs as self-medication, to a startling extent. Jane Carlyle suffered from poor health and insomnia. In 1852 she 'took a great dose of morphia ... and was thankful to get four hours of something like forgetfulness by that questionable means'.[43] She was still taking it in 1862, although it made her 'listless' the next morning. Chloroform could be bought from a druggist. Laudanum, another opium derivative, was, like morphia, freely available from chemists, and never very expensive. It was a mild soporific and painkiller but a supreme sedative, and particularly helpful at deathbeds.[44] In an inquest on a man who had committed suicide by overdosing on it, 'some of the jury remarked that 2 ounces of laudanum was a large quantity for any chymist [*sic*] to sell to an individual', but no blame fell on the chemist, since he knew the man, who had said he wanted it to 'foment his gums, which were swollen and painful ... there was no restriction imposed on chemists in respect of the sale of laudanum and other such sedatives. There was a restriction in the case of arsenic'.[45]

✻

The diseases that afflicted nineteenth century Londoners may have been more accurately diagnosed, but there was little advance in curing them. The Commission on the Employment of Children noted, in 1864, that London children of seven or eight, by when children in the poor parts of London would have started work, were 'stunted in growth, their aspect pale, delicate, sickly ... the diseases most prevalent being of the nutritive organs, curvature and distortion of the spine, deformity of the limbs and especially of the lungs, ending in atrophy, consumption and death'.[46] The terrible infectious diseases – diphtheria, measles, scarlet fever, whooping cough and mumps – from which children nowadays are largely protected, were often fatal. In 1862 a pandemic of diphtheria reached a peak in London. There were repeated epidemics of scarlet fever, the 'leading cause of death among the infectious diseases of childhood'.[47] Infantile diarrhoea wiped out many babies before their first birthday. 'Convulsions' – a favourite term used on death certificates – were probably caused by tuberculous meningitis.[48] Rickets, which can be prevented by a good diet and sunshine, flourished in the murky atmosphere of London. Perhaps as many as 15 per cent of children had deformed legs and pelvises, which for a girl could spell difficult childbirth when she grew up.[49]

'The Irish fever' came over with the starving immigrants, in 1847; it was probably typhus, from which over 1,000 Londoners died in the last three months of 1848. It recurred in 1856 and 1864. There was a severe epidemic of influenza in the winter of 1847–8, affecting small children and old people; just for once, it was 'a disease of the richer classes'.[50] Pneumonia carried away old people of all classes. 'Consumption' as a cause of death was a term shunned by the grieving relatives, because it had overtones of a family history or a sinful way of life. In 1869 its causes were listed as including 'an incontinent search for pleasure', improper clothing, masturbation (that favourite Victorian all-purpose bogey) celibacy, alcoholism and smoking.[51] To die of 'bronchitis' was much more genteel.

Whatever you called it, it carried off over 15,000 Londoners a year, and the efforts of the vaunted quartet of chest hospitals hardly counted.[52] The rich were advised to try a trip to Egypt or Spain, which at least would make their last months of life more enjoyable. Dr Travers of the Brompton Hospital advised antimony, creosote, and boaconstrictor excreta, the price of which illustrated its rarity. He also recommended a 'patent gas mixture' to be injected into the rectum, 'whence they [the gases] were sure to reach the lungs'. Treatment cost only one guinea. The tubercular poor just died. Unspecific fevers and stomach infections were endemic even in middle-class districts, and often fatal in poor slums.

Recurrent epidemics of smallpox still caused suffering, disfigurement and death, despite the vaccination that was available without charge. A Londoner looking back to his childhood in 1850–60 remembered how

persons badly pitted by the disease were too numerous to excite remark, while those blinded by it were many ... Persistent [i.e. repeated] vaccination was then much less satisfactory than now, for lymph was taken from one person to use on another, and mothers were wont to be cheered by the family doctor saying that he knew a splendidly healthy baby 'coming on' and she might depend on her own darling getting a supply from it ... had it not been for the forgetfulness and carelessness inherent in British human nature, the disease would have probably entirely disappeared [which, at last, it has]. And conscientious objectors helped ... in keeping it alive.[53]

An Act of 1853 making smallpox vaccination compulsory was not strictly enforced, although Isabella Beeton, writing in 1861, could say that 'fortunately the state has now made it imperative on all parents to have their children vaccinated before ... the twelfth week ... Though vaccination has been proved not to be always an infallible guard ... the attack is always much lighter, should it occur, and is seldom, if indeed ever, fatal after the precaution of vaccination'.[54] The 1853 Act was strengthened in 1867, and enforced. But vaccination did not stop poor Jenny Marx from catching it, with one of her children.

The child died, Jenny survived with all her good looks gone, her face 'disfigured by scars and a dark purple-red tinge'.[55]

Venereal diseases flourished. There was no cure for syphilis, but its early symptoms could to an extent be palliated in some cases by the mercury treatment which had been used for centuries. Gonorrhoea was a less appalling infection but for that, too, there was no reliable cure.

Cholera was endemic in the Indian sub-continent. In 1820 it had shot up to pandemic proportions, and threatened Europe, but stopped at the Caspian Sea. The next wave began in 1829, this time sweeping through Europe. In 1832 it reached London for the first time; 18,000 people died of it. It was

> a shocking way to die. Internal disturbances, nausea and dizziness led to violent vomiting and diarrhoea, with stools turning to a grey liquid ... until nothing emerged but water and intestinal membrane. Extreme muscular cramps followed, with an insatiable desire for water, followed by a 'sinking stage' during which the pulse dropped and lethargy set in. Dehydrated and nearing death, the patient displayed the classic physiognomy: puckered blue lips in a cadaverous face.[56]

No-one knew what caused it, nor how to treat it. Miss Nightingale believed in stimulating her patients in the Middlesex Hospital with exterior warmth from poultices and hot-water bottles, and internal stimulants such as brandy and laudanum,[57] but without success.

She, with many others, believed in the miasma theory. A bad smell directly caused people to be ill. That was why she insisted on her new hospital of St Thomas's being well ventilated, to avoid the miasma of stuffy wards. Edwin Chadwick, an early pioneer in public health reform, believed in it too:

> The sense of smell ... which generally gives certain warning of the presence of ... gases noxious to the health, appears often to be obliterated in the labourer by his employment ... there is scarcely any stench which is not endured to avoid slight cold ... these adverse circumstances tend to produce an adult population short-lived, improvident, reckless and intemperate, and with habitual avidity for sensual gratification [they took to bed, if they had one, where they begot still more children] ... these habits lead ... to the overcrowding of their homes ... Primary and most important measures ... [to be taken] are drainage, the removal of all refuse of habitations, streets and roads,

and the improvement of the supplies of water ... better supplies of water are absolutely necessary.[58]

So the 1839 cholera had really been the fault of the poor, for being dirty and smelly. In January 1849 cholera recurred. In London alone, there were 14,000 deaths or more.[59] In July 1849 the Board of Health ordered 'all streets, mews, alleys ... to be effectually cleansed every 24 hours and ordure removed, and nuisances e.g. swine, dung, animals kept in or under dwelling houses [be removed] ... the owner or occupier must cleanse and whitewash and abate and remove nuisances'. But this miraculous transformation did not, predictably, happen. The clerk to the governors of St Pancras Union carefully minuted their decision that 'at present the order of the Board of Health ... need not be acted on in this Union', on the same day that he recorded a notification that cholera had arrived in their parishes.[60]

In August there were over 4,000 deaths, in September over 6,500. Chadwick had unwittingly made its fatal path easier by advocating the flushing of drains into the Thames. The river, which then supplied a large part of London's drinking-water, became a receptacle for all the infected sewage.[61] In two poor riverside parishes, one in every 56 inhabitants died in Bermondsey, one in every 38 in Rotherhithe. It remained a mystery why Bethlehem Hospital (better known as Bedlam) in Lambeth should not have had one case among its 700 inmates. Could it be anything to do with the fact that it had 'an abundant supply of pure water from a deep well'?[62]

The next epidemic began quietly, in September 1853, but deaths rose inexorably. By now Dr John Snow, who had been considering the cause of cholera since the 1849 epidemic, was reaching the conclusion that it was a water-borne disease. In August 1854 a baby was seriously ill with diarrhoea, in a house in Broad Street, Soho. Her distracted mother washed her soiled nappies, and threw the washing water into the cesspit under the house, which was connected to a drain under the street. The baby's illness was misdiagnosed as just another case of infantile diarrhoea. When it was recognised as having been cholera, the drain and the well near it which supplied a pump in the street were all examined, but again the vital evidence was missed. The drain, the pump and the well were all found to be soundly built, so the disease could not be water-borne. Snow, however, persisted. They were looked at again.

Sure enough, crumbling brickwork was found which had allowed sewage and the washing water from the cholera-stricken baby's nappies to percolate from the drain to the well. Armed with this evidence, Snow reported to the relevant authority, the Parish Vestry of St James's, which promptly ordered that the handle of the pump in Broad Street be removed. The outbreak began to fall. The case of Mrs Eley gave further proof of the cause of the outbreak, if such were needed. She used to live in Broad Street, where her family had a business making percussion caps. She liked the taste of the water from her local well. When her husband died, she moved to Hampstead, but her loving sons saw to it that she had a regular supply of her favourite water. Hampstead was clear of cholera in 1854 – except for Mrs Eley, who died of it.[63]

Yet the miasma theory still influenced medical thinking. Near Golden Square 'the gutters were flowing with a thick liquid, partly water and partly chloride of lime', a strong-smelling disinfectant, adding to the usual stinks.[64] The miasma theory still held on, until the Great Stink of 1858, when the smell from the Thames was so bad that it made parts of the Palace of Westminster uninhabitable, and at last prompted proper drainage, and Bazalgette, and his marvels. If ever there was a time when bad smells could be shown to cause disease, it was then; but no epidemic happened.

※

To turn from these horrors to a middle class domestic sickroom is almost a relief. In the fashion of the times, Thomas Webster in his 1,264-page *Encyclopaedia of Domestic Economy*, published in 1844, included advice on home nursing. For measles 'very little can be done' and for whooping cough a doctor should be summoned. Wine does you good in moderation, but 'the most pernicious spirit is English gin … smoking produces indolence and blunts the appetite …'. Having considered the merits of various kinds of baths, he recommends exercise as 'absolutely necessary to preserve the health', for instance walking 'combined with the use of the dumb-bells', which must have enlivened the City streets, and reading aloud, which is 'one of the best [exercises] that can be taken'. Turning to 'severe diseases' he remarks that 'the active principle of willow bark, termed by medical men "salicine"' was good for ague, 'and may be procured from the London druggists'. (Good for him. Salicin had been discovered in

1763, when a parson noticed that people suffering from the agues and rheumatic fevers endemic in marshy districts benefited from a preparation of willow, which God had kindly planted in such districts for just that purpose, having – surely unkindly – created fevers in the first place. His discovery was not widely noticed. Salicin was rediscovered by two Italians in 1826, and by 1899 it had acquired the name Aspirin.)[65]

Arsenic could be useful, too; it could be bought from the druggist, as 'Fowler's Solution', but an overdose was dangerous. 'Continued fever' or 'putrid fever' (probably typhoid) is 'the most difficult to treat', but he makes no suggestions. Consumption should be treated as soon as possible, with cold baths and sea-bathing, in summer; what about the winter? (The fashion for Egypt was after his time). Then he turns to accidents. To revive someone apparently dead from drowning, get a bellows, but if none is quickly available, apply what we know as the 'kiss of life'. Arsenic 'is the most common of all poisons'. Opium and laudanum are 'most frequently taken by suicides'. And that is all he says about 'family health'.

Miss Nightingale had suffered from the ladies who went with her to the Crimea. She needed to dispel the middle-class self-image of some of them, as 'ministering angels'. Her *Notes on Nursing* came out in 1859 and was never out of print for decades. The first edition was priced at 5s, and sold 15,000 copies in a month. Later reprints cost only 7d. She wrote the *Notes*, as she wrote everything, with a burning conviction and a clear, easy style. If you have ever been ill, and bedbound, you too would want your bed to be placed so that you can see out of the window – such an easy thing to arrange, but for the Victorian housewife how surprising – the bed had always stood in a certain place. You too would be glad if no-one went just out of earshot to whisper. 'Apprehension, uncertainty, waiting, expectation, fear of surprise, do a patient more harm than any exertion'. 'A small pet animal is an excellent companion for the sick. A pet bird in a cage is sometimes the only pleasure of an invalid confined to the same room for years'.

She loved babies, and recommended visits from them – 'No better society for babies and sick people for each other'. On children: 'Don't treat your children like sick [people], don't dose them with tea. Let them eat meat and drink milk, or half a glass of light beer. Give them fresh, light, sunny and open rooms, cool bedrooms, plenty of outdoor exercise ... plenty of amusements and play; more liberty, and less schooling, and examining, and training; more attention to food and less to physic'. On nursing in general: 'No man, even a doctor, ever gives any definition of what a nurse should be other than this – "devoted and obedient". This definition would do just as well for a porter. It might even do for a horse. It would not do for a policeman ... it seems a commonly received idea among men ... that it requires nothing but a disappointment in love, or incapacity in other things, to turn a woman into a good nurse.'

By the time Isabella Beeton's *Household Management* was published in 1861, she felt able to give her usual authoritative guidance on the illnesses of babies and infants. A baby suffering from thrush would benefit from a home-made mixture containing laudanum. Chickenpox could lead to smallpox, so other children with chickenpox should be avoided. 'The whole treatment resolves itself into the use of the warm bath, and a course of gentle aperients [laxatives]'. Cases of measles, 'this much-dreaded disease', needed a cool room and bleeding, by two or more leeches 'according to age and strength of the patient', on the chest. In really bad cases, treat as for typhus, with wine 'and even, spirits'. Whooping cough 'is only infectious through the faculty of imitation' so it should not be encouraged. If necessary, however, apply the usual remedies – aperients and leeches – combined with 'keeping up a state of nausea and vomiting'. Croup, which can still be terrifying, was 'by far the most formidable and fatal of all the diseases to which infancy and childhood are liable ... Place the child immediately in a hot bath up to the throat [she assumes that hot water would be immediately available] and give an emetic ... should the symptoms remain unabated after a few hours, apply one or two leeches to the throat ...'. Perhaps it helped.

Her next chapter is headed 'The Doctor'. It begins with a long list of drugs and home-made mixtures that should be kept in the house. (She missed salicin.) Then come directions for first aid, and a gruesome list of 'common poisons and their antidotes'. But there is no list of common diseases and their suggested treatment, on the lines of the section on childhood diseases. Her closing paragraphs recommend tomatoes, and washing '*all* the skin every day', and ventilating gas-lit rooms, which was probably very sensible – and that is all. Disappointing, from that omniscient lady.

CHAPTER 16

Amusements

Rat pits and dog fights · penny gaffs · music halls · the Alhambra ·
the opera · musical concerts · the pleasure gardens · Vauxhall ·
Cremorne · public parks · Victoria Park · Battersea Park · the royal parks
· destitutes and rats · Green Park and St James's Park · Hyde Park ·
Kensington Gardens · Regent's Park · the Zoo · Surrey Gardens ·
Kew · Wyld's 'Monster Globe' · museums · Buckingham Palace

The brutal blood sports that had delighted Londoners in Hogarth's
day had been banned, since 1835. No longer could you enjoy bear-
baiting or bull-baiting, or throwing sticks at a tethered cock for fun.
But there were some 70 places scattered through the poorer parts of
London where, if you knew the ropes, you could watch rats fighting
dogs, or dogs fighting each other.

In Bunhill Row, near Moorgate, 'in one two-roomed house is a
notorious dog-trainer, who keeps a dog-pit. It was in his upper room,
reached by a ladder through a trap-door. All the windows were
boarded up'.[1] The 'pit' was 'a small circus 6 feet in diameter, gas-lit'.
There was a large cage full of rats, from which 12 were let out and
set against an untrained dog, but it did so badly that it was not sold.
A good ratter could fetch a high price. Next, 50 rats were loosed
against a bull terrier, and various other dogs were tried. This 'sport'
went on till midnight. One publican bought 26,000 live rats for 3d each,
every year, mostly from the country round Enfield. 'I've had noble lords
and titled ladies come here to see the sport – on the quiet'.[2]

There were theatres and music halls to suit all tastes. Slum children
always seemed to have the necessary cash to get into a 'penny gaff',
their kind of neighbourhood theatre. 'On a Monday night as many
as 6 performances will take place [in the same room] each having its

200 visitors ... [they are] a platform to teach the cruellest debauchery'
fulminated Mayhew. The audience was aged between eight and
twenty, and – surprisingly – mostly female. Perhaps the men were at
the rat-pit. There were 'filthy songs, clumsy dancing and filthy dances
by men and women'.[3] 'The true penny gaff is the place where juvenile
poverty meets juvenile crime ... the foulest, dingiest place of public
entertainment I can conceive ... the odour is indescribable ...
Demands for gin assailed us on all sides, women old and young, girls
and boys in the most woful [sic] tatters ... some cried for a pint,
others for half a pint, others for a glass.'[4] Gory stories of violent crime
were most popular, such as the Murder of Maria in the Red Barn,
or the robberies of Jack Sheppard the highwayman. The capital
outlay was minimal – a platform of some sort, and a piano. They
were held in the back rooms of public houses all over the poor districts
of London. The pub landlords did well out of them, and the audience
came away with its mind filled with desirable role models, as well as
gin.

By the late 1860s penny gaffs were being supplanted by theatres
and music halls. There were 33 theatres in London, mostly playing
comedy and melodrama, and some of them famous for 'the impro-
priety of costume of the ladies in the pantomimes'.[5] At the Garrick
Theatre, conveniently sited next to the Whitechapel police station, a
penny got you into the pit and a box would only cost 2d or 3d. In its
repertoire 'virtue is always rewarded', which certainly made a change
from the penny gaffs.[6] The Royal Victoria Theatre across the river
in Waterloo Road (now 'the Old Vic'), with a seating capacity of
1,200, presented melodramas for the local populace, with occasional
spectacles such as a 'masquerade ball' for 'the lowest class, orange
girls, coster girls, servants and the like'.[7] A gallery seat cost only 4d,
for which, when there was a play 'with a good murder in it', the
crowd began to queue hours before opening time.

Astley's Amphitheatre in Lambeth could be relied on for spectacular
equestrian performances with dancing horses, and sometimes even
elephants. It had a round circus ring, as well as a proscenium stage.
The Drury Lane Theatre (which is still there) put on Christmas
pantomimes 'in dumb show. Not a word could we hear. The fights
in pit and gallery were frequent. The shower of orange peel from the
gods into the pit was quite astounding'.[8] It is mildly surprising to find
Munby in the gallery at the Haymarket Theatre, having 'waited with
the mob at the gallery door ... to sit in the gallery among the

"roughs" and drink with [Hannah, his working-class mistress] out of the same bottle, between the acts'.⁹ Yet it was here, in 1860, that he noticed in the stage box 'two quiet ladies in black', with the Count of Flanders, a relation of both of the royal pair through the King of the Belgians. 'The Queen was with them, half-hid by a curtain, but laughing consumedly at the farce', so she *could* be amused. She had probably taken as normal 'the guard of red-coated and bear-skinned grenadiers who marched up and down in front of the building with gleaming bayonets ... it was said that soon after the theatre had been built such a guard was requisitioned for a special occasion ... no cancellation was received so the sentries have been there ever since'.¹⁰

Performances were long. 'At most theatres the curtain rose at 7 or 7.30 ... the performance began with a short piece, farce or operetta, followed at about 8 by the principal attraction, which, if not very long, was succeeded by a second farce ... there was usually a refreshment bar'.¹¹ When Madam Vestris, a famous music hall star, appeared at the Lyceum Theatre, the doors opened at 6.30, the performance began at 7, and was promised to 'terminate as near 11.30 as possible'. Seats in the dress circle were 5s, in the upper boxes 4s, in the pit 2s and in the gallery 1s.¹² I have found no reference to that plague of modern theatres, the queue for the ladies' cloakroom during the interval, nor, indeed, to ladies' lavatories.

There were music halls where for 6d you could drink and smoke while you watched acrobats and listened to 'operatic selections' and black-face minstrels, for which there was a vogue.¹³ The Theatre out at Sadler's Wells had used water from the New River Head next door to make a vast tank 90 feet long, under the stage, in 1804. In 1823 it even added machinery to whisk the stage and scenery up to the roof, so that 'acquatic performances' could be mounted without an interval.¹⁴ Someone wanting to express his artistic genius might frequent the Albert Saloon, in Tothill Street, just east of Victoria Station, where there was no set programme and members of the audience could 'oblige' with their favourite turns – like karaoke nowadays. There were underground haunts such as the Cave of Harmony, also known as Evans's, in Covent Garden, 'a cellar for shameful song-singing, where members of both Houses, the pick of the Universities, and the bucks of the Row [fashionable Rotten Row, in Hyde Park] were content to dwell in indecencies for ever,' and 'vulgarity woke roars of laughter, and the heads of the first families rapped the tables with their empty tumblers, calling for the slang chorus again'.[15] The Judge and Jury Court was even more notorious for vulgarity:

> It is difficult to imagine anything more low and blackguard than this ... parody of a Court of Justice ... there is a long low room opposite Covent Garden ... lit with candles and furnished with benches; opposite those benches a railed-off space for the Bar and Jury, and an elevated desk for the Judge. You pay one shilling entrance, which entitles you to a cigar and a glass of rum or gin and water, or beer ... they deal in very gross indecencies.

Thus wrote a member of the aristocracy in 1842.[16] (In those days, the proceedings in the Matrimonial Courts were reported in full, and could contain some very lurid details, which were woven into the proceedings in the Judge and Jury Court.)

The most famous of the music halls was the Alhambra. It was a vast building holding four to five thousand, built in the Moorish taste, complete with minarets, on the east side of Leicester Square (where the Odeon cinema is now). It had begun in 1854 as The Royal Panopticon of Science and Art, but the public stayed away in their thousands, so it closed and reopened as a circus in 1858. It made a perfect display arena for daring feats of horsemanship. When Victoria brought her family to see 'Black Eagle, the Horse of Beauty', its success was guaranteed. It expanded into a music hall in 1860. 'The Alhambra has set the fashion [for] dancing and music and gorgeous scenic representations. The principal attractions ... are ballet dancing, and such performances as those of Leotard' on his Flying Trapeze. His act caused 'a real sensation ... the ease, the grace, the unerring certainty ... his 3 swinging bars suspended by long ropes carried him right across the auditorium and stage of the vast building'.[17]

Leotard's act lasted for ten minutes, and the audience had to wait for it from 8, when the doors opened, until 11, when he appeared. Meanwhile they were regaled with 'a dance forbidden in Paris' – can this have been the original no-knickers can-can? – and a corps de ballet of 200 girls 'all painted to look, at a distance, as attractive as possible, and wearing the scanty costumes patronised by dancers of the opposite sex'. There were 40 magnificent chandeliers, and an orchestra of 60 players, but they were 'almost drowned in the noise of the promenading patrons, male and female, who are more inclined to lounge about the many little bars ... and "liquor up"'. Surely they must have watched the stage when the 'Titanic Cascades' poured tons of water from the top of the building down to a tank under the stage, and thence to the sewers. But perhaps they went back to liquoring up when an innocuous version of the can-can came on, danced by Finette of Paris but without the 'offensive features of the can-can in petticoats'.[18] The whole place was 'beautifully fitted up … light and cheerful … there is something pleasant in the sight of an immense crowd enjoying itself … here you may move about, or attempt to do so, and talk, and laugh, ad lib … it is the resort of women who have to live by their charms of person … a market place and Royal Exchange of vice'. (The Royal Exchange was a shopping mall in the City – nothing to do with Albert and Victoria.) There was a refreshment room downstairs known as the Canteen, where 'forty or fifty ballet girls [could be seen] standing chatting, or seated in company with their male admirers … if she is chaste, she cannot long be expected to remain so'.[19] In 1859 a ballet dancer was prosecuted for trying to supplement her wage, 9s a week, by petty crime; most preferred part-time prostitution.

No wonder the Alhambra was not, in respectable circles, 'a place for a young man to frequent' – but they did. A ticket admitting you to the 'body of the hall, where artisans and working men congregate, and not infrequently bring with them their wives,' cost only 6d, but it cost 1s to enter the main part of the building, where

in the boxes and balconies sat brazen-faced women, blazoned in tawdry finery, and curled and painted … there is no mistaking these women … [behind the refreshment bars] superbly-attired barmaids vend strong liquors … besides these there are … small private apartments to which a gentleman desirous of sharing a bottle of wine with a recent acquaintance may retire. [At the long bar] any night may be seen dozens of prostitutes enticing simpletons to drink … in dozens, in scores, prostitutes every one, doing exactly as they do in the infamous and prosecuted Haymarket dens, and no one interferes.[20]

It cost only 1s for standing-room – or wandering-about room – and 2s 6d for a seat.[21]

Munby went there in 1862, and saw a 'female gymnast', aged 10, dressed in the abbreviated shorts and low bodice appropriate for gymnastics. The Alhambra's reputation as the haunt of prostitutes attracted the notice of Parliament; one wonders how many Honourable Members had sampled its delights in person. The Select Committee they appointed was reassured by the evidence of Strange, the owner/manager, that only 3 per cent of his audience were prostitutes. (Suppose a nearly full house, 4,000 people: only 3 per cent of them, i.e. 120, were prostitutes, according to Strange. How did he collect his statistics? His conclusion seems improbable.)

✳

The upper classes – except for Victoria, and I doubt if she went to the Haymarket often – would not normally dream of attending a theatre; they went to the opera. There were three principal opera houses. Covent Garden Opera House staged no fewer than eighteen first London performances of opera, in the period 1840–70, including Berlioz's *Benvenuto Cellini*, directed in 1841 by Berlioz himself. Her Majesty's Opera House in the Haymarket (Her Majesty's Theatre now occupies part of the site, New Zealand House the other part) was almost as vast as La Scala in Milan. It staged fifteen first London performances in the period 1840–70, including a succession of Verdi operas; the London debut of Jenny Lind, the 'Swedish Nightingale', in Meyerbeer's *Robert le Diable* in 1847, and Offenbach's *Orpheus in the Underworld* in 1865. 'Many of the double boxes on the grand tier have sold for as much as £7,000 or £8,000. A box on the pit tier, £4,000'.[22] These colossal sums would allow the owner to sublet to others, for a season, but even so, opera-going was an expensive hobby.

The Theatre Royal in Drury Lane came third in the league of first London performances of opera, with ten. Wagner just scrapes into our period with *The Flying Dutchman* there, in 1870. Opera was occasionally put on in other theatres. In 1857 Auber's *Fra Diavolo* was staged in the Lyceum Theatre (constantly threatened with closure but still there, in Wellington Street near the Aldwych), and in 1869 *Orpheus in the Underworld* was revived at the St James's Theatre in King Street (the site is now occupied by an office block).[23]

Music lovers were well catered for in London. On Sundays the choral singing by the children of the Foundling Hospital near Gray's Inn was worth going to hear.[24] 'The Psalms were chanted by upwards of 1,000 children ... there was a most fashionably dressed congregation'.[25] There were regular concerts in the Hanover Square Rooms. In 1855 a concert there raised all of £130 'for the sick and wounded at Scutari' (Florence Nightingale's hospital during the Crimean War). Every Friday during the London Season the 500 members of the Sacred Harmonic Society performed sacred oratorios, 'the greatest treats which the lover of good music can enjoy', in Exeter Hall in the Strand.[26] Hector Berlioz, in London as one of the judges in the Great Exhibition, was impressed by this 'well organised mass of amateurs assisted by a small number of professional musicians', who could sing 'the most difficult music of Handel and Mendelssohn'.

Berlioz also remarked approvingly on the instrumentalists of the Philharmonic Society and the Beethoven Quartet Society. But he was moved to tears by the charity school children's annual concert in St Paul's Cathedral. The sound of 6,500 young voices singing in unison was 'the most extraordinary thing I have ever seen or heard'. Someone had recognised him, and pushed him into a surplice over his black coat, and he took his place with the seventy or more Cathedral singers.

> Banners were placed in different parts of the vast amphitheatre [of specially built tiers of seats] indicating the place appropriated to each school, bearing the name of the parish ... the dark blue of the coats of the little boys on the higher seats and the white frocks and caps of the little girls ... the boys wearing on their waistcoats, some a brass plate, others a silver medal, produced by their motion a continual scintillation ... [The girls wore green and red ribbons] which made this part of the amphitheatre ... resemble a mountain covered with snow amid which peeped out here and there blades of grass and flowers ... everywhere prevailed order and devotional silence.[27]

There were concerts in the Crystal Palace at Sydenham, where 2,000 massed voices belted out Handel oratorios, but they 'were not so agreeable as the smaller concerts in Exeter Hall' in the Strand.[28]

The pleasure gardens of the previous century still survived, in Vauxhall and Cremorne. Vauxhall (where the southern end of Vauxhall Bridge now is) still had its 'gloomy avenue of trees' and its 'illuminated rivulet', but the 'pond with a gigantic Neptune and 8 white sea-horses' was now lit by gas. There were tableaux of Wellington and Nelson, and a circus with horses, but 'the most brilliant exhibition of the evening' was the fireworks.[29] But it was not what it had been and after no less than seven 'farewells' it closed in 1859. Cremorne (across the river in Chelsea; now built over. Its entrance was from the King's Road) was a late comer, opened as pleasure gardens in the 1840s, with a theatre, a banqueting hall, 'delightful lavender bowers', and an American bowling saloon, the first (or second) in London, its competitor in the Strand claiming to be the first in May 1849.[30] 'The gardens are beautiful ... adorned with really fine trees, and watered by the Thames, here almost a silver stream ... on a summer evening the air is fresh and balmy, the amusements are varied, the company are genteel in appearance ... the women are well-dressed and well-behaved.'[31] In 1856 a visiting Frenchman, Francis Wey, was impressed. The gardens offered

> a variety of attractions. One moves on methodically from the one to the other at the sound of a large bell which a man rings as he leads the way, the crowd trotting along behind him ... In a Chinese bandstand an orchestra struck up a scottische. A minute later the carefully levelled open space was filled with couples ... people here dance with their hips and their shoulders, seeming to have little control over their legs ... frivolous young things improvise all sorts of indecorous antics.[32]

Throughout the Season it was open fifteen hours a day, and charged only a shilling. During daylight there were tableaux and pageants and balloon ascents, and as darkness fell, fireworks which lit up the sky for miles.

In 1855 there was a hideous accident during one of the pageants. Jane Carlyle described how she met eight soldiers, in the King's Road, 'carrying, high over their heads, a bier. Twenty yards further on, another. I asked a working man what had happened. "It was a great night at Cremorne, the storming of Sevastopol [a recent battle in the Crimean War]; 30 or 40 soldiers were storming, when the scaffold broke, and they all fell in on their own bayonets".'[33] In 1864 Goddard, the 'Flying Man', rose to 5,000 feet in his balloon from Cremorne, but he came down on the spire of St Luke's Church in Chelsea, and was killed.

There is a lyrical description of Cremorne in a book on prostitution:[34]

> The most beautiful public garden London can boast. Fifteen thousand have been known to be present, nightly visitors are 1,500 to 2,000 ... By about 10 o'clock age and innocence had seemingly all retired ... leaving the massive elms, the grass-plots and the geranium beds, the kiosks, temples, 'monster platforms' and crystal circle ... to flicker in the 1,000 gas lights ... You heard very plainly the sigh of the poplar,

the surging gossip of the tulip-tree, and the plash of the little embowered fountain.

The writer then returns to his subject, prostitution. There were 1,000 men of the upper and middle classes still in the gardens, after ten o'clock, and 300 prostitutes, but it was all very discreet, there was no soliciting and the prostitutes were 'pretty and quiet'.

The London parks were open to all. The East End was not well supplied with open spaces; the fields of Spitalfields had been built over long ago. In 1841 Victoria Park was begun, on 290 acres acquired out beyond the built-up area of Hackney, to 'serve as a lung for the North East part of London'.[35] The site was marshy, but the soil was consolidated by earth from the excavations for the London docks.[36] It took a remarkably long time to achieve its full glory, but already by 1850 it had 'added to the health of the inhabitants of Spitalfields and Bethnal Green'.[37] There was 'a large sheet of water cut out, and very pretty diversified walks made, nicely planted and tasty [*sic*]';[38] and a football field, used by the City of London School team, among others, in 1865,[39] and cricket pitches, and a boating lake, with an island crowned by a Chinese temple; but there was still room for the 'poor labouring men who were out strolling on the Sabbath morning' to have peace and quiet, except from the 'infidels who seek to proselytise', such as atheists.[40] A woman looking back to her Bethnal Green childhood had an idyllic recollection of Victoria Park. She was born in 1855, the seventh child of fourteen:

My fourth sister and I always stayed away from school on washing day, to mind the babies. In the summer it was real sport, because everybody had large families and generally kept the elder girls, and sometimes the boys, at home to mind the little ones. We used to ... go out all together with our babies and prams, into Victoria Park. Very few people had prams of their own, but [they] could hire them at 1d an hour to hold one baby, or 1½d for two. The single pram had always to accommodate 2, and the double pram 3 or more ... We would picnic on bread and treacle under the trees in the Park and return home in the evening a troop of tired but happy children.[41]

She gave no date for these happy occasions, but she went out to service in 1867, so it was before then. She must have been in time to enjoy the drinking-fountain paid for by that untiring benefactor, Angela Burdett Coutts, in 1861.

Battersea was another new park. Its site, on the south bank of the river opposite Chelsea, was unpromising: a 'swamp of dank pools'[42] separated from the river only by a narrow raised causeway, and frequently flooded. Before 1846 the area had been the haunt of the riff-raff of London, and the site of weekly horse fairs run by the resident gypsies. It became so notorious that in 1846 the Commissioners for Improving the Metropolis acquired 320 acres of land there, of which 198 were to be a public park, the rest to be used for housing. The park was opened in 1853, and acquired its beautiful lake (which is still there), in 1860, and a sub-tropical garden (which is not) in 1864.

The old-established royal parks led through central London like a green necklace, from St James's Park at the foot of Buckingham Palace, round the Palace by Green Park, and across the traffic at Hyde Park Corner into Hyde Park, with Kensington Gardens further west. Regent's Park lay to the north, at the edge of the built-up area. Friedrich Engels, who was always looking on the dark side, saw 'an average number of 50 human beings of all ages who huddle together in the parks every night, having no other shelter'.[43] For once he missed the true, darker picture. Munby, walking through St James's Park in July 1865 at four o'clock one afternoon, saw all the open spaces 'covered with ragged men and ragged women'. The park-keeper told him that 'they are men out of work, and unfortunate girls, servant girls many of them, what has been out of place and took to the streets till they've sunk so low that they can't get a living even by prostitution ... they come as soon as the gates opens'. Munby again – 'Every pose expressed an absolute degradation and despair ... on one side of the path there were 150 of them'.[44] A Government rat-catcher told Mayhew that 'the parks is much infested' with rats.[45]

And yet Hippolyte Taine thought St James's Park was 'a real piece of English country; enormous ancient trees, real meadows, a lake peopled by ducks and wading birds; cows, and folded sheep graze the eternally fresh grass'.[46] The lake was indeed 'peopled' with 21 species of ducks, more than 300 birds. They belonged to the Ornithological Society, which occupied a lodge on an island in the lake, where its members sat at meetings, and hatched eggs. In 1857 a suspension bridge was built over the lake, which gave, as its successor still does, one of the most magical views in London. St James's Park was lit by gas, but perhaps not brightly enough; it has always had a *louche* reputation for cruising Guardsmen from the nearby barracks, as well as muggers. Yet what could be more innocent than the milk-sellers, duly licensed by the Home Secretary, with eight cows in eight stands (half that number in the winter) where infants and 'delicate people who had been prescribed new milk' could enjoy it fresh from the cow?[47] Green Park serves as a *cordon sanitaire* between St James's Palace and Buckingham Palace, and the traffic of Piccadilly. Nothing much happens there. 'Green Park and St James's Park are the recreation grounds of the middle classes, who, having to go on foot and not disposing of much leisure, cannot go further afield'.[48] Tourists down from the north to see London and the Great Exhibition greeted them with relief; 'after wandering about a while we lay down on the grass and I had a short snooze'.[49]

'Wealthy people owning carriages patronise Regent's Park and Hyde Park.'[50] Hyde Park is a vast area of green, 340 acres of grass and trees. No wonder a little of it could be spared, temporarily, for the Great Exhibition. 'It is a unique experience, in the very heart of a large city, to embrace at a glance pompous equipages with powdered attendants and magnificent horses, and rustic herds of cows, sheep and goats with elegant women trailing silks and laces among them'.[51] In the London Season 'all the wealth and fashion and splendid equipages of the nobility of the country were to be seen there, between 5.30 and 6.30 every evening'.[52] Hippolyte Taine again:

> Hyde Park is a country gentleman's park transported to the heart of the capital. Round about two in the afternoon the principal road through it becomes a riding school ... tiny little girls, and boys not more than eight years old, ride their ponies beside their father's horse. I have seen massive and dignified matrons at the trot ... girls and ladies ride in the park even when it is raining.[53]

The massive matrons at the trot along Rotten Row must have been unnerving to a foreign visitor, but the 'girls and ladies' could look superb on horseback. A foreign journalist paints the picture:

> On fine summer evenings all the youth, beauty, celebrity and wealth of London may be seen on horseback in Rotten Row. [The Duke of Wellington] with his horse walking at a slow pace ... everyone takes off his hat; and the Duke smiles to the right and to the left ... All of a sudden a couple come forward at a quick pace. There is room for them and their horses in the midst of Rotten Row, however full it may be, for everyone is eager to make way for them: it is the Queen and her

husband, without martial and splendour, without a single naked sword in sight.[54]

Miss Walters, universally known as 'Skittles', the leading London prostitute in 1862, did not enjoy – perhaps did not want – such consideration. 'The crowd who assembled in Hyde Park to watch her drive by seriously incommoded the traffic'.[55]

Hippolyte Taine was charmed by 'whole families of the common people picnicking on the grass in Hyde Park: they neither pulled up nor damaged anything'. He did not see, or at least did not remark on, a more remarkable sight: 'the number of persons who frequent the Serpentine (the lake in Hyde Park) for the purposes of ablution ... not less than 7,000–8,000 daily immerse themselves in this water alone'.[56] This number is hard to swallow. I can only say that it was in the context of an article on the need for public baths and washhouses. In the winter this immersion was undertaken only by devoted – demented? – swimmers (as now), who were unworried by six inches of ice: they borrowed some gunpowder from their washerwomen (who habitually used it to clear the soot from the chimneys of their washing-coppers) and blew up the ice.[57]

There was a curious low, round building near the Serpentine, with no windows.[58] This was the Magazine: the Government store of gunpowder. 'Upwards of a million rounds of ball and blank ammunition are kept ready for immediate use'.[59] Fortunately it was not needed to disperse the Chartists' rally in the Park in 1855, to protest against the Sunday Trading Bill, which would have shut the pubs and the shops on Sundays, depriving the working man of his quiet pint and his wife of a chance to do the shopping in peace. Karl Marx, who was there, was convinced that 'the English Revolution began yesterday in Hyde Park', but after some skirmishes with the police the 'revolutionaries', disappointingly, went home.[60]

Further west, Hyde Park merges with Kensington Gardens, even more elegant than Hyde Park. Nathaniel Hawthorne was American Consul in Liverpool between 1853 and 1858. He got to know London well. His comments tended to be less than enthusiastic; the only time he really let himself go was in Kensington Gardens – 'the most beautiful piece of artificial woodland and park scenery that I have ever seen'.[61] In 1865 Munby, who preferred working girls to women of his own class, was scathing: 'a troop of exquisites sat motionless on their well-trained steeds ... as they spoke and simpered languidly with

Applicants for Admission to a Casual Ward painted by Luke Fildes in 1874 from sketches from the life made in 1870. Even here, the central figure wears a battered top hat.

The milk-woman in this 1864 photograph looks far too slight for the heavy churns of milk she carries on her wooden yoke.

A posed photograph of 1860, 'Lighting the Grate'. This maid looks suspiciously as if she is wearing a crinoline: see page 126.

Servant girls could look surprisingly elegant. The girl in the silk dress (1861) shows off her pretty hands and bracelets. The challenging girl beside her (1856) seems to be wearing her working dress and apron. Below, the young woman with the elegant flower-trimmed bonnet and lace collar (1861) is hiding her nails, but the country servant girl (1862) up in London to see the sights seems almost proud of her pathetically ugly hands.

SLAVES OF THE NEEDLE.

It is almost 1 o'clock in the morning, but the young dressmakers work on by candlelight under the unforgiving eye of their supervisor, in this 1853 print. One young girl droops, near to exhaustion (see page 254).

The dress they are making will need a crinoline petticoat under its voluminous skirt. These are dated 1864. Earlier ones made a circular shape.

Society at play: a state ball at Buckingham Palace in 1848. Note the matched pair of footmen, the kilted Highlander, and the galaxy of Army uniforms.

Society on horseback: Rotten Row in Hyde Park (detail from hand-coloured engraving published in 1867). The women ride side-saddle. The men wear frock coats and light-coloured trousers. Both sexes wear top hats. The building behind the trees is St George's Hospital and the statue on the sky-line is the Duke of Wellington.

The interior courtyard of the Reform Club (see page 104), a sanctuary for middle-class bachelors, built in 1841 by Charles Barry.

Women prisoners in Brixton prison (1860), sewing shirts, in silence, watched by female wardresses. If they could not sew when they came in, they surely could when they were released.

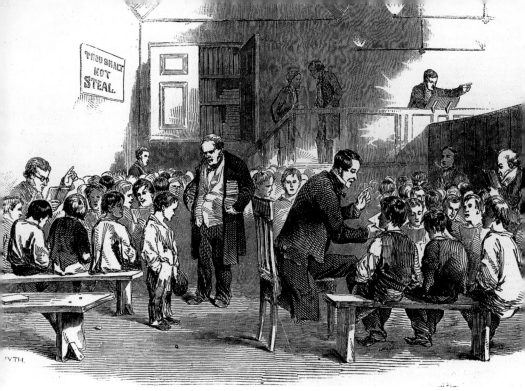

A Ragged School in 1846. These boys seem to be docile and fairly decently dressed. This was far from the norm – see page 236.

Mutes standing outside the front door of a middle-class home which had suffered a bereavement; one of the many funereal ceremonies dear to the Victorians. The bare-footed children gaze at them with astonishment.

the yet more languid belles who lay supine under a cloud of pink and white fluff in the barouches'.[62]

Regent's Park and its gleaming stucco terraces had been planned by Nash as a complement to his graceful Regent Street. They were not finished until the 1820s, and the park was not opened to the public for another twenty years. The Royal Botanic Society took over eighteen acres (now the site of Queen Mary's rose garden) and built a glass and iron conservatory big enough for 2,000 visitors, as well as a rockery and other horticultural delights. At the north end of the park you can still visit the Zoo. In 1828 the Zoological Society had opened its collection to the public, for 6d a head on Mondays, 1s on other days. Despite the low entrance fee, it was a fashionable resort.[63] The layout had been planned by Decimus Burton, with iron-barred cages where, in the words of Nathaniel Hawthorne, 'the creatures are as comfortable as could be'.[64]

The world's first reptile house opened there in 1843; the keeper mistakenly thought he could charm a cobra but he died of snake bite within hours. Still, you might be able to watch 'a boa constrictor seize a duck and squash it', as well as a rhinoceros and a 'hippoppotamis' [*sic*], and a kiwi from New Zealand that was said to live on snails.[65] An aquarium was added in 1849. An orang-utan joined the collection of primates the next year. There was a parrot walk, with parrots on perches strung between the trees at head height (which sounds risky, especially if you were wearing some stuffed birds in your hat), and a pair of elephants called Jumbo and Alice. In 1849 there were nearly 170,000 visitors, and 1,352 animals: 'the giraffes and rattlesnakes are very rare and fine'.[66]

There was another zoo over the river, in Surrey Gardens in Walworth, where for a shilling you could not only view the animals, but enjoy all the usual amenities of a pleasure garden. It was worth timing your arrival carefully: there was 'feeding of the carnivores at 5, the pelicans at 5.30, a concert at 6.15, and the pyrotechnic Exhibition at dusk ... At the close of the evening's amusements omnibuses to all parts are in attendance'.[67] But the Crystal Palace put it out of business. The animals were sold in 1855, and the proceeds used to build a vast concert hall where Spurgeon, a popular preacher, once held an audience of 9,000 enthralled for 45 minutes, preaching on Sin. The hall was destroyed by fire, and the gardens were sold for redevelopment in 1877.

One Great Exhibition tourist took time out to go to Syon House, the Duke of Northumberland's country house at Isleworth, where the spectacular lily Victoria Regia was in flower; and then on, by river, to Kew Gardens, which were even better than the gardens of Syon House.[68] Since 1840 the gardens, properly called the Royal Botanic Gardens, had been controlled by the Department of Woods and Forests. Between 1841 and 1856 they had grown, under the directorship of Sir William Hooker, from 15 to 250 acres. As well as rare trees, swathes of immaculately kept lawns and brilliant massed carpet-bedding designs, the visitor could enjoy vestiges of the previous century when the gardens were a royal amusement, and William Chambers had been employed to design the Chinese Pagoda (163 feet high and still surviving, although deprived of the bells that used to tinkle from every storey), and the Orangery near the entrance gates, as well as miscellaneous temples and a ruin in eighteenth-century taste. Also, charmingly, the visitor wearied by perambulating the gardens could rest from time to time in the alcoves built for the royal family for just that purpose (two survive, near the Lion Gate and at the Brentford Gate).

The Great Palm House designed by Decimus Burton took four years to build, from 1844. It is still there. It is 363 feet long, 100 feet wide and 62 feet high at its apex, built of iron and curved sheets of glass. Burton also designed the Temperate House, which was begun in 1860 but not completed until 1899, and the grand entrance gates bearing the arms of Queen Victoria. Under Hooker's direction, the gardens were opened to the public for the first time in 1840, every weekday from noon to six, and the lake was created, in 1861.

More urban pleasures could be identified in the countless guidebooks to the London of the Great Exhibition. There was even a fabric map the size of a large handkerchief, usefully showing not only the location of various sights but also whether they were free or not.[69] 'A floating (swimming) bath had for many years been moored on the upper south side [of Blackfriars Bridge] ... it was well frequented for many years, and was known from the quantity of flowers all over its decks in pots which were kept bright by means of red ochre'.[70] Wyld's 'Monster Globe' in Leicester Square was an ingenious geography lesson; the surface of the world in relief was shown *inside* the huge structure, viewed from a series of iron steps and galleries. It was intended to last only as long as the Crystal Palace in Hyde Park, but it survived for ten years.[71]

The Victorian tourist was indefatigable. A schoolteacher down from Manchester to stay with his uncle in 1858 put Kensal Green cemetery top of his list of sights; 'the Duke of Sussex and Princess Sophia are buried there'. He and his uncle then covered the West End, St Paul's Cathedral, and Covent Garden Market, arriving at London Bridge, where they took a steamer down the river – 'there were a great number of sailing vessels and steamers of all sizes' – with a cursory look at Brunel's *Great Eastern* ship in its dock, and a quick trip round Greenwich Hospital, and the Deptford dockyard, and an inspection of the Thames Tunnel – 'it is a very fine place'. Then round the Tower of London and the Mint ... 'Uncle thinks we must have walked 20 miles' all on one day. After several days of hectic sightseeing, including Madame Tussaud's Waxworks in Baker Street (1s entry, 6d extra for the 'Chamber of Horrors') – where 'there was very fine music', and a memorable replica of 'Marie Antoinette lying asleep, breathing' – he was perhaps beginning to tire, so he took the extreme step of washing his feet and putting on clean socks, and off they go to the Zoo, where he found the monkey house so smelly that he could not stay.[72]

In 1869 Munby went to see the Siamese Twins, 'two small elderly Mongolian men, grizzled and wizened ... they lean on each other as they walk ... the flesh bond that connects them (5 ins long and as thick as a strong man's wrist) is just visible through their open shirt-fronts'. (Poor men; nowadays, surely, an attempt would be made to sever them. As they were, they each got married. One twin died before the other, who mercifully did not survive for long.)

If the new sport of bicycling interested you, two 'French Female Velocipedistes', dressed as men in short breeches, were performing at the Royal Gardens in Woolwich in 1869.[73] When you visited Westminster Abbey, be sure you had your penknife with you. Emerson was surprised to find the royal tombs 'cut and scrawled with penknives, and even in the Coronation Chair in which for hundreds of years the Kings and Queens of England have been crowned, Mr Butter, Mr Light and Mr Abbott have recorded their humble petition to be remembered: "I Butter slept in this chair" is explicitly recorded by that gentleman's penknife on the seat'.[74]

Museums catered for the Victorian passion for self-improvement. The British Museum was open three days a week, from 10 to 4 in

winter, 10 to 7 in summer. The museum of the Royal College of
Surgeons preserved all sorts of horrors for the delight of members
and 'visitors introduced by them personally'. The Prince Consort
opened the Museum of Practical Geology in 1851, all lined in marble,
in Jermyn Street (demolished 1936). The East India Company, which
governed India until 1854, opened its museum in Leadenhall Street,
in the City, every Saturday from 11 to 3; there you could see 'Hindu
idols in silver and gold ... and an emblematic organ (a tiger on a
man) contrived for the amusement of Tippoo Sahib'.[75] It was possible
to watch banknotes being made in the Bank of England, and the
'inmates' of the Blind School in St George's Fields working. Ladies
would enjoy window-shopping, or even strolling through the big new
department stores. Their husbands might prefer to look in to Christie's,
the auctioneers, in King Street, or assess the horses at Tattersall's sale
rooms near Hyde Park Corner. The energetic with heads for heights
might like to visit St Paul's Cathedral, and climb up past the
Whispering Gallery, admission 6d, up another 616 narrow winding
steps – 'a dirty and somewhat fatiguing task' – to the ball, which,
according to the writer of a popular guide book, 'is in diameter 6 feet
2 inches and will contain 8 persons, "without", it is said, "particular
inconvenience". This however may well be doubted'.[76]

But the summit of sightseeing would be Buckingham Palace; 'mode
of admission: order from the Lord Chancellor, granted only when the
Court is absent'.[77] The Queen was in London, of course, during the
Great Exhibition, but she was nearly always away. What splendour.

CHAPTER 17

The Great Exhibition

⁓᪉⁓

*The right conditions · the Chartists · the Royal Society of Arts · the site
· the aim of the Exhibition · the building · the opening · tickets ·
refreshments · the lavatories · the exhibits · the statues · the Koh-i-noor
· criminals and revolutionaries · the visitors · the Queen · the Duke
of Wellington · railway excursions · the Penzance pedestrian ·
attendance figures · closing day*

At last, with everything in place, we can go to the major event of the
century: the Great Exhibition of the Industry of All Nations.¹ Not
quite straight away. There have to be plans, and discussions, and
dissension and squabbles and tension. The opening date, 1 May 1851,
comes closer and closer and nothing is quite ready ...

1848 has become known as 'the year of revolutions', as unrest flared
all over Europe. In England the Chartists were passionately advocating
social reform, but their great meeting in Kennington, a southern
suburb, from which a march to the Houses of Parliament was planned,
fizzled out. All the bridges across the Thames were blocked, and the
middle classes had been mobilised in strength. O'Brien, the Chartist
leader, realised that his supporters could not win, and told them to
go home quietly, which they did. He was allowed to take their petition
across the river in three cabs, and leave it at the House of Commons.

When the Chartist petition, which was supposed to be supported by
five million signatures, underwent the scrutiny of Parliament, it was at
once seen that there were only about a million and a half of signatures.
Many of these were impudent forgeries. The Duke of Wellington's
name appeared seventeen times, whilst amongst other great personages
who ... were the warmest supporters of the 'Charter' and showed it
by signing their names several times, appeared the Queen, Prince

Albert ... and 'Punch'! Many apparent signatures turned out to be obscene and disgusting words, slang phrases, or gross ribaldry. The whole movement, therefore, is covered with scorn and ridicule.[2]

The Chartists' grievances continued to simmer, but the danger of revolution was past. The year 1849 marked the beginning of an economic boom. England had vast resources of natural materials such as coal and iron, and a steady trade in imported cotton. The new young queen had re-established the popularity of the monarchy, and the fertility of the royal pair ended any danger of a regency, or even of another female monarch. There were two small clouds in the sky. The first was that Albert, whom Victoria had married in 1840, was – not to put too fine a point on it – only a foreigner. The other, not so obvious, was the increasing possibility of trade competition from America and the European nations, in particular France.

The French seemed to have a knack of designing things that worked better – looked better – *sold* better, than our products, no matter how stalwart they were. John Bull would have been content to stand on his reputation for solid worth, and ignore the foreigners. For just that reason the Society for the Encouragement of Arts, Manufactures and Commerce had been founded in 1754. The usual abbreviation of its title to the Society of Arts (it became 'Royal' in 1847) obscures its influence in the manufacturing and commercial worlds, especially in industrial design, which it encouraged with prizes and competitions. Albert, who was far better-educated and internationally minded than his royal spouse, found this *modus operandi* familiar and admirable; this was the way things were done in Germany. He accepted the Presidency of the Society in 1847.

Exactly where and when the idea of the Great Exhibition crystallised, has been much discussed. Whoever had the final say, Henry Cole, of the Royal Society of Arts, and Albert, Prince Consort, between them generated the initiative which produced the Great Exhibition. A Royal Commission was appointed in January 1850, under the presidency of Albert, with members carefully drawn from every aspect of British life except, of course, the working class. The Exhibition was due to open in 17 months.

It needed financial backing. It needed a building. It needed a site. It needed publicity. The money came in, after energetic fundraising in which Albert was understandably reticent in case people should say 'Who does he think he is?' The building was, inevitably, the subject of a competition, but none of the plans submitted really pleased the Commission. With a slight bending of the rules, and astonishing speed, Joseph Paxton, the Duke of Devonshire's head gardener who had constructed a magnificent glasshouse for him at Chatsworth, submitted a design, which was accepted. But where could it be erected? Battersea Fields? Victoria Park? Kew? Hyde Park? Certainly not Hyde Park. It would frighten the horses in Rotten Row, disturb the peace of that plutocratic neighbourhood, destroy the trees ... Out of the question. But somehow, all the alternative sites turned out to be unsuitable, and Hyde Park it was. After all, it would be there for only a few months. The last objection, that the trees would be cut down to make room for it, died away when Paxton tweaked his design and roofed them in, like gigantic conservatory plants.[3] They all survived.

It remained to sell the idea to the general public, on whom the success of the whole project would depend. Albert had lofty ideals, as well as an astute political sense. In a speech at the Mansion House to launch the project, he said 'Nobody ... who has paid any attention to the peculiar features of our present era, will doubt for a moment that we are living at a period of most wonderful transition, which tends rapidly to accomplish that great era to which, indeed, all history points – the realisation of the unity of mankind.'[4]

On a more pragmatic level, the Exhibition would show the world – or that part of it that came to Hyde Park – all that was best in raw materials, industrial design and new inventions, which in turn would lead to improvements in public taste and in technical education, both badly needed in England. The implicit message would lie in the excellence – it was hoped – of the British exhibits, which would tell their own story. It was never intended to be a glorified trade fair. Some of the exhibitors objected to the rules forbidding trade, but they had to be content with taking enquiries which might result in a sale; no prices were to be displayed. More than 17,000 exhibitors took part, showing more than 100,000 exhibits. The theory behind the choice of exhibits was that there should be five classes: raw materials, machinery, manufactures, fine arts and that invaluable classification, Miscellaneous. In the event these tidy lines tended to be blurred by logistic considerations – would a large piece of machinery go up the stairs?– so that I doubt whether many visitors were always conscious of the logic behind what they saw.[5]

The press kept its readers abreast of the developments in Hyde

Park. Interest was so great, and such a nuisance to the contractors, that tickets were issued to watch the construction. To discourage free viewing a hefty wooden palisade was erected round the site. (It was used as part of the floor when the great building was nearly finished). Charles Pugh, a respectable official in the Law Courts, was not to be thwarted. In April 1851, two weeks before the official opening day, after 'a pretence of going to the office' for an hour and a half, he 'took a walk round the Crystal Palace ... at all the crevices I peeped in I saw nothing but confusion'.[6]

As May 1851 came nearer and nearer, the public became increasingly intrigued. Londoners were familiar with the use of glass for hothouses. Loddige's plant nursery in Hackney was famous for his huge collection of orchids and palms, housed in a glass paraboloid with narrow iron ribs, 80 feet long, 60 feet wide and 40 feet high at its apex. By the 1830s the palms had outgrown their living space, and Paxton was engaged to design a new hot-house for them, using laminated wood and curved glass. Decimus Burton had used iron and glass for his vast Palm House out at Kew, begun in 1844. Glass was still costly, because of the tax on it, which even impelled some houseowners to blank out windows in a façade, to save duty. In 1845 the duty was abolished, creating a surge in demand which in turn inspired new production technology. By 1850 Britain's principal glass manufacturer, Chance Brothers of Birmingham, could accept Paxton's demand for the 900,000 square feet needed for his building, in panes of 49 inches by 10 inches, 16oz per square foot.

New machines and techniques appeared as the work progressed. Paxton devised a trolley system running on his newly invented roof gutters, which enabled 80 men to instal 18,000 panes in a week.[7] Since the building was, under the terms of the Commission, to be temporary, no foundations needed to be dug, except for the main upright beams. The whole edifice was delicately put in place like a gigantic house of glass cards. The first batch of iron columns was delivered in September 1850. Work went on rapidly from then. The labour force quickly rose to 2,000 men, and a crowd of men waited at the site every morning hoping to be taken on. A strike was called, but it was smartly quashed, the strikers being dismissed and replaced by foreigners. The building profession was not happy with this smooth glass monstrosity constructed out of endless prefabicated modules. Where were the curlicues and ornaments, the terracotta frou-frou that ought to clothe any self-respecting building – and add satisfactorily to its cost? The 'Crystal Palace', as it was christened by *Punch*, was merely an engineering work.

Critics foresaw gloomily that the glass would break in any storm, and the building would collapse under the weight of spectators, so tests were run. One of the galleries was installed a few feet from ground level, and 300 workmen were summoned to do their worst by running and jumping and walking on it; nothing happened. Then a detachment of soldiers were paraded on it, and ordered to run and march on the spot, in step; again, nothing happened. Finally boxes each containing 36 loose 68-lb shot were rolled about on a gallery already installed; still, nothing happened.[8] As to storms, heaven obliged two days before the opening, and sent a violent hailstorm. Not a pane was broken. The public took the Crystal Palace to their hearts, and stood up in the omnibuses passing the site, craning their necks to see the latest state of play.

Meanwhile exhibits were agonisingly slow in arriving, sometimes going on display weeks after the Exhibition had opened. Visitors who had already, as they thought, viewed everything, might always be surprised by an addition. The delay was understandable in the case of some Russian exhibits held up by adverse weather. American items, too, had vast distances to travel, without Government funding. Some of the French, Italians and Portuguese were slow to recognise the potential of the Exhibition. But it is hard to justify the tardiness of any of the British exhibits.[9] In theory, the exhibits from each participating country demonstrated its level of industrial achievement. In practice, it is hard to see, for example, how a collection of anthropomorphic stuffed frogs being shaved, and kittens seated round a table having tea, from the German Customs Union, could represent any aspect of industrial development, although I am sure they were very difficult to do.

The day before the opening, the Queen wrote in her diary 'My poor Albert is terribly fagged. All day some question or other, some difficulty, all of which my beloved one takes with the greatest quiet and good temper'.[10] When at the last moment the arrangements were found to be a little backward, Lord Granville (in charge of the Royal Commission, under Albert) was seen, broom in hand, vigorously sweeping up the refuse scattered about the dais, half an hour before the time fixed for the arrival of the royal personages – the whole family, come to see how things were going, which cannot have been very helpful. 'There is still, certainly, much to be done'. But on the magic day, 1 May 1851, Victoria surpassed herself as a diarist:

> This day is one of the greatest and most glorious of our lives ... it is a day which makes my heart swell ... The Park presented a wonderful spectacle, crowds streaming through it, carriages and troops passing, quite like the Coronation Day ... The day was bright, and all was bustle and excitement. At half past eleven the whole procession in nine state coaches was set in motion. Vickie [aged eleven: Victoria's eldest child] and Bertie [aged ten: the future Prince of Wales] were in our carriage, Vickie ... looked very nice, Bertie was in full Highland dress. The Green Park and Hyde Park were one mass of densely crowded human beings, in the highest good humour ... A little rain fell, just as we started: but before we neared the Crystal Palace the sun shone and gleamed upon the gigantic edifice ... The glimpse through the iron gates of the Transept, the moving palms and flowers, the myriads of people filling the galleries and seats all around, together with the flourish of trumpets, gave a sensation I shall never forget ... The tremendous cheering, the joy expressed in every face, the vastness of the building, with all its decorations and exhibits, the sound of the organ (with 200 instruments and 600 voices, which seemed nothing) and my beloved Husband the creator of the great 'peace Festival' ... was indeed moving ... After the National Anthem had been sung, Albert left my side, and at the head of the Commissioners ... read the Report to me, which is a long one, and I read a short answer. After this the Archbishop of Canterbury offered up a short and appropriate prayer, followed by the singing of Handel's Hallelujah Chorus.

Little did Victoria know the feuding and wrangling that lay behind this triumphal surface. And a certain amount of ceremony had to be ad-libbed. China had inscrutably refused to send an exhibit, but some kind of display had been cobbled together from contributions from private British individuals. It was the more puzzling that at the moment that the Hallelujah Chorus rang out, 'a Chinaman, dressed in magnificent robes, suddenly emerged from the crowd and prostrated himself before the throne. Who he was nobody knew'. After a hurried consultation involving even the royal couple 'it was thought best to place him between the Archbishop of Canterbury and the Duke of Wellington. In this dignified position he marched through the building to the delight and amazement of all beholders'[11] – and no doubt his own, being merely the captain of a Chinese junk moored in the river as a tourist attraction.

Tickets had been on sale for weeks. It made sense to buy a season ticket for 3 guineas, if you planned to come more than once. 'The wonders of its contents exhibit themselves more forcibly at every visit', wrote the same man who had tried so hard to see through the palisade.[12] For the first two days the charge was £1, then 5s a day until 24 May when the plebs would be admitted at 1s. It was shut on Sundays. 'Saturday morning until noon is reserved for the infirm and invalids, who are drawn in small carriages, and of those there are a great number'.[13]

Albert had hoped that 'the first impression which the view of this vast collection will produce upon the spectator will be that of deep thankfulness to the Almighty for the blessings which he has bestowed upon us ... and the second, the conviction that they can only be realised in proportion to the help which we are prepared to render to each other; therefore, only by peace, love and ready assistance, not only between individuals but between the nations of the earth'[14] – a forerunner of the United Nations, in Hyde Park. But most people were more materialistic. Their first reaction was of astonishment at the expanse of airy space filled with visual excitement. Hector Berlioz was one of the judges invited from France. He 'said "Hug" like a Mohican [*sic*], the first time I entered the edifice. I uttered an English exclamation that I need not repeat, on entering a second time; and I so far forgot myself as to suffer a French "sacrebleu" to escape me on my third visit.'[15]

Even Charlotte Brontë, notoriously shy of crowds, came five times: 'it is a marvellous, stirring, bewildering sight – a mixture of a genii palace and a mighty bazaar'.[16] When your eyes began to focus, you took in columns painted in vertical stripes of blue, white and yellow, contrasting with red-painted signs, red drapes and red canopies everywhere. 1851 was a hot summer; the visual effect of all that red must have been stifling. Taking as deep a breath as your stays would allow, you advanced. Possibly the most sensible thing to do was to have a cup of tea or a glass of lemonade while you acclimatised. The Commission had decided not to allow any alcohol to be sold in the Palace, which considering the British working man's propensity for getting drunk, was probably wise. But the refreshments that were on offer caused an outcry. Here is a visiting Frenchman's view: 'There are several buffets, where there are all kinds of fearful pastry and horrible creams that would be ices ... there are several fountains of filtered water ornamented with small drinking cups ...'[17] in case you did not fancy, or feel like paying for, the mineral waters and lemonade supplied by Messrs Schweppes.

As word got round, most excursionists brought their own food and – alcoholic – drink, which they disposed of sitting comfortably on the bases of the exhibits. Their tickets did not allow re-entry, so they could not join the happy throngs picnicking on the grass outside. Then, the perennial problem: but due to George Jennings's commercial foresight, there were 'retiring rooms and washrooms' available for a penny, which were used by over 827,000 people, not counting the free urinals for men.[18] Mr Jennings in a letter to the Commissioners had prophesied that 'the day will come when Halting Stations will be constructed in all localities where numbers assemble'.[19] These public lavatories were an example of so many things we take for granted, without which life would be, to say the least, uncomfortable, and we never pause to thank the Victorians for them.

Suitably strengthened, into the Exhibition. Most people went straight up the central aisle to the famous crystal fountain made by Osler of Birmingham, 27 feet high, 4 tons of pale pink glass faceted and carved with superlative skill, jetting water high into the air, catching the light magically wherever you stood. It was a useful meeting-point – you couldn't miss it. But if you did, 'the police office is every day encumbered with objects that have been lost, from umbrellas to children'.[20] Where to go next depended on your tastes. Dr Dionysius Lardner, a serious scientist with a particular interest in railways, concentrated on the process of photography and the electric telegraph system; the railway engines and rolling stock; the eight-cylinder *Times* printing machine; calico printing machines operated by one man and a boy which could produce four-colour prints in the same time as 200 men would have taken before; and the new era of precision engineering, which dealt in tolerances of a millionth part of an inch.

Dr Lardner's book about the Exhibition, published after it had closed, referred to the new steam-propelled passenger liners, the 'steam marine'. A transatlantic service had begun in 1836 but had 'signally failed'. In 1851, however, Samuel Cunard, a Canadian, was granted an annual subsidy of £145,000 to run a weekly transatlantic service to New York with his fleet of nine steamships. Dr Lardner seems to have missed the prototype of a facsimile machine,[21] but he was lyrical about the electric telegraph machine. There was a scale model of Liverpool Docks, with 1,600 fully rigged ships. The Americans had sent a McCormick reaping machine and the Colt revolver, as well as a sewing machine – not yet Mr Singer's – and a most useful artificial leg, a bed that could be carried in a suitcase, and a coffin designed to enable the funeral to be postponed until distant relatives could attend it.

Your taste may lie more in the visual arts. By one of the inscrutable rules of the Commission, paintings were not allowed, but statues were, and they made a lasting impression. Who could forget a statue of the Prince Consort dressed as a Greek shepherd? A north-country visitor compiled an elaborate record of his visit to London, complete with prints and newspaper articles carefully gummed into a handsome leather-bound volume. He was 'much pleased with the sculpture, especially the veiled female figures'.[22] What veils they were wearing were skilfully rendered so as to seem transparent, and you do not see many nude women in Newcastle. He was not the only man to be pleased by the female statues. An American sculptor had sent a delightful figure of a Greek slave, naked except for a strategically placed length of chain. The interest she caused may of course have been wholly evoked by her political significance. Stained glass was exhibited in an upstairs gallery, so that the light shone through the panels. It would be sensible to see them on a fine day, when the brilliance of the colours was at its best, and the gallery was not quite so crowded as the main floor.

For a feast of exotic splendour the India exhibit was unparalleled: silks embroidered with precious metals and gems, a throne glittering with gold and silver, even a howdah, displayed on a stuffed elephant.[23] While in oriental mood, you must see the Koh-i-noor, the famous diamond acquired by England in 1850, after the Sikh Wars of 1845–9 and the annexation of the Punjab.[24] Its previous owner, the wife of Shah Sooja, when asked to estimate its value, replied 'If a strong man were to throw four stones, one north, one south, one east, one west, and if the space between them were to be filled up with gold, all would not equal the value of the Koh-i-noor'.[25] She must have been sorry to see it go. It was displayed in an ignoble metal 'birdcage' safe 6 feet high and lit by gas jets, but it still did not glitter as expected. (It was recut later, and set in the royal crown).

The French exhibit was almost as gorgeous, and more relevant to

British trade. It visibly benefited from French experience in display technique, with which British exhibitors were struggling. The French had booked a bigger space than any other foreign participant, and used it magnificently. The luxury goods in which France excelled, including textiles and fashionable garments, were complemented by the machinery used to create them, and backed by a whole room full of furniture and another of Sèvres porcelain, and tapestry and carpets from Gobelins and Beauvais.

Visitors commented on the festive appearance of the park. 'The Serpentine was a picture. There was a small man of war, a three-master, hung over with flags and the sailor men all over the yards [which must have been uncomfortably crowded, on a miniature ship as this was] and many small boats rowing about.'[26]

There had been dire predictions of international criminals congregating in the park and spreading their depredations all over London. And not only criminals, but political agitators and revolutionaries. Russia stopped issuing passports. Naples tried to prevent its citizens from 'having their minds tainted with revolutionary doctrines' by coming to London. King Frederick William of Prussia forbade his brother, the future Kaiser, to come to his cousin's apotheosis because of the revolutionaries. Albert – who rises in my estimation the more I know of him – wrote back scathingly:

> As far as England is concerned, I can only assure Your Majesty that we have no fear here either of an uprising or an assassination, that certainly very many political refugees are accommodated here and perhaps also conspire with each other, but that they in reality behave peacably, live in great poverty, and probably have come to the conclusion from their own experience that the English people have nothing in common with their views and that London is perhaps the worst terrain in Europe for their plans to take root.[27]

In the event 200 soldiers and 300 policemen, some being plain-clothes detectives lent by foreign forces to identify any known bad-hats, patrolled the throngs of visitors. Only twelve pickpockets were arrested during the whole Exhibition. Several of the foreign detectives decided that duty called them to the racecourses, since trade was so slack in the Crystal Palace, or spent their evenings checking on the nightlife in Soho and the Haymarket, but they often decided that home-grown crime was worthier of their attention, and went home.

So who did come? Famously, the Queen. She adored her husband and was transparently, and rightly, proud of the acclaim he had earned. Possibly she really was interested in the American display of machinery and 'very curious inventions', which seems unlikely, but her visit pleased the Americans enormously. She spent two hours looking at machinery, which again would be beyond most Victorian women unless their dear husbands were engrossed beside them. She managed to buy a quantity of Sèvres porcelain, despite the rules; but one could hardly remind one's monarch of them. She probably spent 50 hours at the Exhibition, in repeated visits. She began the royal walkabouts which have buttressed the royal family's popularity ever since. The doors opened at 9, but she would be there before then, and leave as the day visitors were beginning to crowd in. Sometimes Albert came too, sometimes she had only her usual entourage with her – no obvious police guard or military escort. When visitors recognised this diminutive figure, she would smile and nod happily. So much for the gloomy prophesies of the Prussian King. Her calmness was the more remarkable when one remembers the various attempts to assassinate or harm her.[28]

The Duke of Wellington often strolled along from his house at Hyde Park Corner. Seven days after the Exhibition opened, he wrote to a friend, 'whether the Show will be of any use to anyone may be questioned, but of this I am certain: nothing can be more successful'.[29] The Iron Duke had a crowd-pulling power comparable only to Diana, Princess of Wales. It landed him in personal danger when on his last visit his fans almost mobbed him, and others rushed to see what was happening; and he had to be removed by the police for his own safety.[30]

The railways ran crowded excursion trains from all over England, after a price-cutting war that reduced the cost of a ticket to London to 5s. Conditions on the trains were appalling, the companies seeing no reason to provide for the excursionists anything better than glorified cattle trucks open to the weather, without any kind of facility. Still the throngs came. Thomas Cook is estimated to have conducted 150,000 people to see the Great Exhibition, including 3,000 Sunday-school children. Albert 'insisted upon all the children at the schools being sent to see the Glass Palace, which certainly augments the crowd and is remarkably inconvenient as they move in strings'.[31]

Victoria sent all the sailors serving on the royal yacht. She noted in June that

> we saw three whole parishes ... from Kent and Surrey, (800 in number) walking in procession, two and two, the men in smock frocks, with their wives looking so nice ... they subscribed to come to London to see the Exhibition, it only costing them 2s 6d [she was wrong, they paid only 1s 6d, the rest of the cost being subsidised by the local gentry] ... numerous firms from the North sent their people ... an agricultural implement maker in Suffolk sent his people in two hired vessels provided with sleeping berths, cooking apparatus and every comfort ... which were drawn up to a wharf in Westminster.[32]

The workers from two factories came in a convoy of coaches decorated with flags and greenery, each drawn by four horses.[33] Groups of exotically dressed foreigners added to the colour. An 84-year-old fisherwoman from near Penzance walked to London to see the Exhibition. It took her five weeks, and the journey home daunted her because she had only 5½d left. Very wisely she applied to the Lord Mayor of the City – someone must have tipped her off – and he gave her a sovereign.

Daily attendance figures were breathlessly reported by the press. An average figure for the 1s days was 50,000, but two days from the closing date it rose to a breathtaking – literally – 109,915. The total by the end of the Exhibition on 11 October was over six million. By then, the daylight hours were getting shorter and some of the exhibits were getting tatty. How did Herr Lindt keep his Swiss chocolate in prime condition? How bad was the water damage? The roof never had been totally rainproof. The elm trees that had caused such dissension were yellow now, and beginning to shed their leaves. It was time to close. The beautiful Osler fountain was turned off, an official waved a red flag, bells were rung, and slowly but obediently the public left.

CHAPTER 18

The Crystal Palace at Sydenham

ষ্টিক্ষ

*The move to Sydenham · access · construction · aims to educate the masses
· the Architectural Courts · alcohol and Sunday opening · the nude statues ·
Paxton's waterworks · the extinct animals · popular entertainments ·
music · the 1936 fire*

The workmen moved in to pack up the exhibits, the Osler fountain
was carefully dismantled, masses of straw billowed in the chilly wind,
the elms dropped their leaves. The great structure glimmered in the
October mists, while its future was debated. It had never been
intended to be permanent, but what should happen to it now? Should
it after all be saved for the future? It would make a wonderful 'winter
garden' for Londoners, or a concert hall, which London lacked; but
the acoustics would be terrible. Albert was not in favour of preserving
the building, with the expense of upkeep that would entail. He
intended all the very considerable profit – £186,000 – of his Great
Exhibition to be devoted to what became known as Albertopolis, the
complex of museums in South Kensington. On 29 April 1852 the
House of Commons finally ordered that the palace had to go.

By 17 May the Crystal Palace Company had been formed, the
major shareholder being the London, Brighton and South Coast
Railway. The Chairman of the Company, and of the Railway, was
Samuel Laing. Six of the promoters, including Paxton, had been
involved with the Hyde Park Exhibition. The public was invited to
subscribe by a prospectus promising huge dividends, finance had been
raised, and the Crystal Palace was bought, as it stood, in Hyde Park,
for £70,000 in cash.[1] It was to be re-erected on a 350-acre site on top
of Sydenham Hill in Norwood, about 6 miles south of London. Its
magnificent site would be a free advertisement visible to all travellers
on Laing's railway. It could not fail.

There were to be two railway stations, both serving the London, Brighton and South Coast Railway. Crystal Palace Low Level was at the foot of the hill, which meant a long walk up a glass-covered colonnade. The displays of flowering plants on the way did not always compensate for the exertion, on a hot day. The other station, Crystal Palace High Level, was connected to the palace by an ornate pillared subway built by Italian bricklayers. This station was opened in 1865. First-class passengers travelled in style, if there were enough first-class carriages. If not they had to put up with a second-class carriage 'open at the sides. (Sheep truck is a more appropriate name for it.)'[2] They might well prefer to use their own coaches, postilion and all. Third-class passengers came in the usual cattle trucks. Some people travelled by omnibus, taking an hour and a quarter from Paddington if all went well. Buses were scheduled to run every ten minutes from Clapham.

The demolishers came to Hyde Park, but not with their customary wrecking-ball. With astonishing patience and skill the whole house of glass cards was taken to pieces, packed, and carried through London and out to its new home. Where it had been was a vast area of long, yellowed grass. In time the park recovered as if Albert's apotheosis had never happened. The transport of materials to Sydenham was achieved by teams of horses – what else? Two at a time they laboured up Sydenham Hill pulling 2-ton loads. Gradually 400 tons of glass and all the reusable iron, more than 4,000 tons of it, arrived at the new building site. Some glass was inevitably broken, but it was returned to Chance Brothers for remaking. Meanwhile an even more spectacular load was making its way from Loddiges' Nursery in Hackney, which was closing down. Paxton bought most of its stock, including a 50-year-old palm tree weighing with its rootball 15 tons, and as high as a three-storey house. It was loaded on to a special transporter with wide wheels – even so, one wonders how much damage 15 tons inflicted on the streets – and pulled through London and up Sydenham Hill by a team of 32 horses.[3]

Building there began in August 1852. Where the Hyde Park building had sprung into life in eight months, with a labour force of at most 2,260, the new Crystal Palace, a permanent building on a difficult site, took nearly two years to complete, with a labour force of up to 6,400. It was higher, it contained nearly twice as much space, and was clad in almost twice the surface of glass. It was more – of everything. It was, despite its transparency, massive. Although it was much admired, and continued to be throughout its life, the pictures of it convey to me – but tastes differ – an overbearing, looming presence. It was visible from great distances. 'I have seen it shining, even in winter, from Wormwood Scrubs' (north of Hammersmith).[4]

There were three storeys, again using the elegant modules that had been so successful in Hyde Park, but this time arranged with three huge vaulted transepts. Because it was built on a steeply sloping site, strong foundations were needed, and a basement was designed to house an unprecedented heating system using 50 miles of hot-water pipes. (Time and again one stops to admire the innovative energy of the Victorians). All did not go smoothly. There were four structural collapses, and seventeen fatal accidents. But by May 1854 it was more or less finished. If the opening had been much delayed, the fashionable Season would have come and gone, so arrangements went ahead for the royal opening on 10 June 1854.

Did the royal pair stifle a yawn and think 'Not again! This can't be as good as Albert's magical Great Exhibition'? History does not relate. The Queen allowed her Prime Minister to tell the Directors that she had taken special pleasure in the music; it was 'the finest effect that her Majesty had ever heard'. Whether Albert enjoyed it so much can perhaps be doubted; the sound of 1,800 singers belting out the Hallelujah chorus would have made Handel turn in his grave. All the great and the good were there. Dickens thought it was 'the most gigantic Humbug ever mounted on a long-suffering people's shoulders'. Ruskin on the other hand thought that 'it is impossible to estimate the influence of such an institution on the minds of the working classes, pursuits, health, intellects roused into activity within the crystal wall'.

The ethos of the new Crystal Palace was to be the education of the masses, by giving them an 'Illustrated Encyclopedia'. To that end, a historical theme park awaited them, with prehistory in the grounds, and the march of time in ten 'Architectural Courts', each one a reconstruction, in plaster, of ancient buildings and figures, incorporating the latest archaeological expertise. A thoughtful progression through them, armed with the relevant guidebook, would give the visitor an overall grasp of the whole history of civilisation.

There was an exact reproduction of the Court of Lions in the

Alhambra court, and an authentic copy of an elaborate Moorish stalactite-honeycomb roof, in 5,000 separate pieces of gelatine. The Pompeian and Italian courts exploded with colour. The Assyrian Palace was guarded by gigantic winged and bearded figures. The Egyptian court glowed with the original colours of Pharaonic temples, of which only tiny faded fragments still remain. The pillars in the Temple of Karnac were built much shorter than they really are, which enabled their elaborate capitals to be studied. Two of the colossal figures at Abu Simbel were reproduced in painted plaster, 51 feet high, towering into the vaulted transept roof. The Greek court was peopled with white plaster casts of ancient statues, the damage which time had inflicted on the originals made good in Sydenham. The Roman court was walled with multicoloured marble. The Byzantine court included a copy of an eighth-century cloister in a museum in Cologne. The Medieval court encouraged the Victorian passion for Gothic. There was a separate court for historical and contemporary sculpture.

But somehow this grand design got tangled up with Paxton's gardening bent, and zoological collections, and freak shows, and the Directors' concern to make money. The many beautiful illustrations show greenery dripping from every projection, and palm trees everywhere. There were bazaars selling anything from shawls to pianos, toys to furniture. Birmingham and Sheffield had their own courts marketing their own productions. Attentive visitors in search of enlightenment found themselves confronted by models of grotesque people and a collection of stuffed animals, including a hippopotamus. 'The figures of various outlandish tribes brandishing spears in their native jungle' loomed over the refreshment room tables.

Looking back to his boyhood, the clearest recollection of one visitor seems to have been the refreshments – what parent has not found well-meant efforts to imprint culture foundering in fast food?

> It was here that I tasted my first ice-cream, and a jolly big one it was. They used to put the creams in glasses in vertical stripes of pink and white. Round-bottomed soda-water bottles were likewise novelties ... One [or one's parents] had to decide how much one was going to spend for lunch, tea or dinner, pay the amount at a window, obtain checks for the amount and hand these to the waiter, who rationed accordingly.[5]

And what parent has not heard a desperate plea to find a lavatory?

At first Mr Jennings, who had so obligingly furnished facilities in the Crystal Palace when it was in Hyde Park, was told severely that 'persons would not come to Sydenham to wash their hands', but common sense eventually won and Mr Jennings's installations at Sydenham produced a revenue of £1,000 a year.[6] At least alcohol was allowed, after a titanic struggle. Another battle raged over Sunday opening. Since the avowed aim of the whole enterprise was mass education, it seemed ridiculous to such men as Mayhew to close it on Sundays, the only free time in which the working classes could come. It took six years to win this battle.

There was an urgent crisis caused by an array of well-endowed male statues. The spotlight had shifted from the busty Greek slaves of Hyde Park, to male statues wearing not even a piece of chain. A bevy of bishops, including the Archbishop of Canterbury, and several peers, wrote to *The Times* on 8 May 1854, less than a month before the opening date, averring that such sights would not only destroy 'that natural modesty which is one of the outworks of virtue ... which Nature herself has placed in the way of Crime', Nature apparently not having realised the side effects of genitals, but also, and more seriously, it would endanger the profits of the Crystal Palace Company, because 'tens of thousands [would] assert their disapproval by the absence of themselves and their families'. It may have been all right for the ancient Greeks and Romans, but 'we protest against the adoption of this usage in Christian and Protestant England'.

The bishops only wanted a small amendment to the classical casts: 'the removal of the parts which in "the life" ought to be concealed, although we are also desirous that the usual fig leaf may be adopted' – whether over the amputation or covering the offending member is unclear. This caused a minor panic. Despite a desperate search for plaster fig leaves, 50 statues were still unamended at opening day.[7] Meanwhile, what publicity. (When you think of it, the bishops had something. Female anatomy above the waist was visible every night at the opera, and on all the public buildings in Whitehall. Men might be familiar with the sight of naked prostitutes, but women did not have a comparable opportunity. Respectable spouses performed marital intercourse wearing their enveloping night attire. Women may have had no idea what a man's penis looked like. Once they did – and these would be tidy ones reposing in neatly curled pubic hair – their expectations might have changed. But not, surely, so far as to commit crimes.)

The waterworks in the grounds were created by Paxton with almost maniacal zest. Ponds, basins, lakes, reservoirs and cascades, water temples and fountains needed far more water than the local water company could supply. No matter, Paxton had a well dug at the foot of the site, and pumped the water up to water towers he designed at the top of the site, which collapsed, and had to be replaced by two designed by Brunel. Paxton's waterworks became more and more elaborate – and expensive. There were 11,000 jets, including *two* plumes of water soaring to 280 feet, unequalled anywhere in the world. In June 1856 Paxton was able to show his achievement to his Queen, and to thousands of spectators. A contemporary observer noted:

> Between the temptation of the fountains and the expected arrival of the Queen, the elegant crowd did not know which way to look or what sight to sacrifice. The uncertainty was soon put an end to by a heavy shower of spray, which, carried by the wind, came down on the devoted bonnets with stormy drenching violence ... Those who had umbrellas used them but those who were less fortunate took to their legs.[8]

Paxton then retired from the management of the palace, replete with pride but perhaps a little worried that his extravagance with water had almost ruined the Company. Thereafter the wonderful display, the 'Grand System', was given only four or five times a year, on fine days, and then you had to pay extra to see it. By 1894 there was little left of it to see.

But you could still enjoy the 33 'extinct animals' displayed in appropriate settings in the grounds. One of the iguanodons was 34 feet long, big enough for twenty gentlemen to sit inside the mould prepared for it and enjoy a splendid dinner, in 1853. All the animals were meticulously modelled according to the latest, exciting discoveries of palaeontology. (The absence of other dinosaurs, which are so familiar to us, was because they had not yet been discovered). The extinct animals may not have looked pretty, but they were certainly educational, and impressive too.

To begin with, all seemed to be set fair. In its first year, and despite the bishops, there were 1,322,000 visitors, including 71,000 children. But Paxton had depleted the funds by his waterworks, the receipts from refreshments were disappointing, and there was much financial mismanagement. The Directors struggled to maintain the high ideals which had inspired the Architectural courts, but a disastrous fire in 1866 destroyed the colossal Abu Simbel figures, which were never restored, and much of the north transept, including the display of tropical animals. The stuffed hippopotamus ended up like 'a big dried sausage'.

Gradually the character of the vast site tipped from educational to popular. The 'Foresters' Fetes' attracted 90,000 people in Lincoln green with bows and arrows, pretending to be Sherwood Foresters. There were famous horticultural competitions and rose shows. The boy who had relished his 'jolly big' ice cream remembered 'a photographic artist who made you stare unblinkingly for some two minutes ... then you took away your portrait on glass'. (This need for an unblinking stare during a long exposure accounts for the sullen or preoccupied expression of early photographs). But the excellent memory of this writer did not recall any educational sights.

Another visitor's account was even less improving; 'the first thing of any importance was a number of Hottentots etc [*sic*]'. His party found somewhere to sit and rest 'in front of the organ ... an ugly, unfinished instrument', then set off to see ship models, a Chinese war junk, the Lord Mayor's barge, a burlesque show of Punch and Judy, a conjuror, and 'a number of other things which I cannot write down as I am in no humour for doing it' – the fate of most travel diaries.[9] Munby, that extraordinary man who moved in fashionable artistic circles when he was not pursuing servant girls, visited the Crystal Palace in the summer of 1861, and all he found to say was that 'a large circle had been formed for Kiss in the Ring – the women were chiefly shop-girls and servants'.[10]

Blondin, the famous tightrope walker, enthralled nearly two million people that summer, jumping and sitting down and somersaulting, and pretending to fall, on a rope stretched the length of the central transept, and even cooking an omelette on a stove which he carried on his back. (Surely this was one of Soyer's Magic Stoves, so compact that it could be used in a railway carriage?) Miss Leona Dare in sequinned tights held a trapeze in her teeth and was lifted into the air by Signor Eduardo Spelterini's balloon. 'Mr Green's great balloon *Le Continent*, hero of dozens of ascents, stood inflated in the north nave ... One summer's evening a fine balloon crossed St James's Park and was greeted with a chorus of "Ha-ba-balloons" ... Balloons frequently went up from the Crystal Palace or one or other of the pleasure gardens.'[11]

Henry Croxwell, the official Crystal Palace aeronaut, took passengers up to 2,000 feet in his balloon, filled with gas from the Sydenham gasworks. He charged £5 for an ascent in his later 'Mammoth Balloon', 80 feet high and 50 feet in diameter. A distinguished scientist with whom he was studying the weather described the experience:

> When one mile high the deep sound of London, like the roar of the sea, was heard distinctly ... At the height of 3 or 4 miles ... the plan-like appearance of London and its suburbs; the map-like appearance of the country generally; and the winding Thames ... were sharply defined. Railway trains were like creeping things, caterpillar-like. Ships ... looked like toys.[12]

Wombwell's Menagerie arrived in 1864. In 1865 Charles Brock persuaded the Company to allow a competition between different firework manufacturers, which he won. Thereafter the magnificent firework displays put on by his family firm could be enjoyed every Thursday evening. Twenty thousand people had paid to see the first display, but you could view most of them from your bedroom window if you lived in the right place.

Promoters of musical performances were not deterred by the obvious acoustic drawbacks of this vast open space enclosed in metal and glass. Encouraged, no doubt, by the royal enthusiasm for the singing at the opening ceremony, the management put on concerts of sacred and classical music. (Remember there was no Albert Hall yet). Albert must surely have enjoyed the Schiller and Mendelssohn Festivals of 1859 and 1860, held out of doors, with torchlight processions. Visiting brass bands and military bands gave regular concerts, and the resident orchestra gave daily concerts of popular music, with classical concerts every Saturday. The Handel Festivals in 1857, 1858 and 1859 and thereafter triennially were immensely popular. The choruses of 2,500 voices may have been audible, but how could a soloist make her or his finer flourishes heard in that vastness? Increasing the number of singers to 3,600 (by 1883, 4,000 singers and 4,441 instrumentalists) was not the whole answer.[13] No piano could bridge those huge gaps, obviously an organ was needed, and it duly arrived in 1857, weighing 20 tons.

Although those 'monster' concerts may now seem grotesque, they included the first English performances of many works, such as all of Schubert's symphonies. The Crystal Palace was the centre of musical culture, and it remained a vibrant part of London life until its dramatic destruction by fire in 1936. It has now almost completely disappeared from popular memory. No-one except historians knows about the Architectural courts. Paxton's Great Display has no echo now. Ask the average man in the street what he knows about the Crystal Palace and he will give you the latest score of the football team.

Education

To right-minded citizens, education was to be the panacea for London's woes. The working classes might or might not emerge from the Crystal Palace at Sydenham better-versed in the history of mankind than when they went in, but there were other ways of turning them into well-informed and well-behaved citizens. The first essential was to catch them young.

The Ragged Schools are among the least known of Victorian achievements. They took ragged – verminous and naked – children and clothed and fed them, and taught them rudimentary social skills, let alone the three Rs plus a fourth, religion, instead of leaving the children to fester in the gutter. They had many critics, and indeed to us their religious ethos may not be wholly congenial; but instead of looking at them from our viewpoint, consider the scene before they existed. There was no way for a destitute child to learn anything, except crime and begging. No one concerned themselves with the welfare of these children, except the dreaded workhouse guardians. The police were against educating them: 'we are teaching the thieves to prig [steal] the articles marked at the highest figures'.[1]

Some teachers were private individuals who did what they could, with what lay to hand. The first was Robert Raikes in Gloucester, who opened a Sunday school in 1783 to give poor children basic religious instruction, and taught them to read so that they could read the Bible. John Pounds, a Portsmouth cobbler, invited poor children to come and play with his crippled nephew, and by 1818 was teaching 30 or 40 of them to read. Quintin Hogg, ex-Etonian, the fourteenth child and seventh son of Sir James Hogg, was apprenticed to a city tea merchant and living comfortably at home in Carlton Gardens:

> My first effort was to get a couple of crossing-sweepers whom I picked up near Trafalgar Square, and offered to teach how to read. In those days the Thames Embankment did not exist, and the Adelphi Arches were open both to the tide and the street. With an empty beer bottle for a candlestick and a tallow candle for illumination, ... and a couple of Bibles as reading books ... we had not been engaged in our reading very long when I noticed a twinkling light. 'Kool ecilop' shouted one of the boys [in Cockney back-slang], at the same time 'doucing the glim', and bolted with his companion.

Hogg satisfied the policeman that he was no malefactor, and decided to add Cockney back-slang to the Greek and Latin he had acquired at Eton. He learned at first hand how the poor lived, by disguising himself as a boot-black boy, and sleeping rough where he could. In 1863, when he was eighteen, he took a room in Of Alley (leading off Villiers Street; there used to be a complex of streets named after the previous owner of the site, George Villiers, Duke of Buckingham, of which Of Alley was the smallest) and set up a Ragged School, with a woman teacher in charge. He was snugly at home in Carlton Gardens when a desperate summons came from Of Alley. When he got there he

> found the whole school in an uproar, the gas fittings had been wrenched off and were being used as batons by the boys for striking the police, while the rest of them were pelting them with slates ... I felt rather alarmed for the safety of the teacher, and rushing into the darkened room called out for the boys to instantly stop and be quiet. To my amazement the riot stopped immediately.

From then he took personal control of the school. Every evening, for two sessions of one and a half hours each, he taught two classes of 30 boys simultaneously, perched on the back of a form, one set of boys in front of him learning to read, the others, when he turned round, learning writing or arithmetic, and he expected his pupils to listen to ten minutes of religious instruction at the end of each class. He enlisted the help of some of his ex-Etonian friends and work colleagues. In three years the school grew to two rooms and a separate 'doss house' for homeless boys.

Hogg's methods could be described as 'hands-on'. He enforced discipline with Etonian-type thrashings. He personally shaved the heads of boys with lice, and scrubbed them from head to foot. (This was beyond the London City Missionaries, who sent them away if they were 'literally loaded with vermin').[2] Some boys had no clothes. Five arrived wearing only their mothers' shawls pinned round them. All the more credit to them for having come at all, whatever their motives. Somehow clothes and food were found, and the gas bill for lighting was paid.

One of Hogg's sisters took on a class for girls and women. The girls were as wild as the boys – they came in turning catherine wheels, sometimes with the police in hot pursuit.[3] Lady Frederick Cavendish found the same, when she tried to teach a class of girls at a Sunday school run by St Martin-in-the-Fields parish church. 'I was a good deal taken off my legs by the coolness and talkativeness of my pale-faced cockney damsels ... the row was great, and my numbers un-manageable, so I did not make a satisfactory start.' She tried again later, and was 'driven nearly wild by 8 obstreperous ragamuffin boys'.[4]

Many of the teachers were professed Christians working for Church organisations such as the London City Mission (founded 1835). The biggest LCM school was at Clerkenwell Green, founded in 1846. By 1850 it was running a free day school with a daily attendance of 160, an evening school with an average attendance of 100, an infant school with 60 children a day, and a Sunday school with an average attendance of 155.[5] Some were in dangerously criminal districts, such as the one opened in 1853 in Spitalfields, attended by 350 children aged between four and fifteen.[6] Some schools became considerable enterprises. There was one in the East End with 400 pupils, who each got a basic meal every day.[7]

There was no state aid, except for the 'industrial training', usually tailoring or shoe-making for boys, for which a small subsidy was available in a few schools. But was such training always a good thing? It was impossible, in the conditions of a Ragged School, to train a boy up to the high standard of a master tailor. If he learned enough to scrape a living at it, he was undercutting properly trained apprentices. Girls were taught sewing and knitting, which sounds so limited; surely the girls would have learned that at home? But this illustrates the achievement of the schools. It is almost impossible to imagine life at the very bottom of the pile, which was their catchment area. The children's mothers *could not* sew or knit, because they in turn had never been taught how to. So the pictures of children dressed in remnants of torn, ragged garments were not a matter of artistic licence. The clothes might have been salvaged at an earlier stage of decrepitude, by mending them – but no-one knew how. It was not a thing that very poor people did, unless someone showed them how to do it.[8]

Many children valued the chance to attend a Ragged School as we would prize a lottery win. One little girl began to earn her living at the age of ten, as a baby-minder, for 1s 6d a week 'and my tea', working a twelve-hour day – except twice a week when she left an hour early to go to a Ragged School.[9] The boy who made his living by selling birds' nests (see page 83) told Mayhew 'I go to a Ragged School three times a week if I can ... I should like to know how to read'.[10] And their lives were not all dreary. Hippolyte Taine met a clergyman 'who was in the habit of taking bands of Ragged Schools children for a day in the country. He took 2,000 on one occasion ... the whole thing cost about £100, made up by voluntary subscriptions.'[11] An ex-pupil remembered how 'most of the boys was thieves ... after we came out of school at 9 o'clock at night some of the bad boys would go a-thieving ... the master was very kind to us. They used to give us tea-parties and to keep us quiet they used to show us the magic lantern ... '.[12] Sometimes there were singing and drawing lessons, and 'travel stories'.[13]

In 1844 nineteen of the Ragged Schools in London joined to form a Ragged School Union, with Lord Shaftesbury as its President. This gave the movement considerable clout and attracted publicity and funds. In its first year, the Union drew up a list of those children whom it hoped to reach:

1. Children of convicts who have been transported.
2. Children of convicts in prisons at home.
3. Children of thieves not in custody.
4. Children of the lowest mendicants and tramps.
5. Children of worthless and drunken parents.
6. Children of stepfathers and stepmothers; often driven by neglect and cruelty to shift for themselves.
7. Children of those suitable for the workhouse but living a vagrant semi-criminal life.

8. Children of honest parents too poor to pay for schooling or to clothe the children so as to enable them to attend an ordinary school.

9. Orphans, deserted children and runaways, who live by begging and stealing.

10. Workhouse lads who have left it and become vagrants.

11. Lads of the street-trading classes, ostlers' boys and labourerers' assistants, who would otherwise get no schooling.

12. Girl-hawkers working for cruel and worthless parents.

13. The children of poor Roman Catholics who do not object to their children reading the Bible.

This list reads almost like an entrance examination; in practice, it seems that any child who could get to a Ragged School and wanted to learn would be welcomed. By 1861 there were 150 day schools affiliated to it, teaching nearly 20,000 children, with 2,000 unpaid teachers,[14] and 207 Sunday schools teaching another 25,000. Almost every school ran a Penny Savings Bank, yet another new concept, begun in 1849.[15] By 1869 there were 195 schools in the Union. This was the zenith of the movement, which crumbled after the 1870 Education Act established government-funded Board Schools. In the words of a contemporary, 'there was free schooling in England for all willing to accept it'.[16] The religious instruction which underlay a Ragged School education might itself have been a model for inter-denominational unity; the Anglicans and Dissenters joined together to satisfy 'one great instinct in every human breast, the weary longing for kindness from our fellow men, and the delight in finding it'.[17] Not many of these children had seen much kindness in life.

The real achievement of the movement, over just thirty years, was not the gift of a smattering of book learning, religious knowledge, and industrial skills. It was the conversion of unemployable young savages into well-behaved – mostly – young people with rudimentary social skills, self-respect, and a chance to leave the only world they knew, of crime and poverty.

The workhouses provided some education for the unfortunate children who had not managed to escape the beadles. 'If the teacher does not reside in the workhouse, and is not provided with rations, the Guardians must allow the teacher £15 ... [A teacher who lived in] must have convenient and respectably furnished apartments [and] rations, the same ... as are supplied to the master of the workhouse.' If the Inspector found that a Poor Law school did not have the 'necessary books and school apparatus, the guardians must provide them'.[18] This sounds faintly like a counsel of perfection; some Poor Law schools never attained the standards expected by Matthew Arnold as one of Her Majesty's Inspectors of Schools. Some workhouses shunted their school-age children to the Central London District School for Pauper Children out at Hanwell, which was known as the 'Monster School' because of its size – it had 1,000 pupils – not its inmates. Those with 'zeal, skill, attainments and gentleness of disposition' were given five-year apprenticeships as pupil-teachers.[19]

Above the financial and social levels of the Ragged Schools were the schools run by the National Society and the British and Foreign School Society, usually called the British Society. The National Society was Anglican. The children got a heavier dose of religion in National Schools than in Ragged Schools, since they had to learn the liturgy and the catechism. The British Society was Nonconformist, largely Wesleyan, and its schools taught 'useful learning' as well as basic Christian religious knowledge.

Curiously, each society simultaneously developed the 'monitorial system', whereby one teacher could impart some learning to selected pupils ('monitors') who in turn passed it down, each to a group of pupils who in turn ... John Lancaster, of the British Society, ran a school in Borough, in Southwark, teaching 1,000 children by 60–70 monitors. It may have looked workable on paper, and it was certainly cheap, but each snatch of education lasted only fifteen minutes, and the potential for 'Chinese whispers' errors must have been immense.[20] The monitorial or 'Lancaster' system was replaced by properly apprenticed pupil-teachers in 1846. These children were the brightest of their classmates, but they were sometimes no older than eight.

From 1852 all elementary schools, including those in workhouses and those run by private individuals, were subject to annual inspection by Government-appointed Inspectors. The National Schools, being Church of England, were inspected by ordained clergymen. All the other schools, including those run by the Jews and the Wesleyans, were inspected by laymen such as Matthew Arnold, whose annual reports make fascinating reading.[21]

The Wesleyans charged each child a weekly fee of between 2d and 8d, which meant that their pupils came from the lower middle class, not from the poor. Arnold was frequently scathing. 'There is no class of children so indulged, so generally brought up without discipline, that is, without habits of respect, exact obedience, and self-control, as the children of the lower middle class'. He fulminated that 'ornamental needlework should be prohibited in schools', and replaced by the plain needlework which parents did not teach their daughters. The system of pupil-teaching, while a vast improvement on the monitorial system, was overcrowded by girls, since 'the field of employment open to them is less wide than for boys, who can earn so much, and earn it so young, that their parents are unwilling to permit their engagement as pupil-teachers at the present rate of remuneration'. He regretted the poor standards of grammar, parsing and paraphrase, and urged that poetry and prose passages should be learned by heart. The books provided as reading books 'should inspire ... scholars with a real love of reading' – unlike the trash they were given, which included such useful gems as 'the crocodile is viviparous', and, as poetry, a nauseating poem about England:

> ... No men than hers are braver,
> The women's hearts ne'er waver
> I'd freely die to save her
> And think my lot divine ...

(Poor Arnold, having to read that rubbish, which went on for four verses, while his own noble poems could have replaced it). He quoted two letters written by children, one at a public elementary school – delightful, simple and grammatically correct – and another from a boy writing home from a private middle-class school, unbelievably turgid: '... and time has sped fleetly since reluctant my parting steps crossed the threshold of that home whose indulgence and endearment their temporary loss has taught me to value more and more ...'. He criticised the examination system. A child could pass by learning the set book by heart, and still be unable to read. 'A child who has never heard of Paris or Edinburgh will tell you the measurements of England in length and breadth till his tongue is tied. I have known a class, presented in English history ... [which] took the period from Caesar's landing to the reign of Egbert ... but only one of them had heard of the Battle of Waterloo'.

At least he was happier with the teacher training college run by the British Society in Southwark. 'The distinctive spirit of the place seems to me to be one of active-mindedness'. But he returns to his hobbyhorse of female education: 'Women teachers would be reluctant to use their time in the laundry, the bakehouse etc ... in this middling class of society girls grow up with a lamentable ignorance ... of domestic economy, but this is not the ignorance which their parents send them to school to remove ...'. By 1861 there was a 'really beautiful' laundry there – he could enthuse when he approved – and 'a practising kitchen has been provided but it is not yet in operation'. By then there were two training schools, for schoolmasters and for schoolmistresses. By 1870 the masters had a gym, but the mistresses had to be content with callisthenics.

The National Society opened a teacher training college in Battersea in 1843. The syllabus was hair-raising. The teachers rose at 5, worked in the garden from 6 to 7, and put in an hour's study of such subjects as ecclesiastical history, before breakfast at 8. They then divided their time, in half-hour slots, between music, mechanics, scripture, mental arithmetic, chemistry, mathematical geography (?), geometry, the practice of chanting, algebra, grammar, penmanship, and drawing, with 45 minutes for midday dinner and the same for supper. After an hour of prayer, they fell into bed at 10. Saturdays made a pleasant change: two exam papers, each one and a half hours long, and an hour of 'household work'. The average age of the students was 22, and the average length of stay twenty one months They must have been the best-educated 22-year-olds in England.[22]

It is perfectly possible to read accounts of Victorian life and not be aware of the existence of the admirable schools run by the Jews and the Freemasons. The Jews' Free School, usually known as JFS, had opened in 1817, near Petticoat Lane in the East End.[23] Despite its name, it charged 1d a week to its pupils, but a child who could not produce his penny was never turned away. By 1822 it was offering a 'religious, moral and useful education' to 600 boys and 300 girls. The youngest children were taught writing and numbering by trays of sand, smoothed with a flat-iron, on which they traced the letters and figures with their forefingers. Only when they could do this well, were they promoted to slates.

The girls' education was slanted towards domestic training. Matthew Arnold, who inspected the school every year, thought highly of Moses Angel, the Headmaster of JFS from 1842 to 1897. They must have had a lot in common. Angel's view was that 'every young woman is the better for knowing how to mend, wash, make clean, scour, polish, and cook. No lady needs to be ashamed to know how to tell when such labour is properly done'. The girls did get a chance to perpetrate Arnold's bugbear, 'ornamental needlework' but they were also taught to knit and do plain sewing and make their own clothes.

Angel was an astonishing man. He had been a gifted pupil at University College School and his future seemed assured, but in 1839 his father Emmanuel, known as 'Money Moses', and a sister, Alice, were accused of conspiring with two others to steal gold valued at £4,600. All four were tried at the Old Bailey, in a sensational trial, and found guilty. Alice was sentenced to four months' hard labour, but her father was transported to Australia for fourteen years, and died there soon after he arrived, in 1841. At about the same time, Angel was appointed to the staff of JFS at the age of 22, and also took on the post of English editor of the recently founded *Jewish Chronicle*. Soon afterwards he was made Master of the school, at a salary of £140 a year, a handsome sum for a schoolmaster in those days.

He was a strict disciplinarian, timing the arrival of teaching staff and pupils to the minute, but his punishments were rarely more than a reprimand. Teachers were allowed 'to tap, not to flog'. He kept meticulous log books which recorded events in the daily life of the school:

> At 5 o'clock the mother of Schwab of no. 6 room made a great disturbance because her son was kept [in]. As she would not desist, [I] directed the porter to remove her from the premises. On his endeavouring to do so she attacked him violently, bit him till the blood flowed copiously, and made use of very bad language to him and to me. Ultimately [I] let the boy go and told her not to send him to school here again. She continued her abuse and violent language for some time longer and was joined by her daughter who was also very violent.

Moses Angel had a phenomenally wide knowledge, and profound teaching and leadership skills. He taught a range of subjects at every level throughout the school including reading, writing, grammar, geography, the history of England from the earliest period up to the latest date, with some Greek and Roman history, arithmetic including 'the extraction of square root', algebra, and chemistry, and he personally trained his pupil-teachers in Hebrew, Latin, French and literature, after they had already spent a long day teaching. He was perhaps a trifle intolerant at times. In his evidence to a Parliamentary Select Committee he characterised Sunday-school teachers as 'narrow, bigoted sectarianists, as incapable of instilling that universal charity and sympathy which should permeate all true religion as they are wilfully blind to all moral excellence without the pale of their own peculiar creed'. His own pupils were taught the Jewish faith, with 'universal charity'.

He believed in prizes, and occasional treats. One August day in 1845 he took the most deserving boys to the British Museum, and then across the river to the Surrey Zoological Gardens, and they all had a picnic on the road verge, which was less polluted in those days. The children and their bearded, revered Headmaster sitting on the grass by the road enjoying their meal together must have been a remarkable sight. In 1847 there were 419 boys and 276 girls in the school. By 1853 the number of girls had risen to 500. From the 1850s JFS was the largest educational establishment in the United Kingdom. By 1870 it had 2,400 pupils, and was perhaps the largest school in the world – and yet non-Jewish sources could, and do, ignore it. It flourishes still, as a mixed comprehensive school in Harrow for the children of orthodox Jews, with 1,500 students aged between eleven and eighteen.

If your father was a Freemason who had fallen on hard times, and you had passed your eighth birthday, you could apply to the Freemasons for help with schooling.[24] The 'Freemasons' Charity for Female Children' had been founded in 1788. From 1850 it was housed in Wandsworth, which was then 'open country [with] a plentiful supply of water ... easy access by rail [it was next to Clapham railway station] or road'. The school uniform was a long blue serge dress, summer and winter (and it was probably unwashable), a white apron known as a 'pin-before' – a much better name than a pinafore – and a frilled white cap, with a straw bonnet over it, and a cape, for the rare occasions when a girl left the school premises. Each girl was issued with four shifts, and shoes with pattens (iron platforms under the shoes to save wear and tear on them and keep the long skirts from trailing in the mud). As the dresses were outgrown they were handed down to the next in line, and each girl had to keep her dress properly mended.

Parental visits were discouraged. There were no holidays until 1853, when suddenly the girls were given six weeks' holiday, divided between summer and winter, which must sometimes have been difficult for the indigent parents, just as long school holidays can be a mixed blessing for parents now. The school made some income from taking in 'plain work' – making shirts and shifts, for which 2s 3d to 3s was charged – but in 1856 this was seen as unfairly undercutting seam-stresses who depended for their livelihood on their needle, so it was stopped. The food was remarkably good for those days – meat and vegetables every day, for the midday meal – but the only other food the girls got was bread and butter for breakfast and tea.

They went to church twice on Sunday, and on Good Friday and Christmas Day and the anniversary of the founding of the school, and they had to learn the collect for the day and the catechism: not an undue burden, for those days. As well as 'domestic duties' the girls were taught reading, writing, arithmetic, needlework, and from 1858 French, drawing and music (piano-playing), which would be mar-ketable skills for governess jobs. The teaching standards must have been high, since the school entered six candidates for the Cambridge Board exam in 1868 and they all passed.

The Royal Masonic Institution for Boys was founded ten years after the girls' school. To begin with, the boys were put into schools near their homes, but in 1857 a school was built for them at Wood Green. By 1865 there were 100 boys there, being taught, by only two teachers, Greek, Latin, French, German, mathematics, history and geography. The school day began at 6, with an hour's study before breakfast – two pieces of bread stuck together with a small pat of butter, and watered milk or cocoa – then school until dinner at 12.30. The afternoon was for 'recreation' – the school was keen on cricket – until tea at 4.30, the same as breakfast, then more free time until 6, when the boys prepared for the next day's lessons. Bed at 8.30. The Headmaster was a keen flogger.

The apprenticeship system was still operating. Pupil-teachers were formally bound apprentice for five years. The Company of Watermen and Lightermen of the River Thames had 2,140 apprentices in 1858.[25] They would be sure of a living if they served their time and became freemen. The 'shop assistants' listed in censuses may often have been apprentices. It is surprising to see how much of the formal Indenture of Apprenticeship used in the sixteenth century survived in the nineteenth-century form:[26]

[during the six- or seven-year term] the apprentice his Masters faithfully shall serve, their lawful commands everywhere gladly do ... he shall not contract matrimony within the said term, nor play at cards or dice tables ... he shall not haunt taverns or playhouses, nor absent himself from his said Masters service day or night unlawfully ... [his father] will find the said son during the said term sufficient washing, clothing medical attendance and other necessaries and ... [the Masters] engage to instruct the said apprentice in the Art of a draper ... finding unto the said Apprentice sufficient Meat, Drink and Lodging...[27]

In other words, his father still had to pay towards his keep, and he earned nothing for six years: a considerable burden to his family.

The makers of cheap clothes – the slop masters – took apprentices from the workhouses and the Refuge for the Destitute, because of the £5 premium which came with each boy. 'We had no allowance in money – only board, lodging and clothing. Of the seven [bound at the same time as the speaker] only one served his time out.'[28] There was no limit on the number of apprentices a master could take. Another master, a cabinet-maker, had eleven. They were a useful source of cheap labour to the master. Probably few of these apprentices served out their time. But an apprentice to a master who was a member of the Amalgamated Society of Engineers, in the new fields of civil engineering and railway construction, would acquire a valuable marketable skill, demand for which showed no sign of slackening, so he would be likely to stay the course.[29]

The City of London School was founded in Milk Street, in the heart of the City, in 1835. Its pupils were at first the sons of City freemen and householders, but this was soon extended to include the sons of professional, commercial or trading people who could produce a nomination by a City Alderman or Common Councilman. They could be Dissenters or Anglicans, Catholic or Jewish, there was no religious bar. The syllabus included the classical languages, but also Shakespearian studies – unique at that time – modern languages, singing, book-keeping, chemistry 'and other branches of experimental philosophy', and as optional subjects Hebrew, physics and logic – all for an annual fee of just over £12. By 1861 there were 640 boys.[30]

The medieval Livery Companies' foundations such as the Mercers' and the Merchant Taylors' schools were smaller: 70 and 260 boys, respectively. The newly established University College and King's College had their own schools, attracting pupils from the professional and business classes. King's College School had 600 pupils in the early 1850s.[31]

The ancient public schools in London, St Paul's, Charterhouse and Westminster, pursued their habitual way of life unperturbed by modern developments. The Headmaster of Westminster claimed that half of his sixth form could read Xenophon at sight. (This may have prompted Victoria, no classical scholar herself, to warn Gladstone that education was ruining the health of the upper classes.)[32] The Headmaster told a Parliamentary Commission examining the public schools in 1868,

> The teacher's object should be to provide such a training as may best discipline the powers [of a boy] for their future task whatever it may be – and for this purpose no system appears to me likely to be so effective as one which takes as its groundwork the grammatical and logical study of the language and literature of ancient Greece and Rome, to which should be added a fair amount of history, geography and modern languages.

One can only trust that the 'literature of ancient Greece' omitted Plato's recommendation of homosexual love. 'Modern languages' seem to have been confined to French. 'A few boys who have learnt French in their childhood or have the prospect of travelling abroad, keep up and improve their knowledge. The rest neglect the subject ... it is almost indispensable that the Master should be French by birth: ... he is sure to find it a hard task to manage English boys.'
One's heart bleeds for the unfortunate Frenchman.

For working people who had reached adulthood without realising their intellectual potential, there were countless evening classes and educational institutes, such as the London Mechanics' Institution founded in 1823 by Francis Place and Dr George Birkbeck, in the City (later Birkbeck College), offering courses on scientific subjects, Latin and shorthand, with a membership of 1,000 (by 1850 there were 650 Mechanics' Institutions), and the Working Men's College founded in 1854 in Red Lion Square, where the syllabus was much the same.

One wonders why Latin was included. It seems a curiously useless subject for a working man after a long day. Perhaps he wanted to be even with 'his betters'. Munby, that extraordinary diarist who straddled the worlds of working-class women and London artistic circles, taught Latin at the Working Men's College.[33] His lover – eventually wife – Hannah Culwick learned French at the Working Women's College opened in Queen Square for teachers, shopgirls and even servant maids.

The Polytechnic opened in Regent Street in 1838 'for the advancement of practical science'. At first it was a rather confused collection of practical experiments, including a pool deep enough to accommodate a famous diving bell, in the basement. A visitor to it in 1859 'had a lecture in chemistry and a recital of comic songs and a man going down in the diving bell and a harp recital and some dissolving views'.[34] By 1861, under the guidance of the same Quintin Hogg who had concerned himself at such an early age with Ragged Schools, it housed the Metropolitan Evening Classes, later the City of London College, where 900 students learned anything from modern languages to shorthand and book-keeping. (It is now the University of Westminster.)

Short of attending lectures, there were many ways to educate yourself, in London. Nathaniel Hawthorne, visiting the British Museum for the third time ('it quite crushes a person to see so much at once') noticed 'in all the rooms I saw people of the poorer classes, some of whom seemed to view the objects intelligently and to take a genuine interest in them. A poor man in London has great opportunities of cultivating himself ... I saw many children there, and some ragged boys'.[35]

Girls' education was struggling to emerge from the exclusively domestic sphere. Queen's College in Harley Street was founded by the Governesses' Benevolent Institution in 1848, for girls over twelve, to give future governesses a recognised training and status. No 'ornamental needlework' was taught there. Its students included the formidable pair, Miss Buss, who became Headmistress of Cheltenham Ladies' College, and Miss Beale, who became Headmistress of the North London Collegiate School in 1850, where 'a liberal education and the accomplishments necessary for ladies can be obtained at a very moderate expense'. Its syllabus included Latin and science.

A 'Ladies' College' was opened in Bedford Square in 1848, 'a recent institution much wanted and likely to succeed'.[36] But in 1867

one of the countless Select Committee reports of the time could still
lament

> the general deficiency in girls' education ... the want of thoroughness
> ... the want of system; slovenliness and showy superficiality, inattention
> to rudiments; undue time given to accomplishments ... an educated
> mother is even of more importance to the family than an educated
> father ... [in the middle classes] the most material service may be
> rendered to the husband in the conduct of his business ... by a wife
> trained to a life altogether different from that of mere gentleness and
> amiability.[37]

The Public Libraries Acts of 1850 and 1855 enabled vestries to build
and equip libraries, but these powers were rarely used. Private
subscribing libraries, however flourished. Mudie's Lending Library
had a phenomenal success. It opened in 1840, in King Street,
Bloomsbury, for subscribers paying 1 guinea a year. The middle
classes took to it with enthusiasm. By 1852 it moved to New Oxford
Street, with 25,000 subscribers. By 1861 it had to move to new
premises, still in New Oxford Street, to house its 800,000 books.
Nearly half of the books borrowed were fiction, of the rest history
and biography accounted for 28 per cent, travel and adventure books
13 per cent.

In 1841 the London Library opened in Pall Mall, moving four years
later to its present premises in St James's Square. Its prime mover
was Thomas Carlyle, who had got bored with waiting for the books
he wanted to read in the British Museum. Its objects were stated to
be 'the supply of good books in all departments of knowledge. Books
in the lighter departments of literature and new books will necessarily
be included else the library will not be complete; but books will not
be bought merely because they are new, and much discrimination
will necessarily be exercised as to the lighter literature which is the
grand stock-in-trade of the ordinary circulating libraries' – such as
Mudie's. It remains a superlative example of all that is best in
Victorian scholarship. Of all its virtues, the greatest is that a member
may take out as many books as anyone is reasonably likely to need
at one time, and read them in peace at home. There is a generous
time limit, after which the reader is sent a gently reproachful enquiry,

or a slightly more pressing request for the return of a book wanted by another member. The entrance even in these security-conscious times is a dream of Victorian solidity and mahogany.

London University had begun in 1828 as University College, for Dissenters excluded from the ancient universities of Oxford and Cambridge. King's College opened a year later as the Church of England's riposte. In 1836 the two colleges were amalgamated as the University of London for 'all classes and denominations' except, of course, women, who were not allowed to sit for degrees until 1878. The province of learning shifted from exclusively Oxford and Cambridge to include London, where an excellent medical education was available at the teaching hospitals, the Inns of Court provided some legal training, and the teaching profession benefited from training colleges.

The success of the Victorians' drive for education was shown by the figures in the decennial census. In 1845 33 per cent of males and 49 per cent of females were illiterate. By 1871, these figures had fallen to 19 per cent and 26 per cent: surely an outstanding achievement.[38]

CHAPTER 20

Women

There was always work for a poor woman. There was no housework to be done in the slum room which was home to her and her family, and possibly several other families as well. She was better out of her home, earning an honest – if possible – penny. One woman washed the dishes for a fashionable restaurant in Leicester Square from noon till nearly 10 at night, in 'a low, rude, foul-smelling cellar ... windowless, lighted by a flaring gas jet, and in full view ... a larder hung with raw meat, on the other [side] a common urinal'.[1] There must have been many like her, in pubs and hotels and restaurants.

There was always piecework to be had, such as making matchboxes or covering umbrella frames, but the pay was pitifully low. Top hats were finished by pieceworkers, putting on the silk covers and the bindings at home. Sacking was issued by the warehouses near Billingsgate, to girls who 'carried immense loads of sacking on their heads' back to Bermondsey, where they lived, to be made into sacks.[2] There were a few female crossing-sweepers. A fourteen-year-old girl had a pitch from King Charles's statue at Charing Cross down to Spring Gardens. 'She plies her daring broom under the wheels [of the traffic] ... is ever ready to conduct the timid lady or nervous old gentleman through the perils of the crossing ... she drops you a quiet curtsy and says "Please, Sir" holding out her hand and leaning on her well-worn broom.'[3]

Some girls were cheeky enough to compete with the boys selling newspapers in the streets, 'running after the omnibuses'.[4] Girls who lived in Clerkenwell could find work making artificial flowers for the big shops in the City and the West End. They were slowly poisoned by the arsenic used for the pretty green of the leaves.[5] There was a fleeting fashion for 'frosting' the flowers with fine glass, broken into minute chips which clung to the fabric, hung in the air, and ruined the girls' lungs. 'The more weakly died of galloping consumption.'[6]

The 'slop trade', producing cheap mass clothing and uniforms, employed thousands of women – over 11,000 'females under 20' according to the 1849 Census. The Army Clothing Depot in Pimlico alone employed over 700 women. One 'slop worker' told Mayhew she earned about 6s for the six working days, but she had to pay out 2s 6d a week for coal to heat the irons to press her work. Shirts were paid for at the rate of 6s a dozen, but a woman could make only one shirt in a long day, and had to pay for thread and buttons, and candles to see by in winter, so she rarely cleared more than 2s a week. Trousers were a better bet, at 10s a dozen, but with the seamstress providing her own thread etc. she would only get 4s 5d a week clear, for eight pairs.[7] Mayhew called a meeting of women in the slop trade, in 1849. A thousand of them turned up; so did (uninvited) Lord Shaftesbury, who suggested that 'the only remedy was emigration'.[8]

The advent of the sewing machine in 1856 improved the lot of most of these women, if they could learn this unfamiliar technique. From the second report of the Children's Employment Commission, in 1864:

> The sewing machine ... now performs the work formerly known as the most miserable, and even notorious, of all occupations, under the name of 'slop work', in which grown women, by working long hours, could only earn, as in some of the poorest branches they still do, from 4s to 6s a week ... the wages of machinists average 14s to 16s a week ... the introduction of the machine has necessitated the employment, on the whole, of older children and girls, the usual age for commencing being about 14

– and therefore, under the Factory Act, 'entitled' to work full-time.[9] What became of the older women who had scraped a 'miserable' living from slop work before?

Moving up the social scale, there were plenty of posts for barmaids. If a woman could manage to look respectable, she might get a job with the London General Omnibus Company, as a 'watcher', riding round and round in the company's buses to see whether any conductor was cheating.[10] She would need to look respectable, and even sober and well fed, if she hoped to land a job as a wet-nurse – the prime qualification being, of course, that she was lactating, either because her baby had died or because she had farmed it out and was still able to suckle another woman's child. There was nursing work to be had in workhouse infirmaries, and in the general hospitals. Florence Nightingale's residential school for nurses opened in 1860.

The Society for Promoting the Employment of Women encouraged women to be clerks, telegraphists, shop assistants and nurses, but 'the texture of English society is such, that the number of reputable employments for females in the middle and humble ranks is very small.'[11] There were four or five mercantile houses in the City which employed female copying-clerks, who were, of course, paid less than men doing the same work; but at least they got £1 a week, and a female head clerk got 30s. The Victoria Press in Farringdon Street employed fifteen or sixteen female compositors, as well as men.[12] The Electric Telegraph Company took on six female 'operators' in 1850, who were such a success that by 1870 there were 200 of them at the London headquarters of the company.[13]

If they were lucky, these girls lived in one of the hostels run by the Young Women's Christian Association. The first one had been opened in 1855, for Florence Nightingale's nurses en route for the Crimea. By 1863 there were four hostels providing 'a home life based on Christian principles and at moderate charge [10s 6d a week for board and lodging, with a lending library and other amenities] for girls from the country working in London'.[14]

It has been calculated that there was an increase of 33 per cent in the jobs open to women in the two decades 1851–71, but in the same period men's employment increased by 67 per cent.[15] Still, it was a beginning.

Shops needed more and more staff as the middle classes found more ways to spend their money. Most staff lived in, at first in rooms above the shop, then as trade boomed and the value of fashionable sites rose, in hostels round the corner but still within easy walking distance. Munby picked up a 'draper's shopwoman' one Sunday evening, in Hyde Park. She was one of eight staff, four men and four women, all living in except one man. They had the use of a basement room next to the kitchen, and a 'drawing room parlour' at the top of the house. 'Sometimes when you've gone down to get dinner the shop bell rings and up you've to come without tasting a thing.' They worked from 8 in the morning until 9 at night. 'I stand behind the counter – we have one counter and the men the other ... On Sundays we all dine with the master; we go to church, and have to be in at all meals unless we ask leave; but we have the [Sunday] evenings to ourselves from 6.30 to 11.' She was paid £20 a year, with the prospect of a rise the next year, so no wonder she said that 'it's much better than service ... we have to dress smart for the shop of course, but he don't like us to be too smart'. She was two or three years into her apprenticeship, which was normally six years.[16]

This patriarchal staff management seems to have been usual. The staff of nineteen at Robert Sayle, in Cambridge, all lived in. Before the store opened, the floor had to be swept and the counters and showcases dusted. 'Each employee must pay not less than one guinea per year to the church and attend Sunday School every year. Men are given one evening a week for courting purposes and two if they go to prayer meetings regularly.' A copy of an apprenticeship indenture of 1885 is a curious mixture of the medieval form – '... the said apprentice ... shall not haunt taverns or playhouses ... ' – and the contemporary: 'the said apprentice shall ... (1) absolutely abstain from all intoxicating drinks, (2) regularly attend Divine Service in [a specified] Chapel morning and evening (3) attend family prayers each evening and (4) never be out of the premises after 10 o'clock without having obtained special permission from the firm'.[17]

The other opening for women in London was dressmaking – the other end of the spectrum from the poor slop workers, but exploited just as remorselessly. The salons producing those elaborate Victorian gowns worked under inhuman pressure during the summer months of the London Season. A customer expected her new ball dress to be delivered the day after she had ordered it, even before the advent of the sewing machine. This meant a twenty-hour day for the sewing women.[18]

Mayhew gave a vivid account of life behind the scenes, once a customer in a magnificent Regent Street salon had decided on the design and the fabric of the dress she wanted, and had been bowed out to her carriage. The hierarchy in the salon was headed by the 'show-room women' in the salon, of whom there might be five or six, and the same number of 'first hands' in the workrooms, all earning between £40 and £100 a year, down to the unpaid apprentices. A 'first hand dressmaker' goes to the customer's house to take her measurements. Then another 'first hand' cuts it out, in the workroom, and puts the material on a table where 'the young ladies', the apprentices, sit. One of them dares to ask who it is for: 'it's for Lady So-and-So and she wants it tomorrow morning ... she must have it, so we must sit up all night again'. They begin work on the bodice and sleeves, but the skirt, which needs less fitting, is given to 'a ragged dirty little creature' to take to his mother's workroom in a slum in nearby Carnaby Street, with orders to get it done by 9 the next morning. He manages to get the heavy bundle of fabric safely there, without dropping it or having it stolen. His mother and six other women, 'dirty, thinly clad, with pale and hollow countenances' are sewing, round a deal table in a garret. The small boy tells his mother that the skirt 'is to go in at 9'. She is appalled because she already has six skirts to go to the City by 8, but if she delivers late she will get no more work from that salon.

Meanwhile work goes on in the salon workroom to finish the bodice and sleeves, with short breaks for a snack of bread and butter and tea 'of very good quality', and supper of cold meat, cheese and light ale at 10. Six hours later the girls stop and go to bed in a dormitory at the top of the house, sharing eight beds between sixteen. They have three hours of sleep, because breakfast (tea, bread and butter) is at 7.30 and the working day begins at 8. The skirt duly arrives and is checked for any bugs or fleas, for which the slum seamstresses would be fined. The two parts are joined up, checked on one of the girls, packed up in a wicker basket and sent off by a porter.

The pressures on those unfortunate girls finally caused a scandal, when a twenty-year-old girl, Mary Ann Wakley, died after being made to work more than 26 hours without a break. Her death led to the founding of the Association for the Aid and Benefit of Dressmakers and Milliners, to 'induce' the principals of dress-making establishments to adopt a twelve-hour day, and to 'induce ladies to allow sufficient time for the execution of orders'. The Association had no power to compel, but its inducements seem to have had some effect.[19] Probably more effective was Mayhew's campaign; he shocked the middle classes by demonstrating that if these girls were to survive at all, it was no wonder that they supplemented their incomes with part-time prostitution.[20]

✳

Prostitution was the Great Social Evil, a subject that both fascinated and repelled the Victorian middle class. Ladies were supposed not to know about it, gentlemen only knew the theory, not, of course, the practice. Shocking figures of brothels and prostitutes were bandied about in male gatherings, at the same time as the addresses of fashionable *poules de luxe*. In the swirling clouds of prurient rumour it is not easy to find hard facts. Sensationalism sold newspapers.

A fairly firm starting-ground is a *Return of the number of Brothels and Prostitutes within the Metropolitan Police District, as nearly as can be Ascertained* in May 1857, which conveniently compares the figures with those for 1841. Even here we have to pause: these were houses, and women, known to the police. There was no clear law defining a prostitute. The local bobbies probably knew the women in their patch who were on the game, but they could only pull them in if they were making a nuisance of themselves. The same with brothels; it was an offence at Common Law to keep a brothel, but if the owner and the girls were discreet, many brothels probably stayed out of trouble. But still, the police return is an objective record. There were seventeen police districts. 'A District' covered Whitehall, the parks, palaces and Government offices; there were no brothels or prostitutes known to the police, there. By far the greatest number – 209 brothels and 1,803 prostitutes – were in 'H District', Spitalfields, Houndsditch, Whitechapel and Ratcliff, the very poorest and most deprived part of London. At least the police could take pride in the comparison between the figures for 1857 and 1841: the total number of brothels had gone down from 3,325 to 2,825, and the total number of prostitutes known to the police from 9,409 to 8,600.

To dispel some of the nebulous generalities which bedevil the subject, it is possible to look at the Social Evil in three different places and on three different levels: the poor women in the slums, the more prosperous ones working the Strand and the Haymarket, and the *grandes horizontales* of the West End. In her autobiographical sketches published in 1895, Elizabeth Blackwell, the pioneer of medical qualification for women, looked back to the London of 1850: 'At all hours of the night I see groups of our poor wretched sisters standing in every corner of the streets, decked out in their best, which is generally a faded shawl and tattered dress, seeking their wretched living.'[21] Hers is a lone voice, expressing pity for her 'wretched sisters'. In 1839 that redoubtable French lady Flora Tristan, 'accompanied by two friends armed with canes', went down to The Cut, the road that leads south from Waterloo Bridge, not quite as rough as Whitechapel but not exactly salubrious.[22] 'This neighbourhood is almost entirely inhabited by prostitutes and people who live off prostitution ... It was a hot summer evening; in every window and doorway women were laughing and joking with their protectors. Half-dressed, some of them *naked to the waist* [her italics] they were a revolting sight.'[23]

Despite the cheerfulness of that evening, an East End prostitute had the worst of all worlds. Any man using a prostitute may be violent, brutal, perverted, diseased and drunk; East Enders were poor as well. The police were unlikely to protect her from them. The gruesome murderer nicknamed Jack the Ripper in 1888, because of his mutilations of his victims' bodies, was never identified; he was a psychopath, but plenty of other murderers of prostitutes went undetected before his time.

If a woman caught syphilis or any other sexually transmitted disease she would be lucky if she were admitted to the 'foul ward' of a hospital, or to a Lock Hospital specialising in venereal diseases.[24] The treatment was rarely successful. It was still based on mercury, and would remain so until the discovery of Salvarsen in 1910. Mercury is poisonous. It loosens the teeth and makes the hair fall out. It may have alleviated the most obvious symptoms, but did little to eradicate the disease, which could recur for years, if the girl lived that long. Having no other means of livelihood she went back to her trade as soon as she was discharged, and infected another set of men. What she earned would depend on the market, but with luck it would keep her in gin and food. Eight prostitutes in an eight-room house in Ratcliff Highway, Wapping, used as a brothel had to pay the house-owner 2s for every trick they turned, and make a living as well.[25] The slum-dwellers of Whitechapel probably worked where they lived.

But prostitutes did not keep to tidily demarcated districts. The ones who could muster a tolerably respectable wardrobe migrated west. After Flora and her two friends had explored 'all the streets in the vicinity of Waterloo Road',

we sat upon the bridge to watch the women of the neighbourhood flock past, as they do every evening between the hours of eight and nine, on their way to the West End, where they ply their trade all night and return home between eight and nine in the morning. They infest the promenades and any other place where people gather, such as the approaches to the Stock Exchange, the various public buildings and the theatres, which they invade as soon as entry is reduced to half-price [usually halfway through the piece] turning all the corridors and foyers into their receiving-rooms.

The Strand and the Haymarket and nearby streets would be crowded with women commuting from their East End homes, joining girls based in brothels there or nearby. These appeared on the streets with a minder employed to see that they let no chance of a paying customer slip, and did not themselves escape. The most publicised milieu for prostitution was the 'lamentable Haymarket march past'.[26] A religiously inclined young medical student was taken out for his 26th birthday treat, in 1857, by some less priggish friends. He recorded in his diary afterwards that by 2.30 a.m., after a performance of *The Tempest*, 'which cannot but be considered interesting', and calls at various cafés and clubs, they ended up in the Haymarket, 'gratifying only an unworthy curiosity and not edified or satisfied by the proceeding ... and not excited beyond a certain pitch ... '.[27]

Whatever the young man really meant – and from his subsequent history I think it very unlikely that he had sexual intercourse with a prostitute there – it was clear that the Haymarket at night was one of the sights of London. There was a brisk trade in children. Fyodor Dostoevsky was in London in 1862: 'I noticed mothers bringing their young daughters to do business. Little girls about 12 years old take you by the hand and invite you to follow them.'[28] Mayhew estimated at 400 the number of individuals who made a living from 'trepanning' – abducting – girls aged between eleven and fifteen.[29] (The famous publicity stunt by a journalist, W. T. Stead, who 'bought' a thirteen-year-old girl for prostitution – under very careful supervision – was not until 1885.) The Secretary of the London Society for the Prevention of Juvenile Prostitution, founded in 1835, referred to the 'corruption of young boys', who could fetch up to £10 on this infamous market.[30]

Hippolyte Taine was shocked, not by the existence of so many prostitutes, but by their improvidence: 'they do not know how to be thrifty and save, how to buy, or get themselves given, a little place of their own ... as they do in Paris'. He should have talked to Munby, who met a girl whom he recognised from the days when she had been a maid servant.[31] 'Her dress was handsome and good.' She had enjoyed her life as a prostitute, for three years, and then bought a coffee house with her savings. This was the goal of so many girls when they began, but was so rarely realised. There was no security in the trade. Another girl complained to Munby that 'all my gentlemen have left town [it was August] and I shall have to give up my lodgings'. She had exchanged her country life as a farmer's daughter for prostitution in London, of her own accord.

It was rare for women to take their customers home: 'their landlords would object and besides their lodgings are unfit. They take their "captures" to the houses reserved for their trade.'[32] 'Throughout the day, in the Strand and Haymarket, a large number of shops and more or less respectable-looking houses display this notice "Beds to let".'[33] Every now and then attempts were made to clean the place up, but they did not last. According to Munby, writing in 1859, 'the clearance, so called, of the Haymarket and Casinos produced a large and still flourishing crop of secret dens and night haunts.'[34] The casinos included the Argyll Rooms, where the usual fee to a prostitute was between two and three guineas. Flora again, on her favourite hobby horse, the sins of the aristocracy:

> The 'finish' is as much a part of life in England as ... the elegant café in France. In the tavern the clerk and the shop assistant ... get drunk with tawdrily dressed women; in the gin-palace, fashionable gentlemen drink ... French and Rhenish wines, smoke excellent Havana cigars, and flirt with beautiful young girls in splendid gowns. But in both places scenes of orgy are acted out in all their brutality and horror ... From the outside, these 'gin-palaces' with their carefully fastened shutters seem to be quietly slumbering; but no sooner has the doorkeeper admitted you by the little door reserved for initiates than you are dazzled by the light of a thousand gas lamps ... Towards midnight the regular clients begin to arrive; several finishes are frequented by men in high society, and this is where the cream of the aristocracy gather ... the orgy rises to a crescendo; between four and five in the morning it reaches its height ... what a worthy use these English lords make of their immense fortunes! How ... generous they are when they have lost the use of their reason and offer fifty, even a hundred guineas, to a prostitute if she will lend herself to all the obscenities that drunkenness engenders ... One of the favourite sports is to ply a woman with drink until she falls dead drunk upon the floor, then to make her swallow a draught compounded of vinegar, mustard, and pepper;

this invariably throws the poor creature into horrible convulsions, and her spasms and contortions provoke the honourable company to gales of laughter ... [35]

It is hard to picture the reaction of the other 'initiates' to this eagle-eyed Frenchwoman soberly observing them, accompanied by her two non-participating friends. You may have noticed a certain prejudice in her account. She assured her readers – who of course were French – that she was describing what she saw with her own eyes. 'What goes on in these places ought to be seen, for it reveals the moral state of England better than any words could express'. Neither Dickens nor Mayhew described the 'finish' from inside, as she did; nor did her compatriot Monsieur Taine, nor that amiable man-about-town Munby, although he did describe the Haymarket at 4 in the morning, with 'several half-drunken prostitutes, one of whom, reeling away, drops her splendid white bonnet in the gutter'. Was she making it all up, as a study in Anglophobia? She may have overstated her case slightly, but I incline to accept it on the whole.

Hippolyte Taine found very few high-class prostitutes – but perhaps he did not have the right *entrée*. One of them, whom he did not name, 'at the top of the profession, entertains lords ... her friends smoke in her house, and *cross their legs*' (my italics), clearly a place where anything was permissible. She may have been the famous 'Skittles', Catherine Walters. She was the mistress of Lord Hartington, heir to the Duke of Devonshire, between 1859 and 1863, and even had her portrait painted by Landseer and hung in the Royal Academy.[36] It was bad enough to desecrate the Academy, but it was even worse for Skittles and her sisters to appear in the sacred precincts of Hyde Park, where the aristocracy were wont to display themselves. Skittles rode impeccably, or sometimes drove an incomparable pair of ponies. Many high-class prostitutes chose to ride, showing off their figures in beautifully tailored habits. Any attractive woman who could ride was allowed to enter the park on horseback, although she would have been denied access on foot (after all, a lady would have her own carriage, so a female pedestrian invited the suspicion that she was a prostitute). So, go to a good tailor, learn to ride, hire a horse from a livery stable – and try your luck.[37] In the evening, their gowns and jewels could rival any respectable dowager's. One woman wore diamonds said to be worth £5,000. She charged £25 for twenty minutes.[38]

There seems to have been a passion for flagellation in high-class Victorian circles. Pornographic literature could be bought everywhere, except on the railway stations, where Mr W. H. Smith kept his stock respectable. The stereoscopic views and cartes-de-visite which ladies and gentlemen collected for viewing in the drawing room had their less innocent counterparts – and yet they seem so very innocent to a twenty-first-century eye. Munby had had a photograph taken (he was no photographer himself) of one of his favourite subjects, a Paddington dustwoman. The 'doorsman' of the studio, mistaking Munby's motives completely, offered to get him a girl from a pub nearby 'who would have a picture of her taken with her clothes up'. A vendor approached him: 'Beg pardon, Sir, but was you in want of any ballet girls or *poses plastiques*? I am a theatrical agent. I can supply you with girls at an hour's notice'. Munby 'thanked him coldly'.[39] Another time, he was offered pictures of nude and semi-nude women at 2s each. The models were not prostitutes; 'a girl has no need to go on the streets when she can earn £5–£6 a week by this ... and sitting to the Academy'.

William Dugdale, a prolific publisher of smut, used a variety of marketing ploys. *The Exquisite; a Collection of Tales, Histories and Essays, Funny, Fanciful and Facetious*, came out every week between 1842 and 1844. It could be bought as weekly parts, for 4d or 6d each, with an engraving and eight pages of text, or the engravings could be bought separately, in colour, for a shilling each; or the whole run could be bought in three bound volumes – covering the market, from the casual customer buying a shilling's worth of dirty picture, to aristocratic library shelves.[40]

Inevitably, Victorian reformers set about reforming prostitutes. William Gladstone used, famously, to invite them home to tea. The London Society for the Protection of Young Females was especially concerned for girls under fifteen. The Female Mission to the Fallen was founded in 1858 to work among the urban working class, and managed to send half the cases it dealt with back to their families, and jobs, and the other half to residential homes.[41] The most picturesque institution was the Midnight Mission, set up in 1853.[42] 'An elderly gentleman of almost clerical appearance' invited the passing prostitutes in the Haymarket to come into the meeting-hall and have a cup of tea, and something to eat, and listen to hymns and prayers, after which 'any who want to stay are offered a home'.[43] By 1861, 4,000 women had come to the meetings – whether to take the weight off their feet and enjoy a cup of tea and a bun, or for higher interests, was impossible to know – and 600 of them had been 'restored to their friends', or found safe jobs.[44]

Charles Dickens knew a newsworthy project when he saw one. He interested the rich philanthropist Angela Burdett Coutts in these 'fallen women', and collaborated with her in setting up a home for a few of them in 1848, which was good for an article in his journal *Household Words*. It was called 'Urania House', after Venus Urania, the goddess of love in her spiritual aspect, as opposed to Venus Aphrodite, the goddess of physical love. Ralph Waldo Emerson met Dickens at a dinner that year:

> Charles Dickens said Miss Coutts had undertaken to establish an asylum for vicious girls taken out of the street. She had bed [*sic*], clothed, schooled them, and had them taught to sew and knit and bake, that they might be wives for the Australians. Then she proposed to send them out, at her charge, and have them provided for until they married. They liked all this very well until it came to sailing for Australia. Then they preferred going back to the Strand.[45]

For a gently bred woman whose world suddenly fell apart – perhaps her husband died leaving nothing, or deserted her, or she never married and family support dried up – prostitution was not the answer. She had to find employment as a governess. There was no other middle-class opening for her.

She would be well advised to get her duties clearly stated when she began, and not left as – 'she is to cram a certain number of troublesome spoiled children with French, music and sundry other accomplishments while in return she is to receive an inadequate salary'.[46] Once she was engaged, she had the prospect of secure employment for a year, and if she was dismissed before the year end without reasonable cause – which she would have to prove, an almost impossible task, one would think – she was entitled to her salary up to the end of the year.[47] After many hints on the same lines – 'all admirable, but how can a trembling young woman badly in need of a job face up to a prospective employer and demand to have her holiday entitlement specified? – *The Magazine of Domestic Economy* helpfully told her to 'be of good cheer, for though your good works may not be seen or acknowledged ... there is compensation – if not in this world, assuredly in a better'.[48] Surely an admission that a governess's lot in this life was beyond redemption.

Her working life was not likely to last more than 25 years, at a starting salary of £25, rarely reaching £80. Even if a string of children in the same family meant that she was kept on for several years, there was no pension at the end of them. Although her salary sounds as if it should be enough, considering that she lived in, she could not be sure of steady employment, and she was often supporting aged parents, or helping to educate younger siblings; and since she was expected to be on duty in the evenings, and had little or no time to herself, she could not do as most girls with little money did, and make her own clothes, yet she always had to be respectably dressed.

In 1843 the Governesses' Benevolent Institution was founded, which attracted enough money to open a 'temporary home for governesses out of situation', housing 52 of them in its first six months, with a free registry to which prospective employers could refer. It was able to fund annuities for them when they were too old to work; by 1858 there were 43 annuitants.[49] But these were stopgaps; the real advance came in 1848, when the Institution founded Queen's College in Harley Street, 'for general female education and for granting to governesses certificates of qualification'. The syllabus included English literature and grammar, French, German, and Italian: Latin, astronomy and theology; mechanics and natural philosophy (roughly speaking, science), the new science of political economy and even, for a while, a course on the Method of Teaching.[50]

Young women over fourteen, chaperoned by 'Lady Visitors', were taught by nine lecturers from King's College, including F. M. D. Maurice, a Christian Socialist and Professor of Theology, and Charles Kingsley, who later became Professor of Modern History at Cambridge. At first they gave evening lectures, which were free. From 1850 fees were charged, for daytime lectures, but prospective governesses could attend for half fees, and there were four free places. Most pupils, including the governesses, took only a few of the courses. The teaching staff charged no fees for examining and awarding certificates. These middle- to upper-class girls who attended were better-educated than many of their brothers, and the governesses had something to show prospective employers.

※

The Elements of Social Science was written by a respected medical writer, George Drysdale. It was published in 1854 and went into many editions.[51] After a clear description of the male sexual organs, and a guess that the clitoris was 'probably' the 'chief organ of sexual enjoyment' in women, he considered the problems arising from the long interval between adolescence and the age of matrimony – perhaps ten years out of a young man's life. What was he to do? Abstinence was bad for him, and so was masturbation, that bogy of the Victorian era. He suggested a utopian expedient which if practicable would commend itself to any young man at any time. 'The true and only remedy for the evils arising from abstinence is a moderate indulgence in sexual intercourse, together with ... freedom from study, exercise and amusements in the open air.' But if unmarried women insisted on preserving their virginity, where could he find this therapeutic 'moderate indulgence' except with prostitutes?

Women too had their problems; 'it is a common remark among men seeing a girl languid and sickly, that what she needs is venereal gratification'. (*That* was what they talked about over the port.) Prostitution 'should be regarded as a temporary substitute for a better state of things', that better state being one where 'every man and every woman should have a fair share of the blessings of love and of offspring' so long as the offspring did not outnumber their parents. Then, after this prolonged sowing of wild oats by both sexes, they could enter the blessed state of matrimony with quiet minds. Divorce should be easily obtainable, 'neither man nor woman should ever pretend to be constant when they are not', and – the greatest blessing of all – 'the introduction of truer views of sexual morality among us would ... draw us nearer in sympathy with the French and the other continental nations'. It has yet to happen.

At last we get to wedding bells and wedded bliss ...

A poor woman would be welcomed into her husband's family to look after him and preserve his wage-earning capacity with healthy cooking and clean, mended clothes. Her wedding festivities would be modest – friends and neighbours round for a meal, and a trip to the parish church for the ceremony. The guests would be expected to contribute to the cost, in cash or in kind, so that the young couple did not begin life together with a burden of debt. The bride might have a new dress for the occasion, which would be kept for 'best' and last her for many years.

Most middle-class girls married between 20 and 25. By 30, their chances of matrimony had diminished to vanishing point. 'This is not a marrying age ... to sell one's independence for gold is repugnant to all correct feeling. It is too often done, notwithstanding that unhappiness is the secret or evident result' observed *The Magazine of Domestic Economy* in 1843.[52] Yet the same writer goes on: 'we are no advocates for improvident marriages. Love in a cottage is very delightful, but it must be a cottage ornée, and if with a double coach house the love will be the more enduring'.

But the double coach house took some negotiating. 'A gentleman will often give his daughter a dowry amounting to no more than his eldest son's future income for one year; moreover he insists that the gentleman who marries his daughter make a settlement on her, two hundred, three hundred or four hundred pounds a year ... this requirement discourages many suitors.'[53] While her father battled with the suitor in his study, the hopeful bride tried her best to live up to the current image of a desirable bride:

> It would be a miracle if the object of being attractive to men had not been the polar star of feminine education. And, this great means of influence over the minds of women having been acquired, an instinct of selfishness made men avail themselves of it to the utmost as a means of holding women in subjection, by representing to them meekness, submissiveness and resignation of all individual will into the hands of a man, as an essential part of sexual attractiveness ... The wife is the actual bond-servant of her husband.[54]

So there she sat, in the drawing room, meekly embroidering, while her future was decided for her in her father's study.

The middle-class male Victorian's ideal of married life was that he went out into the rough world to earn the family income, and the wife stayed at home making it beautiful, and comfortable for him when he came home from his exhausting day. She should never trouble him with domestic worries or anxiety about the children; while buttressing her husband's illusion that she was only his sweetly submissive bond-servant, she had to deal with all such crises on her own. When he was inclined for sexual intercourse, she should be available. As William Acton noted in *The Functions and Disorders of the Reproductive Organs* (1865):

The sexual act is ordinarily attended with great pleasure. I am speaking here ... of the pleasure experienced by the male ... even in the healthiest person a feeling of fatigue immediately follows ... sickly men have died in the act ... taking a hard-working intellectual man residing in London as the type, sexual congress ought not to take place more frequently than once in seven to ten days. [More often leads to backache.] I should say that the majority of women are not much troubled with sexual feeling of any kind ... love of home, children and domestic duties are the only passions [women] feel. As a general rule, a modest woman seldom desires any sexual gratification for herself.[55]

Impotence could be caused by badly fitting trusses, or by obesity, in which case Mr Banting's diet, avoiding dairy fats, bread, potatoes and beer, should produce results. A general tonic, such as cantharides, strychnine or phosphorus, or even electricity, could often improve things.[56] I have found no advice for immodest women who went so far as to desire some sexual gratification for themselves.[57]

Contraception was certainly not practised by Victoria and Albert, although it is difficult to believe that as a well-read and scientifically minded man Albert did not know of it. At the other end of society, Munby was chatting to a young woman whom he had known when she was a milkmaid, one of his favorite types. She told him she was now married, with a baby. He said ' "it came at the right time, I hope?" "Oh yes," says Norah, with the pride of an honest wife, "I took care of that".'[58] Perhaps Norah had come across Francis Place's advice, in his pamphlet *To the Married of Both Sexes of the Working People*, widely circulated from 1823 onwards: either the husband should practise *coitus interruptus*, or the wife should insert a sponge 'as large as a green walnut or a small apple', tied to a length of ribbon, into her vagina before intercourse and withdraw it immediately afterwards. He refined his advice in a further 'handbill' addressed to 'the Married of Both Sexes in Genteel Life'. 'A little practice and care in the use of the sponge will render all other precautions unnecessary.'

This belief was surely over-optimistic, but it was a step in the right direction, and it had the advantage of being the responsibility of the woman, since 'any preventive means, to be satisfactory, must be used by the woman, as it spoils the passion and impulsiveness of the venereal act if the man has to think of them', which would never do.[59] Some medical practitioners advocated the 'safe period', but unfortunately the cycle of ovulation and menstruation was imperfectly understood and their advice pinpointed just the wrong period.

Condoms were available 'which [are] so thin as not very greatly to interfere with the venereal enjoyment and yet [they are] ... comparatively seldom used in this country ... [they are] sold only in a few shops which have a low moral character, and in an underhand way ... *care should be taken that the same sheath should not be used frequently, as it becomes less trustworthy*'.[60]

※

Until 1857 divorce was obtainable only by private Act of Parliament. In a case of 1845 where a man had been found guilty of cohabiting with another woman after his wife had deserted him, the sentencing judge said:

> You should have gone to the ecclesiastical court and there obtained ...
> a decree *a mensa et thoro* [judicial separation]. You should then have
> brought an action in the courts of common law and recovered ...
> damages against your wife's paramour. Armed with these decrees you
> should have approached the legislature and obtained an Act of Par-
> liament ... It is quite true that these proceedings would have cost you
> many hundreds of pounds, whereas you probably have not as many
> pence. But the law knows no distinction between rich and poor.[61]

The sentence was one day's imprisonment, which had already been served. The offender was released and legal opinion was convulsed. Twelve years later the Matrimonial Causes Act 1857 set up a new court to hear divorce cases, which for the first time came 'within the reach of people with moderate incomes', at only £25 or £30.[62] But a woman could not divorce her husband unless she could prove that he had not only slept with another woman but also that he had committed incest, buggery, bestiality, cruelty or rape, while a man had only to prove that his wife had slept with another man. After the 1857 Act a divorced wife no longer forfeited all her property, and she might keep any income she managed to earn; but the court was unlikely to award her custody of her children. Divorce was not lightly undertaken. By 1872 only about 200 decrees were being granted annually.[63]

The proceedings of the Court for Divorce and Matrimonial Causes were fully reported, to the delight of the gutter press. Members of the public struggled to get into the court, especially when a famous name was involved, and few could be more famous than Viscount Palmerston. In 1863 he was joined as co-respondent in a case brought by a disreputable Irishman, O'Kane, who alleged that Palmerston, then aged 80, had committed adultery with Mrs O'Kane. Palmerston had what O'Kane most wanted – money – and would surely pay, he thought, to have the action settled out of court. But Palmerston was far too well advised. Enquiry agents discovered that 'Mrs O'Kane' was not legally married after all. Palmerston did not even appear in court to deny the ungentlemanly, if flattering, conduct imputed to him – such a disappointment to the waiting crowds.

Another case was more fun. A very senior Admiral, Sir Henry Codrington, sued for divorce on the grounds of his wife's adultery, in 1863. When the Admiral had been posted to the Crimea, in 1854, his wife had very properly employed Miss Emily Faithful as her companion/chaperone. But when the Admiral returned, his wife still preferred Miss Faithful's company in the bedroom to his own. The story gathered pace when the Admiral was posted to Malta, and his wife went too. He was busy doing whatever admirals do, which left her often at a loose end, so she embarked on a gay social life, often crossing the Grand Harbour at night with one of her swains, in a small 'gondola' which the boatmen always found to be out of trim ... Shock! Horror! The Admiral's wife was sitting beside her swain! – And on at least one occasion the gondola was almost capsized ...

At one breathless stage in the evidence, a female witness was asked about conversations between her and Lady Codrington, during which she had pleaded with Lady Codrington to behave herself. 'I was horror-struck', she faltered, blushing, in the witness box, 'at what I then discovered'. 'What was that?' asked Counsel, while the public strained their ears for the answer. 'That the – er – climax of evil had already occurred'. Not exactly earth-shattering, compared to evidence tossed off lightly nowadays, but certainly a strain on a Victorian lady, no matter how disappointing for the public. Miss Faithful had again joined the Codrington household, in Malta, and when the Admiral alleged that his wife had been unfaithful with one or two of her swains, Lady Codrington cross-pleaded with an allegation that he had been unfaithful with Miss Faithful. Things looked up slightly when Miss Faithful deposed that the Admiral had come into her room one night wearing only his nightshirt. She feared the worst, but he explained that he only wanted to poke the fire.[64] The jury needed only an hour to find for the Admiral on all points.

Were the Victorians happily married? Other people's marriages are impossible to analyse, in any era. And our expectations are so different. As well as that 'good sense of humour' so essential to lonely hearts advertisers, we expect some form of sharing partnership, not a relationship of master and 'bond-servant'. We hope for mutual honesty, kindness and forbearance, supported by a foundation of sexual attraction. Women are not desperate to find husbands. If they are overwhelmed by maternal longings, they can even satisfy those, without a living-in father for the child. They may decide to pursue a rewarding career instead of, or combined with, matrimony. A Victorian middle-class woman who had not married was expected to be the companion and nurse of her parents, always at their beck and call. After they died, the best she could hope for was the life of a useful maiden aunt, handed round the family and lodged grudgingly in bleak spare bedrooms. Marriage, even to a tight-fisted autocrat totally uncongenial in bed, was probably preferable.

CHAPTER 21

Crimes and Punishments

Thieving was constant. 'There are thousands of neglected children loitering about the metropolis and prowling about the streets, begging and stealing for their daily bread.'[1] Some of the thieves were only six years old. As they grew up, young women graduated to stealing clothes, whole rolls of carpet, and even fenders, tucked under their voluminous clothes.

Shoplifters were usually women between 14 and 60. 'The skirt of their dress was lined from the pocket downward, with an opening in front where they can insert a small article, which is not observed in the ample crinoline.'[2] Three out of four prostitutes were 'addicted to stealing', according to Mayhew, especially if their customers were drunk. Children sent out with washing to be delivered to the washerwomen, or taking the clean laundry back to the sender, were easy prey for a thief, so were well-dressed little girls and boys who somehow had become separated from their minders; they were lured into a back street and stripped naked. Washing put out to dry in the garden was at risk, and even the copper boiler in which it had been laundered, as well as copper pipes and lead roofing in empty houses.

Between 7 and 8 in the evening was a favourite time for house thefts. The family would be at dinner, and the servants − if they were not themselves involved − preoccupied with serving the meal. The early evening had the added advantage, to the thieves, that if they were detected, they could be charged with robbery but not burglary, which applied only to crimes committed after 9 at night. A servant in a grand house might be suborned to participate in a robbery, or might have been placed there by a gang well before the robbery took place.

It was a foolish man who walked in a London street with his watch or his pocket book on view. A favourite technique then, as now, was to create some kind of disturbance to distract the victim's attention, and filch his valuables while he was not looking. Often thieves operated in gangs, one taking the goods and handing them immediately to another member of the gang, who escaped. Sometimes the 'hue and cry' was raised by the thief himself, indicating a false scent while his accomplice made off in the opposite direction with the goods.[3]

A distinguished Egyptian archaeologist, Joseph Hékékyan Bey, was sheltering from the rain in Regent Street, 'under a portico, where there was a crowd. ... [Later] I found that my purse, which I carried in my left waistcoat pocket, was missing ... it is as well I did not lose my watch also, which was in the other pocket ... I passed an unpleasant night at the thought that I had been so careless.'[4] This was not just 'dipping' into an outside pocket, such as the pockets in a man's coat tails, which were asking to be picked; the thief was skilled, to reach into a man's waistcoat undetected. 'A lady generally carried her gold or silver watch in a small pocket in front of her dress, possibly under one of the large flounces', but if she were jostled in a crowd, or getting into an omnibus, her watch was just as vulnerable as her husband's. For other spoils the thieves 'generally insert the whole hand, as the ladies' pockets are deep in the dress'. The victim's voluminous petticoats, or her crinoline, would prevent her from feeling this intrusive hand.

Railway stations were prime sites for thieves; people had their minds on catching the right train, and did not see the pickpockets 'hanging about stations looking as if they might take a train' until too late. Luggage on the backs of cabs and carriages collecting passengers from the railway terminal could be cut from the securing straps, sometimes with the connivance of the driver. There was a nice line in stolen lapdogs. First, lure it away by parading a bitch on heat past it, or stupify it by dropping a piece of doctored meat beside it. Then, answer the advertisement by its distracted owner, return the dog which you had 'found', and collect the promised reward. You could always steal it all over again ... If no reward was promised, keep the dog for a while, and maybe change its appearance slightly, then sell it. An easy West End livelihood with no unsocial hours.

House thieves were after silver and gold articles, which would be in the fence's hands within fifteen minutes of removal from the house, and immediately thrown into the waiting crucible to be melted down to an unidentifiable mass. Coiners had sophisticated methods, involving melting base metals such as old spoons, pouring the result into prepared moulds, and electroplating them to look like silver using nitric and sulphuric acid, cyanide, copper and a galvanic battery. This could be particularly nasty in a police raid, when the coiners would throw the acids at the police. Nitric acid was a horrible weapon used by some criminals.[5]

'Crime is developing itself into a mania ... London has ceased to be a city which one can traverse at night with mind at rest and the hands in the pockets', wrote a French visitor in 1866.[6] Even by day, and in fashionable districts, it was not safe. Hugh Pilkington, MP was walking along Pall Mall in broad daylight one day in 1862, when two men attacked or 'garotted' him, one beating him while the other stole his watch.[7] In the same year, a Frenchman was walking in Hyde Park just before 4 in the afternoon, when four 'garotters' attacked him. They did not know their man, who had served in the French Army. He knocked out two of them and the others fled. 'Not everybody has served in the Zouaves'.[8]

The Inland Revenue is not generally thought of as a calling endangering life and limb, but in 1861 an unfortunate Collector was murdered by a man whom he had assessed to tax for the keeping of a dog.[9] Duelling was illegal, but in 1843 Lieutenant Munro and his brother-in-law Colonel Fawcett managed to shoot at each other in a field near the Camden Road, over a silly quarrel, and unfortunately Fawcett was killed. Munro 'surrendered himself and has been tried and sentenced to death, but this punishment the Queen has commuted to twelve months' imprisonment in Newgate'.[10] Karl Marx resented bad reviews so bitterly that he threatened to challenge the reviewers to a duel, but somehow nothing came of it, which was just as well because he was so short-sighted he would undoubtedly have missed.[11]

Much more to the public taste was the trial of Mr and Mrs Manning for the murder of Patrick O'Connor. Manning was a very shady character, suspected of thefts of bullion worth £4,000 from the

Great Western Railway on which he was employed as a guard, but he had escaped prosecution. Maria Manning was a Swiss woman employed as a lady's maid by a daughter of the Duchess of Sutherland. She had been courted by two men, Patrick O'Connor and Manning. She married Manning in 1847 but she and her husband cultivated O'Connor, having designs on his property. O'Connor was about as crooked as Manning, with whom he seems to have planned various fraudulent schemes. By now the Mannings were living in a terraced house in Bermondsey. For a while a medical student lodged with them, whom Manning asked about the effect of chloroform and the most vulnerable part of the human skull. Then they gave him notice; invited O'Connor to dinner; shot him and beat his head in, just where the medical student had advised; and buried his body under the floor of the basement kitchen, covered in vitriol and quicklime. O'Connor was missed from his employment, and after a splendidly sensational detective investigation his corpse was found, decomposed but still identifiable by his false teeth. The Mannings had meanwhile fled, Maria to Edinburgh where, after an exchange of telegraphs from the police involved, she was arrested. Her husband was arrested in Jersey.[12]

Poisoning frequently appears in the annals of Victorian crime. An astonishing number of poisons were ready to a murderer's hand in the average home, which explains why Isabella Beeton gave her full attention to common poisons and their antidotes in her book on *Household Management*. They ranged from sulphuric acid or 'vitriol', nitric acid or 'acqua fortis', and prussic acid, for which 'very little can be done ... as death takes place so quickly after the poison has been swallowed', to arsenic, 'corrosive sublimate.. .a most powerful poison' and laudanum, a derivative of opium. (Curiously she does not mention strychnine, unless under another name which I have missed.) From the poisoner's point of view the best bet was prussic acid.

In 1845 John Tavell was tried for murdering Sarah Hart, in Slough, by poisoning her with prussic acid.[13] He was a colourful villain who had served fourteen years' transportation in Australia, made a fortune there, and returned to England. He affected Quaker dress, 'his whole appearance and manner impressed one with the notion of his being a very saintly personage'. There was some relationship between him and Sarah Hart, which made him decide she would be better out of his way, so he went to a chemist in Bishopsgate Street in the City and bought two drachms of a proprietary medicine, 'Scheele's Prussic

Acid', which he said he wanted to apply to his varicose veins. The purchase was duly entered in the poison book as the law required. He came back the next day and bought some more, saying he had broken the first bottle. He took the train from Paddington, arrived at Sarah Hart's cottage, gave her the poison in a drink of beer, and hurried out of the house and back to the station. But his misdeed was quickly discovered and 'a signal was made by the electric telegraph ... only very lately established on the line of the Great Western railway'.

Tavell was traced from Paddington to his home, arrested, in due course found guilty and hanged. In another case of poisoning by prussic acid, a medically qualified son gave his old mother a properly measured dose of Scheele's prussic acid 'as a remedy for violent attacks of vomiting to which she was subject', but she died. There was no strict quality control of drugs, and this particular bottle of it was too strong. He was tried for her murder, but acquitted.

William Palmer of Rugeley near Stafford used strychnine to perpetrate an insurance fraud involving murder in 1856. He was found guilty and executed in Stafford jail. During his trial, which was widely reported, evidence had been given that strychnine could not be identified in a dead body. This inspired William Dove of Leeds to murder his wife with it. He persuaded a pupil of his general practitioner to give him enough to poison the rats which he said infested his house. It took several doses of it, in 'medicine', to kill his wife. He had been wrong about the post-mortem traces: 'large quantities' were discovered in her body. He was found guilty and hanged in 1856.

Arsenic had many innocent uses, such as in paint, as Scheele's green, which was a nice bright emerald, pretty for cake decorations, artificial flowers and wallpaper. 'Such papers certainly give off arsenical dust', so the rumours about Napoleon's death being caused by the wallpaper in his room on St Helena were not so ludicrous then as they seem now, although the amount of arsenic in the 'dust' was infinitesimal. It was also handy for worming horses, poisoning rats, and killing flies. A solution of it could be used as a depilatory. So arsenic could be found all over a normal house and stable, and many cases of death by 'gastric upsets' may well have been murder by arsenic.

Anyone who was anyone wanted to be in court while a notorious trial was proceeding. The Central Criminal Court provided seating beside and below the trial judge, where on ordinary days the Aldermen attended, 'reading the daily newspapers or writing letters'.[14] But for notorious trials the City of London Sheriffs could issue much-prized tickets.[15] In 1840, when Courvoisier was tried for the murder of his employer Lord William Russell, the Duke of Sussex, two earls, two lords, two ladies and an Honourable all squeezed into the 'places set apart for persons of rank'. Courvoisier was an 'alien' or foreigner, and entitled to a jury of six compatriots as well as six Englishmen, but he chose not to exercise that right. On the last day the Duke had lost interest, but 'the attendance of ladies of rank was more numerous'. Perhaps it was their presence which overwhelmed the Chief Justice, so that in pronouncing the death sentence he was 'interrupted by his own sobs'.

The Mannings were tried in the Central Criminal Court in 1849. The trial lasted two days and, again, admission to the body of the court was by ticket only, where 'several ladies were present on the bench, ... [and others] were provided with seats in the dock', and various foreign ambassadors and other 'distinguished visitors' were found seats elsewhere. The jury took just 45 minutes to find both Mannings guilty.

Two years later Society sensation-seekers had a field day, when ex-Etonian ex-Hussars Viscount Frankfort de Montmorency took the witness box in the trial of Alice Lowe, whom he accused of stealing jewellery from him in scandalous circumstances, 'scandalous' being the Victorian shorthand for 'as a prostitute'. She had been brought to a house in Paddington, which he kept as a separate establishment from the matrimonial home and unknown to his wife. Her 'visit' lasted nearly two months, during which she was prevented from leaving. One evening when the noble Lord left to go to his club, she seized her opportunity, and the jewellery she said he had given her, and escaped. The jury found her not guilty, and Lady Frankfort understandably obtained a judicial separation from her husband.

Ten years later Lord Frankfort was back in court, this time in the dock, charged with 'publishing an indecent communication' in the shape of a letter 'to the peeresses and the daughters of the nobility and gentry', offering to arrange for them to entertain their lovers in their bedrooms while their husbands spent the night in a drugged sleep. This missive, beside which our 'junk mail' pales into insignificance, was enclosed with a list of apparent associates, one of whom, Lord Henry Lennox, brought the case against Lord Frankfort, the originator of the stunt. One of the recipients was a prominent clergyman who, of course, opened the letter addressed to his wife, and was scandalised. When he was called to the witness box, he asked that all ladies in court – who included many of his parishioners – should be asked to leave before he gave evidence, but the judge merely suggested that they should not listen. Lord Frankfort was sentenced to twelve months imprisonment in Coldbath Fields House of Correction in Clerkenwell, but he was spared the usual prison routine; 'on undertaking ... to pay 5 shillings a week towards the cost of his maintenance, he was exempted from oakum picking and the treadmill'.[16]

Sentences were savage and apparently arbitrary. The Newgate Calendar for 1853, recording all the cases heard that year in the Central Criminal Court, shows wide variations in sentencing. A 15-year-old box-maker and his accomplice, a 21-year-old shoe-maker, together stole a handkerchief worth 1s. They were both transported for seven years. Two other pickpockets, who each stole a handkerchief, worth 3s and 2s, were sentenced by the same judge, one to a month in a house of correction, the other to four years' penal servitude. Someone who nicked a bottle of gin worth 2s 1d got only fourteen days in Newgate. One bigamist got fourteen days in Newgate, another got a year in a house of correction. For 'having carnal knowledge' of a girl under ten a man was sentenced to six months imprisonment, but for raping a girl aged between ten and twelve another man got a year in a house of correction.

A man found guilty, as the report put it, of 'b-----y', at that time a capital crime, landed two years in a house of correction; but another, a 53-year-old labourer, was transported for life. So was a fourteen-year-old servant found guilty of accusing a man (her employer? the summary does not say) of the crime of b-----y with intent to extort £100. The great majority of defendants were described as 'labourers', but in one case two surgeons and a chemist were accused of having carried out an abortion. One of the surgeons was sentenced to transportation for fifteen years, the other surgeon and the chemist being found not guilty. A minor crime peculiar to those days, 'uttering forged turnpike toll tickets, for 4d and 6d', landed the offender in a house of correction for eighteen months.

There was nothing approximating to our non-custodial sentences, such as probation or antisocial behaviour orders. The prison population was estimated at about 6,000.[17] Bridewells, the lowest in the hierarchy of prisons, were used for sentences up to three months. The original Bridewell beside the River Fleet survived until 1860, and others were built at Holloway, Wandsworth Common and Coldbath Fields, and at Tothill Fields for boys and women. Those sentenced for up to two years were sent to prisons known as houses of correction. There was one housing 1,100 or more at Coldbath Fields, next to the Bridewell there.[18] Longer sentences were served in Millbank, Pentonville, Brixton prison for women, or the hulks.

Jeremy Bentham, the prophet of Utilitarianism, who advocated that government should achieve the greatest possible good for the greatest possible number, had spread his reforming zeal to prison design in the 1820s. Instead of gloomy blocks such as Newgate, prisons should be built on his 'Panopticon' plan, with separate wings arranged in a star shape, converging at a central point where guards and other services could be concentrated, with easy access to all the cells in each wing: economic and healthy, and conducing without doubt to the greatest possible good of all concerned. The prison at Millbank (on the site now occupied by Tate Britain), the largest prison in London, was a Panopticon design, with six radiating wings, built in 1821 on 7 acres of marshy, damp land beside the river. A former inmate described it as 'a terribly gloomy place – gloomy walls, gloomy faces, gloomy silence ...'.[19] Each cell was furnished with a small table, a 'slop tub' with a lid, a hammock and a rug, and 'a stick painted red one end and the other end black ... in the wall at the corridor side was a narrow slit and when you wanted anything you thrust your stick through the slit and kept it there until it happened to catch the eye of the warder on duty. If he saw the black end out, he knew that you wanted work, if the red end, your wants were of a more personal nature'.[20]

Pentonville was built in 1842, at a cost of £85,000, on a 7-acre site at the edge – then – of the built-up area, out at Holloway, on the Caledonian Road. Hippolyte Taine called it an 'admirably contrived hive made of iron'.[21] There were four radial wings on a semi-circular plan, with three exercise yards between them, each wing containing 130 cells on each of its three floors. Each cell was 9 feet high, 13 feet long and 7 feet wide, with a water closet, a copper washbasin, a stool, a table and gas lighting. The prisoners slept on hammocks, with mattresses and blankets. Once a fortnight they got clean shirts and drawers and even a bath – a new experience for many.[22] The first impression the prison made on a visitor was of 'perfectly Dutch-like cleanliness ... [it was] extremely bright and cheerful ... it strikes the mind on first entering it as a bit of the Crystal Palace'. And 'almost every gentleman placed in authority over the convicts appears to be activated by the most humane and kindly motives towards them'.[23] The prisoners were taught a trade, such as tailoring, shoe-making and weaving, at which they could earn as much as 8d a week. 'Some long-sentence men have as much as £20 to receive on getting their liberty, and then they have a good suit of clothes given them as well – according to their station – in order that they may have a fair start in the world again.' Once a day, unless it was raining, they were taken out of their cells for exercise, walking 'at a brisk walking pace', 130 at a time, in two circles, every man holding on to a rope which was knotted at 15–foot intervals, so that no prisoner was ever near another prisoner. In theory they observed silence in the chapel and at school, but they managed to talk to each other without moving their lips.[24]

Here we come to what we would see as the negative aspect of this idyllic scene, the 'separate system'. The Surveyor General of Prisons defined it thus: 'each individual is confined in a cell, which becomes his workshop by day and his bedroom by night ... not only to prevent the prisoner from having intercourse with his fellow prisoners, but to compel him to hold communion with himself' – which would lead, inevitably, to moral redemption. The prisoners were known only by number. When they did emerge from their cells, for exercise or to attend daily service in the chapel, they each wore a cap with a flap over their face, with holes over their eyes, so that they could not recognise or be recognised by their fellow-inmates.[25] The best-behaved prisoners were allowed the huge privilege of working in the bakehouse or the kitchen 'with the cap-peak up' – in silence, of course – as well as receiving extra food, and visits. But lack of co-operation was punished by solitary confinement in a 'refractory cell', in total darkness, usually for no more than two or three days, but sometimes for as long as three weeks. After this conditioning, prisoners were transferred to prisons at Portsmouth, Woolwich and Portland to labour at 'public works', which must surely have been a relief to most of them.

In retrospect it was all so well intentioned. The clean conditions and individual space were better than most inmates had ever experienced in the outside world, but the psychological effect of the 'separate system' must have been disastrous. The average age of prisoners was between 15 and 25; imagine how they reacted to being shut off from humankind like pariahs. The authorities did notice an unusual number of suicides, at first, but it was halved by increasing the amount of (masked) exercise. It was still higher than at other prisons.

Brixton prison for women housed 700 prisoners, and was almost wholly staffed by women.[26] The Prison Medical Officer observed sadly, in 1854, that 'female patients do not bear imprisonment as well as the male prisoners', but 'all at Brixton was done more gently and feelingly, and yet not less effectively, than at other prisons'. The women were known by their names, not by numbers. There was a nursery for babies born to prisoners while in Brixton, although their other children were sent to the workhouse. Their prison dress was a loose claret-brown gown, a blue-checked apron and neckerchief, and a small close-fitting white linen cap. Exercise was taken in pairs, pacing round grass plots and flower beds, and 'chattering' (my italics). 'The majority of the poor creatures fared more sumptuously under their punishment than they possibly could have done outside', and the food in the infirmary included such luxuries as fish, and chops. The women worked at making flannel underwear, and stitching stays, and doing the washing and ironing contracted for by the prison management, and making shirts, some for sale to Moses and Son and such suppliers. 'No wonder', thought Mayhew and Binny, 'that honest women cannot live by the labour of shirt-making.'

Up to 1853, an average of 460 convicts were transported to Australia annually.[27] By 1853 there were over 6,000 convicts in Australia, and 2,650 in Bermuda and Gibraltar. The sentence was usually for seven years, but could be for ten, fourteen, or fifteen years. In rare cases the records show the chilling entry 'death recorded and transported for life' – the convict had legally ceased to exist in England. At least the transported man or woman had some chance, however illusory, of making a new life. After 1853, when the colonies understandably refused to act any longer as the refuse bin for English criminality, penal servitude in this country was largely substituted for transportation abroad. Convicts already sentenced to seven and ten years' transportation faced four or six years' penal service in England, instead. Only convicts sentenced to fourteen years or life were still transported.

As usual, there was a shortage of prison accommodation here, so some prisoners were sent to the hulks at Woolwich, half an hour away by rail. These were old battleships which had first been used to house convicts as long ago as 1779, when labour was needed to dredge the Thames. 'Originally adopted as a make-shift under pressing circumstances, these old men-of-war have remained nearly half a century the receptacles of the worst class of prisoners from all the jails in the United Kingdom.'[28] In 1841 they housed 3,552 convicts. The hulks were constantly wet, dark and verminous. Of those at Woolwich, the *Defiance* was the biggest, a 74-gun ship with 500 inmates on three decks, sleeping in hammocks which were so tightly packed that they touched. The *Warrior* was also a 74-gun ship. (The number of guns signified the size of the ship. The guns had of course been removed long ago, as had most of the masts, and the rigging.) It housed another 450 prisoners. The *Unité* was a hospital ship which could hold up to 58 patients in comparative luxury: they got iron bedsteads, extra tea and 2 oz of wine, and half a sheep's head every day, with milk and bread and butter. Lastly, the *Sulphur* was the washing hulk. It had been a 30-gun sloop, but was now degraded to a floating laundry, where three washermen washed the convicts' clothes and hung them out to dry on ropes between the stubs of the masts, like flags when a ship is 'dressed over all'.

In some ways perhaps, the life on board a hulk was not too bad. The men got a change of clothes every week, and they could receive visits and letters once in three months. They worked from 7.30 to 5 (4 in the winter), with an hour for a midday meal, compulsory school and prayers from 6.45 to 8.30, and bed – or rather hammock – at 9, or 8 in the winter. The midday meal was 6 oz of meat, a pound of potatoes and 9 oz of bread. Breakfast and supper were bread and cocoa or gruel. They were supposed to have three hours' schooling a week, an hour of reading, another of writing, and another of arithmetic. They earned 'gratuities' for the labour they did – mostly repairing the banks, and dredging the river bed. It might be as much as 6d a week, which was kept for them until discharge, when they received half the pay due, with a suit of clothes and a set of underwear, and they could draw the rest after two or three months. This does sound sensible; the impulse to go on a spending spree on release must have been almost irresistible. But they were not allowed to talk to their fellow-inmates except for an hour after chapel on Sunday, they were taught no skills which might help on discharge, and the graves of any who died were dug in the surrounding marsh, with no gravestone to mark where they lay.

A prisoner whose sentence included 'hard labour' in prison might be set to work on a treadmill, which had been used in British prisons since 1817. 'The general idea was that a cylinder was kept revolving by the weight of persons on boards, who then had to keep stepping forward ... prison warders who might turn a ratchet to make the work harder were promptly nick-named by the inmates "screws".'[29] They were hated by prisoners, who called them 'grinding the wind' – totally futile. Every day, twelve men at a time would step up 24 steps, 8 inches apart, for fifteen periods of fifteen minutes a day, punctuated by rest periods: all in silence, of course.

'Crank labour' was just as pointless, but had the advantage – to the authorities – that it could be done in the prisoner's cell and preserve the isolation in which he lived. There was a lever which revolved a drum with a series of cups inside it to scoop up sand and empty it at the top of the cycle. In eight hours it was possible – and expected – to do 10,000 turns of the crank. For outside labour, there was 'shot drill' every day for an hour or more. The first man in a line picked up a heavy cannon ball and gave it to the next man, who put it on the ground and picked it up and gave it to the next man ... when it got to the end of the line it went all the way back again.

Picking oakum was a standard punishment in prisons, women's as well as men's, and also a work test in poorhouses. The only difference, for a convict on hard labour, was that he had to do three times as much – 6 lb a day – as the others. At least, it was not soul-destroyingly futile. The spaces between the planks of wooden sailing ships had to be plugged, and the best material was the mass of loose fibres from old unravelled ropes – oakum.

※

By 1861 only murder and treason were punishable by death. Very few murderers were in fact hanged. In 1854 only five went to the gallows; the annual average varied between nine and sixteen.[30] The 'procession to Tyburn' (near Marble Arch) of the previous century had been abolished, with all its ribaldry and passion, but executions were still public occasions, held where the prisoner was incarcerated. In 1849 the Mannings were hanged, on the roof of Horsemonger Gaol near the Elephant and Castle, where they had been imprisoned. Thirty thousand people came to watch, including Charles Dickens. 'We have taken the whole of the roof [of a house overlooking the prison] and the back kitchen, for the extremely moderate sum of 10 guineas.' The night was passed by the drunken crowd in 'every variety of offensive and foul behaviour ...'.[31]

After the Mannings' death, Dickens wrote to *The Times* urging that executions should no longer be public; but this macabre spectacle went on for another twenty years. Dickens also suggested that Calcraft, the hangman, 'should be restrained in his unseemly briskness, in his jokes, his oaths and his brandy'. But at least, the 'hanging days' were changed to Wednesdays from Mondays, when any number of workmen might decide to take a 'Saint Monday' (a day off) to attend. Mrs Manning wore black satin for her execution, which caused 'society [to lay] away its black satin dresses for the season'.[32] Dickens gave a macabre sidelight on Victorian clothes: of 'the two forms dangling on the top of the entrance gateway [to the prison] the man's [was] a limp loose suit of clothes, as if the man had gone out of them; the woman's, a fine shape so elaborately corseted and artfully dressed that it was quite unchanged in its trim appearance as it slowly swung from side to side'.[33]

CHAPTER 22

Religion

❧

*The 1851 religious census · absentees · the working class · Anglicanism
· the Broad Church · Newman's Oxford Movement · the Anglo-Catholics
· St Alban's Church · Queen Victoria, Days of Fast, and Days of Humiliation
and Prayer · the Low Church · building new churches ·
Roman Catholicism · Nonconformist sects · Spurgeon
· the Quakers · Spiritualism · the Jews*

In 1851 a thunderclap broke over middle-class England. For the first –
and last – time, a 'religious census' attempted the impossible task of
delineating the current state of religious belief, by counting the number
of 'attendances' at any place of worship on a specified Sunday (30
March) and checking whether there were enough seats for whoever
did go. The report was a sensation; 21,000 copies were sold. Its
conclusions affronted the self-image of the mid-Victorians, as upright
God-fearing members of the Church of England. Less than half the
population of England had attended any church or chapel at all, and
of them, less than half had attended an Anglican church. The
author of the report, Horace Mann, concluded gloomily that 'a sadly
formidable portion of the English people are habitual neglecters of
the public ordinances of religion'.[1] In the benighted parish of Bethnal
Green, in the East End of London, only 6,024 had attended any
service, out of a population of over 90,000. Where were the others?

By concentrating on a Sunday, the census ignored the 20,000
London Jews. But the biggest category of absentees was the working
class.[2] Unlike a middle-class office worker, a skilled artisan's working
day started at 6, and was twelve hours long, except for Saturdays
when more and more employers were granting a half holiday (and
except for 'Saint Monday' if the employee thought he could get away

with it). On Saturdays, he and his wife did the shopping and used what remained of the day for amusement and relaxation. Just once a week, they could have a late night out, since the next morning did not have to start before dawn.

When it came to Sunday, the wage-earner was likely to find the delicious treat of a lie-in irresistible. Sunday dinner was a sacrosanct family occasion. The woman of the house would be busy in the kitchen all morning, preparing the culminating meal of the week. For the man, now was the time to walk round to the barber's for his weekly shave, discussing the news of the day with other customers. The pubs were shut during the hours of morning service, but if he felt in need of a pick-me-up or a hangover cure, the barber would sell him a medicinal nip of spiced rum or brandy for 3d.

'If a working man whose appearance makes it evident that he is a working man does go into a church, he is put into a free sitting ... while any well-dressed individual is obsequiously shown into a pew.' The 'well-dressed individual' might well have paid for his comfortable seat. Pew rents were a considerable part of the income of a parish. Lady Frederick Cavendish and her husband moved into a house within the parish of St Martin-in-the-Fields in 1865, and 'as the service was very respectably conducted and the sermon good, we have decided, it being our future parish church, to take sittings in it for ourselves and our servants ... and were considerably disgusted by the drive-a-good-bargain fashion in which the official did it; certainly putting before one the odiousness of the pew system in most lively colours'.[3]

Some clergy tried their best to persuade working men to come to church, even in their working clothes, but the feeling of not being welcome was hard to dispel. In 1849 a Congregational minister delivered a scathing description of middle-class church attendance:

Here in Great Britain we carry our class distinctions into the house of God ... the poor man is made to feel that he is a poor man, the rich reminded that he is rich ... the square pew, carpeted, perhaps, and curtained, the graduated scale of other pews, the free-sittings, if there are any, keep up the separation between class and class ... we have distinct places for the pennyless, for we have a morbid horror of poverty ...[4]

Horace Mann, a firm upholder of the Church of England, had to agree. For both the middle class and the upper class, 'a regular church-attendance is now ranked among the regular proprieties of life ... it is observable how absolutely insignificant a portion of the congregation is composed of artisans'.[5]

❃

The old parochial organisation of London, where people attended their parish church as a matter of course, had lapsed. For those who decided to go to an Anglican service, the Church of England could now provide a bewildering variety of worship, loosely grouped under the headings of Broad, High and Low; or to satirists, High, Dry, Low and Slow, with a late entry by the Ritualists coming in as Fast.[6] Christ Church, in Lisson Grove, Marylebone, exemplified the Broad Church. Its middle-class congregation could still sit comfortably in their high-backed pews, in their good Sunday suits and bonnets, and compose themselves for meditation, or sleep, unseen, and safe from intrusion by strangers, or even worse by the poor – who knew what they might be harbouring? – while the familiar cadences of the Anglican service rolled over their heads. The aristocrats of Berkeley Square had their own chapel nearby, equally Broad in doctrine although exclusive in membership. St James's Chapel in Marylebone, another Broad church, was usually filled to its capacity of 1,500 on a Sunday. (The name 'chapel', which often denotes a Non-conformist place of worship, does not have that meaning here). Any doctrinal doubts could be satisfied, if really pressing, by reading the 39 Articles at the back of the Book of Common Prayer, which had been hammered out in Tudor times and reaffirmed by Charles II on his restoration. The familiar language of the Authorised Version of the Bible, and the Book of Common Prayer, was incomprehensible at times, but the general meaning was clear, and always had been.

The firm foundations of the Broad Church of England trembled slightly between 1834 and 1842, when John Henry Newman, Vicar of the University church of Saint Mary's, Oxford, preached the 'Parochial Sermons' urging his congregation to adopt 'deeds, not words and wishes', and actively remedy the current lethargy which allowed the state to encroach on the proper province of the Church. He repeated his message in a series of published *Tracts for the Times Against Popery and Dissent*. By the time he got to Tract 90, in 1841, he alarmed many of his readers by suggesting that the 39 Articles, to which every Anglican clergyman had to subscribe, were compatible with traditional Catholicism.[7] This was too much for the Establishment, and he was persuaded to stop there. But the 'Tractarian' or Oxford Movement had made a powerful beginning.[8] It began to train its own clergy in the theological college at Cuddesdon near Oxford, where its trainees invited attention by wearing 'jampot' collars (nowadays called dog-collars), so-called 'mark of the Beast' waistcoats buttoning up to their cravats, and long, straight, black coats as near to a Roman Catholic priest's habit as possible. They were said even to cultivate a peculiar gliding gait, and a way of intoning the service in a high nasal voice. They were a gift to the caricaturists working for *Punch*.

Newman believed that 'material phenomena are both the types and the instruments of real things unseen':[9] how the clergy dressed in church, the rituals and ceremonies they used, all should remind the congregation of the great 'things unseen'. In 1868 Lady Frederick Cavendish, a devout member of the Anglican Church, attended a church where 'it was interesting to see the vestments for the first time, the three officiating clergy all wearing them ... I learn gradually to like much of the "advanced" ritual ... It all depends on whether one sees, enters into, and *approves* the symbolism.'[10] Holy Communion was referred to as the Mass in some circles, scandalising more old-fashioned communicants. Churches could be beautified with ornament. Ladies took the opportunity, at feasts of the Church such as Christmas and Easter, to decorate their churches, not just with flowers – on which an especially devout and well-off parishioner might spend considerably more than a poor person's annual income – but also with 'cotton wool letters and powdered alum on the ivy leaves', to look pretty. Some ladies risked life and limb, at Christmas, to climb ladders and fix garlands to the gas brackets – creating a fire risk as well as endangering their modesty.[11] (Definitely a day for wearing petticoats, not a crinoline; such a pity Mrs Bloomer's practical costume was not socially acceptable.)

The wave of prosperity that had filled middle-class drawing rooms with expensive clutter rolled into their churches, too. Crosses appeared on or near altars. The clergy blossomed into sumptuous vestments. Mrs Little's Ecclesiastical Warehouse advertised for sale 'chasubles, dalmatics, copes, albs, surplices, girdles ... stoles ... Gothic lace in all widths'.[12] More seriously, the doctrine of 'auricular confession'[13] with penance and absolution, which was allowed by the Book of Common Prayer but had rarely been practised in the Anglican Church, was adopted enthusiastically by the Anglo-Catholics. This outraged every Victorian paterfamilias. What would his wife or his daughter confide to this outsider about his matrimonial habits, or his fatherly domination? In any case who did he think he was, purporting to give absolution?

More abstruse doctrines also favoured by the Anglo-Catholics, such as baptismal regeneration, the apostolic succession and the Real Presence (the elements of the Eucharist being transmuted into the real body and blood of Christ), did not cause such uproar, but many people found some Tractarian practices hard to stomach. The Rector of St George's, down in the East End, tried to introduce Eucharistic vestments and the intoning of services in 1859, but his parishioners vociferously objected and rioted, week after week, until a posse of Anglo-Catholic gentlemen from outside the parish had to come and protect him. Nothing would placate his congregation until he was forced to retire. In the Church of St Jude out at South Kensington, 'among the fast disappearing lanes and market gardens of a receding rusticity',[14] the middle-class congregation were content to follow varying ways. The choir appeared in their ordinary clothes, but some members of the congregation turned to the east to recite the Creed, and more still bowed their heads at the name of God. The not-so-High objected to so much 'singing'. The ritual was indeed 'a little high',[15] but the vicar, the Reverend Forrest, took a firm line. 'It was his opinion that the Psalms should be sung and while he remained Vicar such would be the law', and that was that.

The most extreme Anglo-Catholic ritual was to be found in St Alban's Church just off Holborn. In 1866 Lord Shaftesbury, a member of the Low or Evangelical Church who was said to 'represent the conscience of Victorian England', went on a sight-seeing trip. He found:

A *High Altar* reached by several steps, a cross over it – no end of pictures. The chancel was very large, and separated from the body of the Church by an iron grill. Abundance of servitors, etc. in Romish apparel. Service intoned and sung, except the lessons, by priests in white surplices and green stripes ... three priests in green silk robes, the middle priest having on his back a cross embroidered, as long as his body ... Such a scene of theatrical gymnastics, of singing, screaming, genuflections, and a series of strange movements of the priests, their backs almost always to the people, as I never saw before even in a Romish Temple. Clouds upon clouds of incense, the censer frequently refreshed by the High Priest, who ... swung it about on a silver chain

... the communicants went up [to the altar] to the tune of soft music, as though it had been a melodrama, and one was astonished, at the close, that there was no fall of the curtain.[16]

This all sounds like a bad case of conspicuous consumption. And yet here, as in many Anglo-Catholic churches, 'the poor were decidedly in the ascendant [in the congregation], and fully on a par with the rich'. Father Stanton ran a club for working men at St Alban's, in which beer and spirits were sold, religious newspapers were banned, and card-playing was allowed; and at the Mothers' Meetings he read them the latest Dickens novel, *Nicholas Nickleby*, without any prayer or homily.[17] His predecessor, Father Mackonochie, had been prosecuted in 1867, when the Judicial Committee found him guilty of such crimes as elevating the Eucharistic elements and using incense; but the Ritualists carried on despite the judgment.[18] Another Anglo-Catholic priest, Father Lowder, worked tirelessly among the poor and derelict of the dock area. He ran a loan society, a sick benefit association, a soup kitchen and a coal club, and in January 1868 100 members of his congregation sat down to a hot supper and bowls of hot punch.[19]

Queen Victoria was 'shocked and grieved' to see 'the higher classes and so many of the young clergy tainted with this leaning towards Rome'.[20] Perhaps she never noticed that Prince Albert often went to evensong at St Margaret's in Margaret Street, another Ritualist stronghold, even taking one of his daughters with him.[21] Victoria was decidedly of the moderate Church. She was averse to declaring a public Day of Fast in 1847 for the potato blight in Ireland and the general scarcity of food, a Day of Thanksgiving for the removal of the cholera in 1849, and a Day of Humiliation and Prayer in 1854 to remind God of his duty to England when the war in the Crimea began, and again in 1857 to mark the Indian Mutiny.

Her ministers persuaded her, however, that they would be proper gestures by the Crown. The 1854 Day of Humiliation was in the end only a Fast Day. Victoria thought the whole idea was 'absurd'. If it had to be done she suggested that it should take place with the least possible disruption to public life, on a Sunday, but this would not do. Trade and normal life had to suffer, on a weekday. One diarist recorded that 'the shops were all closed and the churches well attended'.[22] There was a subtle difference between a 'Day of Fast' and a 'Day of Humiliation': on a Fast Day the banks could carry on business, whereas on a Day of Humiliation they had to close, creating all kinds of complications about the dates when bills of exchange became payable. By shifting the Crimea intercessionary prayers from Humiliation to Fast, 'the religious part of the community' and the financial interests of the City were reconciled.[23]

The Low or Evangelical Church kept its services simple, and believed in the literal truth of the Bible. Just as the Anglo-Catholics leaned towards Rome, the Evangelicals found some common ground with Nonconformists, but had an advantage over them, for young men, in that they did not impose on their congregations the intense and narrow-minded scrutiny of some Nonconformist elders. The Sabbatarian movement, which managed to close the British Museum and the National Gallery on Sundays, and the Temperance movement, which pressed for the limitation of licensed hours in public houses, both drew their strength from the Evangelical Church.

※

In 1836 the Bishop of London had hoped to attract private funding for fifty new churches, but the main result was a privately funded group of ten churches built in 1859 in Bethnal Green, which so clearly needed special attention. Not all of them were a success. The incumbent of one described some of the others:

> The present incumbent ... tells the very few people who attend him that they should read nothing but the Bible and the newspaper – the destinies of the French Empire form the perpetual theme of his sermons ...
>
> [Another incumbent] tormented and defrauded the Clergy by marrying for 2s 6d (including all charges) thus he brought people from all parts of London to be married at his Church, and used frequently to join together 50 couples per diem ...
>
> [Another incumbent] left head over heels in debt ... and was succeeded by [another] who had an aversion to coming in contact with poor people ... he was a sort of perpetual blister to good Mr Cotton [who had provided the funds to build the churches]
>
> [Another incumbent] was so out of health that for the most part he was compelled to be [away] from home ... and his wife was a forward, meddling and quarrelsome person ... the present incumbent ... is only a slug in the Lord's Vineyard.[24]

The 1851 census, which compared the theoretical number of church attenders with the adequacy of existing church accommodation, provoked a burst of church-building, almost exclusively in the 'Gothic' taste, the only suitable architectural style for prayer. Many existing churches were 'restored', often unfortunately in the view of modern critics, who may deplore the ubiquity of Gilbert Scott, and his gift for converting medieval saints into likenesses of Prince Albert. Minton encaustic tiles covered the floors, the chancel was raised to mark the distinction between the congregation and the clergy, and steps to the altar marked the distinction between the clergy and God. Organs were installed, and from 1860 they thundered out *Hymns Ancient and Modern*. The numbers of Anglican clergy rose from, in round numbers, 14,500 to 20,500 between 1841 and 1871.[25] The standard of religious observance gradually rose from 1849, when a contemporary wrote:

> there are many ministers in the Church Established in England whose religious character ranks deservedly high. But of three quarters of them it may be remarked ... that they are practically ignorant of the great spiritual principles of the Gospel ... the office they sustain allies them with the aristocracy, and a benefice ensures to them, in most cases, a certain, and in not a few, an ample income.[26]

This was a little unfair, considering that half of all incumbents received less than £200 a year, and thousands of curates existed on half that sum.[27] On the other hand, many of the Anglo-Catholic clergy did come from the aristocracy, and their private incomes enabled them to serve as unpaid curates.

Roman Catholicism had raised the hackles of dyed-in-the-wool Anglicans since Queen Elizabeth imposed the Protestant religious settlement on England. The ranks of the 'old' Catholics had been swollen in 1847–50 by the hordes of destitute immigrants fleeing the famine in their native Ireland, who did not endear themselves to the prim and proper middle classes. Victoria was unusually broad-minded, for her time: 'Sincerely Protestant as I have always been ... I cannot bear the abuse of the Catholic religion',[28] and there was a great deal of abuse about. Newman and Henry Edward Manning, another leading figure in Anglo-Catholicism, were converted to the Roman Catholic faith in 1845 and 1851. From the lamentations and hand-wringing of the Anglican middle classes, one might have concluded that the new converts proposed to bring in Papal rule of England at a stroke, instead of merely transferring their personal allegiance from the Archbishop of Canterbury to the Pope.

In 1850 Pope Pius IX added, as it seemed, insult to injury by appointing a hierarchy of bishops to replace the Vicars-General who had represented him in England since the sixteenth century: result, predictably, a further outcry against such 'papal aggression'. *The Times* thundered about 'an Italian Priest' being allowed to 'restore a foreign usurpation over the consciences of [English] men'. There were 'No Popery' placards everywhere, and effigies of the Pope were burned as well as Guy Fawkes on 5 November.[29] The Ecclesiastical Titles Act was added to the statute book in 1851, to prevent Roman Catholic priests from taking hierarchical titles, but it was never enforced, and was repealed by Gladstone in 1871. In 1865 Manning, who was universally respected, became Archbishop of the Catholic diocese of Westminster, and the hullabaloo began to expire.

The Roman Catholic Church, like the Anglo-Catholics, welcomed the poor. That indefatigable cleric the Reverend C. H. Davies, who wrote descriptions of the 'orthodox' and 'unorthodox' churches in Victorian London, was struck by this when he attended the service of 'Blessing the Palms' commemorating Christ's entry into Jerusalem, on the first Sunday in Holy Week, in the Pro-Cathedral in Kensington. (Westminster Cathedral was not yet built). 'Huge bundles' of 'very large branches' of real palm trees were blessed and distributed to the clergy and to every member of the congregation. It must have been a splendid sight, reminiscent of the woods coming to Dunsinane, as the Archbishop wielded his 10-foot-high branch and lesser clergy wrestled with theirs. 'Though situated in the centre of the wealthiest suburb of London, the Pro-Cathedral has a large congregation of poor among its regular attendants ... as is ever the case at Catholic churches, [they] received equal attention, and went away happy with as big a piece of palm as the wealthiest member of the congregation'.[30]

For anyone who, for historical or personal reasons, felt unable to join either of the two main Churches, there was a plethora of Non-conformist Christian faiths to choose from.[31] The most charismatic preacher of the time was Charles Haddon Spurgeon, a Baptist. He attracted huge congregations. In 1856 he hired one of the halls at the Surrey Gardens, with a capacity of 10,000, but 12,000 forced their way in, and 7,000 had to wait outside.[32] Three years later he regularly filled the 6,000-capacity Tabernacle near the Elephant and Castle that was purpose-built for him. He must have been a brilliant organiser as well as preacher, for he ran an orphanage where 220 boys were boarded, clothed and educated, living in separate houses presided over by matrons in the best twenty-first-century style; and almshouses, and a Pastors' College giving free training for the Baptist ministry. He had 4,200 members on his Church books, and 'each member has a set of 12 communion tickets all ready perforated, with dates printed, one of which he or she is bound to tear off and put in the plate each month, to attest presence at "the Ordinance"'. Failure to do so was censured and could even lead to excommunication.

Another Baptist chapel in Bloomsbury held, charmingly, a 'Midsummer morning Sermon' at 7 a.m., for 'young men and maidens'. The Strict Baptists went in for baptism by total immersion, in their Tabernacle near Spurgeon's. The Particular Baptists had a chapel in Notting Hill Gate. Spurgeon's Tabernacle was also used by the Primitive Methodists, or 'Ranters' – mainly of a lower social class, as evidenced by the vans and carts waiting outside (rather like judging a meeting today by the kind of battered cars parked outside). They were given to frequent, loud interjections of 'Hallelujah' and 'Glory be to God'. The Children of God, or 'Walworth Jumpers', functioned in an arch of the London, Chatham and Dover Railway. Their distinguishing mark was the 'good whacking kiss' exchanged between them. They did not exactly jump, but sometimes members of the small congregation would go into a trance, and dance.

The Catholic and Apostolic Church – not, of course, to be confused with any other Catholic Church, whether Anglo- or Roman – were also known as the Irvingites, after their founder. They had seven churches in London, in each of which an ornate service with vestments and incense 'higher than the most advanced Ritualistic churches' was celebrated twice a day. The Swedenborgian or 'New Testament' faith had five churches in London, with the main one in Argyle Square near King's Cross. They believed that the dead are immediately resurrected, the spiritual body being the true self; with this body (*faute de mieux*), marriages are consummated in Heaven.

The Plymouth Brethren had three meeting-places in London. They celebrated Communion with a loaf of home-made bread cut into four and passed round the congregation, each member helping himself by breaking off a piece, while wine was handed round in large, ordinary tumblers. The Christadelphians met in a dancing academy in Gower Street. They too practised baptism by total immersion. 'I was amazed to hear working men read and expound from their thumbed [well-worn] Bibles'.

The Moravians had 5,532 members in Britain, although only one chapel in London, in Fetter Lane. They traced their history back to the fifteenth-century Hussites. Their foreign missions covered an astonishing area of the globe, such as Labrador, Greenland, the Aborigines of Australia and the Indians of North America. The Sandemans or Glassites, remarkable mainly because that eminent scientist Faraday was a member, believed in salvation by faith, not works. At their 'love-feasts' each person had to kiss the neighbour on each side; just as you are imagining the careful jockeying for position to avoid smelly old men or spotty young ones – the seats were allocated by lot.

The Methodists, who had been the foremost Dissenting body in the previous century, were preoccupied by schism from 1845 onwards, but remained the largest and most powerful Nonconformist denomination.[33] Unfortunately, the enquiring parson whose descriptions of more esoteric sects form the basis of this section did not visit them. He did visit the Society of Friends, or 'Quakers', in a meeting-house in St Martin's Lane, 'a little, unpretentious building, very clean'. He got there early, and found a congregation of 150 people, men and women sitting separately, 'the young ladies not in grey, but in silks and "killing" bonnets, and the men sitting with their hats on. At 11 sharp, the beginning of the "silent service" was signalled by the men removing their hats.' Silence was unbroken for nearly an hour, then the 'officiating minister, who was dressed in full Quaker costume, was moved by the Spirit'. Then silence fell again for twenty minutes, after which a 'clerically-dressed gentleman' preached for twenty minutes. Silence fell again, until 'suddenly at the stroke of 1 o'clock, hats were resumed' and the congregation returned to the normal life of any congregation emerging from Sunday service.

'It may possibly strike some persons as strange that Spiritualism should be classed among the religions of London, however unorthodox. They have been accustomed to associate this subject only with dancing tables and locomotive furniture in general ... [but] to a very large number of persons indeed, Spiritualism is in the most solemn and serious sense a religion.'[34] It had been imported from America in the early 1850s. To begin with, it was restricted to the moneyed classes: 'one at least of the reasons why the pursuit of modern spiritualism ... is so largely confined to the "upper 10,000" lies in the high price at which the spirits have hitherto consented to vouchsafe "manifestations" ... it is not everybody who can afford a crown [5s]'.[35] But the price came down, and the vogue spread. One of the first mediums was Mrs Hayden, who arrived from Boston in 1852 and took up residence in Queen Anne Street, 'where spiritual phenomena would be forthcoming from 12 to 3 p.m. and from 4 to 6 daily'. She was quickly exposed as a fraud, and returned to the States. Another medium, Daniel Home, managed to persuade Elizabeth Barrett Browning that he had levitated, at a seance which she and her husband attended in 1859. Robert Browning's reaction, however, was to publish his poem 'Mr Sludge, the Medium', in 1864. A notorious case involving Home ended in the Law Courts, when an elderly woman, Mrs Lyon, wanted her money back from him. She won, but the court ordered her to pay Home's costs, implying that she should have known better. The terrible mortality in cholera epidemics and the Crimean War made many credulous people seek comfort in the possibility of communicating with dead loved ones, but their pathetic needs were turned to cash by unscrupulous manipulators.

In the East End of Victorian London Jewish habits were obdurately non-English, and prone to arouse criticism, on that ground alone. For instance Jews did not share the Englishman's devotion to getting drunk and knocking his wife about, nor did they leave their poor and sick to the tender mercies of the parochial poorhouse; they drank little, and looked after the weaker members in their community. There were two traditions: the Sephardim, who could trace their descent back to the Jews of Spain and Portugal, and the Ashkenasim from eastern Europe, who comprised 90 per cent of London Jews. Up to the end of the eighteenth century there had been a certain amount of friction between the two, which had died away by the Victorian era, although some Sephardic Jews still claimed superiority to their Ashkenasim brothers. Disraeli was at pains to claim Sephardic descent.[36] His grandfather, a merchant in Italy, had joined the Sephardic community when he came to London. But the Rothschilds, surely the most famous of Jewish families, were Ashkenasim, from Frankfurt.

Until the terrible pogroms of the 1880s, there were only, on average, 200 Jewish immigrants a year.[37] Most London Jews had been born in England. The clothes dealers of the East End were Ashkenasim. They often began as itinerant hawkers and pedlars, and buyers and sellers of old clothes. Hats were valuable, in those days, and when an 'old clo' man' acquired one he would put it on top of his own, for safe keeping, and successive purchases on top of that; which accounts for the 'triple tiara' appearance of Jews in anti-Semitic cartoons, of which there were all too many. By hard work, acumen and careful living, Jewish itinerant traders often amassed enough capital to set up shops selling clothes, fruit and Kosher food, or workshops making jewellery, watches and furniture. The immense emporium of Moses and Son in the East End sold clothes to the aristocracy as well as to the working classes. Jews had a virtual monopoly of the second-hand markets round Petticoat Lane.

As they became more prosperous, Jewish traders often joined the middle-class exodus westwards to the suburbs, building synagogues there but retaining a loyalty to the old synagogues in the City. The synagogue at Bevis Marks near Aldgate, in the City, had been built for the Sephardim in 1700. The 'Great Synagogue' in Duke's Place, nearby, had been built by the Ashkenasim in 1722,[38] a 'spacious building' lit only with candles. The music was 'singularly beautiful'.[39] In 1841 the Reform Jews, disillusioned with 'the ritual [of the Orthodox Jews, which was] burdened with pages of the private works of pious rabbis, and with polemical and metaphysical discussions quite alien to the spirit of prayer',[40] seceded, and inaugurated a simpler form of service. They used at first a synagogue in Burton Street in the West End of London, near their congregation, which was for the most part middle-class. By 1871 they were able to open an 'exceedingly hand-some' synagogue in Upper Berkeley Street, Portman Square, with a capacity of 1,000, the men on the ground floor and the women in the gallery.

Jews had long been subject to various civic disqualifications, but the bars were gradually falling. Sir David Salomons was elected Sheriff of the City of London in 1835, but his election was 'annulled' by the Court of Aldermen. The same thing happened when he was elected by another City ward. But he was successfully elected an Alderman in 1845, and reached the pinnacle of City life when he became Lord Mayor in 1855. In 1847 Baron Lionel de Rothschild was elected by the City as its Member of Parliament, but the Commons ejected him because he refused to swear the oath taken by all Members, which invoked the name of Christ. An undignified wrangle broke out between the City, who steadfastly supported their candidate, and the Commons and the Lords. At last a compromise was found: either House could resolve to modify the form of oath to be required from its Members. Twenty-five days later Rothschild took his seat: a considerable victory for the Jewish party.

The Jewish Board of Guardians, on which both Orthodox and Reform Jews served, administered long lists of Jewish charities. The Rothschild family were munificent benefactors, to the Jewish Free School, the Jewish Hospital and numerous other schools, sheltered housing and homes for old people. One expense which daunted many Christian families, the cost of funerals, was not incurred by a Jewish family. 'Jewish burials are of the severest ceremony. Rich and poor alike are laid in plain deal coffins, the hearses are without plumes, and the monuments of the plainest character'.[41]

The Rothschilds successfully negotiated the social rapids of anti-Semitism by taking up hunting and horse-racing, and becoming English gentlemen and sportsmen – a feat Disraeli never accomplished. But he did, after all, become Prime Minister.

Death

'Wretched as these people were, they would struggle to bury the dead
without assistance from the parish, for there is nothing the poor have
such a horror of as a pauper's funeral'.[1] According to Engels, 'the
corpses [of the poor] have no better fate than the carcasses of
animals'.[2] The Economic Funeral Company was sure of a market.[3]
'Some undertakers perform the last offices for the poor on condition
of being paid at the rate of 18d a week.'[4] Since it could cost as much
as £4 to bury an adult[5] – less for children – the dreary weekly debt
must have dragged on for ever.

Sometimes the bereaved family could not afford even a down
payment, and the corpse stayed in the family's one-room home until
they could. Sometimes the neighbours took pity on the family and
clubbed together to pay for a dead man's funeral.[6] One of the
achievements of Dr Rogers, as workhouse medical officer, was to
persuade the parish to build a mortuary for corpses awaiting burial –
the first in London.[7] Sometimes the very poor formed funeral clubs,
many of which, 'conducted by designing vilains who preyed upon the
general infirmity, cheated and wronged the poor most cruelly'.[8]

A working man in regular employment was likely to belong to a
trade union or a Benefit Club. A member of one of the earliest trade
unions, the Amalgamated Society of Engineers, could reflect with

relief that his weekly due of 1s would cover not only unemployment and sickness benefits, but also his funeral costs, up to £12. If his wife died before him, he could opt to be paid £5 for her funeral, leaving £7 payable on his own death.[9]

Where were they to be buried? Churchyards within London had been crammed to overflowing as long ago as 1665, after the Plague. There were 88 overcrowded churchyards in the City alone. Many churches had acquired separate burial grounds but they, too, were full. The great social reformer Edwin Chadwick had exposed their horrors in the 1830s: 'on spaces of ground which do not exceed 203 acres, closely surrounded by the abodes of the living, 20,000 adults and nearly 30,000 youths and children are every year imperfectly interred'.[10] In 1843 a privately run burial ground near – all too near – the New River Head, in Islington, exemplified the problem. It had space for about 2,700 burials, but the proprietors had allowed 80,000 in 50 years: more than 20,000 burials in one year alone.

> Coffins were hardly in the ground before they were disinterred and broken up to fuel the stove in the workmen's hut. New graves were dug by cutting down through recent burials, severing arms, legs and heads in the process. A gravedigger ... had been 'up to my knees in human flesh by jumping on the bodies, so as to cram them in the least possible space at the bottom of the graves, in which fresh bodies were afterwards placed'.[11]

Surely there was a better solution.

Kensal Green Cemetery – on the Harrow Road, roughly two miles north-west of Paddington – was opened in 1833 by a private company, the General Cemetery Company, with parliamentary approval. Its 56 acres offered decent burial spaces for both Anglicans and Dissenters, with just 7 acres reserved for paupers. The grounds were pleasingly landscaped, with wide carriageways. By 1842 it had accommodated 6,000 burials.[12] In 1843 the Cemetery Company had an astonishing stroke of luck. The Duke of Sussex, Victoria's uncle, died. He was entitled to be buried in the royal vault in Windsor, but he had been appalled by the badly organised funeral there of his brother William IV in 1837, and in any case he wanted his mistress to be buried beside him when her time came. So he specified in his will that he should be buried in Kensal Green. This appealed to the populace, who had not seen very much of him in his lifetime but rallied to his funeral at his death. 'The late Duke of Sussex did a national service when he desired to be laid, in the equality of death, in the cemetery of Kensal Green, and not with the pageantry of a State Funeral in the Royal vault at Windsor.'[13] (He was refreshingly unstuffy. In his copy of *The Book of Common Prayer* he wrote in the margin beside the Athanasian Creed, 'I don't believe a word of it.'[14] He had married Lady Augusta Murray morganatically. She died in 1830 and he then married his mistress, Lady Cecilia Buggin, but that marriage was also invalid under the Royal Marriage Act. In the end, after much jockeying for position, Victoria created her Duchess of Inverness.)

The Duke of Wellington wrote to the Prime Minister of the day, Peel, 'the Queen's command might overrule the Duke's desire to be buried at Kensal Green ... but there will be no end to the complaints of interference by authority on the part of the Freemasons [the Duke had been Grand Master of the Freemasons' United Grand Lodge since 1813] and of those who will take part with the Duchess of Inverness ...',[15] so it was decided to follow the Duke's unconventional wishes. His funeral, on 5 May 1843, was brilliantly organised. The procession from Kensington Palace, where he had died, to Kensal Green about three and a half miles away, was headed by an advance guard of the Royal Horse Guards, then 'four of the Queen's marshalmen, on foot, in scarlet uniforms'. If they walked the whole way, the rest of the procession must have gone at a slow walking pace behind them.

They were followed by four 'mutes' on horseback – undertaker's men dressed in deep black with silk scarfs and long trailing hat-bands – and then what must surely have been a rather boring procession of fifteen empty mourning coaches, each drawn by six horses 'caparisoned in black velvet and feathers', until at last the band of the Horse Guards came by, playing gloomy music. After them, the hearse, pulled by eight horses and escorted on each side by troops of Horse Guards, so that a spectator would see only the horses and uniforms, not the coffin. Then more mounted Guards, and another collection of beplumed horses and mourning carriages, 50 in all, more cavalry, and 'a strong cordon of police ... which effectually kept back the immense crowd'.[16] Indeed, police crowd-control was imaginative and efficient.

By the time the procession got to Paddington station it 'passed along at rather a rapid rate' – maybe the marshalmen had got a lift in a mourning coach by then – and the atmosphere was noticeably lighter. After all, the Cockney residents of that part of London were unlikely to see such a spectacle ever again, so they took a day off work and enjoyed themselves. Print-sellers and ballad-singers were out in force, and refreshment booths were doing a roaring trade selling 'beer and backy' or, for the more refined, gingerbread and currant wine. The hopefuls who had put up rickety-looking stands of seats were not doing so well; the more enterprising of them tried to attract custom by alleging that 'This is the safe stand', or it was 'Approved by the Surveyor of the Woods and Forests', but most people relied on seeing what they could from the pavement, or convenient trees and lamp-posts. After the funeral had passed the stand sellers cut their losses, converted their stands into dancing booths, and catered for the 'day of jollity like a country fair'.

Meanwhile the procession arrived at the cemetery gates, where the state mourners were set down, to join other prominent people including Prince Albert and most of the Cabinet, who had come by another route. The Cemetery Company must have had a paroxysm of cleaning and decorating. The chapel, 'a neat little edifice on the summit of the hill ... done up for the occasion ... festooned with black material', filled up with the great and the good. The coffin was put on a bier directly over the catacomb below the chapel. During the service it was lowered, in two stages – the Cemetery Company's directors' hearts must have been in their mouths, but the machinery worked smoothly – into the catacomb, where it was bricked up until an appropriate vault could be built. The Cemetery Company had nothing suitable that was ready, not having expected this largesse. Spaces near the Anglican chapel promptly shot up in price.[17]

The royal duke was followed six years later by his sister Princess Sophia. The success of Kensal Green was guaranteed, and it soon became one of the tourist sights of London. The sophisticated Greville was 'not surprised that people who go to visit this spot, and see the cheerfulness and the beauty it exhibits, feel a longing to take their last rest in it'.[18] A teacher from Manchester went straight to it when he arrived to 'do' London in 1858, and recorded his impressions in his diary. 'The Duke of Sussex and the Princess Sophia are buried there. There are a great number of tombs, most splendidly polished etc. A great number of gentry have taken ground and put vaults on it'.[19] When Lieutenant-General Pasley's wife (daughter? – sister? – 'poor Magdalene') died on 26 December 1844, the first thing to do after the undertaker had brought the coffin was to go out to Kensal Green and choose a vault 'for 12 coffins, adjoining that of Sir George Matthias Cox'; even in death, one needs to be choosy about one's neighbours.[20]

The General would not have been pleased to read *On the Laying Out, Planting and Managing of Cemeteries*, published the previous year, in which John Claudius Loudon, the famous garden designer, referred to 'burying in vaults' as 'a mark of wealth or distinction [which] for that reason is adopted by many of the London tradesmen'. There were extensive catacombs (underground galleries with shelved recesses for coffins) as well as vaults and single grave spaces. Somewhere in the catacombs are two coffins still in the packing cases in which they made the journey from India in the 1860s.[21] Loudon was buried in Kensal Green in 1844. The Brunel family, Marc Isambard and his wife Sophia (1849) and their son Isambard Kingdom (1859) were buried there, also James Miranda Barry, Inspector General of the Army Medical Department, who at his death was found to be a woman.[22]

Kensal Green was followed by other privately owned cemeteries, Norwood (39 acres) in 1837, Highgate (37 acres), in 1839, Brompton (39 acres) in 1840, Abney Park (32 acres) the same year, Nunhead (52 acres) and Tower Hamlets (33 acres) in 1841. 'The keeping of the new London cemeteries is in general good [but] in some it is highly discreditable, sheep being admitted to eat the grass.' This seems a good idea, imparting a rural look and sparing the gardeners the difficult task of trying to scythe uneven ground; but Loudon disapproved.

Highgate cemetery, owned by the London Cemetery Company, became 'London's most fashionable necropolis'.[23] It was built on a 37-acre site on a hillside sloping down to Swain's Lane, and the designers used the gradient to produce multi-layered effects. The Egyptian Avenue was a narrow, sloping street entered through iron gates under a massive Pharaonic arch, 12 feet below ground level. It was bordered by cast-iron doors to sixteen vaults, each containing twelve coffins on stone shelves. In 1878 the cost of a vault was 130 guineas (£136 10s). The Avenue led to the beautiful Circle of Lebanon, well below ground level, with twenty vaults along both sides of the circular path, each housing fifteen coffins. The circle was built round a magnificent cedar tree which had grown there since at least 1693.

There was room for 30,000 graves in the main part of the cemetery, each containing, on average, three coffins, and each grave costing at least £2 10s. Two acres were left unconsecrated, for atheists and Dissenters. There were catacombs along the north wall, in a gloomy underground gallery 80 yards long, lined with 840 recesses. They could be hired pending plans for the final disposal of the coffin, or bought outright for £10. By 1854 the enterprise had proved so successful that the company expanded in the only possible direction, by buying 19 more acres on the other side of Swain's Lane. The chapels on the original site were also used for burials on this new site, but Swain's Lane was a fairly busy road, and it was unthinkable to expect coffins to negotiate the traffic. It must have been bad enough for the mourners.

The solution, typically Victorian in its use of new technology, was to install a bier for the service in the chapel, which lowered the coffin by hydraulic power into a basement leading to a tunnel under the Lane, emerging in the new site. The very first occupant of the original site was Elizabeth Jackson, buried in a plot 2 feet 6 inches wide, 6 feet 6 inches long and 10 feet deep, for which her family paid 3 guineas (£3 3s). Four more coffins joined hers later. The last one to go in cannot have been far from ground level.

More famous patrons included George Wombwell, the menagerie proprietor, who died in 1850, and Tom Sayers, the last bare-knuckle pugilist, who died in 1865. Another famous sportsman buried there was F. W. Lillywhite, the famous cricketer, who died in 1854 having invented what was then called 'round-arm' (over-arm) bowling. And this was where Lizzie Siddal, Dante Gabriel Rossetti's wife, was buried in 1862. In the extremity of his grief he put a manuscript of his poems into her coffin. On second thoughts he wanted it back, so in 1869 the coffin was opened and the book duly retrieved; cost of labour 2 guineas.[24]

Brompton cemetery was opened in 1840 by the West of London and Westminster Cemetery Company, hoping to emulate the prosperity of Kensal Green. But the company ran out of money, and had to be bought out by the General Board of Health in 1852, becoming the first London cemetery under state control. The founder of Charing Cross hospital, Dr Benjamin Golding, was buried there in 1863, followed two years later by the architect of the Albert Hall, Francis Fowke.

Abney Park cemetery in Stamford Hill, Stoke Newington, had been opened in 1840, when Bunhill Fields, 'which had been so many years the "God's Acre" for Nonconformists of all classes, was filled to repletion'.[25] George Loddige, whose huge plant nursery and arboretum was nearby in Hackney, took shares in the Abney Park Cemetery Company, and used the site to advertise his own business. 'A named Arboretum has been planted by Messrs Loddiges, which contained every hardy tree and shrub, varieties as well as species, that was in their collection a year ago. The names are on brick, the same as in the [Loddige] arboretum'. It included 'all the hardy kinds of rhododendrons, azaleas and roses in Messrs Loddiges' collection; and ... dahlias, geraniums, fuchsias, verbenas, petunias, etc are planted out in patches in the summer season'.[26] By the time the cemetery opened in May, 2,000 trees and shrubs had already been planted, a mixture of broadleaved and conifer trees bordering the winding paths. Magnolias and rhododendrons would go in during the autumn. It was the largest collection of trees in Britain, after Loddige's own arboretum.[27] It sounds a lovely place, a universe away from the squalid burial grounds of inner London, but Loudon thought it looked like a 'pleasure ground' and disapproved; still, as he said, 'people insist'. One does begin to suspect some professional jealousy here. The detailed and fascinating 'Lists of Trees, Shrubs and Perennial Plants adapted for Cemeteries and Churchyards' appended to his book *On the Laying Out, Planting and Managing of Cemeteries* recommends a nursery at Fulham – not Loddiges.

Nunhead cemetery was another venture by the London Cemetery Company. It was known as the 'Cemetery of All Saints'. A memorial to the five 'Scottish Martyrs' who were transported in 1793 for their campaign to reform Parliament was erected in 1851. It was inscribed 'the experience of all ages should have taught our rulers that per-secution can never efface principles' – taken from the defence speech of one of the 'Martyrs'.

Tower Hamlets cemetery was opened by the City of London and Tower Hamlets Cemetery Company in 1841. It was consecrated by the Bishop of London, and received its first funeral that same day. It soon became overgrown, providing a green haven in the East End of London.

West Norwood cemetery was opened by the South Metropolitan Cemetery Company on 40 acres in this outlying hamlet, in 1837. Famous names there are Sir William Cubitt (1861), Mrs Beeton (1865), and Dr William Marsden, founder of the Royal Free and Royal Marsden Hospitals (1867).

In 1854 the London Necropolis Company opened their cemetery at Brookwood, with a 'daily funeral express, down and back', for the mourners, and a charge per coffin of 2s 6d, via South Eastern rail from the 'Necropolis Station' just outside Waterloo.[28]

In 1852 Parliament passed the Metropolitan Burial Act, enabling local authorities to open cemeteries if existing burial grounds were insufficient or dangerous to health. Four years later the City opened a cemetery in Ilford in Essex, to take not only all new burials but also the disinterred burials from demolished churches, and from churchyards which were being cleared and made into public gardens. By a complicated legal process the City's purchase of those 200 acres led indirectly to the preservation of Epping Forest for public use. Other local authorities including St Pancras and Islington, Camberwell, Greenwich, Tottenham and Woolwich also opened cemeteries. It must have seemed then that the demands of London's dead had been met for the foreseeable future, but this was not to be. The situation was eased by the introduction of cremation, but not until the 1880s.

Loudon's book on cemeteries had been refreshingly down-to-earth.[29] It began: 'The main object of a burial ground is the disposal of the remains of the dead in such a manner as their decomposition ... shall not prove injurious to the living.' The best way to achieve that, he advised, was by interment in a single grave, 5 or 6 feet deep. The Quakers and the Jews buried only one coffin in a grave, which was never disturbed. But in most large cities, graves were deeper, and up to twelve coffins were piled in on top of each other, even fifteen in the case of paupers' graves. Loudon was scathing about the measly 7 acres offered by the directors of Kensal Green for the paupers of seven London parishes, 'which exceed 1,000 annually ... one would think that the poor were considered as animals of a different species'. On the matter of coffins, he warned that lead coffins, such as Lieutenant-General Pasley had bought, were never totally air- and moisture-proof. Sometimes 'a corpulent body is ready to burst the coffin even before being taken from the house ... in the public catacombs of the new London cemeteries, explosions have been known to take place' which made such a terrible smell that 'the gravediggers have to be plied constantly with rum'. Bones last for centuries, but the fleshy body becomes, as he delicately said, 'unsuitable for dissection' after eight or nine weeks of interment. It was a good idea to cover each coffin over, with a lead or stone cover, to prevent disturbance by later burials in the same grave (and, I imagine, to make it harder for grave-robbers, arriving before the eight or nine weeks had elapsed).

The traditional wood for coffins was elm, which resists damp better than most others. An elm coffin was usually covered with black or coloured velvet or felt, fixed on by brass-headed nails. 'A very familiar street sound of those days was the tack, tack, tack of the undertaker's hammer.'[30] In the 1860s, when domestic furniture began to shine with the glossy finish of French polish, elm was dropped in favour of oak in the graveyard as well; it would take the new polish, but elm would not.[31] Embalming was still rare. It was usual to be buried in a shroud or winding sheet, although normal clothes were sometimes used, especially in the case of young brides, whose bodies might wear their wedding dresses. Sometimes pathetic souvenirs were buried with the corpse in the coffin, such as Dante Gabriel Rossetti's poems, which he retrieved later, or General Chesney's favourite boots, forage cap and uniform jacket, carefully arranged round and over the body of his second wife Everilda, in 1841.[32]

Not everyone could immediately clothe themselves from head to foot in funereal garb, although many probably kept a standby set in their wardrobes, in case of emergency.[33] Hannah Culwick was a general servant when her aunt died. Her employer's maid gave her an old black dress, and she spent 15s 9d on a black and white shawl, and 9s on flannel – in the context, presumably black – for two petticoats. She was a hard-working and practical woman; for her to lay out nearly 25s from her annual wage of £16 shows how important mourning clothes were. For the middle classes, 'in the present day our ashes must be properly selected, our garments must be rent to pattern, our sackcloth must be of the highest quality'.[34] Messrs Lush and Cook, dyers, advertised in 1842: 'We dye blacks every day, and special mourning orders can be executed in 24 hours when necessary. Please note: only superior feathers look well after being dyed black.'[35] So it might not be a good idea to have your feather boa put into mourning.

A serviceable but faded black dress might be still refurbishable at home: 'to a pint of boiling water add 2/3 of a pint of ox-gall'.[36] Jay's Mourning Warehouse in Regent Street, established in 1841, was invaluable.[37] They even sold a 'Patent Euthemia, a self-expanding bodice ... in cases of sudden bereavement ... when a ready-made and stylish dress is required at a moment's notice'.[38] You could send your maid round to get one, and a ready-made black skirt, which would suffice until a proper wardrobe could be assembled. 'Black' Peter Robinson's 'Family Mourning Warehouse' (so called to distinguish it from Mr Robinson's other shop, also in Regent Street) 'offers advantages to the Nobility and Families of the Highest Rank [in huge letters], also [in much smaller print] to those of limited means ... the stock of Made-up articles is the Most Extensive that can be seen in any one establishment. Goods sent on approval to all parts of England, free of carriage'.[39]

So with the new telegraph system, and delivery by railway, country mourners need not have to wait too long, and that obliging Mr Robinson had a carriage ready at all times, with two fitters, to show a lady bereaved in London the latest fashions in mourning wear, and take her measurements for her new black clothes. In case the neighbours might think such preoccupations improper in a house of mourning, the carriage, the coachman and the fitters were all in decent black.[40]

A bereaved lady worrying over the subtleties of What to Wear in Fashionable Mourning needed help. In 1844 a lady went into a shop – it could have been Jay's, but the account of her visit is not wholly reliable. The following conversation took place:

LADY: I wish. Sir, to look at some mourning,

SHOPMAN: Certainly ... How deep would you wish to go, Ma'am? Do you wish to be very poignant? ... We have the very latest novelties from the Continent. Here is one, Ma'am, just imported – a widow's silk – watered, you perceive, to match the sentiment. It is called 'Inconsolable', and is very much in vogue in Paris for matrimonial bereavements. And we have several new fabrics introduced this season to meet the demand for fashionable tribulation.

LADY: And all in French Style?

SHOPMAN: Certainly – of course, Ma'am. They excel in the funèbre. Here, for instance is an article for the deeply afflicted. A black crape – makes up very sombre and interesting ... Or would you prefer a velvet, Ma'am?

LADY: Is it proper, Sir, to mourn in velvet?

SHOPMAN: O quite! – certainly. Just coming in. Now here is a very rich one – real Genoa – and a splendid black. We call it 'The Luxury of Woe' ... only 18s a yard, and a superb quality – in short, fit for the handsomest style of domestic calamity.

LADY: And as to the change of dress, sir; I suppose you have a great
  variety of half-mourning?

SHOPMAN: Oh! Infinite – the largest stock in town. Full, and half, and
  quarter, and half-quarter, shaded off, if I may say so, like an India-
  ink drawing, from a grief *prononcé* to the slightest *nuance* of regret.[41]

It was not only domestic calamity that called for the public
demonstration of grief. When the Queen's mother died, in 1861, the
Court went into mourning for six weeks, and the public in general
was expected to follow suit for three. 'This is very considerable, as
trade must suffer greatly.'[42] When Albert died, on 14 December six
months later, the wave of black almost submerged the City. A modest
Chancery clerk with five daughters and a wife to dress in mourning
found it a severe financial strain.[43] For a whole week 'every shop in
London has kept up mourning shutters, and nothing is to be seen in
all drapers', milliners', tailors' and haberdashers' shops but black'.[44]
Even the brass door plates were covered with black crape.[45] It was
bad luck on shopkeepers anticipating the Christmas rush. On the day
of Albert's funeral in Windsor, 23 December, the City shops were
mostly closed.[46] They may have managed to retrieve a little of their
trade the next day. A church had been 'draped in black' for the day
of the funeral, but 'the black was removed on the next day, and the
Church very prettily decorated for Christmas'.[47]

Getting to the cemetery could present problems unless you were able
to take the Necropolis express train. Some cemeteries were served by
the growing network of railways. Buses might take you part of the
way, but their routes were planned to take in the nearer suburbs, not
the outlying districts where the new cemeteries were. Horse-drawn
hearses slowly plodded their way out, followed by a miscellaneous
flock of vehicles. Horses need a rest and a drink from time to time;
so did their drivers and passengers. One cemetery 5 miles from the
City gates had an enormous trade, providing employment for 70 or
more gravediggers.[48] On some Sundays there were 70 or more
funerals, and on weekdays the average number was 40 or more. The
nearest public house was the 'Jolly Sandboys', a 'regular house-of-call
for mourners'. At four o'clock on a Sunday there might be fifteen
hearses and undertakers' coaches gathered there, each with their two

big black horses, 'the hearse drivers in merry groups ... with glasses of gin and pewter pots of beer'. The mourners were 'engaged precisely as were the coffin-bearers and hearse-drivers'. Some were in the pub, others were eating and drinking in the coaches. 'The uproar was just that to be met any Saturday night in a Whitecross [East End] gin-shop.'

Such sociable grieving was to some extent curtailed by Mr Shillibeer's patent hearses, which 'convey the coffin and six mourners to the place of interment' for a charge of £1 1s for one horse, 10s 6d more for two. When the funeral was over the vehicle closed up, on a screw mechanism; the space for the coffin disappeared, and it turned into a normal carriage in which the six mourners could go home as if nothing had happened. Although Loudon approved,[49] professional undertakers must have deplored them. Greville wrote about the funeral of his sister-in-law in 1841: 'I was unutterably disgusted with the ceremony, with the bustling business of the undertaker ... the decking us out in the paraphernalia of woe, and then dragging us in mourning coaches through crowds of curious people by a circuitous route, [so] that as much of us as possible might be exhibited to vulgar curiosity.'[50]

When George Birkbeck, the respected educationalist, died in 1841, 1,000 people followed his coffin all the way from his house in Finsbury Square in the City to Kensal Green. Tom Sayers the last bare-knuckle pugilist, attracted a far greater crowd. The route of his funeral was lined by 100,000 mourners, from Camden Town to Highgate. The hearse, drawn by four horses, was followed by his phaeton, with his dog sitting in the driving seat. Then came an amazing collection of vehicles, from four-wheeled carriages to two-wheeler cabs, farm wagons, costers' carts, a brewer's dray and a donkey cart.

The grandest funeral of all was that of the Duke of Wellington. Everybody had known his face, with that beak of a nose, and everyone, it seemed, had loved him. At a concert in Exeter Hall one evening in 1842, 'the finest thing was when the Duke of Wellington came in ... the whole audience rose, and a burst of acclamation ... saluted the great old man, who is now the Idol of the people'.[51] He was still as popular when he sauntered round the Great Exhibition from time to time, in 1851, and was mobbed by his admirers. He died at Walmer Castle in Kent, on 14 September 1852. The funeral, over which Prince Albert exercised a distant influence, took an unconscionable time to organise. His son was 'not unnaturally annoyed at his father's funeral

being put off so long'.[52] At last his body was brought to London by
train on 11 November, and lay in state for a week in the Royal
Hospital, Chelsea, a fitting place for this most eminent of old soldiers.

People waited for five hours and more, in bitter weather, to pay
their last respects. One of them recorded in his diary that it was 'a
wet drizzling day – in an awful crowd for 4 hours before getting in –
a grand sight but not worth the trouble'.[53] At least three people were
crushed to death in the crowd. Meanwhile the 'traders in Death', as
Dickens called them, had a field day:[54]

> To be let, a second floor, of three rooms, two windows, having a good
> view of the procession. Terms, including refreshment, 10 guineas.
> Single places, including bed and breakfast, from 15s ...

> Seats and Windows to be let, in the best part of the Strand, a few
> doors from Coutt's banking-house. First floor windows, £8 each;
> second floor, £5 10s each; two plate-glass shop windows, £7 each ...

> To be let, a shop window, with seats erected for about 30, for 25
> guineas ...

> Cockspur Street, Charing Cross ... a few seats still disengaged ... also
> a few seats on the roof ...

> Notice to Clergymen – T.C. Fleet Street has reserved for clergymen
> exclusively, upon condition that they appear in their surplices, FOUR
> FRONT SEATS at £1 each; four second tier at 15s each; four third
> tier at 12s 6d; fourth tier, at 10s [by when surely the view would have
> been very limited if any, ... and so on, all the way up to the sixth tier
> at 5s.]

Dickens was particularly scathing about 'this enterprising tradesman's
anxiety to get up a reverend tableau in his shop window of four-and-
twenty clergymen all on six rows'. The son of the local hair-cutter at
Stratfield Saye, the Duke's country house, was in the fortunate position
of being able to offer for sale, through his parent's foresightedness, 'a
small quantity of HAIR that his father cut from the Duke's head' –
well, so he said, but who could prove it?

On 18 November the coffin was transported to St Paul's Cathedral,
in a magnificently ornate procession which surely the Duke would
have hated.[55] An estimated one and a half million people watched it
pass: the splendid coaches of Church and state dignitaries, the
marching bands, 83 Chelsea Pensioners who must have got very

weary even though they had to walk only from Charing Cross, the heralds Bluemantle and Rouge Dragon wearing their brilliantly coloured medieval tabards, more dignitaries, Prince Albert alone in a coach and six ... By now the tension was mounting. At last, the Band of the Grenadier Guards, and the Funeral Car.[56] This might have been a disaster. It was 'tawdry and clumsy', the size of a small house, 27 feet long, 10 feet wide and 17 feet high, weighing 18 tons and drawn by twelve horses borrowed from a brewery. In Pall Mall the six wheels sank into the mud and the whole creaking edifice was stuck fast until 60 strong men heaved it free.

The next obstacle was Temple Bar, where part of the superstructure had to be lowered to pass underneath. The machinery for this worked, but when the whole contraption arrived at St Paul's Cathedral the machinery to transfer the coffin to the waiting bier refused to function for more than an hour, while a piercing wind blew through the open west door. The congregation included many eminent but rather bald gentlemen. They eventually, in self-preservation, covered their heads with their handkerchiefs, or even their hats.

Following the coffin was the Duke's horse, led by his groom, with those famous boots in the stirrups, facing backwards. The crowds along the route had watched the procession silently, many in tears. As the catafalque passed they raised their hats in respect. The effect, according to an onlooker, was of the sudden rising from the ground and settling again of a huge flock of birds.

What You Got For Your Money

A farthing was enough to hire an iron, in a parish washhouse.

1d took you by steamer from Woolwich to London Bridge, or a mile on Gladstone's Parliamentary trains, or it paid for a bath and doing your washing in Smithfield Wash House and Laundry, or it bought three oysters, or got you into a 'penny gaff', or you could buy breakfast of 'coffee' and bread and butter in Billingsgate, or a sparrow from a street seller, or pay for a lavatory in the Great Exhibition.

2d would buy you a 'second class warm bath' in Whitechapel.

4d would buy a gallery seat in the Old Vic.

6d was the bus fare from the suburbs such as Bayswater, to the Bank, or it would buy a good cotton dress for a servant, or a ticket for a music hall, or admission to the Zoo.

1s was the admission charge to a Chinese junk, in 1851, or the bus fare to the Bank from the outer suburbs, or the cost of lunch in a tavern, or admission to the Alhambra, or Cremorne Gardens, or the Great Exhibition on a cheap day. It was the cost of a toothbrush.

1s 6d a week was earned by a ten-year-old, in Bethnal Green, for six twelve-hour days. It would buy a pair of black silk hose.

4s 5d was earned, net, for making eight pairs of trousers.

4s 9d would buy a tartan waistcoat.

5s a week was the rent for a three-room flat provided by Angela Burdett Coutts, or the price of dinner in a London club.

5s 6d would buy a good silk top hat, but many cost much more, up to 12s.

6s 6d was the charge for a table d'hôte dinner in Soyer's Symposium, or the cost of a crinoline.

9s a week was the wage of a milk woman, with her meals.

10s 6d was charged by a fashionable dentist for two fillings.

15s was the cost of a first-class excursion return rail ticket from York to London.

16s a week was the top wage for a sewing-machinist; it would buy an umbrella.

£1 was the average weekly income of a coffee-stall keeper, or a female copying-clerk in the City, or a general labourer.

£1 1s was the cost of getting to the cemetery in Mr Shillibeer's one-horse patent hearse.

£1 8s would buy a portrait in daguerreotype.

£1 10s or more was the weekly wage of a skilled shipbuilding workman.

£1 14s was the weekly wage of a bus driver.

£1 15s or more was the weekly wage of a skilled engineering workman.

£3 would buy a man's mourning suit in an East End tailoring establishment.

£3 3s would buy a season ticket for the Great Exhibition.

£3 9s 6d would buy one of Thomas Crapper's water closets.

£3 10s would buy a 10-inch-wide lawn mower.

£3 16s was what Emerson paid for a frock coat.

£4 was the minimum cost of a funeral.

£5 would buy a 5-foot monkey puzzle tree.

£5 5s was the price of dinner in a first-class restaurant.

£6 was the annual wage of a maid-of-all-work, living in.

£12 was charged by a baby-farmer to 'adopt' an unwanted child.

£16 a year was the wage of a general servant, living in.

£17 16s would furnish three rooms for a schoolteacher.

£20 a year was the wage of a female shop assistant, living in.

£21 should buy a full set of false teeth.

£25 for twenty minutes was charged by a top-class prostitute.

£42 was the annual wage of a manservant.

£48 would buy a 48-inch-wide lawn mower, with an additional £1 4s for the boots for the horse.

£60 bought a 'clarence' (carriage) for Jane Carlyle.

£90 was the annual salary of a junior clerk, second class, in the Post Office.

£136 10s was the cost of a twelve-coffin vault in Highgate cemetery in 1878.

£140 was the average annual stipend of an Anglican parson.

£161 would buy a hothouse 64 feet by 25 feet.

£400 was the annual salary of the Governor of the Bank of England.

£1,000 was the 'regulation' price of a Cornetcy in the Foot Guards.

£8,000 was the cost of a double box in Her Majesty's Opera House.

£9,000 was the 'regulation' price of a Colonelcy in the Foot Guards.

£30,000 was granted by Parliament annually to Prince Albert.

£40,000 was said to have been paid by the Earl of Cardigan, to command the 11th Hussars.

£100,000 was the amount the Duke of Bedford was said to save every year.

£150,000 was Lord Derby's annual income.

£250,000 was the Duke of Westminster's annual income from his London estate.

Currency and Measurements

Copper or bronze coins in circulation began at a farthing, worth a quarter of a penny, then a halfpenny (pronounced 'haypenny'), a penny, a two-penny piece and a four-penny piece. There were twelve pennies in a shilling.

Silver coins in circulation began at a three-penny (pronounced 'thripenny') bit, then a sixpence, a shilling, a florin worth 2 shillings, a half-crown and a crown worth 5 shillings. There were 20 shillings in the £.

Gold coins in circulation were half-sovereigns and sovereigns. A sovereign was worth £1. It was about the size of a modern £1 piece, but heavier.

A guinea was used to express professional fees and in other prestigious spheres. It was not a coin. It was worth £1 1s.

After 1844 all banknotes were issued by the Bank of England, for £5, £10, £20, £100, £200, £500 and £1,000.

There are 12 inches in a foot, 3 feet in a yard. An inch equals 2.54 centimetres. A foot equals approximately 30 centimetres. A yard is shorter than a metre, being approximately 90 centimetres.

A mile is 1.609 kilometres. A kilometre is 0.621 miles. An acre is 4,840 square yards, or 0.405 of a hectare. A hectare is 10,000 square metres.

The Retail Price Index, 1840–1870

How much you could buy in today's prices with £1 then:

Year	Value		Year	Value
1840	43.96		1856	44.73
1841	45.01		1857	43.93
1842	48.70		1858	47.51
1843	54.89		1859	46.57
1844	54.94		1860	43.03
1845	52.40		1861	43.42
1846	50.39		1862	43.83
1847	44.98		1863	49.42
1848	51.16		1864	47.11
1849	54.62		1865	45.67
1850	58.35		1866	43.62
1851	58.83		1867	42.00
1852	57.81		1868	43.79
1853	49.81		1869	45.45
1854	44.69		1870	45.56
1855	44.38			

Source: The Retail Price Index, November 2004 (Office for National Statistics).

Notes

The many references to Henry Mayhew's four-volume *London Labour and the London Poor* are by volume only. For a fuller explanation, see Preface.

Preface (pp. xiii-xvi)

1 Friedrich Engels *The Condition of the Working Class in England*, trans. and ed. W. O. Henderson and W. H. Chaloner, Oxford, 1958.
2 Flora Tristan, *Promenades dans Londres 1840 et 1842*, Paris, 1842, described the London she saw in 1839 and earlier. She disapproved of the English aristocrats, and dedicated her book to the 'Men and Women of the Working Class'. It was translated into English by Jean Hawkes, with introduction and notes, and published in London in 1982: hereafter it is referred to as *The London Journal of Flora Tristan*. Possibly she over-egged her omelette from time to time, and her *Promenades* slightly preceded the period we are looking at, but on the whole, and applying a large pinch of salt, I think she was a reliable witness.
3 Edward Hyams (trans. and ed.), *Taine's Notes on England*, London, 1957.
4 A modern reproduction with introductory notes by Ralph Hyde was published in 1980 by Harry Margary of Lympne Castle, Kent, in association with Guildhall Library, London.

Chapter 1: Smells (pp. 1-8)

1 Edwin Chadwick, an energetic Victorian sanitary reformer, calculated that 'in one year the liquid and solid excrements of a man would produce 16.41 lbs of nitrogen, sufficient for ... 800 lbs of wheat ... or 900 lbs of barley': *Report on the Sanitary Condition of the Labouring Population of Great Britain*, 1842.
2 Stephen Halliday, *The Great Stink of London*, Stroud, Gloucestershire, 1999.
3 Home Office papers, HO35, 59.
4 Report of the Surveyor, Holborn and Finsbury District of Sewers, 27 January 1843 in HO44/39, National Archives.

5   Mayhew, Vol II.
6   Ibid.
7   Ibid.
8   Ibid.
9   Friedrich Engels, *The Condition of the Working Class in England*, trans. and ed. by W. O. Henderson and W. H. Chaloner, Oxford 1958. Engels was in London for only a few weeks, and may have allowed himself to paint the conditions he found blacker than they were. But his editors suggest that where he was using the evidence of his own eyes he was reliable.
10   G. A. Sala, *Twice Round the Clock*, London, 1859.
11   An undated letter quoted in L. T. C. Rolt, *Isambard Kingdom Brunel*, London, 1957.
12   Charles Dickens, *Dictionary of London 1880*, London, 1880. The writer was a son of the novelist.
13   Stephen Halliday, *Making the Metropolis*, Derby, 2003.
14   Kathleen Tillotson (ed.), *Charles Dickens, Letters*, Vol.V, 1848 and 1849, Oxford, 1977.
15   There is an intriguing story in the annals of the Bank of England relating to sewers: the Directors had ignored an anonymous letter warning them of an imminent raid on the Bank's bullion, but they finally agreed to meet their informer, at night, in the vault where the bullion was stored. Sure enough, the miscreant emerged through the floor, before their very eyes. The Bank's records include – 'in May 1836, having reason to apprehend danger from our sewers, it was discovered that an open and unobstructed sewer led directly from the gold vaults down to Dowgate'. The informant, a working man who had heard of the plot while he was repairing the sewers, was awarded £800. W. Marston Acres, *The Bank of England From Within*, London, 1931.
16   *The Illustrated London News*, 27 August 1859.
17   *Illustrated Times*, 14 December 1861.
18   *The Illustrated London News*, 30 November 1861.
19   From the unpublished diary of Thomas Rogers, in the Guildhall Library, MS 19,019, listed in Heather Creaton, *Unpublished London Diaries*, London, 2003.
20   The chimneys – minarets – were demolished in the 1930s. The interior is as exotic as the outside.
21   *The Illustrated London News*, 21 May 1864.

Chapter 2: The River (pp. 9–21)

1   Edward Hyams (trans. and ed). *Taine's Notes on England*, London, 1957.
2   Generally known as the Watermen's Company. I am indebted to the Company and its secretary for making its *History* available to me. This magnificent work, which covers in 4 volumes almost 700 years of life on London's river, was compiled by Henry Humpherus, clerk to the Company for 33 years in the mid-19th century. It has been edited by Jack N. King, W. Barrett and G. Wilson of the Watermen's Company and John L. Dawson of Cambridge University and

reprinted in 1999 in Lavenham, Suffolk. I will refer to it in this chapter as *Humpherus*. Quotations not otherwise attributed are from its annals.

3   A. R. Bennett, *London and Londoners in the 1850s and 60s*, London, 1924.

4   Humpherus, op. cit. From that date on, Henry Humpherus devoted most of his energy and skill to fending off the Board. His efforts are recorded in his *History*, but from about 1857 his entries concerning collisions and fires and other river happenings tend to give place to the latest dastardly doings of the Board. There is no reason to suspect, however, that steamers suddenly ceased to collide with each other, or try to do down the Watermen.

5   Mayhew, Vol. III.

6   *The Magazine of Domestic Economy*, 1840, Vol. 5.

7   Bennett, op. cit.

8   Gustave Doré and Blanchard Jerrold, *London*, London, 1872.

9   Ibid.

10 This must account for a family legend that an ancestor of mine, a clipper captain almost certainly coming from Aberdeen, was carried aboard his ship in China, mortally ill. His mate asked anxiously whether they ought not to delay, for the sake of his health. 'Sail, damn you' was the reply. Unfortunately the story stops there. I don't know whether he survived long enough to get his £100.

11 Bennett, op. cit.

12 *The Times* quoted in John Richardson, *The Annals of London*, London, 2000.

13 Although this, like so much in this chapter, is quoted from Humpherus, I would give the reference to Dickens if I knew it, but I don't. Possibly he was as usual exaggerating, in the interests of a good story. My own deduction is that the 'dozen English sailors' had spotted a commercial opportunity for milking the London tourist trade, and themselves arranged the voyage and hired these picturesque Chinamen.

14 W. S. Bell's unpublished diary of his visit to the Great Exhibition, Museum of London accession no. 52.25, listed in Heather Creaton, *Unpublished London Diaries*, London, 2003.

15 Bennett, op. cit.

16 Quoted in L. T. C. Rolt, *Isambard Kingdom Brunel*, London, 1957, which I have found the most readable and informative of the many books about Brunel. But unfortunately Rolt doesn't give the name of the reporter, or his paper.

17 Bennett, op. cit.

18 The unpublished diary of J. A. Patterson, 1858, Wellcome Institute MS 73537, listed in Creaton, op. cit.

19 George Dodd, *Days at the Factories*, London, 1843.

20 Humpherus, op. cit.

21 *The Illustrated London News*, 8 April 1865.

22 Ibid., 18 May 1867.

23 Bennett, op. cit.

24 For more information on the hulks see Chapter 21, Crimes and Punishments.

25 Bell, op. cit.

26 Hyams, op. cit.

Chapter 3: The Streets (pp. 22–33)

1   It would be impossible to correlate present-day and Victorian London without constantly referring to Ben Weinreb and Christopher Hibbert, *The London Encyclopaedia*, London, 1983 (2nd ed).

2   Ralph Hyde, *Printed Maps of Victorian London, 1851–1900*, London, 1975.

3   It can still be bought: Ralph Hyde (introd.), *Stanford's Library Map of London and its Suburbs, 24 sheets on the scale of 6 inches to a mile*, Lympne Castle, Kent, 1980.

4   Edward Hyams (trans. and ed). *Taine's Notes on England*, London, 1957.

5   M. L. Davies (ed.), *Life as We Have Known It*, London, 1931.

6   Shown on a map which was part of Bazalgette's preliminary studies for the intercepting drains. They were mixed with stables, a smithy and a 'cab yard'.

7   *Gardeners' Chronicle and Agricultural Gazette*, 1865.

8   G. A. Sala, *Gaslight and Daylight*, London, 1859.

9   Thomas Beames, *The Rookeries of London*, London, 1850.

10 John Richardson, *The Annals of London*, London, 2000.

11 The Metropolitan Police had power to control traffic, but it seems rarely to have been used.

12 Mayhew, Vol. II, quoting the City Surveyor's figures.

13 Report of the Select Committee on Metropolitan Communications, 1854.

14 A. R. Bennett, *London and Londoners in the 1850s and 60s*, London, 1924.

15 For this and many other topographical references I have relied gratefully on Edward Jones and Christopher Woodward, *A Guide to the Architecture of London*, London, 1983, as well as Weinreb and Hibbert, op. cit.

16 Stephen Halliday, *Making the Metropolis*, Derby, 2003.

17 *Illustrated Times*, 8 August 1866.

18 Richardson, op. cit.

19 Ibid. The quotation is from the *Express* newspaper. The Italian for traffic light is *semaforo*.

20 Dionysius Lardner, *The Great Exhibition and London in 1851*, London, 1852.

21 Bennett, op. cit.

22 Charles Knight, *London*, London, 1844.

23 Matthew Sweet, *Inventing the Victorians*, London, 2001.

24 J. E. Ritchie, *The Night Side of London*, London, 1869.

25 Republished by Harry Margary, Lympne Castle, Kent, in association with Guildhall Library, London, 1980. Margary and the Guildhall also published *The A to Z of Victorian London* in 1987, but unfortunately it is based on a map of 1888, too late for my purposes.

26 Bennett, op. cit.

27 Ibid.

28 Max Schlesinger, '1820–85: Saunterings in and about London', trans. Otto Wenkstern, London, 1853, excerpts included in Xavier Baron, *London 1066–1914, Literary Sources and Documents*, Vol. II, Robertsbridge, East Sussex, 1997.

29 Reminiscence of a City of London Schoolboy, in A. E. Douglas-Smith, *The City of London School*, Oxford, 1965 (2nd edn).

30 Unpublished diary of Lt-Gen. Pasley, British Library Add. MS 41991, listed in Heather Creaton, *Unpublished London Diaries*, London, 2003.

31 There are detailed descriptions in Thomas Webster, *An Encyclopaedia of Domestic Economy*, London, 1844.

32 Webster, op. cit.

33 J. A. Froude (ed.), *Mrs Carlyle's Letters*, London, 1883. She died in her clarence, as the coachman was driving her round Hyde Park. He was waiting for directions, and when none came he looked into the carriage and saw his employer, peacefully sitting there, dead.

34 Webster, op. cit.

35 On any occasion on which the Queen will be watched on television riding in a state coach, she is never shown getting in or out of it.

36 Warren Pugh's diary, Bodleian MS Misc. d.472, listed in Creaton, op. cit.

37 Mayhew, Vol. III.

38 Ibid. It was still possible, if you were strong enough to brave the driver's clear disinclination, to have a taxi's leather hood 'raised or lowered at pleasure', in 1949.

39 T. C. Barker and Michael Robbins, *A History of London Transport*, London, 1963. In 1854 the Select Committee on Metropolitan Communications found that 15,000 people came into London every day by steamboat, 6,000 by rail, and 200,000 on foot. The authors estimated that 20,000 came in by omnibus.

40 Mayhew. He gives the total number of licensed omnibuses as 3,000.

41 Unpublished diary of Charles Pugh, Bodleian MS Eng. Misc. d.465–73, listed in Creaton, op. cit.

42 Bennett, op. cit.

43 Froude, op. cit.

44 Ibid.

45 Bennett, op. cit.

46 The French and the English vied with each other in public transport. I had always thought that 'omnibus' was derived from the Latin meaning, *for everyone*. But it came from a Frenchman, M. Omnes, whose trading slogan was *omnes omnibus* – Omnes for everything. Shillibeer, prominent in the early days of buses, whom we shall meet in connection with his patent hearse, pressed for the plural of omnibus to be *omnibii*, a construction guaranteed to drive a Latinist to despair.

47 Bennett, op. cit. This was before the invention of the bicycle as we know it, and Amelia Bloomer and her outrageous bicycling pantaloons.

48 Thea Holme, *The Carlyles at Home*, Oxford, 1965.

Chapter 4: The Railways (pp. 34–44)

1 Dionysius Lardner, *The Great Exhibition and London in 1851*, London, 1852.

2 Matthew Sweet, *Inventing the Victorians*, London, 2001.

3 This quotation is from Ben Weinreb and Christopher Hibbert, *The London Encyclopaedia*, London, 1983 (2nd edn), on which I have gratefully relied, as ever, for topographical and historical data.

4 Henry Mayhew and John Binny, *The Criminal Prisons of London and Scenes of Prison Life*, London, 1862.

5 M. L. Davies (ed.), *Life as We Have Known It*, London, 1931.
6 John Richardson, *The Annals of London*, London, 2000.
7 Edward Hyams (trans. and ed.) *Taine's Notes on England*, London, 1957.
8 For railway buffs who probably know this already, a chronology of the opening
   of the mainline stations, and the lines they served, would read:

> 1836 London Bridge: Deptford and Croydon Railway
> 1837 Euston: London and Birmingham Railway
> 1838 Paddington (temporary structure): Great Western Railway
> 1839 Mile End: Eastern Counties Railway, extended to Shoreditch 1840
> 1840 London Bridge: Greenwich line, London and Brighton Railway
> 1841 Fenchurch Street: Blackwall Railway
> 1848 Waterloo: South Western Railway including Twickenham and
>   Richmond
> 1850–54 Paddington (permanent): Great Western Railway
> 1852 King's Cross: Great Northern Railway
> 1850–53 North London line between the docks and the western suburbs
> 1860 Victoria: London, Brighton and South Coast Railway
> 1862 Victoria: London, Chatham and Dover Railway
> 1864 Blackfriars: South Eastern Railway, London, Chatham and Dover
>   Railway
> 1864 Charing Cross: South Eastern Railway
> 1866 Cannon Street: South Eastern Railway
> 1868 St Pancras: Midland Railway

   The 'missing' ones are Liverpool Street, built 1875, and Marylebone, 1899.
9 A. R. Bennett, *London and Londoners in the 1850s and 60s*, London, 1924.
10 Lardner, op. cit.
11 *The Magazine of Domestic Economy*, 1844.
12 Andrew Williamson, *The Golden Age of Travel*, London, 1998.
13 Unpublished journal, W. S. Bell, Museum of London, accession no. 52.25, listed
   in Heather Creaton, *Unpublished London Diaries*, London, 2003.
14 W. L. Burn, *The Age of Equipoise*, London, 1964.
15 James Bland, *The Common Hangman*, London, 1984.
16 T. C. Barker and Michael Robbins, *A History of London Transport*, Vol. 1, London,
   1963.
17 D. Hudson, *Munby: Man of Two Worlds*, London, 1972.
18 'Hints to Railway Travellers' in *The Magazine of Domestic Economy*, NS Vol. 2,
   1844.
19 Lardner, op. cit.
20 Mayhew, Vol. II.
21 Ralph Hyde, *Printed Maps of Victorian London 1851–1900*, London, 1975.
22 Bennett, op. cit.
23 Mayhew, op. cit.
24 James Burn, *The Beggar Boy: an Autobiography*, London, 1888.
25 Hyams, op. cit.
26 Ibid.
27 Bennett, op. cit.

28 G. A. Sala, *Twice Round the Clock*, London, 1859.

29 John Hollingshead, *My Lifetime*, London, 1895.

30 Barker and Robbins, op. cit.

31 The last of the crosses marking the route taken by the coffin of Edward I's wife, Eleanor, in 1290 had stood in the hamlet of Charing, close to her final destination in Westminster Abbey. It had become derelict by 1647 and was demolished. The present version, in the forecourt of the station, was designed by Barry and built in 1863.

32 The best view of its medieval spires and turrets is from the forecourt of the British Library. If you stand outside the sordid sheds cluttering up the outside of King's Cross Station and look across at the skyline of St Pancras from the other direction, starting at the clock tower and moving right, you can spot a statue of Britannia, on her own little pinnacle.

33 *Illustrated Times*, 18 January 1862.

34 The following account is taken from Andrew Saint and Gillian Darley, *The Chronicles of London*, London, 1994. The writer is identified only by his initials, C. L. E.

35 Barker and Robbins, op. cit.

36 *Illustrated Times*, 2 February 1869.

Chapter 5: Buildings (pp. 45–58)

1   James Burn, *The Beggar Boy: an Autobiography*, London, 1888.

2   John Richardson, *The Annals of London*, London, 2000.

3   John Hollingshead, *My Lifetime*, London, 1895.

4   Stephen Halliday, *Making the Metropolis*, Derby, 2003.

5   *The Illustrated London News*, 8 April 1865.

6   I owe the information about George Peabody to the kindness of the Archivist of the Peabody Trust. The interiors of Peabody Buildings throughout London have been modernised, and the exteriors cleaned and redecorated, but the Trust has retained almost all the Victorian holdings except for Bermondsey (bombed in 1940), Westminster (disposed of in 1922) and Spitalfields (sold in the 1970s).

7   John Hollingshead, *Ragged London in 1861*, London, 1861.

8   Thomas Wright, *Some Habits and Customs of the Working Classes*, London, 1867.

9   Richardson, op. cit.

10 G. A. Sala, *Twice Round the Clock*, London, 1859.

11 E. P. Thompson and Eileen Yeo (eds), *The Unknown Mayhew – Selections from the Morning Chronicle 1849–50*, London, 1971.

12 There is one in a little alcove beside the front door of my Victorian terrace cottage. I asked a builder what he thought it was, and after some thought he guessed that it was a dog kennel.

13 Kathleen Tillotson (ed.), *Charles Dickens, Letters*, Vol. 4, 1844–6, Oxford, 1977.

14 Quoted in Lawrence Wright, *Clean and Decent*, London, 1960: an invaluable work.

15 Thea Holme, *The Carlyles at Home*, Oxford, 1965.

16 Chapter 23 verse 13, which, to save trouble, I append: 'And thou shalt have a paddle upon thy weapon; and it shall be, when thou wilt ease thyself abroad, thou shalt dig therewith, and shalt turn back and cover that which cometh from thee'. It does seem a long shot.

17 *Gardening Chronicle and Agricultural Gazette*, 1865.

18 To the question about lavatory paper that trembles on most lips, I can answer – newspaper, cut into tidy squares. Or any other paper, including grocers' bags. How Victorian drains coped with solid wodges of insoluble paper must be another subject.

19 Halliday, op. cit.

20 For the early history of the Grosvenor estates see the author's *Dr Johnson's London*, London, 2000.

21 John Raymond (ed.), *Queen Victoria's Early Letters*, London, 1963 (rev. edn; first pub. 1907).

22 Ralph Hyde (introd.), *Stanford's Library Map of London and its Suburbs*, Lympne Castle, Kent, 1980.

23 Round one corner, well worth spotting, is a modern lift leading to modern lavatories. It is reticently signposted; ask the staff for guidance.

Chapter 6: Practicalities (pp. 59–69)

1 There are some marvellous books on the history of London. My own favourite is Steven Inwood's *A History of London*, London, 1998. For the history of specific places and institutions *The London Encyclopaedia*, ed. Ben Weinreb and Christopher Hibbert, London, 1983, is invaluable. For a year-by-year view often quoting contemporary accounts, read John Richardson's *The Annals of London*, London, 2000. For a topographical guide collating geography and history try Edward Jones and Christopher Woodward, *A Guide to the Architecture of London*, London, 1983.

2 Peter Cunningham, *Handbook of London*, London, 1849: the version I read was the second edition published the next year.

3 Mayhew, Vol. II.

4 Henry Mayhew and John Binny, *The Criminal Prisons of London and Scenes of Prison Life*, London, 1862.

5 Cunningham, op .cit.

6 John Fisher Murray, 'Physiology of London Life', published in *Bentley's Miscellany*, Vol. XV, 1844.

7 D. Hudson, *Munby: Man of Two Worlds*, London, 1972.

8 Gustave Doré and Blanchard Jerrold, *London*, London, 1872.

9 Thomas Beames, *The Rookeries of London*, London, 1850.

10 M. L. Davies (ed.), *Life As We Have Known It*, London, 1931.

11 E. P. Thompson and Eileen Yeo (eds), *The Unknown Mayhew – Selections from the Morning Chronicle 1849–50*, London, 1971.

12 Edward Hyams (trans. and ed.), *Taine's Notes on England*, London, 1957.

13 R. W. Vanderkiste, *A Six Years' Mission Among the Dens of London*, London, 1854.

14 Ibid.

15 Hyams, op. cit.

16 Mayhew, Vol. II.

17 Ibid.

18 See the author's *Elizabeth's London*, London, 2003.

19 Cunningham, op. cit.

20 Anne Hardy, 'Parish Pump to Private Pipes', in W. F. Bynum and Roy Porter, *Living and Dying in London*, London, 1991.

21 Beames, op. cit.

22 Stephen Halliday, *The Great Stink of London*, Stroud, Gloucestershire, 1999.

23 Mayhew, op. cit.

24 S. E. Finer, *The Life and Times of Sir Edwin Chadwick*, London, 1952.

25 Hardy, op. cit.

26 Richardson, op. cit.

27 Thea Holme, *The Carlyles at Home*, London, 1965.

28 Robert Ward, *London's New River*, London, 2003.

29 Inwood, op. cit.

30 George Dodd, *Days at the Factories*, London, 1843.

31 R. H. Mottram, 'Town Life', in *Early Victorian England*, London, 1934. Gas was replaced by electricity, but there were gas lamps in the Temple as late as the 1970s.

32 Beames, op. cit.

33 A. R. Bennett, *London and Londoners in the 1850s and 60s*, London, 1924.

34 Mayhew, op. cit.

35 Graham Storey, Kathleen Tillotson and Nina Burgis (eds), *The Letters of Charles Dickens*, Vol. 6, Oxford, 1988.

36 They were used in the production of Prussian blue.

37 James Greenwood, *The Wilds of London*, London, 1881.

38 Hudson, op. cit.

39 John Hollingshead, *My Lifetime*, London, 1895.

40 Hawthorne, 'The English Notebooks', in Xavier Baron, *London, 1066–1914*, Vol. II, Robertsbridge, East Sussex, 1997.

41 Hyams, op. cit.

42 Unpublished diary of Robert James Lee, MS 3224, Wellcome Institute, listed in Heather Creaton, *Unpublished London Diaries*, London, 2003.

43 Richardson, op. cit.

44 Unpublished diary of Thomas Cobb, Guildhall MS 18,770, listed in Creaton, op. cit.

45 Bennett, op. cit.

46 Theodor Fontane, 1844–59, trans. Dorothy Harrison, London, 1939, included in Xavier Baron, op. cit.

47 Bennett, op. cit.

Chapter 7: Destitution and Poverty (pp. 70–80)

1 For Mayhew, see the Preface, page xiv. For those daunted by the sheer immensity of Mayhew's original volumes, I recommend the three books edited by Peter

Quennell, *Mayhew's Characters* and *Mayhew's London*, both selections from the first three volumes, published in 1951, and *London's Underworld* from the fourth volume, published in 1950.

2 Gustave Doré and Blanchard Jerrold, *London*, London, 1872.

3 G. A. Sala, *Gaslight and Daylight*, London, 1859. Henry Mayhew and John Binny, *The Criminal Prisons of London and Scenes of Prison Life*, London, 1862.

4 Mayhew and Binny, op. cit.

5 James Greenwood, *The Seven Curses of London*, London, 1869.

6 M. L. Davies (ed.), *Life as We Have Known It*, London, 1931.

7 Greenwood, op. cit.

8 Mayhew, Vol IV.

9 G. A. Sala, *Twice Round the Clock*, London, 1859.

10 John Raymond (ed.), *Queen Victoria's Early Letters*, London, rev. edn 1963.

11 John Hollingshead, *Ragged London in 1861*, London, 1861.

12 R. W. Vanderkiste, *A Six Years' Mission Among the Dens of London*, London, 1854.

13 Greenwood, op. cit.

14 Hollingshead, op. cit.

15 Thomas Beames, *The Rookeries of London*, London, 1850.

16 Helen Morris, *Portrait of a Chef. The Life of Alexis Soyer*, Cambridge, 1938. Soyer also organised soup kitchens for the poor of Dublin, which were very successful. He is better-known for his tenure as chef at the Reform Club, and for revolutionising Army catering during the Crimean War.

17 Joseph Rogers, *Reminiscences of a Workhouse Medical Officer*, ed. Thorold Rogers, London, 1889.

18 The Workhouse was the new name, since the 1834 Poor Law Act.

19 Hollingshead, op. cit.

20 His account is included in M. B. Smedley (ed.), *Boarding-out and Pauper Schools Especially for Girls*, London, 1875.

21 James Kay-Shuttleworth, *Four Periods of Public Education*, London, 1862.

22 Ralph Hyde (introd.), *Stanford's Library Map of London and its Suburbs*, Lympne Castle, Kent, 1980.

23 Edward Hyams (trans. and ed.), *Taine's Notes on England*, London, 1957.

24 John Bailey (ed.), *The Diary of Lady Frederick Cavendish*, London, 1927.

25 The rules about 'settlement' were relaxed slightly after the Union Chargeability Act of 1865, but were still harsh and arcane.

26 Thompson and Yeo, op. cit.

27 James Greenwood, *The Wilds of London*, London, 1881.

28 Hollingshead, op. cit.

29 Ibid.

30 James Greenwood, *The Seven Curses*, op. cit.

Chapter 8: The Working Class (pp. 81–94)

1 Thomas Wright s.n. The Journeyman Engineer, *The Great Unwashed*, London, 1868.

2   Peter Vinten-Johansen et al., *Cholera, Chloroform and the Science of Medicine: a Life of John Snow*, Oxford, 2003.

3   John Hollingshead, *Ragged London in 1861*, London, 1861.

4   W. B. Tegetmeier, *A Manual of Domestic Economy*, London, 1867.

5   Thomas Beames, *The Rookeries of London*, London, 1850.

6   These eelboats had been trading in the Thames for a long time. Although eels were caught in the Thames, the Dutch seem to have cornered the market. 'There are two companies in Holland each having five vessels. Their vessels are built with a capacious well in which large quantities of eels are preserved alive until wanted. One or more of these vessels may be constantly seen lying off Billingsgate' – Thomas Webster, *An Encyclopaedia of Domestic Economy*, London, 1844.

7   G. A. Sala, *Twice Round the Clock*, London, 1859.

8   Ibid.

9   Mayhew, Vol. I. These astonishing towers of baskets carried on the heads of the porters could still be seen when I was there in 1955, but I imagine they have long been obsolete.

10   D. Hudson, *Munby: Man of Two Worlds*, London, 1972.

11   Mayhew, op. cit.

12   George Dodd, *Days at the Factories*, London, 1843.

13   Ibid.

14   Ibid.

15   Peter Cunningham, *Handbook of London*, London, 1850 (2nd edn).

16   Jean Hawkes (trans. and ed.), *The London Journal of Flora Tristan*, London, 1982.

17   Dodd, op. cit.

18   Gustave Doré and Blanchard Jerrold, *London*, London, 1872.

19   Most of these details are taken from Ben Weinreb and Christopher Hibbert, *The London Encyclopaedia*, London, 1983.

20   Vinten-Johansen, op. cit. There was a brewery in Broad Street, Soho, for example, employing 80 workers.

21   Dodd, op. cit.

22   John Richardson, *The Annals of London*, London, 2000.

23   T. C. Barker and Michael Robbins, *A History of London Transport*, London, 1963.

24   *The Illustrated London News*, 30 November 1861.

25   *The Builder*, quoted in Stephen Halliday, *Making the Metropolis*, London, 2003.

26   In addition to Dodd I have been able to use information kindly supplied by the Archivist of the Leathersellers' Company, Jerome Farrell, including excerpts from Penelope Hunting, *History of the Leathersellers' Company*, London, 1994.

27   Dodd, op. cit.

28   Ibid.

29   Thomas Wright, *Some Habits and Customs of the Working Classes*, London, 1867.

30   Wright, *The Great Unwashed*, op. cit.

31   Wright, *Some Habits*, op. cit.

32   E. P. Thompson and Eileen Yeo (eds), *The Unknown Mayhew – Selections from the Morning Chronicle 1849–50*, London, 1971.

33   Thompson and Yeo, op. cit.

34 Wright, *Some Habits*, op. cit.

35 Samuel Smiles, *Self-Help with Examples of Conduct and Perseverance*, London, 1859. Another quote – 'Although English officialdom may often drift stupidly into gigantic blunders the men of the nation generally contrive to work their way out of them with a heroism almost approaching the sublime'. He was writing three years after the Crimean War.

Chapter 9: The Middle Class (pp. 95–108)

1 Dudley Baxter, *National Income 1868*, quoted in J. M. Golby, *Culture and Society in Britain 1850–1890*, Oxford, 1986.

2 Quoted in G. Kitson Clark, *The Making of Victorian England*, London, 1962.

3 C. R. Penny, *The Victorian Post Office*, Woodbridge, Suffolk, 1992.

4 My paternal grandfather, who was an estate factor in the nineteenth century, used copying ink and a huge screw press in which the letters stayed all night, producing a thin copy in purple ink the next morning. It was also invaluable for pressing little girls' collections of flowers.

5 M. L. Davies (ed.), *Life as We Have Known It*, London, 1931.

6 Penny, op. cit. In Trollope's *Autobiography*, published after his death, in 1883, he remembered bitterly how he 'came up to London [in 1834] purporting to live a jolly life upon £90 per annum. I remained 7 years in the General Post Office, and when I left it my income was £140. During the whole of this time I was hopelessly in debt.'

7 Kitson Clark, op. cit.

8 Anthony Trollope, *An Autobiography*, London, 1883.

9 This section is largely based on W. Marston Acres, *The Bank of England From Within*, London, 1931.

10 G. A. Sala, *Twice Round the Clock*, London, 1859.

11 W. O. Henderson, *J C. Fischer and his Diary of Industrial England 1814–51*, London, 1966.

12 Edward Hyams (trans. and ed.), *Taine's Notes on England*, London, 1957.

13 The autobiography of James Coss, included in M. B. Smedley (ed.), *Boarding-out and Pauper Schools Especially for Girls*, London, 1875.

14 Francis Wheen, *Karl Marx*, London, 1999.

15 Judith Flanders, *The Victorian House*, London, 2003.

16 *The Magazine of Domestic Economy*, Vol. 5, 1840.

17 The Eyre estate was full of these delightful houses, with and without the bolt-holes I have described. All of them were built on 99-year leases which ended in the mid-twentieth century, when the whole area was totally redeveloped. Until it could be, individual houses were boarded up and street after street in St John's Wood gradually decayed: a melancholy sight.

18 J. A. Froude (ed.), *Mrs Carlyle's Letters*, London, 1883.

19 Geoffrey Best, *Mid-Victorian London*, London, 1971.

20 For once I have not studded this account with notes.

21 Max Schlesinger, *Saunterings in and about London*, trans. Otto Wenkstern, London, 1853.

22 Francis Wey, *Les Anglais Chez Eux*, Paris, 1856, trans. Valerie Price as *A Frenchman Among the Victorians*, Yale, 1936, included in Xavier Baron, *London 1066–1914*, Vol. II, Robertsbridge, East Sussex, 1997.

23 It would be invidious, not to say tedious, to anecdotalise all these majestic clubs, but you may like to know that once, when I was entertained in the Ladies' Annexe of the Athenaeum, I was checking that my hat was straight, in the ladies' cloakroom – it was so long ago that one wore a hat – when a bishop's wife admired it, and we all had a jolly session of trying on each other's hats. The 'sanitary ware' was a deep ecclesiastical purple.

24 Peter Cunningham, *Handbook of London*, London 1850 (2nd edn).

25 For most of the details of gentlemen's clubs I have gratefully relied on Ben Weinreb and Christopher Hibbert, *The London Encyclopaedia*, London, 1983.

26 Ibid.

27 The average age of marriage for professional and upper-class men between 1840 and 1870 was 29.93 years: J. A. Banks, *Prosperity and Parenthood; a Study of Family Planning among the Victorian Middle Class*, London, 1954.

28 Edwin Chadwick had reported to the Poor Law Commissioners that the average age at death of the gentlemen residents in Bethnal Green – and there were some – was 45, while that of the working population was only 16.

29 Unpublished diary of Charles Pugh, Bodleian MSEng. Misc.d.465–73, listed in Heather Creaton, *Unpublished London Diaries*, London, 2003.

30 Henry Mayhew and John Binny, *The Criminal Prisons of London and Scenes of Prison Life*, London, 1862.

31 Ibid.

32 Wheen, op. cit.

33 A ready reckoner in *The Magazine of Domestic Economy* for 1843 set out the amounts due for the 'New Tax upon Income'. An income of £1,000, which would be a very comfortable amount, attracted just £29 34s. Those were the days.

34 Froude, op. cit.

Chapter 10: The Upper Class and Royalty (pp. 109–119)

1 Florence Nightingale, *Cassandra*, written in 1852 but not published (in London) until 1928. Miss Nightingale allowed a few copies to be privately printed, but she constantly revised the original, until the last version – the one that was published in 1928 – lacked the fire of her original essay.

2 John Bailey (ed.), *The Diary of Lady Frederick Cavendish*, London, 1927.

3 Alison Aldburgham, *Shops and Shopping 1800–1914*, London, 1981.

4 (Editor unnamed), *Society, Politics and Diplomacy 1820–1864; Passages from the Journal of Francis W. H. Cavendish*, London, 1913.

5 Merton M. Sealts (ed.), *Ralph Waldo Emerson, the Journals and Miscellaneous Notebooks*, Vol. X, 1847–8, Cambridge, Mass., 1973.

6 The section that follows is an amalgam of Anthony Bruce, *The Purchase System in the British Army 1660–1871*, London, 1980; Byron Farwell, *For Queen and Country*, London, 1981; and the 1844 edition of *The Queen's Regulations and Orders*. I would not have been able to write it without the help of Dr Alastair Massie, Archivist

of the National Army Museum, to whom I am most grateful. If I have misinterpreted the information he made available to me, the mistakes are entirely my own.

7 Farwell, op. cit.

8 Marion Harding (ed.), *The Victorian Soldier*, London, 1993. One of the exploits of this amazing little man was to lead an expedition in 1835–6 to prove his theory that the Euphrates was navigable from a point near Antioch, to the Persian Gulf, which he did by transporting two iron-clad steam launches overland from the coast of Turkey to the river. One of them sank, later, but Chesney finished the trip on a raft.

9 Another being, of course, the shock-horror about prostitution while patronising prostitutes.

10 Bruce, op. cit.

11 *The Times*, 23 December 1854, quoted in Bruce, op. cit.

12 Farwell, op. cit.

13 Ibid.

14 Bailey, op. cit.

15 Thea Holme, *The Carlyles at Home*, Oxford, 1965.

16 It survives, on the opposite side of Piccadilly from the Ritz and a little further west. It still – when I last saw it – had the words 'In' and 'Out' painted on the two pillars of the carriage drive. After Palmerston's death in 1865 it was taken over by the Naval and Military Club, always known as the 'In and Out Club'.

17 Bailey, op. cit.

18 A note by the editor, in S. M. Ellis (ed. and annot.), *A Mid-Victorian Pepys: the Letters and Memoirs of Sir William Hardman*, London, 1925.

19 Cecil Woodham-Smith, *Queen Victoria, her Life and Times*, vol. 1, *1819–1861*, London, 1972.

20 'Eon and his collar', *The Times*, 27 September 1975.

21 See note 4.

22 John Raymond (ed.), *Queen Victoria's Early Letters*, London, 1963 (rev. edn).

23 The list of royal Freemasons kindly supplied by the Library and Museum of Freemasonry includes Victoria's father the Duke of Kent, her uncles the Dukes of Cumberland and Sussex, and her three sons, Edward Prince of Wales (later Edward VII), Arthur Duke of Connaught and Leopold Duke of Albany. The tradition was continued by Edward VIII and George VI. The present Duke of Edinburgh, whose position is somewhat analogous to that of Prince Albert, is a Freemason.

24 John R. Davis, *The Great Exhibition*, Stroud, Gloucestershire, 1999.

25 This marriage had been planned by the royal couple for dynastic reasons, although Victoria insisted that her daughter had fallen in love with 'Fritz', and he with her. Fritz was the first potential suitor the young Princess had met. The announcement of their engagement was delayed until the Princess had been confirmed. A faint suspicion crosses my mind that another reason for delay was that at sixteen she may not yet have been physically mature; menarche came later, in those days, than now. No matter how much in love she was, the exchange of letters between her and her father as she left for Germany still moves the heart.

26 Henry Vane, *Affair of State. A Biography of the 8th Duke and Duchess of Devonshire*, London, 2004.

27 A. L. Kennedy (ed.), *'My Dear Duchess', Social and Political Letters to the Duchess of Manchester 1858–69*, London, 1956.

28 Ibid.

29 Stella Margetson, *Victorian High Society*, London, 1980.

30 *Oxford Dictionary of National Biography*, 2004.

31 Ibid.

32 Bailey, op. cit.

Chapter 11: Domestic Service (pp. 120–130)

1 M. L. Davies (ed.), *Life as We Have Known It*, London, 1931.

2 Evidence of Louisa Twining, the founder of the Workhouse Visiting Society, to the Select Parliamentary Committee on Poor Relief, quoted in *The English Woman's Journal*, March 1861.

3 Mrs Isabella Beeton, *The Book of Household Management*, London, 1861.

4 Davies, op. cit.

5 Liz Stanley (ed.), *The Diaries of Hannah Culwick*, London, 1984.

6 Kathleen Tillotson (ed.), *Charles Dickens, Letters*, Vol. 4, 1844–6, Oxford, 1977.

7 Thomas Webster, *An Encyclopaedia of Domestic Economy*, London, 1844.

8 Ibid.

9 J. A. Froude (ed.), *Mrs Carlyle's Letters*, London, 1883.

10 Webster, op. cit.

11 I had just drafted this paragraph when I saw a letter in the *Guardian* Review Section of 24 July 2004, part of which read: 'Not so long ago ... butchers used to keep all the gall bladders (where bile is stored) from the animals they cut up and put them in a pail of water. They used this to wash the surfaces and floors, because it was such an effective detergent.'

12 I have taken the description of the family wash from *The Magazine of Domestic Economy*, Vol. 6, 1841.

13 Webster, op. cit.

14 Webster, op. cit.

15 *The Magazine of Domestic Economy*, New Series, 1844.

16 John Bailey (ed.), *The Diary of Lady Frederick Cavendish*, London, 1927.

17 Webster, op. cit.

18 John Burnett (ed.), *Useful Toil*, London, 1974.

19 Edward Hyams (trans. and ed.), *Taine's Notes on England*, London, 1957.

20 C. S. Peel, 'Homes and Habits' in *Early Victorian London 1830–65*, Vol. I, London, 1934.

21 *The Magazine of Domestic Economy*, Vol. I, New Series, 1843.

22 In the distant days when I employed a nanny, I once heard ours conferring with a friend about advertisements in *The Lady*, then the current source of jobs. 'Fun-loving' meant that she would be expected to sleep with the husband.

'Foreign holidays with the family' meant that she stayed in every evening, while the family gallivanted.

23 Mayhew, Vol. III.
24 Quoted in Burnett, op. cit.

Chapter 12: Houses and Gardens (pp. 131–147)

1   James Greenwood, *The Seven Curses of London*, London, 1869.
2   Asa Briggs, *Victorian Things*, Stroud, Gloucestershire, 2003 (rev. edn).
3   Mayhew, Vol. II.
4   W. B. Tegetmeier, *A Manual of Domestic Economy*, London, 1867; particularly useful because he was writing for 'female students in [teacher] Training Institutes', not the middle classes whom such writers as Mrs Beeton were addressing.
5   Tegetmeier, op. cit.
6   Jean Hawkes (trans. and ed.), *The London Journal of Flora Tristan*, London, 1982.
7   Thomas Webster, *An Encyclopaedia of Domestic Economy*, London, 1844.
8   Ibid.
9   Ibid.
10 *The Magazine of Domestic Economy*, Vol. 6, 1841.
11 The long-running saga of Carlyle and the piano is set out in Thea Holme, *The Carlyles at Home*, Oxford, 1965.
12 Matthew Sweet *Inventing the Victorians: What we Think About Them and Why We're Wrong*, London, 2001; a fascinating book.
13 Webster, op. cit.
14 The desk at which I write belonged to my great-grandfather. It is a splendid bit of Jacobethan wishful thinking, much improved since I gently levered off the heavily carved swags of masks and fruit which dug into my knees. If any of the family reads this – I have them carefully put away.
15 Charlecote Park, the home of the Lucy family, was built in 1558. Like most houses, it was tinkered with by sucessive owners but remained mostly unchanged until a Welsh heiress, Mary Elizabeth Williams, married the then owner George Hammond Lucy, in 1823 and set about converting it back to the way it had been in the sixteenth century. Even after his death in 1845 she continued their joint plans to recreate Charlecote as it had been under Elizabeth, with of course necessary amendments such as plumbing: when she arrived there had been only two earth closets serving the whole building. She achieved a magnificent monument of Victorian 'Elizabethan taste' which has to be seen by anyone interested in the subject, but in doing so she almost obliterated the ancient building of 1558. Only the gatehouse and garden turrets, which are Tudor gems, survive.
16 Charles Newton, *Victorian Designs for the Home*, London, 1999.
17 George Dodd, *Days at the Factories*, London, 1843.
18 Charles C. Oman and Jean Hamilton, *Wallpapers*, London, 1982; the catalogue of the wallpaper collection in the V&A. The following descriptions of wallpapers are taken from that collection.

19 James Burn, *The Beggar Boy; an Autobiography*, London, 1888.

20 I have been fortunate enough to discuss wallpapers with Dr Saunders of the V&A, Christine Woods of the Whitworth Art Gallery in Manchester, and Allyson McDermott, conservation consultant, who has been concerned with Linley Sambourne House, 18 Stafford Terrace, London W8. The expertise and enthusiasm of these three ladies, and their generosity with their time, were invaluable to me. The interior of the house is a monument to late-Victorian taste, too late for my purpose. The house can be viewed on application to the Royal Borough of Kensington and Chelsea Library and Art Service.

21 Some can still be seen on the front of Linley Sambourne House.

22 Samuel Beeton, *Book of Garden Management*, London, 1872, quoted in John Marshall and Ian Wilcox, *The Victorian House*, London, 1986.

23 'Encaustic' means 'using pigments mixed with hot wax, which are burned in as an inlay': *Concise Oxford English Dictionary*. Minton had exhibited them at the Great Exhibition, but they never caught on for domestic interiors, except for hallways.

24 Webster, op. cit.

25 Briggs, op. cit.

26 Unpublished diary of Thomas Rogers, Guildhall Library MS 19,019, listed in Heather Creaton, *Unpublished London Diaries*, London, 2003. Louis Daguerre developed this complicated process in 1835. It involved subjecting a silver-coated copper plate to iodine vapour, developing the image over hot mercury, and fixing it in a solution of sodium thiosulphate and gold chloride. To begin with, the sitter had to be braced into immobility for as long as fifteen minutes but this was gradually cut to one minute. Only one print could be made from each photograph. From 1851 daguerrotypes were replaced by the wet collodian process which enabled more than one print to be made (Stephen Van Dulken, *Inventing the 19th Centuryi*, London, 2001).

27 Briggs, op. cit.

28 Six hundred of his collection have survived, as a unique archive of social types. Michael Hiley, *Victorian Working Women: Portraits from Life*, London, 1979.

29 *The Magazine of Domestic Economy*, New Series, Vol. 2, 1844.

30 Mayhew, op. cit . Three wholesale dealers sold to 'the wealthy suburbs'.

31 A. R. Bennett, *London and Londoners in the 1850s and 60s*, London, 1924.

32 Tegetmeier, op. cit. Argand was the name of the inventor. These are the lamps one often sees converted to electricity. They are fairly tall, to spread light over a table, and they have the characteristic glass reservoir for oil. One end of the wick was in the reservoir, the other came up through a holder which could be adjusted to regulate the height of the flame. A glass 'chimney' sat on top, which had to be kept very clean. They were tricky to operate, and they did smell a bit, but they gave a lovely mellow light.

33 Ibid.

34 *The Magazine of Domestic Economy*, New Series, Vol. 2, 1844.

35 Tegetmeier, op. cit. Do you know where your maincock is? When will the gas-fitter arrive?

36 Marshall and Wilcox, op. cit.

37 J. C. Loudon, *The Suburban Horticulturalist*, London, 1842.

38 Loudon, op. cit. When I lived in Tanganyika, as it was then, I became accustomed to male dinner guests 'seeing Africa' in a row, backs to the company, while the women used the bathroom, but I don't remember anyone thanking the men for their contribution to the garden fertility.

39 Shirley Hibberd, *The Amateur's Kitchen Garden*, London, 1877.

40 Advertised in the 1865 volume of *Gardening Chronicle and Agricultural Gazette*.

41 *The Floral World* (bound volume of monthly parts), 1863.

42 Advertisement on the flyleaf of J. C. Loudon, *The Horticulturalist*, London, 1871.

43 Unpublished diary, H. R. Silvester, Wellcome Institute MS 5689, listed in Creaton, op. cit.

44 Mayhew, Vol. 1.

45 *The Magazine of Domestic Economy*, New Series, Vol. 2, 1843. The magazine was ahead of its time; the Royal Horticultural Society ran a trial of garden path surfaces in 1852, and found that the 'newly-introduced asphalt' was best: Brent Elliott, *The RHS – A History*, London, 2004.

46 Mayhew, op. cit.

47 Ibid.

48 *The Cottage Gardener, or Amateur and Cottager's Guide to Out-Door Gardening*, Vol. I, 1849.

49 David Solman, *Loddiges of Hackney, the Largest Hothouse in the World*, London, 1995. In 1839 George Loddige laid out a model arboretum in Abney Park cemetery, opened in 1840. For family reasons, and because the encroaching built-up area meant air pollution, the nursery closed in 1852–4.

50 Brent Elliott, *Victorian Gardens*, London, 1986.

51 For the list of fashionable flowers I have used both Elliott, *Victorian Gardens*, op. cit., and Maggie Campbell-Culver, *The Origin of Plants*, London, 2001. There was a huge expansion of plant material available to gardeners in the nineteenth century.

52 *The Floral World*, op. cit.

53 Elliott, *Victorian Gardens*, op. cit.

54 Winslow Ames, *Prince Albert and Victorian Taste*, London, 1967.

55 *The Floral World*, op. cit.

56 Ibid.

57 Elliott, *Victorian Gardens*, op. cit.

Chapter 13: Food (pp. 148–161)

1 My copy is of the seventh edition, with the owner's name in it in careful Victorian script. Tessa McKirdy, of Cooks Books, Rottingdean, was kind enough to look for the date of the first edition; her estimate is 1858. It was in print until 1905.

2 Mayhew, Vol. I.

3 Ibid.

4 M. L. Davies (ed.), *Life as We Have Known It*, London, 1931.

5 Mayhew, op. cit.

6 Gustave Doré and Blanchard Jerrold, *London*, London, 1872: shown in a picture

of Dark House Lane, lined with fishmongers' stalls. This notice hung over one of them.

7   Thomas Webster, *An Encyclopaedia of Domestic Economy*, London, 1844.

8   A. R. Bennett, *London and Londoners in the 1850s and 60s*, London, 1924.

9   Thea Holme, *The Carlyles at Home*, Oxford, 1965.

10 James Burn, '*The Beggar Boy*': an Autobiography', London, 1888.

11 Eliza Acton, *Modern Cookery for Private Families*, London, 1856.

12 Mrs Isabella Beeton, *The Book of Household Management*, London, 1861. Either Isabella was fond of blinding her readers with science, or the average middle-class Victorian housewife knew more about chemistry than a modern undergraduate. Pyroligneous acid is a by-product of the production of charcoal, also known as wood vinegar. It is a reddish-brown wood distillate containing acetic acid, methyl alcohol, acetone, and a tarry residue. I would not wish my smoked fish to have been 'washed over' with it.

13 *The Magazine of Domestic Economy*, Vol. II, 1844.

14 Webster, op. cit.

15 Peter Cunningham, *Handbook of London*, London, 1850 (2nd edn).

16 Holme, op. cit.

17 Alison Aldburgham, *Shops and Shopping 1800–1914*, London, 1981.

18 Stephen Van Dulken, *Inventing the 19th Century*, London, 2001.

19 Ibid.

20 Burn, op. cit.

21 For the information on Reckitt & Coleman, see Penelope Lively, *A House Unlocked*, London, 2001. Most of the other information in this and the following paragraph comes from the Internet, except for Huntley & Palmer's biscuits, for which I gratefully acknowledge the help of the Library of Reading University, and Angostura bitters, for which I deciphered the small print on a very ancient bottle in my drinks cupboard.

22 Acton, op. cit.

23 For an explanation of the use of alum in bread, see the author's *Dr Johnson's London*, London, 2000.

24 Webster, op. cit.

25 James Greenwood, *The Seven Curses of London*, London, 1869.

26 Beeton, op. cit. in her section on Poisons.

27 Alexis Soyer, *A Culinary Campaign*, London, 1857.

28 Alexis Soyer designed a lithograph of his wonderful kitchens, complete with a self-portrait as the Head Chef, wearing his characteristic beret rather on one side. The couple to whom he is showing the kitchens are listening entranced, especially the lady. The man stands rather patiently. He is still wearing his shiny silk top hat. Unfortunately the one thing M. Soyer did not take into account was the possibility of reproducing his very detailed lithograph, which is in shades of grey and beige, in a modern book. Copies of it can however still be bought from the Reform Club.

29 Alexis Soyer, *The Modern Housewife*, London, 1851.

30 Holme, op. cit.

31 Soyer, *Modern Housewife*, op. cit.

32 Judith Flanders, *The Victorian House*, London, 2003.

33 Webster, op. cit.

34 Information kindly supplied by Dr Peavitt of the Science Museum.

35 It is, of course, and always has been so far as I know, a delicious mixture of Swiss cheeses melted – *fondu* – in wine, with nutmeg and a good slug of kirsch.

36 Chloride of soda is a mixture of calcium chloride, baking soda and water.

37 Webster, op. cit.

38 Beeton, op. cit.

39 Unpublished diary of Charles Pugh, Bodleian MS Misc. d. 472, listed in Heather Creaton, *Unpublished London Diaries*, London, 2003.

40 G. A. Sala, *Twice Round the Clock*, London, 1859.

41 Soyer, *Modern Housewife*, op. cit.

42 Webster, op. cit.

43 S. M. Ellis (ed. and annot.), *A Mid-Victorian Pepys: the Letters and Memoirs of Sir William Hardman*, London, 1925.

44 Sala, op. cit.

45 John Hollingshead, *My Lifetime*, London, 1895.

46 G. A. Sala, *Gaslight and Daylight*, London, 1869.

47 J. A. Froude (ed.), *Mrs Carlyle's Letters*, London, 1883. Her lunch place should not be confused with Verrey's Restaurant in Regent Street, patronised by the Prince of Wales, Disraeli and Dickens.

48 Nathaniel Hawthorne, *The English Notebooks*, excerpts included in Xavier Baron, *London 1066–1914*, Robertsbridge, East Sussex, 1997.

49 Unpublished diary of W. S. Bell, Museum of London accession no. 52.25, listed in Creaton, op. cit.

50 Cunningham, op. cit.

51 Symposium means a convivial meeting round a dinner table, where men could discuss subjects such as philosophy, as Plato and his friends did. It was a clever choice of title, as long as you could pronounce it.

52 Graham Storey, Kathleen Tillotson and Nina Burgis (eds), *The Letters of Charles Dickens*, Vol. 6, Oxford, 1988.

53 Helen Morris, *Portrait of a Chef. The Life of Alexis Soyer*, Cambridge, 1938.

54 Elizabeth Ray, *Alexis Soyer, Cook Extraordinary*, Lewes, East Sussex, 1991. John R. Davis, *The Great Exhibition*, Stroud, Gloucestershire, 1999.

55 Diary of W. S. Bell, op. cit.

Chapter 14: Clothes and So On   (pp. 162–178)

1 James Greenwood, *The Wilds of London*, London, 1881.

2 Gustave Doré and Blanchard Jerrold, *London*, London, 1872.

3 Greenwood, op. cit.

4 Ibid., and John Hollingshead, *My Lifetime*, London, 1895.

5 Mayhew, Vol. I.

6 Ibid.

7 Ibid.

8 Edward Hyams (trans. and ed.), *Taine's Notes on England*, London, 1957.

9 One of these dealers was Moses Moses, who began with a barrow and ended with a small shop in Covent Garden, in 1860.

10 Mayhew, op. cit.

11 Mayhew, Vol. II.

12 Ibid.

13 Anne and Roger Cowan, *Victorian Jews Through British Eyes*, Oxford, 1986.

14 A full-page advertisement was carefully pasted into the diary of W. S. Bell, who came to see London and the Great Exhibition in 1851: unpublished diary, Museum of London accession no. 52.25, listed in Heather Creaton, *Unpublished London Diaries*, London, 2003.

15 E. P. Thompson and Eileen Yeo (eds), *The Unknown Mayhew – Selections from the Morning Chronicle 1849–50*, London, 1971.

16 A. R. Bennett, *London and Londoners in the 1850s and 60s*, London, 1924.

17 Michael Slater (ed.), '*Gone Astray and other Papers, from Household Words 1851–59*, Vol 3 of *Dickens' Journalism*, London, 1998.

18 James Burn, *The Beggar Boy: an Autobiography*, London, 1888.

19 Thomas Webster, *An Encyclopaedia of Domestic Economy*, London, 1844.

20 Burn, op. cit.

21 *The Magazine of Domestic Economy*, Vol. 2, 1844.

22 Bennett, op. cit.

23 Hollingshead, op. cit.

24 Anne Buck, *Victorian Costume and Accessories*, London, 1961.

25 Bennett, op. cit.

26 Stephen Van Dulken, *Inventing the 19th Century*, London, 2001.

27 Buck, op. cit.

28 Buck, op. cit. The Duke of Wellington habitually wore a plain blue frock-coat. The surviving variants of tail-coats are (1) 'evening tails' in black, with a white bow-tie and waistcoat, worn at very formal occasions such as the annual banquet given by the Lord Mayor of London, (2) the same coat worn with a black waistcoat and black bow-tie by some headwaiters. The 'morning coat' in black or grey, worn at very fashionable occasions such as Ascot, with a black or grey top-hat, its downmarket version hired, often from Moss Bros, for weddings, and the 'tails' worn by Eton boys, differ from tailcoats in the cut at waist level, at the front.

29 Unpublished diary of Thomas Cobb, solicitor, Guildhall Library MS 18, 770/1–11, listed in Creaton, op. cit.

30 Van Dulken, op. cit.

31 Buck, op. cit.

32 *English Woman's Domestic Magazine*, 1865.

33 J. A. Froude (ed.), *Mrs Carlyle's Letters*, London, 1883.

34 Bennett, op. cit.

35 *The Magazine of Domestic Economy*, 1842.

36 Buck, op. cit.

37 Now on view in Carlyle's House, owned by the National Trust.

38 Buck, op. cit.

39 Dionysius Lardner, *The Great Exhibition and London in 1851*, London, 1852.

40 Mayhew, Vol II.

41 Alison Aldburgham, *Shops and Shopping 1800–1914*, London, 1981.

42 Unpublished diary of Thomas Cobb in Creaton, op. cit.

43 *The Magazine of Domestic Economy*, 1841.

44 C. Willett Cunnington, *The Perfect Lady*, London, 1948.

45 Ibid.

46 Leon Radzinowicz, *A History of English Criminal Law*, London, 1968.

47 *The Magazine of Domestic Economy*, 1844.

48 Bennett, op. cit.

49 My maternal grandfather had been an Army officer. As a small child, I remember his sharp-pointed waxed moustache. He expected his grand-daughters to kiss him, but you had to judge your approach run carefully to avoid impalement.

50 Webster, op. cit.

51 Thea Holme, *The Carlyles at Home*, Oxford, 1965.

52 *The Magazine of Domestic Economy*, 1842.

53 Unpublished diary of J. A. Patterson, Wellcome Institute MS 73537, listed in Creaton, op. cit.

54 *The Magazine of Domestic Economy*, 1843.

55 *The Ladies' Cabinet*, 1844, quoted in Buck, op. cit.

56 Diary of William Tayler, in John Burnett (ed.), *Useful Toil*, London, 1974.

57 Buck, op. cit.

58 *The Magazine of Domestic Economy*, 1842.

59 Van Dulken, op. cit.

60 Hyams, op. cit.

61 G. A. Sala, *Twice Round the Clock*, London, 1859.

62 Slater, op. cit.

63 Michael Hiley, *Victorian Working Women: Portraits from Life*, London, 1979.

64 Hyams, op. cit.

65 Buck, op. cit. Anne Buck was the Keeper of the Gallery of English Costume at Platt Hall, Manchester.

66 Cunnington, op. cit.

67 I can quote no historical authority for this supposition, but, given the Victorian passion for Jacobethan, it seems to me likely.

68 Quoted in Aldburgham, op. cit.

69 C. Willett and Phillis Cunnington, *The History of Underclothes*, London, 1951.

70 C. and P. Cunnington, op. cit.

71 Quoted, source unknown, in Aldburgham, op. cit.

72 Ibid.

73 Froude, op. cit.

74 Quoted, source unknown, in C. and P. Cunnington, op. cit.

75 *The Handbook of the Toilet*, 1841, quoted in Cunnington, op. cit.

76 Alex Werner and Roy Porter, *London Bodies*, London, 1998.

77 Ibid. My maternal grandfather served in the Royal Army Medical Corps in India, where the combination of heat and tight stays overcame many ladies at parties. When called to the rescue he simply cut their stay-laces. The ladies quickly recovered, but his reputation for alacrity in divesting them of their stays was slightly ambiguous.

78 *The Magazine of Domestic Economy*, 1840.

79 *The Handbook for the Toilet*, 1841, quoted in Cunnington, op. cit.

80 Quoted in Aldburgham, op. cit.

81 Ibid.

82 Barbara Leigh Smith, *Women and Work*, London, 1857.

83 Pattens were iron under-soles that strapped on to the sole of a shoe to lift the wearer an inch or more from the ground. They were slippery in wet weather and awkward to walk in.

84 E. P. Thompson and Eileen Yeo (eds) *The Unknown Mayhew – Selections from the Morning Chronicle 1849–50*, London, 1971. This detailed account goes on to describe what happens to the 'dresses' when the fitter comes back with the 'measures' and work can start. I have included it in Chapter 20.

85 Holme, op. cit.

86 Judith Flanders, *The Victorian House*, London, 2003.

87 Aldburgham, op. cit.

88 Ibid.

89 Werner and Porter, op. cit.

90 Aldburgham, op. cit.

91 G. L. Browne and C. G. Stewart, *Reports of Trials for Murder by Poisoning*, London, 1883.

92 Merton M. Sealts (ed.), *Ralph Waldo Emerson, the Journals and Miscellaneous Notebooks*, Vol. X, 1847–8, Cambridge, Mass., 1973.

93 Van Dulken, op. cit.

Chapter 15: Health (pp. 179–197)

1   I have relied, in this chapter, on Roy Porter's monumental history of medicine, *The Greatest Benefit to Mankind*, London, 1997, as well as other sources, separately noted.

2   Adam Hart-Davis, *What the Victorians Did for Us*, London, 2001.

3   Elizabeth Longford, *Wellington, Pillar of State*, London, 1972.

4   John Fisher Murray, 'Physiology of London Life', published in *Bentley's Miscellany*, Vol. XV, 1844.

5   S. M. Ellis (ed. and annot.), '*A Mid-Victorian Pepys: the Letters and Memoirs of Sir William Hardman*, London, 1925.

6   Thomas Webster, An *Encyclopaedia of Domestic Economy*, London, 1844. What a thought, leeches in your mouth.

7   Liz Stanley (ed.), *The Diaries of Hannah Culwick*, London, 1984.

8   Peter Vinten-Johansen et al., *Cholera, Chloroform and the Science of Medicine: a Life of John Snow*, Oxford, 2003.

9   Journal of Samuel Boddington, Guildhall MS 10,823/5c, listed in Heather Creaton, *Unpublished London Diaries*, London, 2003.

10 Edwin Chadwick, *Report on the Sanitary Condition of the Labouring Population of Great Britain*, 1842, and Porter, op. cit.

11 Porter, op. cit.: 'the public responsibility thereby undertaken for the sick poor became a basis for the British National Health Service'.

12 Joseph Rogers, *Reminiscences of a Workhouse Medical Officer*, ed. Thorold Rogers, London, 1889.

13 For a brief history of them, see the author's *Dr Johnson's London*, London, 2000.

14 R. W. Vanderkiste, *A Six Years' Mission Among the Dens of London*, London, 1854.

15 D. Hudson, *Munby: Man of Two Worlds*, London, 1972.

16 Joan Lane, 'A Social History of Medicine', in John Woodward and David Richards (eds), *Health Care and Popular Medicine in Nineteenth Century England*, London, 1977.

17 Peter Cunningham, *Handbook of London*, London, 1850 (2nd edn).

18 Edward Hyams (trans. and ed.), *Taine's Notes on England*, London, 1957.

19 Graham Storey and Kathleen Tillotson (eds), *The Letters of Charles Dickens*, Oxford, 1988.

20 Thomas Dormandy, *The White Death: a History of Tuberculosis*, London, 1999.

21 James Greenwood, *The Wilds of London*, London, 1881.

22 Cunningham, op. cit.

23 Jeanne Peterson, *The Medical Profession in Mid Victorian London*, London, 1978. Unfortunately, as the author says, 'information about general practice in London is scarce'.

24 Thea Holme, *The Carlyles at Home*, Oxford, 1965. I am told that such an accident can cause the most agonising pain. No wonder the maid was screaming.

25 Vinten-Johansen, op. cit.

26 Much of the material on Florence Nightingale is taken from Cecil Woodham-Smith, *Florence Nightingale*, London, 1950. There are many more recent books about her, but I needed to make a summary which would show her relevance to life in London – the province of this book – not her achievements all over the world.

27 Diary of Henry Robert Silvester, MD, Wellcome Institute MS 5689, listed in Creaton, op. cit.

28 Quoted in A. J. Rogers, *The Scientific Revolution in Victorian Medicine*, London, 1979.

29 Ulrich Tröhler, 'Modern Surgery', in W. F. Bynum and Roy Porter (eds), *Companion Encyclopedia of the History of Medicine*, London, 1993.

30 Porter, op. cit.

31 Lytton Strachey and Roger Fulford (eds), *The Greville Memoirs*, Vol. V, London, 1938.

32 Kathleen Tillotson, *Charles Dickens, Letters*, Vol. V, Oxford, 1977.

33 In his monumental *History of St Bartholomew's Hospital* published in 1918, Dr Norman Moore does not refer to the 'four or five thousand' anaesthetics administered in his hospital before 1852, when Dr Patrick Black was according to him, appointed the first 'Administrator of Chloroform'.

34 Vinten-Johansen, op. cit.

35 Genesis, Chapter 3 verse 16.

36 Vinten-Johansen, op. cit.

37 George Drysdale, *The Elements of Social Science*, London, 1854.

38 Home Office 35292–3.3.40 in the National Archives, formerly the Public Records Office.

39 *British Medical Journal*, 1868.

40 Mayhew, Vol I.

41 *The Magazine of Domestic Economy*, 1842.

42 J. A. Froude (ed.), *Mrs Carlyle's Letters*, London, 1883. This famous nostrum survived into the 1950s in tropical Africa, and I believe it can still be found. When I tried it, in Tanganyika, it was a white liquid made of kaolin, which certainly soothed the stomach, and morphia, which certainly produced a refreshing sleep. I believe the modern version no longer contains morphia.

43 Froude, op. cit.

44 Dormandy, op. cit.

45 From an undated press cutting in the diary of Charles Pugh listed in Creaton, op. cit.

46 Quoted in Dormandy, op. cit.

47 Charles Creighton, A *History of Epidemics* London, 1965 (2nd edn).

48 Ibid.

49 Alex Werner and Roy Porter, *London Bodies*, London, 1998.

50 Creighton, op. cit.

51 Ibid.

52 Ibid.

53 A. R. Bennett, *London and Londoners in the 1850s and 60s*, London, 1924.

54 Mrs Isabella Beeton, *The Book of Household Management*, London, 1861.

55 Francis Wheen, *Karl Marx*, London, 1999.

56 Porter, op. cit.

57 Vinten-Johansen, op. cit.

58 Chadwick, op. cit.

59 These figures vary between 14,000 and 18,000. It is difficult to tell which is correct, but it hardly seems to matter, looking back to those awful days.

60 G. M. Young and W. D. Handcock, *English Historical Documents*, Vol. XII (1), *1833–1874*, London, 1956.

61 S. E. Finer, *The Life and Times of Sir Edwin Chadwick*, London, 1952.

62 Thomas Beames, *The Rookeries of London*, London, 1850.

63 Vinten-Johansen, op. cit. I had always imagined Snow himself heroically wrenching the handle from the pump. Instead, he achieved something quite as difficult – to persuade a local authority to move fast. They deserve credit for acting so promptly on his advice, in the teeth of the prevalent belief in 'miasma'.

64 John Hollingshead, *My Lifetime*, London, 1895.

65 Porter, op. cit.

Chapter 16: Amusements (pp. 197–212)

1 John Hollingshead, *Ragged London in 1861*, London, 1861.

2 Mayhew, Vol. III.

3 Mayhew, Vol. I.

4 Gustave Doré and Blanchard Jerrold, *London*, London, 1872.

5 Ibid. For an impression of a Victorian music hall, the Hackney Empire is well worth a visit.

6 Doré and Jerrold, op. cit.

7 D. Hudson, *Munby: Man of Two Worlds*, London, 1972.

8   S. M. Ellis (ed. and annot.), *A Mid-Victorian Pepys: the Letters and Memoirs of Sir William Hardman*, London, 1925.

9   Hudson, op. cit.

10 A. R. Bennett, *London in the 1850s and 60s*, London, 1924.

11 Ibid.

12 Unpublished diary of W. S. Bell, Museum of London accession no. 52.25, listed in Heather Creaton, *Unpublished London Diaries*, London, 2003.

13 Hudson, op. cit.

14 Robert Ward, *London's New River*, London, 2003; Peter Cunningham, *Handbook of London*, London, 1850 (2nd edn).

15 Doré and Jerrold, op. cit.

16 Lytton Strachey and R. Fulford (eds), *The Greville Memoirs*, Vol. V, London, 1938.

17 John Hollingshead, *My Lifetime*, London, 1895.

18 Ibid.

19 J. E. Ritchie, *The Night Side of London*, London, 1869.

20 James Greenwood, *The Seven Curses of London*, London, 1869.

21 Ritchie, op. cit.

22 Cunningham, op. cit.

23 The Earl of Harewood and Anthony Peattie (eds), *The New Kobbé's Opera Book*, 1997 (11th edn). The Lyceum is a gorgeous building which should be seen if possible, although it looks a little seedy now. Kobbé is the bible of opera, but it makes little mention of the Lyceum during the period 1840–70, while according to Ben Weinreb and Christopher Hibbert (eds), *The London Encyclopaedia*, London, 1983, to which I have constantly referred for dates and places, 'many brilliant productions' were staged there in the years 1847–55, and 'in 1856–9 it was used by the Covent Garden Theatre Company, whose own theatre had been burned'.

24 Cunningham, op. cit.

25 Unpublished diary of W. S. Bell, listed in Creaton, op. cit.

26 Ibid.

27 Letters of Hector Berlioz, bound in with Dionysius Lardner, *The Great Exhibition and London in 1851*, London, 1852.

28 Strachey and Fulford, op. cit.

29 Max Schlesinger, '1820–85: Saunterings in and about London', in Xavier Baron, *London, 1066–1914*, Robertsbridge, East Sussex, 1997. For a description of Vauxhall in its heyday, see the author's *Dr Johnson's London*, London, 2000.

30 Cunningham, op. cit. for the other bowling saloon, Weinreb and Hibbert, op. cit. for Cremorne.

31 Ritchie, op. cit.

32 Francis Wey, *Les Anglais Chez Eux*, 1856, trans. Valerie Price as *A Frenchman Among the Victorians*, Yale, 1936.

33 J. A. Froude (ed.), *Mrs Carlyle's Letters*, London, 1883.

34 William Acton, *Prostitution*, London, 1870 (2nd edn).

35 Cunningham, op. cit.

36 Adam Hart-Davis, *What the Victorians Did for Us*, London, 2001.

37 Cunningham, op. cit.

38 Unpublished diary of Charles Pugh, Bodleian MS Eng.Misc. d.467, listed in Creaton, op. cit.

39 A. E. Douglas-Smith, *The City of London School*, Oxford, 1965 (2nd edn).

40 R. W. Vanderkiste, *A Six Years' Mission Among the Dens of London*, London, 1854.

41 M. L. Davies (ed.), *Life as We Have Known It*, London, 1931.

42 Pugh, op. cit.

43 Friedrich Engels, *The Condition of the Working Class in England*, trans. and ed. W. O. Henderson and W. H. Chaloner, Oxford, 1958.

44 Hudson, op. cit.

45 Mayhew, Vol. III.

46 Edward Hyams, (trans. and ed.), *Taine's Notes on England*, London, 1957.

47 Mayhew, Vol. II. If you were ever made, as a child, to drink milk fresh from the cow – and full of all kinds of germs – you have my sympathy. It's revolting.

48 Wey, op. cit.

49 Unpublished diary of W. S. Bell, listed in Creaton, op. cit.

50 Wey, op. cit.

51 Ibid.

52 Cunningham, op. cit.

53 Hyams, op. cit.

54 Schlesinger, op. cit.

55 Ellis, op. cit.

56 *The Magazine of Domestic Economy New Series*, Vol. 1, 1843.

57 Bennett, op. cit.

58 It is still there, just on the Kensington Gardens side of the Broad Walk. It is now used as offices for the park staff.

59 Cunningham, op. cit.

60 Francis Wheen, *Karl Marx*, London, 1999.

61 Nathaniel Hawthorne, *The English Notebooks* and *Our Old Home*, London, 1863, excerpts in Baron, op. cit.

62 Hudson, op. cit.

63 Doré and Jerrold, op. cit.

64 Hawthorne, op. cit.

65 Unpublished diary of J. A. Patterson, Wellcome Institute MS 73537, listed in Creaton, op. cit.

66 Cunningham, op. cit.

67 Unpublished diary of W. S Bell, in Creaton, op. cit.

68 Ibid.

69 The Guildhall Museum has a splendid example.

70 Henry Humpherus, *History of the Origin and Progress of the Company of Watermen and Lightermen of the River Thames*, edited by Jack King, W. Barrett, G. Wilson and John Dawson, vol. IV, reprinted Lavenham, Suffolk, 1999.

71 Ralph Hyde, *Printed Maps of Victorian England*, London, 1975.

72 Unpublished diary of J. A. Patterson, listed in Creaton, op. cit.

73 Hudson, op. cit.

74 Merton M. Sealts (ed.), *Ralph Waldo Emerson, the Journals and Miscellaneous Notebooks*, Vol. X, 1847–8, Cambridge, Mass., 1973.

75 Cunningham, op. cit. The man-eating tiger can now be seen in the V&A.

76 Ibid. The very thought makes the blood run cold.

77 Cunningham, op. cit.

Chapter 17: The Great Exhibition (pp. 213–224)

1 There is a vast amount of literature about the Great Exhibition, both contemporary and modern. In the latter category I have particularly relied on, and enjoyed, Michael Leapman, *The World for a Shilling*, London, 2001; John Davis, *The Great Exhibition*, Stroud, Gloucestershire, 1999; and Asa Briggs, *Victorian Things*, London, 1990 (rev. edn).

2 *Society, Politics and Diplomacy 1820–1864: Passages from the Journal of Francis W. H. Cavendish* (editor not named), London, 1913.

3 The idea was not new. In 1849 the Bank of England needed to rearrange the spaces in the building designed by Sir John Soane in 1788. A temporary building was put up in the garden. 'There were two lime trees in the garden and special care was taken to protect them from injury, the roof of the temporary office being built round them and the trunks enclosed in match-boarding. A journalist quipped that "the business ... appears to be carried on in an exotic arboretum".' W. Marston Acres, *The Bank of England From Within*, London, 1931.

4 Quoted in David Newsome, *The Victorian World Picture*, London, 1997.

5 Nor is the reader, without reference to Leapman's book, op. cit. The author, too, found it impossible to pick out the exhibits which would have most appealed to her. English jewellery scored highly, and the Indian and French textiles must have been lovely. It all depended on your individual taste.

6 Manuscript diary of Charles Pugh, Bodleian MS Eng. Misc. d.465-73, listed in Heather Creaton, *Unpublished London Diaries*, London, 2003.

7 J. R. Piggott, *Palace of the People. The Crystal Palace at Sydenham 1854–1936*, London, 2004.

8 Leapman, op. cit. One cannot help but wish that the designer of the Millennium Bridge over the Thames had read about these tests before his notoriously wobbling bridge was installed. The Victorians were thorough.

9 Davis, op. cit.

10 Cecil Woodham-Smith, *Queen Victoria, Her Life and Times*, Vol. I, London, 1972.

11 Memoirs of Lord Playfair, quoted in Woodham-Smith, op. cit.

12 Charles Pugh, listed in Creaton, op. cit.

13 Dionysius Lardner, *The Great Exhibition and London in 1851*, London, 1852.

14 Principal Speeches and Addresses of H.R.H. the Prince Consort, 1862, quoted in J. M. Golby, *Culture and Society in Britain 1850–90*, Oxford, 1986.

15 Letter from Hector Berlioz included in Lardner, op. cit.

16 Elizabeth Gaskell, *The Life of Charlotte Brontë*, London, 1971 (Folio Society edn).

17 Letter from M. Lemoinne included in Lardner, op. cit.

18 Information kindly supplied by Michael Leapman.

19 I once heard it seriously argued that the delay in the emancipation of French women was caused by the lack of public lavatories for them. Certainly when I was a pupil at the Bar the clerk to Chambers, who didn't approve of women barristers, handed me a huge key which he expected me to carry like Excalibur – it was too big to go into any handbag – and advance down King's Bench Walk in the Temple to the row of lavatories, thus publicly announcing my destination.

20 Lemoinne in Lardner, op. cit.

21 Patented by Alexander Bain in 1843. Stephen van Dulken, *Inventing the 19th Century*, London, 2001.

22 Unpublished diary of W. S. Bell, listed in Creaton, op. cit. Poor Mr Bell; he so clearly intended his beautiful book to be a wonderful family heirloom admired by generations, but it turned up in a sale and was − providentially for the historian − bought by the Museum of London.

23 The elephant came not from India but from a museum in Saffron Walden. Leapman, op. cit.

24 The Marquis of Dalhousie wrote to the Queen from Simla on 15 May 1850 about the arrangements for transporting it. He had sent it by the *Medea*. 'One of your Majesty's ships had been ordered to Bombay to receive it, but had not then arrived, and did not arrive until two months afterwards ... The *Medea* however sailed on 6 April [1850] and will, it is hoped, have a safe and speedy passage to England'. John Raymond (ed.), *Queen Victoria's Early Letters*, London, 1963 (rev. edn).

25 Raymond, op. cit.

26 Unpublished diary of Robert James Lee, MS 3224, Wellcome Institute, listed in Creaton, op. cit.

27 Quoted in Davis, op. cit.

28 In June 1840 the royal pair were fired on by a madman, who narrowly missed. Victoria was pregnant, but unperturbed. In July 1850 Robert Pate, an ex-officer, hit her on the head with a cane. Her bonnet saved her from any injury more serious than a bruise, but it would have unnerved a lesser woman.

29 A letter to Lady Salisbury quoted in Christopher Hobhouse, *1851 and the Crystal Palace*, London, 1950.

30 Leapman, op. cit.

31 Wellington, in Hobhouse, op. cit.

32 Woodham-Smith, op. cit.

33 W. O. Henderson, *J. C. Fischer and his Diary of Industrial England 1814–51*, London, 1966.

Chapter 18: The Crystal Palace at Sydenham (pp. 225–233)

1 J. R. Piggott, *Palace of the People. The Crystal Palace at Sydenham 1854–1936*, London, 2004 on which I have most gratefully relied.

2 S. M. Ellis (ed. and annot.), *A Mid-Victorian Pepys: the Letters and Memoirs of Sir William Hardman*, London, 1925.

3 David Solman, *Loddiges of Hackney*, London, 1995.

4 A. R. Bennett, *London and Londoners in the 1850s and 60s*, London, 1924.

5 Ibid. This was the infuriating system operated in Soviet shops, I don't know whether it's still done.

6 Lawrence Wright, *Clean and Decent*, London, 1960.

7 Piggott, op. cit.

8 Quoted from a contemporary source, in Graham Reeves, *Palace of the People*, Bromley, Kent, 1986, a copy of which was most kindly sent to me by the Crystal Palace Park Rangers Service of the London Borough of Bromley, which is

looking after the animals. They have been carefully restored, and can be visited as part of the Crystal Palace Park.

9 Unpublished diary of J. A. Patterson, Wellcome Institute MS 73537, listed in Heather Creaton, *Unpublished London Diaries*, London, 2003.

10 D. Hudson, *Munby; Man of Two Worlds*, London, 1972.

11 Bennett, op. cit.

12 Quoted in Reeves, op. cit.

13 The only comparable experience, perhaps, is to take part in a 'scratch' performance of the *Messiah*, in the Albert Hall – 'scratch' because amateur choirs converge from all over the country to sing together, without rehearsal, leaving little room for non-singing audience. Usually sopranos are segregated from altos, tenors from basses, but the choir I belonged to was able to sit together in a box, and since there was a table at the back of the box we furnished it with bottles and glasses. I'm not sure how we all sounded – the essence of the performance was enjoyment, not musical excellence – but I can say that it is much easier to sing the Hallelujah Chorus when your throat is regularly lubricated by slurps of red wine. The capacity of the Albert Hall is 7,000, a mere nothing compared to the Crystal Palace, but the volume of noise we made seemed to me deafening.

Chapter 19: Education (pp. 234–249)

1 E. P. Thompson and Eileen Yeo (eds), *The Unknown Mayhew – Selections from the Morning Chronicle of 1849–50*, London, 1971.

2 R. W. Vanderkiste, *A Six Years Mission Among the Dens of London*, London, 1854.

3 Most of this information comes from Ethel M. Hogg, *Quintin Hogg. A Biography*, London, 1904, and Ethel M. Wood, *A History of the Polytechnic*, London, 1965.

4 John Bailey (ed.), *The Diary of Lady Frederick Cavendish*, London, 1927.

5 Vanderkiste, op. cit.

6 Mayhew, Vol. IV.

7 John Hollingshead, *Ragged London in 1861*, London, 1861.

8 The only children dressed in rags, that I've ever seen, were in Myanmar (formerly called Burma). The ones wearing their native dress – on the same lines as a sarong – were fine. Their wrap-around cloth was suitable for the climate, easily adjusted for growth, comfortable, and – though I doubt if this worried them – becoming. The ragged children were wearing clothes donated by Western charities, such as T-shirts advertising unimaginable football teams, hot and unsuitable – but dearly prized, and worn till they finally fell to bits. They could have been mended, but no-one knew how. The only beneficiaries from these donations were, to my mind, the donors themselves, salving their consciences by getting rid of unwanted rubbish.

9 M. L. Davies, *Life as We Have Known It*, London, 1931.

10 Mayhew, Vol. II.

11 Edward Hyams (ed.), *Taine's Notes on England*, London, 1957.

12 Mayhew, Vol. II.

13 Caroline Cornwallis, *The Philosophy of Ragged Schools*, London, 1851.

14 Hollingshead, op. cit.

15 Samuel Smiles, *Workmen's Earnings, Strikes and Savings*, London, 1861.

16 A. R. Bennett, *London and Londoners in the 1850s and 60s*, London, 1924.

17 Cornwallis, op. cit.

18 Matthew Arnold, *Reports on Elementary Schools 1852–82*, London, 1908.

19 James Kay-Shuttleworth, *Four Periods of Public Education*, London, 1862. For the story of one boy who went from workhouse to teaching, see Chapter 7.

20 John Burnett (ed.), *Destiny Obscure*, London, 1982. Chinese whispers, as in 'send reinforcements, we are going to advance' which is misheard as 'send three and fourpence, we are going to a dance'.

21 Arnold, op. cit.

22 John Lawson, *A Social History of Education in England*, London, 1973.

23 Gerry Black, *J. F. S. The History of the Jews' Free School since 1732*, London, 1998.

24 Lorna Cowburn, *Polished Cornerstones*, London, 2001. I am grateful to the librarians at the Masonic headquarters, who were most kind and helpful.

25 Henry Humpherus, *History of the Origin and Progress of the Company of Watermen and Lightermen of the River Thames*, edited by Jack King, J. L. Dawson, W. Barrett and W. B. G. Wilson, reprinted 1999, Lavenham, Suffolk. The Company still trains apprentices for the river, and still confines its membership to those having to do with the river, unlike some livery companies who have departed from their original function. It is one of the only two companies which are not, strictly speaking, livery companies, because it does not have a livery or ceremonial uniform, the other being the Company of Parish Clerks.

26 For this see my *Elizabeth's London*, London, 2003.

27 This is taken from an Indenture kindly made available to me by the John Lewis Partnership Archivist. It is dated 1885, and relates to Bainbridges in Newcastle, but I gratefully adopt it as typical of London apprenticeships slightly earlier. The records of John Lewis's London shop were destroyed by war damage.

28 Thompson and Yeo, op. cit.

29 T. Wright s. n. The Journeyman Engineer, *The Great Unwashed*, London, 1868.

30 A. E. Douglas-Smith, *The City of London School*, Oxford, 1965, a copy of which was generously given me by the School's Archivist.

31 Unpublished diary of Robert James Lee, MS 3224, Wellcome Institute, listed in Heather Creaton, *Unpublished London Diaries*, London, 2003.

32 G. M. Young, *Portrait of an Age*, London, 1977.

33 D. Hudson, *Munby: Man of Two Worlds*, London, 1972.

34 Unpublished diary of J. A. Patterson, Wellcome Institute MS 73537, listed in Creaton, op. cit.

35 Xavier Baron, *London 1066–1914*, Robertsbridge, East Sussex, 1997: extracts from Nathaniel Hawthorne, *The English Notebooks* and from *Our Old Home*, published in 1863.

36 Peter Cunningham, *Handbook of London*, London, 1850 (2nd edn).

37 The Taunton Commission. This may provoke a wry smile from today's over-stressed professional woman juggling husband, children, house, office and career. Gentleness and amiability are sometimes in short supply.

38 David Newsome, *The Victorian World Picture*, London, 1997.

Chapter 20: Women (pp. 250–268)

1 Michael Riley, *Victorian Working Women: Portraits from Life*, London, 1979.
2 Ibid.
3 D. Hudson, *Munby: Man of Two Worlds*, London, 1972.
4 Ibid.
5 James Greenwood, *The Seven Curses of London*, London, 1869.
6 *British Medical Journal*, 1868; the fashion was 'a few years ago'.
7 E. P. Thompson and Eileen Yeo (eds), *The Unknown Mayhew – Selections from the Morning Chronicle 1849–50*, London, 1971.
8 Ibid.
9 Evidence quoted in J. M. Golby, *Culture and Society in Britain 1850–90*, Oxford, 1986.
10 Ibid. Men were employed too. They would all have to look respectable enough not to rouse the conductor's suspicions.
11 George Dodd, *Days at the Factories*, London, 1843.
12 Hudson, op. cit.
13 Adam Hart-Davis, *What the Victorians Did for Us*, London, 2001.
14 Ben Weinreb and Christopher Hibbert, *The London Encyclopaedia*, London, 1983.
15 J. A. and O. Banks, *Feminism and Family Planning in Victorian England*, Liverpool, 1964.
16 Hudson, op. cit.
17 Copies of the records of Robert Sayle (now owned by the John Lewis Partnership) and the apprenticeship indenture were kindly made available to me by its Archivist.
18 Hiley, op. cit.
19 Ibid.
20 Thompson and Yeo, op. cit.
21 Dr Elizabeth Blackwell, *Pioneer Work in Opening the Medical Profession to Women (Autobiographical Sketches)*, London, 1895.
22 Jean Hawkes (ed.), *The London Journal of Flora Tristan*, London, 1982.
23 Tristan, op. cit.
24 A Lock Hospital was not a lock-up. Its name is said to have originated in the Middle Ages, from the French word *loques*, the rags used to dress syphilitic sores.
25 Tristan, op. cit.
26 Edward Hyams (trans. and ed.), *Taine's Notes on England*, London, 1957.
27 Unpublished diary of Dr Carter, Wellcome Institute MS 5818, listed in Heather Creaton, *Unpublished London Diaries*, London, 2003. It may have been, of course, that poor young Carter went further than just looking, but on the whole I do not think so. The rest of his diary tells a pathetic story: he took a job with the East India Company, in Bombay. There he was spotted as a good investment by a woman who said she had divorced her husband in the Cape; she seduced him, they married, she bore a daughter whom he loved dearly, but he grew to hate his wife. When, as was normal in those days, the little girl had to be sent home out of the lethal Indian climate, his wife went too. He made over to her

more than he could afford, from his pay. All this time he recorded his many hours of prayer, but in the end God did nothing for him. The diary breaks off with several pages unused. Had he died? Or lost heart? Or lost his diary?.

28 Excerpt in Xavier Baron, *London 1066–1914*, Robertsbridge, East Sussex, 1997.

29 Mayhew, Vol. IV.

30 Tristan, op. cit.

31 Hudson, op. cit.

32 Tristan, op. cit.

33 Hyams, op. cit.

34 Hiley, op. cit.

35 Tristan, op. cit.

36 Trevor Fisher, *Prostitution and the Victorians*, Stroud, Gloucestershire, 1997.

37 Ibid.

38 William Acton, *Prostitution*, London, 1870 (2nd edn).

39 Hudson, op. cit.

40 A list of surviving books, pamphlets etc, is helpfully included in the Bibliography to Liza Z. Sigel, *Governing Pleasures: Pornography and Social Change in England 1815–1914*, New Brunswick, NJ, and London, 2002.

41 M. Mason, *The Making of Victorian Sexual Attitudes*, Oxford, 1994.

42 Mayhew, Vol. IV.

43 J. E. Ritchie, *The Night Side of London*, London, 1869.

44 Mayhew, Vol. IV.

45 Merton M. Sealts (ed.), *Ralph Waldo Emerson, the Journals and Miscellaneous Notebooks*, Vol. X, 1847–8, Cambridge, Mass., 1973.

46 Ibid., 1844.

47 *The Magazine of Domestic Economy*, 1843.

48 Ibid.

49 *The English Woman's Journal*, Vol. I, August 1858.

50 Peter Cunningham, *Handbook of London*, London, 1850 (2nd edn). I am most grateful to Anne Greening, the Archivist of the College, whose kindness supplemented Cunningham's account.

51 It was originally published anonymously, by 'A Doctor of Medicine', but the author was soon named as George Drysdale. I used the twenty-third edition of 1884. The text was basically unchanged.

52 *The Magazine of Domestic Economy*, 1843.

53 Hyams, op. cit.

54 John Stuart Mill, *The Subjection of Women*, London, 1869 (2nd edn).

55 William Acton, *The Functions and Disorders of the Reproductive Organs*, London, 1865.

56 Ibid. Acton had an unnerving habit of digressing into examples from the animal kingdom, for instance the erections of monkeys and guinea pigs, and the reproductive systems of giraffes and glow-worms; interesting, perhaps, but hardly helpful.

57 Going against my own principle of not using fictional sources, I would suggest that poor Dorothea's plight in George Eliot's *Middlemarch* exemplified a Victorian woman's sexual frustration.

58 Hudson, op. cit.

59 Drysdale, op. cit.

60 Ibid.
61 *R.* v *Thomas Hall*, Maule J. Quoted in Young and Handcock, *English Historical Documents*, Vol. XII(1), London, 1956.
62 Hyams, op. cit.
63 K. Theodore Hoppen, *The Mid-Victorian Generation*, Oxford, 1998.
64 Both these trials were exhaustively reported in the contemporary press. Horace Wyndham, *Judicial Dramas, Some Society Causes Célèbres*, London, 1907.

Chapter 21: Crimes and Punishments (pp. 269–281)

1 Henry Mayhew and John Binny, *The Criminal Prisons of London and Scenes of Prison Life*, London, 1862, from which much of what follows is taken.
2 Ibid.
3 The very first case I ever defended in a criminal court involved my trying to convince the jury that my client was carrying a valuable stolen necklace because, out of public duty, he had picked it up when he saw it lying on the ground, while the obvious thief – identity unknown – made his getaway. My client as a good citizen took it into safe-keeping until it could be returned to its rightful owner. Unsurprisingly, the jury did not believe it.
4 Diary of Joseph Hékékyan Bey, in Heather Creaton (ed.), *Victorian Diaries*, London, 2001.
5 In 1853 a 22-year-old labourer threw vitriol at a man, for which he was sentenced to four years penal servitude. National Archives, HO 77.60, Newgate calendar.
6 Louis Blanc, *Letters on England*, London, 1866, included in Xavier Baron, *London, 1066–1914*, Robertsbridge, East Sussex, 1997.
7 Jennifer Davis, 'The London Garotting Panic of 1862', in V. A. C. Gatrell et al. (eds), *Crime and the Law*, London, 1980.
8 Blanc, op. cit.
9 Unpublished diary of Charles Pugh, Bodleian MS Eng. Misc. d. 467, listed in Heather Creaton, *Unpublished London Diaries*, London, 2003.
10 (Editor unnamed), *Society, Politics and Diplomacy 1820–1864*, London, 1913.
11 Francis Wheen, *Karl Marx*, London, 1999.
12 (Author unnamed), *The Bermondsey Murder. A Full Report of the Trial of Frederick George Manning and Maria Manning for the murder of Patrick O'Connor*, London, 1849.
13 G. L. Browne and C. G. Stewart, *Reports of Trials for Murder by Poisoning*, London, 1883, from which I have taken the cases of Tavell and the other poisoners in this section.
14 Mayhew and Binny, op. cit.
15 Annual Register of Law Cases, 1840.
16 Horace Wyndham, *The Mayfair Calendar*, London, 1925.
17 Mayhew and Binny, op. cit. Their survey focused on criminal prisons. The notorious prisons of the Fleet and Marshalsea, which were used for civil cases such as debtors, were abolished in 1842. I have not included them in this section.
18 Peter Cunningham, *Handbook of London*, London, 1850 (2nd edn).
19 Mayhew and Binny, op. cit.

20 Ibid.

21 Edward Hyams (trans. and ed.), *Taine's Notes on England*, London, 1957.

22 James Greenwood, *The Wilds of London*, London, 1881.

23 Mayhew and Binny, op. cit.

24 Greenwood, op. cit.

25 Jane Carlyle attended a service in Pentonville in 1851. The under-chaplain 'read a passage in the Bible and then looked up in a reference book the numbers of the prisoners whose turn it was to be examined ... He read about the young man who ... asked Jesus what he should do to be saved ... and then called out, "Numbers 32 and 78: What shall I do to enter into eternal life?" 32 and 78 answered: "Sell all that thou hast and give to the poor." Now ... did you ever hear such nonsense?' (*Mrs Carlyle's Letters*, ed. J. A. Froude, London, 1883.)

26 The following account is taken from Mayhew and Binny, op. cit.

27 James Greenwood, *The Seven Curses of London*, London, 1869.

28 Mayhew and Binny, op. cit.

29 Stephen Van Dulken, *Inventing the 19th Century*, London, 2001.

30 Leon Radzinowicz, *A History of English Criminal Law*, London, 1968.

31 Kathleen Tillotson (ed.), *Charles Dickens: Letters*, Oxford, 1977.

32 Ibid.

33 Charles Dickens, *'Gone Astray' and other papers 1851–59*, London, 1999.

Chapter 22: Religion (pp. 282–295)

1 Quoted in K. Theodore Hoppen, *The Mid-Victorian Generation*, Oxford, 1998.

2 Eloquently described in Thomas Wright, *Some Habits and Customs of the Working Class*, London, 1867.

3 John Bailey (ed.), *The Diary of Lady Frederick Cavendish*, London, 1927.

4 Edward Miall, *The British Churches in relation to the British People*, London, 1849.

5 From his 'Report on the Religion Census', London, 1851. Interestingly, he suggested that the cure for working-class irreligion might be better housing, and the cause of the middle-class exclusiveness was their 'peculiar isolation in distinct and separate houses'.

6 The Reverend C. M. Davies was a roving ecclesiastical reporter. I have based much of this chapter on his *Orthodox London, or Phases of Religious Life in the Church of England*, London, 1873, and his two volumes *Unorthodox London*, London, 1873 and 1875. I also relied gratefully on the chapter headed 'Godly People' in Hoppen, op. cit.

7 Paul Turner, *Victorian Poetry, Drama and Miscellaneous Prose*, Oxford, 1989, on Newman.

8 I hope I have correctly used the terms Anglo-Catholic – not to be confused with the other, Roman Catholics; Tractarian; Ritualist; and the Oxford Movement – not to be confused with the later Oxford Groups. They seem to me interchangeable, distinguishable possibly by a difference in fashion. 'Tractarian' came from Newman's Tracts, and the 'Oxford Movement' from its starting-point. 'Anglo-Catholic' came later, 'Ritualistic' was a convenient general label.

9 John Henry Newman, *Apologia pro Vita Sua*, Oxford, 1864.

10 Bailey, op. cit.

11 Davies, *Orthodox London*, op. cit.: one of the few occasions on which the writer's impartiality slips.

12 Quoted from the *Church Times*, founded in 1863, the leading organ of Anglo-Catholic opinion, by J. S. Reed, *Glorious Battle; the Cultural Politics of Christian Anglo-Catholicism*, London, 1996. A chasuble is the outermost Eucharistic vestment, worn by the celebrant; hangs from the shoulders, front and back, and was usually ornamented. A dalmatic was an ankle-length robe with wide, short sleeves worn by a deacon. A cope was a vestment reaching to the heels, open in front and fastened at the breast, often highly ornamented with a cape covering the shoulders; worn in processions and solemn occasions other than the Eucharist. An alb is a Eucharistic vestment of white linen, long-sleeved and ankle-length. A stole is a swathe of cloth hanging from the shoulder to the feet, worn by parish priests over the surplice and by other ordained clergy over the alb at the Eucharist. All these definitions are from Reed, op. cit. One can begin to see what fun it must have been to robe appropriately – if you could afford it.

13 Nothing to do with *primula auricula*, save that its name derives from the Latin *aurus*, because its leaves were thought to look like a bear's ears. Here, it means confessing to the ear of a priest *viva voce*, instead of the 'general confession' which is part of the Anglican Order of Service.

14 Davies, *Orthodox London*, op. cit.

15 Ibid.

16 Recorded in his diary, and quoted in Reed, op. cit.

17 Davies, *Orthodox London*, op. cit.

18 James Bentley, *Ritualism and Politics in Victorian Britain*, Oxford, 1978.

19 Reed, op. cit.

20 A letter quoted in Bentley, op. cit.

21 Reed, op. cit.

22 Unpublished diary of Thomas Rogers, Guildhall Library, MS 19,019, listed in Heather Creaton, *Unpublished London Diaries*, London, 2003.

23 Lytton Strachey and Roger Fulford (eds), *The Greville Memoirs*, Vol. VII, London, 1938.

24 Letter by the Reverend Gibson, quoted in Andrew Saint and Gillian Darley, *The Chronicles of London*, London, 1994.

25 Bentley, op. cit.

26 Miall, op. cit.

27 Reed, op. cit.

28 John Raymond (ed.), *Queen Victoria's Early Letters*, London, rev. edn 1963.

29 Dr Elizabeth Blackwell, *Pioneer Work in Opening the Medical Profession to Women (Autobiographical Sketches)*, London, 1895.

30 Davies, *Unorthodox London*, op. cit.

31 Davies, *Unorthodox London*, op. cit. Davies is a mine of information about the Nonconformist faiths. He indefatigably visited as many places of worship as he could, and noted not only what he saw but also, frequently, a synopsis of the sermon he stayed to hear. He did not, and I do not, enter in detail into their articles of faith.

32 A. R. Bennett, *London and Londoners in the 1850s and 60s*, London, 1924.
33 Hoppen, op. cit.
34 Davies, *Unorthodox London*, op. cit.
35 Ibid.
36 Disraeli's father Isaac D'Israeli – the Disraeli spelling came later – had not seen eye to eye with his local synagogue, and had left it, taking his family with him. He had all his children baptised into the Anglican faith. Disraeli played on his Jewishness when it suited him, but he mostly claimed to be an impeccable English gentleman, a claim hard to reconcile with his taste in clothes.
37 Anne and Roger Cowan, *Victorian Jews Through British Eyes*, Oxford, 1986.
38 Todd M. Endelman and Tony Kushner (eds), *Disraeli's Jewishness*, London, 2002.
39 Davies, *Unorthodox London*, op. cit.
40 Quotation from Davies's account of the opening of the West London Synagogue in 1871.
41 Lucien Wolf, 'The Jewish Way of Life' in Cowan, op. cit.

Chapter 23: Death (pp. 296–309)

1 John Hollingshead, *Ragged London in 1861*, London, 1861.
2 Friedrich Engels, *The Condition of the Working Class in England*, trans. and ed. W. O. Henderson and W. H. Chaloner, Oxford, 1958.
3 Thomas Wright s. n. The Journeyman Engineer, *The Great Unwashed*, London, 1868.
4 R. W. Vanderkiste, *A Six Years' Mission Among the Dens of London*, London, 1854.
5 James Burn, '*The Beggar Boy*': an Autobiography, London, 1888.
6 Wright, op. cit.
7 Joseph Rogers, *Reminiscences of a Workhouse Medical Officer*, ed. Thorold Rogers, London, 1889.
8 Charles Dickens, 'Trading in Death', in *Household Words*, London, 1852.
9 Thomas Wright, *Some Habits and Customs of the Working Classes*, London, 1867.
10 Quoted in Roy Porter, *London: a Social History*, London, 1994.
11 *The Times*, 5 March 1843, quoted in Robert Ward, *London's New River*, London, 2003.
12 John Richardson, *The Annals of London*, London, 2000.
13 Dickens, op. cit.
14 A. N. Wilson, *The Victorians*, London, 2002.
15 Included in John Raymond (ed.), *Queen Victoria's Early Letters*, London, 1963.
16 *The Times*, 5 May 1843. The list of who was there, in person or represented by their coaches, had presumably been given to the reporter by Kensington Palace sources. The unfortunate reporter must have followed the procession. He found himself in the nightmare position – for a news reporter – of having to record that 'nothing worthy of the slightest notice happened during its progress'.
17 Information kindly supplied by the Librarian, The Library and Museum of Freemasonry.
18 Lytton Strachey and Roger Fulford (eds), *The Greville Memoirs*, Vol. V, London, 1938.

19 Unpublished diary of J. A. Patterson, 1858, Wellcome Institute MS 73537, listed in Heather Creaton, *Unpublished London Diaries*, London, 2003.

20 Unpublished diary of Lt.-Gen. Pasley, British Library Add. MS 41991, listed in Creaton, op. cit.

21 Julian Litten, *The English Way of Death*, London, 1991.

22 Here as so often I am indebted to Ben Weinreb and Christopher Hibbert, *The London Encyclopaedia*, London, 1983, from which I have taken details about the other London cemeteries I mention below. Their book gives the subsequent, usually sad, history of the cemeteries: a story of dereliction and vandalism, arrested – in some cases – by the action of local or state authorities, and in the case of Highgate cemetery by the concerted action of a group of individuals.

23 Felix Barker, *Highgate Cemetery, Victorian Valhalla*, London, 1984. The photographs, by John Gay, are beautiful.

24 Ibid.

25 Benjamin Clarke, *Glimpses of Ancient Hackney and Stoke Newington*, London, 1894 (the London Borough of Hackney edition, which I used, was published in 1986).

26 J. C. Loudon, *On the Laying Out, Planting and Managing of Cemeteries*, London, 1843.

27 David Solman, *Loddiges of Hackney*, London, 1995.

28 Weinreb and Hibbert, op. cit.

29 So down-to-earth that some readers may prefer to skip this bit.

30 A. R. Bennett, *London and Londoners in the 1850s and 60s*, London, 1924.

31 Litten, op. cit.

32 Marion Harding (ed.), *The Victorian Soldier*, London, 1993. General Chesney had been married to his first wife, and to Everilda, wearing this jacket. It seems a curious choice for post-mortem wear.

33 When the present Queen's father died, she and her husband were in Kenya. She arrived at Heathrow clad in black, which must have been in the royal wardrobe just in case.

34 Henry Mayhew (ed.), *The Shops and Companies of London*, London, 1865.

35 Alison Aldburgham, *Shops and Shopping 1800–1914*, London, 1981.

36 *The Magazine of Domestic Economy*, 1844.

37 More than a hundred years later, when I was looking for a black suit to wear as a trainee barrister, I tried Jay's. It had by then dropped the words 'Mourning Warehouse' from its fascia, but they could still be made out, painted on the side wall. I remember acres of pearl-grey carpet, and deferential assistants, and an atmosphere of profound calm.

38 Aldburgham, op. cit.

39 Ibid.

40 Judith Flanders, *The Victorian House*, London, 2003.

41 Ibid.

42 Unpublished diary of Charles Pugh, Bodleian MS Eng. Misc. d. 472, listed in Creaton, op. cit.

43 Ibid.

44 S. M. Ellis (ed. and annot.), *A Mid-Victorian Pepys: the Letters and Memoirs of Sir William Hardman*, London, 1925.

45 D. Hudson, *Munby: Man of Two Worlds*, London, 1972.

46 Pugh listed in Creaton, op. cit.

47 Unpublished diary of Thomas Rogers, Guildhall Library MS 19,019, in Creaton, op. cit.

48 This account is taken from James Greenwood, *The Wilds of London*, London, 1881. Greenwood was a journalist, but the picture he painted probably had much truth in it. The cemetery 'five miles without the city Gates' was not named, but could have applied to several.

49 Loudon, op. cit.

50 Strachey and Fulford, op. cit.

51 Ibid.

52 (Editor unnamed), *Society, Politics and Diplomacy 1820–64; Passages from the Journal of Francis W. H. Cavendish*, London, 1913.

53 Unpublished diary of Thomas Rogers in Creaton, op. cit.

54 'Trading in Death', in *Household Words*, included in Michael Slater (ed.), '*Gone Astray' and Other Papers*, London, 1998.

55 Vividly described in Elizabeth Longford, *Wellington: Pillar of State*, London, 1972, on which I have relied for my account.

56 For a long time it could be seen in the crypt of St Paul's. It was removed to Stratfield Saye in 1981.

Index